SHORT FICTION CRITICISM:

A Checklist of Interpretation since 1925 of Stories and Novelettes
(American, British, Continental) : 1800-1958

THE SWALLOW CHECKLISTS
OF CRITICISM AND EXPLICATION

POETRY EXPLICATION
by Joseph M. Kuntz

THE ENGLISH NOVEL: 1578-1956
by Inglis Bell and Donald Baird

SHORT FICTION CRITICISM
by Jarvis Thurston, O. B. Emerson,
Carl Hartman, and Elizabeth V. Wright

THE AMERICAN NOVEL
by Donna Gerstenberger and George Hendrick

SHORT FICTION CRITICISM

A Checklist of Interpretation
since 1925 of Stories and Novelettes
(American, British, Continental)
1800-1958

by

JARVIS THURSTON
O. B. EMERSON
CARL HARTMAN
ELIZABETH V. WRIGHT

ALAN SWALLOW, Denver

PREFACE

Although the files of approximately two hundred periodicals, including both "little magazines" and academic quarterlies, and thousands of books were examined in making this checklist, it makes no pretense to completeness; it is hoped, however, that users will not too readily discover significant entries that we have overlooked.

To the users of this checklist we should like to point out the following:

1. The listings cover short stories and novelettes no longer than, approximately, 150 pages.

2. The listings are confined to articles and books in English.

3. The listings are confined to material that has interpretive value. Articles and books dealing with the "environmental" circumstances of literature (biography, genesis, source, etc.) have been cited only when they contain critical material, or "facts" that should prove useful to the practical critic.

4. The page numbers refer to the exact parts of an article or book dealing with a particular story or novelette.

5. Except for a scant dozen entries which we have placed in brackets [ ], every entry has been read or skimmed by at least one of the compilers.

6. Reprintings of articles in books have been indicated whenever we could verify that they contain the same materials; those items that we were unable to verify by comparing article and book (it was not always possible to have both in hand at the same time) are listed as separate entries.

7. At the back of this volume will be found a list of "Sources Consulted," which includes both periodicals and books. The particular edition of a book used in making the checklist may be found by looking for the author's name under "General," or if the book treats no more than four authors, or is devoted to a single author, it may be found under the appropriate name in the "Author Checklists."

8. This volume contains all the entries listed in the checklist published by *Perspective* (Summer, 1953), with the exception of items on Henry James' "What Maisie Knew," which were dropped to conform to our specifications about length.

Since the final selection of entries for the checklist has been in my hands, and since I have assumed the responsibility of preparing the manuscript, my co-editors may not be blamed for any errors or omissions.

JARVIS THURSTON

AGNON, S. Y.

1. A WHOLE LOAF
Joel Blocker, "Literary Export," *Commentary* XXVI (July, 1958),
91-92.

AIKEN, CONRAD

1. GEHENNA
Mark Schorer, "The Life in the Fiction," *Wake* XI (1952), 59-60.
2. LIFE ISN'T A SHORT STORY
Mark Schorer, "The Life in the Fiction," *Wake* XI (1952), 57-58.
3. MR. ARCULARIS
W. P. Albrecht, "Aiken's 'Mr. Arcularis,' " *Explicator* VI (April,
1948), item 40.
Rufus A. Blanshard, "Metamorphosis of a Dream," *Sewanee Review* LXV (Autumn, 1957), 694-702.
Jean Garrigue, "A Consideration of Mr. Arcularis, the Play,"
Wake XI (1952), 73-79.
F. L. Gwynn, "The Functional Allusions in Conrad Aiken's 'Mr.
Arcularis,' " *Twentieth Century Literature* II (April, 1956), 21-25.
D. Heiney, *Recent American Literature*, 515-516.
4. SILENT SNOW, SECRET SNOW
Clifton Fadiman, *Reading I've Liked*, 734-735.
Leo Hamalian, "Aiken's 'Silent Snow, Secret Snow,' " *Explicator*
VII (November, 1948), item 17.
D. Heiney, *Recent American Literature*, 515.
5. STRANGE MOONLIGHT
Conrad Aiken, Comment in Whit Burnett, *This Is My Best*, 85.
Seymour L. Gross, "The Reflection of Poe in Conrad Aiken's
'Strange Moonlight,' " *Modern Language Notes* LXXII (March,
1957), 185-189.

ALEXANDER, SIDNEY

1. THE WHITE BOAT
James B. Hall and Joseph Langland, *The Short Story*, 449-450.

ANDERSON, SHERWOOD

1. ADVENTURE
Stegner, Scowcroft, and Ilyin, *The Writer's Art*, 142-145.

ANDERSON, SHERWOOD, Continued

2. THE BOOK OF THE GROTESQUE
Alwyn Berland, "Sherwood Anderson and the Pathetic Grotesque,"
Western Review XV (Winter, 1951), 135-138.
James Schevill, *Sherwood Anderson,* 101-103.
Lionel Trilling, "Sherwood Anderson," *Kenyon Review* III (Summer, 1941), 296-298. — reprinted, revised, in Trilling, *The Liberal Imagination* (1950), 26-28; (Anchor Books, 1953), 37-38. — reprinted in John W. Aldridge, *Critiques and Essays on Modern Fiction,* 322-323.

3. BROTHER DEATH
Walter Havighurst, *Masters of the Modern Short Story,* xi.
[Earl Hilton, "The Evolution of Sherwood Anderson's 'Brother Death,'" *Northwest Ohio Quarterly* XXIV (1952), 125-130.]
James Schevill, *Sherwood Anderson,* 300-301.

4. DEATH IN THE WOODS
Robert G. Davis, *Instructor's Manual for "Ten Modern Masters,"* 19-20.
Irving Howe, *Sherwood Anderson,* 164-167.
Norman Holmes Pearson, "Anderson and the New Puritanism," *Newberry Library Bulletin,* Second Series, No. 2 (December, 1948), 56-57.
Bernard Raymund, "The Grammar of Not-Reason: Sherwood Anderson," *Arizona Quarterly* XII (Summer, 1956), 146.
William Troy, "Fragmentary Ends," *Nation* CXXXVI (May 3, 1933), 508.
R. B. West, Jr., *The Short Story in America: 1900-1950,* 47-48.

5. THE EGG
Robert G. Davis, *Instructor's Manual for "Ten Modern Masters,"* 19.
Irving Howe, *Sherwood Anderson,* 168-172.
Bernard Raymund, "The Grammar of Not-Reason: Sherwood Anderson," *Arizona Quarterly* XII (Summer, 1956), 140-141.
James Schevill, *Sherwood Anderson,* 164-165.

6. THE FLOOD
Maxwell Geismar, *The Last of the Provincials,* 273.

7. GODLINESS
Jarvis Thurston, "Anderson and 'Winesburg': Mysticism and Craft," *Accent* XVI (Spring, 1956), 126-127.
C. C. Walcutt, "Sherwood Anderson: Impressionism and the Buried Life," *Sewanee Review* LX (Winter, 1952), 34-35. — reprinted in Walcutt, *American Literary Naturalism,* 227-228.

8. HANDS
   Sherwood Anderson, *Memoirs*, 241-243.
   William L. Phillips, "How Sherwood Anderson Wrote 'Winesburg, Ohio,'" *American Literature* XXIII (March, 1951), 9, 15, 20-24.
9. I'M A FOOL
   Robert G. Davis, *Instructor's Manual for "Ten Modern Masters,"* 18-19.
   Irving Howe, *Sherwood Anderson*, 154.
   James Schevill, *Sherwood Anderson*, 187-188.
   C. C. Walcutt, "Sherwood Anderson: Impressionism and the Buried Life," *Sewanee Review* LX (Winter, 1952), 39-40. — reprinted in Walcutt, *American Literary Naturalism*, 233.
10. I WANT TO KNOW WHY
    John Peale Bishop, *Collected Essays*, 239. — reprinted from *Vanity Fair* (December, 1921).
    Brooks and Warren, *Understanding Fiction*, 344-350, 574.
    Irving Howe, *Sherwood Anderson*, 154-157.
    Kenneth Kempton, *Short Stories for Study*, 141-149.
    Simon O. Lesser, "The Image of the Father," *Partisan Review* XXII (Summer, 1955), 381-390. — reprinted in William Phillips, *Art and Psychoanalysis*, 237-246. — reprinted in Lesser, *Fiction and the Unconscious*, 224-234.
    Perry Miller, "A Curious Sense of Dirt," *New Republic* CXXVIII (June 22, 1953), 19-20.
    James Schevill, *Sherwood Anderson*, 162-163.
    Harry Shaw and Douglas Bement, *Reading the Short Story*, 71-72.
    Arthur Sherbo, "Sherwood Anderson's 'I Want to Know Why' and Messrs. Brooks and Warren," *College English* XV (March, 1954), 350-351.
    Lionel Trilling, *The Liberal Imagination* (1950), 24-25; (Anchor Books, 1958), 35. — reprinted in John W. Aldridge, *Critiques and Essays on Modern Fiction*, 321.
    R. B. West, Jr., *The Short Story in America: 1900-1950*, 50-52.
11. LONELINESS
    Herbert Gold, "The Purity and Cunning of Sherwood Anderson," *Hudson Review* X (Winter, 1957-58), 552.
12. THE MAN WHO BECAME A WOMAN
    Herbert Gold, "The Purity and Cunning of Sherwood Anderson," *Hudson Review* X (Winter, 1957-58), 551-552.
    Irving Howe, *Sherwood Anderson*, 160-164.
    Bernard Raymund, "The Grammar of Not-Reason: Sherwood Anderson," *Arizona Quarterly* XII (Summer, 1956), 143-144.

James Schevill, *Sherwood Anderson*, 188-190.

13. THE NEW ENGLANDER

Frederick J. Hoffman, *Freudianism and the Literary Mind* (2nd Edition, 1957), 244-245.

Brom Weber, "Anderson and 'The Essence of Things,'" *Sewanee Review* LIX (Autumn, 1951), 687-688.

14. OUT OF NOWHERE INTO NOTHING

John Peale Bishop, *Collected Essays*, 239-240. — reprinted from *Vanity Fair* (December, 1921).

Irving Howe, *Sherwood Anderson*, 174-175.

15. SEEDS

Trigant Burrow, "Psychoanalytic Improvisations and the Personal Equation," *Psychoanalytic Review* XIII (April, 1926), 173-174.

Frederick J. Hoffman, *Freudianism and the Literary Mind* (2nd Edition, 1957), 235-236.

Irving Howe, "Sherwood Anderson and D. H. Lawrence," *Furioso* V (Fall, 1950), 21. — reprinted in Howe, *Sherwood Anderson*, 179-180.

16. SOPHISTICATION

Beardsley, Daniel, and Leggett, *Aids to Study for "Theme and Form: An Introduction to Literature,"* 20.

Jarvis Thurston, "Anderson and 'Winesburg': Mysticism and Craft," *Accent* XVI (Spring, 1956), 114-115.

C. C. Walcutt, "Sherwood Anderson: Impressionism and the Buried Life," *Sewanee Review* LX (Winter, 1952), 37-38. — reprinted in Walcutt, *American Literary Naturalism*, 230-231.

17. SURRENDER

Maxwell Geismar, *The Last of the Provincials*, 235.

18. THE TEACHER

C. C. Walcutt, "Sherwood Anderson: Impressionism and the Buried Life," *Sewanee Review* LX (Winter, 1952), 36-37. — reprinted in Walcutt, *American Literary Naturalism*, 229-230.

19. THE THINKER

C. C. Walcutt, "Sherwood Anderson: Impressionism and the Buried Life," *Sewanee Review* LX (Winter, 1952), 35-36. — reprinted in Walcutt, *American Literary Naturalism*, 228-229.

20. UNLIGHTED LAMPS

Frederick J. Hoffman, *Freudianism and the Literary Mind* (2nd Edition, 1957), 243.

21. THE UNTOLD LIE

Herbert Gold, "The Purity and Cunning of Sherwood Anderson," *Hudson Review* X (Winter, 1957-58), 551.

ANDERSON, SHERWOOD, Continued

William L. Phillips, "How Sherwood Anderson Wrote 'Winesburg, Ohio,'" *American Literature* XXIII (March, 1951), 26-27.
Jarvis Thurston, "Anderson and 'Winesburg': Mysticism and Craft," *Accent* XVI (Spring, 1956), 119-120.
22. UNUSED
Frederick J. Hoffman, *Freudianism and the Literary Mind* (2nd Edition, 1957), 243-244.

ANDREYEV, LEONID

1. THE SEVEN WHO WERE HANGED
L. Hamalian and E. L. Volpe, *Ten Modern Short Novels*, 273-274.

AVERCHENCO, ARCADII

1. THE YOUNG MAN WHO FLEW PAST
James B. Hall and Joseph Langland, *The Short Story*, 163-164.

BABEL, ISAAC

1. DI GRASSO
Steven Marcus, "The Stories of Isaac Babel," *Partisan Review* XXII (Summer, 1955), 410-411.
2. THE HISTORY OF MY DOVECOT
Irving Howe, "Tone in the Short Story," *Sewanee Review* LVII (Winter, 1949), 151.
3. PAN APOLEK
Steven Marcus, "The Stories of Isaac Babel," *Partisan Review* XXII (Summer, 1955), 401-402.
4. PRISCHEPA'S VENGEANCE
Steven Marcus, "The Stories of Isaac Babel," *Partisan Review* XXII (Summer, 1955), 404-405.

BALZAC, HONORÉ DE

1. ADIEU
Brucia Dedinsky, "Development of the Scheme of the *Comédie humaine*," in Dargan and Weinberg, *The Evolution of Balzac's "Comédie humaine*," 59-61.*

BALZAC, HONORÉ DE, Continued

2. CHRIST IN FLANDERS
   Brooks and Warren, *Understanding Fiction*, 297-300.
   Brucia Dedinsky, "Development of the Scheme of the *Comédie humaine*," in Dargan and Weinberg, *The Evolution of Balzac's "Comédie humaine*," 49-50.*

3. COLONEL CHABERT
   Brucia Dedinsky, "Development of the Scheme of the *Comédie humaine*," in Dargan and Weinberg, *The Evolution of Balzac's "Comédie humaine*," 107-109.*
   Samuel Rogers, *Balzac and the Novel*, 155-160.

4. COMEDIANS WITHOUT KNOWING IT
   (see "The Involuntary Comedians")

5. A COMMISSION IN LUNACY
   Brucia Dedinsky, "Development of the Scheme of the *Comédie humaine*," in Dargan and Weinberg, *The Evolution of Balzac's "Comédie humaine*," 109-110.*

6. THE CURÉ OF TOURS
   (see "The Vicar of Tours")

7. THE DUCHESS OF LANGEAIS
   Richard Aldington, "Introduction," in Aldington, *Great English Romances* (Duell, Sloan, and Pearce, 1946), xxxii-xxxiii.

8. AN EPISODE UNDER THE TERROR
   Edward J. O'Brien, *The Short Story Case Book*, 35-67.

9. GAMBARA
   Brucia Dedinsky, "Development of the Scheme of the *Comédie humaine*," in Dargan and Weinberg, *The Evolution of Balzac's "Comédie humaine*," 119-121.*

10. LA GRANDE BRETÈCHE
    Brucia Dedinsky, "Development of the Scheme of the *Comédie humaine*," in Dargan and Weinberg, *The Evolution of Balzac's "Comédie humaine*," 55-58.*
    Séan O'Faoláin, *The Short Story*, 199-201.

11. LA GRENADIÈRE
    Brucia Dedinsky, "Development of the Scheme of the *Comédie humaine*," in Dargan and Weinberg, *The Evolution of Balzac's "Comédie humaine*," 99-100.*

12. THE HOUSE OF THE CAT AND THE RACKET
    Bonnie Blackburn, "Master and Apprentice: A Realistic Relationship," in E. Preston Dargan, *Studies in Balzac's Realism*, 158-166.

13. THE ILLUSTRIOUS GAUDISSART
    Brucia Dedinsky, "Development of the Scheme of the *Comédie humaine*," in Dargan and Weinberg, *The Evolution of Balzac's "Comédie humaine*," 100.*

BALZAC, HONORÉ DE, Continued

14. THE INITIATE
Brucia Dedinsky, "Development of the Scheme of the *Comédie humaine*," in Dargan and Weinberg, *The Evolution of Balzac's "Comédie humaine*," 160-161.*

15. THE INTERDICTION
(see "A Commission in Lunacy")

16. INVOLUNTARY COMEDIANS
Brucia Dedinsky, "Development of the Scheme of the *Comédie humaine*," in Dargan and Weinberg, *The Evolution of Balzac's "Comédie humaine*," 154-155.*

17. LOUIS LAMBERT
Carl Benson, "Yeats and Balzac's 'Louis Lambert,'" *Modern Philology* XLIX (May, 1952), 242-247.
Brucia Dedinsky, "Development of the Scheme of the *Comédie humaine*," in Dargan and Weinberg, *The Evolution of Balzac's "Comédie humaine*," 75-78.*

18. MADAME FIRMIANI
Brucia Dedinsky, "Development of the Scheme of the *Comédie humaine*," in Dargan and Weinberg, *The Evolution of Balzac's "Comédie humaine*," 73-74.*

19. LES MARANA
Brucia Dedinsky, "Development of the Scheme of the *Comédie humaine*," in Dargan and Weinberg, *The Evolution of Balzac's "Comédie humaine*," 82-84, 93-95.*

20. MASSIMILLA DONI
Brucia Dedinsky, "Development of the Scheme of the *Comédie humaine*," in Dargan and Weinberg, *The Evolution of Balzac's "Comédie humaine*," 121-122.*

21. MASTER CORNÉLIUS
Brucia Dedinsky, "Development of the Scheme of the *Comédie humaine*," in Dargan and Weinberg, *The Evolution of Balzac's "Comédie humaine*," 70-73.*
George D. Morris, "Balzac's Treatment of History in 'Maître Cornélius,'" *Philological Quarterly* X (October, 1931), 356-368.

22. MELMOTH CONVERTED
Brucia Dedinsky, "Development of the Scheme of the *Comédie humaine*," in Dargan and Weinberg, *The Evolution of Balzac's "Comédie humaine*," 114-115.*

23. THE MESSAGE
Brucia Dedinsky, "Development of the Scheme of the *Comédie humaine*," in Dargan and Weinberg, *The Evolution of Balzac's "Comédie humaine*," 55-58.*

BALZAC, HONORE DE, Continued

24. A PASSION IN THE DESERT
Brucia Dedinsky, "Development of the Scheme of the *Comédie humaine*," in Dargan and Weinberg, *The Evolution of Balzac's "Comédie humaine*," 118.*

25. THE PURSE
Brucia Dedinsky, "Development of the Scheme of the *Comédie humaine*," in Dargan and Weinberg, *The Evolution of Balzac's "Comédie humaine*," 58-59.*

26. THE RED INN
Brucia Dedinsky, "Development of the Scheme of the *Comédie humaine*," in Dargan and Weinberg, *The Evolution of Balzac's "Comédie humaine*," 74-75.*

27. THE UNCONSCIOUS COMEDIANS
(see "The Involuntary Comedians")

28. AN UNKNOWN MASTERPIECE
Wayne Conner, "Balzac's Frenhofer," *Modern Language Notes* LXIX (May, 1954), 335-338.
Brucia Dedinsky, "Development of the Scheme of the *Comédie humaine*," in Dargan and Weinberg, *The Evolution of Balzac's "Comédie humaine*," 45-46.*
Mary Wingfield Scott, *Art and Artists in Balzac's "Comédie humaine*," 29-42.

29. THE VICAR OF TOURS
Brucia Dedinsky, "Development of the Scheme of the *Comédie humaine*," in Dargan and Weinberg, *The Evolution·of Balzac's "Comédie humaine*," 61-62.*
Esther Marhofer, " 'Le Curé de Tours': A Study in Topography," in E. Preston Dargan, *Studies in Balzac's Realism*, 91-119.
Martin Turnell, *The Novel in France* (Vintage Books), 246-249.
Rachel Wilson, "Variations in 'Le Curé de Tours,' " in Dargan and Weinberg, *The Evolution of Balzac's "Comédie humaine*," 188-277.

* Brucia Dedinsky's *Development of the Scheme of the "Comédie humaine"*: *Distribution of the Stories* (University of Chicago Libraries, 1943) is a reprint of the piece in Dargan and Weinberg, and retains the same pagination.

BELLOW, SAUL

1. SEIZE THE DAY
Chester E. Eisinger, "Saul Bellow: Love and Identity," *Accent* XVIII (Summer, 1958), 200-202.

BELLOW, SAUL, Continued

Herbert Gold, "The Discovered Self," *Nation* CLXXXIII (November 17, 1956), 435-436.

Paul Levine, "Saul Bellow: The Affirmation of the Philosophical Fool," *Perspective* X (Winter, 1959), 174-176.

John A. Lynch, "Prelude to Accomplishment," *Commonweal* LXV (November 30, 1956), 238.

Ray B. West, Jr., "Six Authors in Search of a Hero," *Sewanee Review* LXV (Summer, 1957), 504-506.

BENCHLEY, NATHANIEL

1. DECK THE HALLS
Kenneth Kempton, *Short Stories for Study*, 141-149.

BENÉT, STEPHEN VINCENT

1. THE DEVIL AND DANIEL WEBSTER
Stephen Vincent Benét, Comment in Whit Burnett, *This Is My Best*, 231.
Charles A. Fenton, *Stephen Vincent Benét*, 293-296.
James A. S. McPeek, "Benét and Monroe's Fourth Reader," *College English* XX (December, 1958), 132-133.

BENSON, SALLY

1. THE OVERCOAT
Kenneth Kempton, *The Short Story*, 142-144.

BERGELSON, DAVID

1. THE REVOLUTION AND THE ZUSSMANS
Judah Goldin, "The Contemporary Jew and His Judaism," in S. R. Hopper, *Spiritual Problems in Contemporary Literature*, 213.

BERRYMAN, JOHN

1. THE IMAGINARY JEW
Mary Orvis, *The Art of Writing Fiction*, 56.

BIERCE, AMBROSE

1. **CHICKAMAUGA**
   M. E. Grenander, "Bierce's Turn of the Screw: Tales of Ironical Terror," *Western Humanities Review* XI (Summer, 1957), 261-262.
2. **A HORSEMAN IN THE SKY**
   Alfred C. Ward, *Aspects of the Modern Short Story*, 67-72.
3. **THE MAN AND THE SNAKE**
   M. E. Grenander, "Bierce's Turn of the Screw: Tales of Ironical Terror," *Western Humanities Review* XI (Summer, 1957), 263-264.
4. **MOXON'S MASTER**
   C. Hartley Grattan, *Bitter Bierce*, 174-183.
5. **AN OCCURRENCE AT OWL CREEK BRIDGE**
   Brooks and Warren, *Understanding Fiction*, 136-137.
   M. E. Grenander, "Bierce's Turn of the Screw: Tales of Ironical Terror," *Western Humanities Review* XI (Summer, 1957), 261-262.
   Sale, Hall, and Steinmann, *Critical Discussions for Teachers Using "Short Stories: Tradition and Direction,"* 5-8.
6. **ONE KIND OF OFFICER**
   M. E. Grenander, "Bierce's Turn of the Screw: Tales of Ironical Terror," *Western Humanities Review* XI (Summer, 1957), 260-261.
7. **ONE OFFICER, ONE MAN**
   M. E. Grenander, "Bierce's Turn of the Screw: Tales of Ironical Terror," *Western Humanities Review* XI (Summer, 1957), 263-264.
8. **ONE OF THE MISSING**
   C. Hartley Grattan, *Bitter Bierce*, 145-151.
   M. E. Grenander, "Bierce's Turn of the Screw: Tales of Ironical Terror," *Western Humanities Review* XI (Summer, 1957), 263-264.

BISHOP, JOHN PEALE

1. **CORPSE IN THE HOUSE**
   Joseph Frank, "Force and Form: A Study of John Peale Bishop," *Sewanee Review* LV (Winter, 1947), 86-88.
2. **IF ONLY**
   Joseph Frank, "Force and Form: A Study of John Peale Bishop," *Sewanee Review* LV (Winter, 1947), 88-89.

BOWEN, ELIZABETH

1. THE DISINHERITED
   A. Desmond Hawkins, "Fiction Chronicle," *Criterion* XVIII (October, 1938), 90-92.
2. THE GOOD GIRL
   Séan O'Faoláin, *The Short Story*, 165-166.
3. THE HAPPY AUTUMN FIELDS
   Winifred Lynskey, *Reading Modern Fiction* (Second Edition, 1957), 41-42.
   Kappo Phelan, "More Books of the Week," *Commonweal* XLIV (July 12, 1946), 311.
4. HER TABLE SPREAD
   Séan O'Faoláin, *The Short Story*, 202-204, 206-210, 229-231.
5. IN THE SQUARE
   Henry Reed, "New Fiction," *New Statesman and Nation* XXX (November 3, 1945), 302.
6. IVY GRIPPED THE STEPS
   Virgilia Peterson, "Like Searchlights in the Sky over England," *New York Herald Tribune Book Review*, (April 7, 1946), 5.

BOWLES, PAUL

1. UNDER THE SKY
   Ludwig and Poirier, *Stories: British and American*, 494-498.

BOYLE, KAY

1. THE CRAZY HUNTER
   R. M. Ludwig and M. B. Perry, *Nine Short Novels*, xvi-xviii.
2. EFFIGY OF WAR
   R. B. Heilman, *Modern Short Stories*, 162-163.
3. KEEP YOUR PITY
   Herbert Barrows, *Suggestions for Teaching "15 Stories,"* 23-25.
4. NATIVES DON'T CRY
   Felheim, Newman, and Steinhoff, *Study Aids for Teachers for "Modern Short Stories,"* 42-44.
5. THEY WEREN'T GOING TO DIE
   Kay Boyle, Comment in Whit Burnett, *This Is My Best*, 1005-1006.
6. THE WHITE HORSES OF VIENNA
   R. B. West, Jr., *The Short Story in America, 1900-1950*, 69-70.

BREUER, BESSIE

1. HOME IS A PLACE
   Bessie Breuer, "Home Is a Place," *Pacific Spectator* IV (Winter, 1950), 97-103. — reprinted in Stegner, Scowcroft, and Ilyin, *The Writer's Art*, 353-358.

BRODKEY, HAROLD

1. SENTIMENTAL EDUCATION
   Anon., "The Eyes of Youth: A Review of *First Love and Other Stories* by Harold Brodkey," *Times Literary Supplement* (July 25, 1958), 421.

BROWN, CHARLES BROCKDEN

1. DEATH OF CICERO, A FRAGMENT
   Harry R. Warfel, *Charles Brockden Brown: American Gothic Novelist*, 163-164.
2. A LESSON ON CONCEALMENT
   W. B. Berthoff, "'A Lesson on Concealment': Brockden Brown's Method in Fiction," *Philological Quarterly* XXXVII (January, 1958), 48-57.
   Harry R. Warfel, *Charles Brockden Brown: American Gothic Novelist*, 176-177.
3. THE MAN AT HOME
   David Lee Clark, *Charles Brockden Brown*, 160-162.
4. THESSALONICA: A ROMAN STORY
   Harry R. Warfel, *Charles Brockden Brown: American Gothic Novelist*, 175-176.

BUNIN, IVAN

1. BRETHREN
   Renato Poggioli, "The Art of Ivan Bunin," *Harvard Slavic Studies* I (1953), 260. — reprinted in Poggioli, *The Phoenix and the Spider*, 140-141.
2. CONVERSATION AT NIGHT
   Renato Poggioli, "The Art of Ivan Bunin," *Harvard Slavic Studies* I (1953), 255-256. — reprinted in Poggioli, *The Phoenix and the Spider*, 136-137.

BUNIN, IVAN, Continued

3. THE CUP OF LIFE
Renato Poggioli, "The Art of Ivan Bunin," *Harvard Slavic Studies* I (1953), 259. — reprinted in Poggioli, *The Phoenix and the Spider,* 139-140.
4. THE GENTLEMAN FROM SAN FRANCISCO
Brooks, Purser, and Warren, *An Approach to Literature,* 174-177.
Willis D. Jacobs, "Bunin's 'The Gentleman from San Francisco,'" *Explicator* VII (March, 1949), item 42.
Maurice B. McNamee, *Reading for Understanding,* 454-456.
Renato Poggioli, "The Art of Ivan Bunin," *Harvard Slavic Studies* I (1953), 257-258. — reprinted in Poggioli, *The Phoenix and the Spider,* 138-139.
West and Stallman, *Art of Modern Fiction,* 117-120.
5. THE GRAMMAR OF LOVE
Renato Poggioli, "The Art of Ivan Bunin," *Harvard Slavic Studies* I (1953), 261-262. — reprinted in Poggioli, *The Phoenix and the Spider,* 141-142.

BURNETT, WHIT

1. SHERREL
Edward J. O'Brien, *The Short Story Case Book,* 461-475.

CABLE, GEORGE W.

1. BELLES DEMOISELLES PLANTATION
Arlin Turner, *George W. Cable: A Biography,* 58-59.
2. CAFÉ DES EXILÉS
Arlin Turner, *George W. Cable: A Biography,* 62-63.
3. DON JOAQUIN
Raymond S. Moore, "'Don Joaquin,' A Forgotten Story by George W. Cable," *American Literature* XXVI (November, 1954), 418-421.
4. THE ENTOMOLOGIST
Arlin Turner, *George W. Cable: A Biography,* 314-315.
5. THE "HAUNTED HOUSE" IN ROYAL STREET
Arlin Turner, *George W. Cable: A Biography,* 239-240.
6. JEAN-AH POQUELIN
Arlin Turner, *George W. Cable: A Biography,* 60-62.
7. MADAME DÉLICIEUSE
Arlin Turner, *George W. Cable: A Biography,* 62.

CABLE, GEORGE W, Continued

8. MADAME DELPHINE
Arlin Turner, *George W. Cable: A Biography*, 105-109.
9. POSSON JONE'
Arlin Turner, *George W. Cable: A Biography*, 63-64.
10. 'SIEUR GEORGE
Arlin Turner, *George W. Cable: A Biography*, 54-57.
11. THE TAXIDERMIST
Arlin Turner, *George W. Cable: A Biography*, 313-314, 315.
12. 'TITE POULETTE
Arlin Turner, *George W. Cable: A Biography*, 59-60.

CALDWELL, ERSKINE

1. KNEEL TO THE RISING SUN
Kenneth Burke, "Caldwell: Maker of Grotesques," *New Republic* LXXXII (April 10, 1935), 232.
Sidney Finkelstein, "What's Happened to Erskine Caldwell?," *Masses and Mainstream* V (August, 1952), 61-62.
Kenneth Kempton, *The Short Story*, 136.
R. B. West, Jr., *The Short Story in America: 1900-1950*, 55.
2. THE PEOPLE VS. ABE LATHAN: COLORED
James B. Hall and Joseph Langland, *The Short Story*, 37-38.
3. THE SACRILEGE OF ALAN KENT
Kenneth Burke, "Caldwell: Maker of Grotesques," *New Republic* LXXXII (April 10, 1935), 232. – reprinted in Kenneth Burke, *The Philosophy of Literary Form*, 350-351.

CALLAGHAN, MORLEY

1. TWO FISHERMEN
Morley Callaghan, Comment in Whit Burnett, *This Is My Best*, 98.

CAMUS, ALBERT

1. THE ADULTEROUS WOMAN
Albert Maquet, *Albert Camus: The Invincible Summer*, 170-171.
Norman Podhoretz, "Books," *New Yorker* XXXIV (March 29, 1958), 115-116.
Philip Thody, *Albert Camus*, 81-83.

CAMUS, ALBERT, Continued

2. THE FALL

Lionel Abel, "Man Without Grace," *Commentary* XXIII (May, 1957), 488-490.

[Louis Allen, "Albert Camus: *La Chute*," *Downside Review* LXXV (1957), 259-274.]

Anon., "Soul in Despair," *Time* LXIX (February, 18, 1957), 102.

Anon., "Intellectual Guilt," *Times Literary Supplement* (February 22, 1957), 109.

Anthony Bailey, "The Isolated Man," *Commonweal* LXVII (October 25, 1957), 92-93.

John D. Boyd, "No Man an Island," *America* XCVI (March 23, 1957), 709.

G. Brée and M. Guiton, *An Age of Fiction*, 229-230.

G. Brée, *Camus*, 98-108, 128-131.

Robert Champigny, "Camus' Fictional Works: The Plight of Innocence," *American Society of Legion of Honor Magazine* XXVIII (Summer, 1957), 179-182.

Max Cosman, Review in *New Mexico Quarterly* XXVII (Spring-Summer, 1957), 129-131.

Robert Gorham Davis, "Exploration into the Guilt of Man," *New York Times Book Review* (February 17, 1957), 1, 33.

Benjamin De Mott, "Agonists and Agonizers, and a Utopian," *Hudson Review* X (Spring, 1957), 144-145.

Harvey Goldberg, "The Violence of Virtue," *Nation* CLXXXIV (March 30, 1957), 278-279.

[Walter Goldstein, Review in *Chicago Review* XI (Summer, 1957), 101-106.]

Ramon Guthrie, "A Brilliant and Powerful Allegory by Albert Camus," *New York Herald Tribune Book Review* (February 17, 1957), 1.

Iain Hamilton, "The Little-ease," *Spectator* CXCVIII (February 22, 1957), 255.

Thomas Hanna, *The Thought and Art of Albert Camus*, 162-179.

Irving Howe, "The Weight of Days," *New Republic* CXXXVI (March 11, 1957), 16-17.

Albert Maquet, *Albert Camus: The Invincible Summer*, 150-167.

Henri Peyre, "Man's Hopelessness," *Saturday Review* XL (February 16, 1957), 16.

Anthony Quinton, "New Novels," *New Statesman and Nation* LIII (February 16, 1957), 213.

C. J. Rolo, "Albert Camus: A Good Man," *Atlantic Monthly* CCI (May, 1958), 32.

C. J. Rolo, "The Outsider," *Atlantic Monthly* CXCIX (March 1957), 84-85.

Ralph Russell, "The Inferno of Albert Camus," *Reporter* XVI (April 4, 1957), 44-46.

F. C. St. Aubyn, "Albert Camus: Dialogue or Monologue?" *Books Abroad* XXXI (Spring, 1957), 123-125.

Philip Thody, *Albert Camus,* 75-81.

Philip Thody, "Albert Camus," *Contemporary Review,* No. 1092 (December, 1956), 349-352.

3. THE GROWING STONE

G. Brée, *Camus,* 134-136.

Irving Howe, "Between Facts and Fable," *New Republic* CXXX-VIII (March 31, 1958), 17-18.

Albert Maquet, *Albert Camus: The Invincible Summer,* 179-182.

Philip Thody, *Albert Camus,* 90-92.

4. THE GUEST

G. Brée, *Camus,* 133-134.

Albert Maquet, *Albert Camus: The Invincible Summer,* 174-176.

Philip Thody, *Albert Camus,* 87-88.

5. JONAH, OR THE ARTIST AT WORK

Albert Maquet, *Albert Camus: The Invincible Summer,* 176-179.

Norman Podhoretz, "Books," *New Yorker* XXXIV (March 29, 1958), 118.

Philip Thody, *Albert Camus,* 89-90.

6. THE OUTSIDER

(see "The Stranger")

7. THE RENEGADE

Robert G. Davis, "Faith for an Age Without Faith," *New York Times Book Review* (March 9, 1958), 1.

Albert Maquet, *Albert Camus: The Invincible Summer,* 171-173.

Norman Podhoretz, "Books," *New Yorker* XXXIV (March 29, 1958), 116-117.

Marian M. Stancioff, "Camus: Solitary or Solidary," *America* XCVIII (January 4, 1958), 396-397.

Philip Thody, *Albert Camus,* 83-85.

8. THE SILENT MEN

Albert Maquet, *Albert Camus: The Invincible Summer,* 173-174.

Philip Thody, *Albert Camus,* 85-87.

9. THE STRANGER

Anon., "A Victim," *Times Literary Supplement* (June 22, 1946), 293.

A. J. Ayer, "Novelists-Philosophers, VIII, Albert Camus," *Horizon* XIII (March, 1946), 164-165.

Jean C. Batt, "The Themes of the Novels and Plays of Albert Camus," *AUMLA* No. 6 (1957), 48-51.

Arthur H. Beattie, "From Despair Toward Hope (The Intellectual Evolution of Albert Camus)," *Arizona Quarterly* IX (Winter, 1953), 335-340.

Haskell M. Block, "Albert Camus: Toward a Definition of Tragedy," *University of Toronto Quarterly* XIX (July, 1950), 355-357.

G. Brée and M. Guiton, *An Age of Fiction*, 220-222.

G. Brée, *Camus*, 86-90, 98-114.

Victor Brombert, "Camus and the Novel of the 'Absurd,' " *Yale French Studies,* No. 1 (Spring-Summer, 1948), 119-123.

Robert Champigny, "Camus' Fictional Works: The Plight of Innocence," *American Society of Legion of Honor Magazine* XXVIII (Summer, 1957), 174-176.

Nicola Chiaromonte, "Albert Camus," *New Republic* CXIV (April 29, 1946), 630-633.

Eleanor Clark, "Existentialist Fiction," *Kenyon Review* VIII (Autumn, 1946), 674-678.

John Cruickshank, "Camus's Technique in 'L'Étranger,' " *French Studies* X (July, 1956), 241-253.

W. M. Frohock, "Camus: Irony, Influence and Sensibility," *Yale French Studies,* No. 4 (1949), 91-96.

Harry R. Garvin, "Camus and the American Novel," *Comparative Literature* VIII (Summer, 1956), 194-197, 202-203.

Herbert S. Gershman, "On 'L'Étranger," *French Review* XXIX (February, 1956), 299-305.

Henry A. Grubbs, "Camus and Graham Greene," *Modern Language Quarterly* X (March, 1949), 33-42.

Philip Hallie, "Camus and the Literature of Revolt," *College English* XVI (October, 1954), 26-28.

L. Hamalian and E. L. Volpe, *Ten Modern Short Novels*, 642-644.

Thomas Hanna, *The Thought and Art of Albert Camus*, 35-48.

Rayner Heppenstall, "New Novels," *New Statesman and Nation* XXXI (June 29, 1946), 474.

Katherine Hoskins, "A Novelist of the Absurd," *Partisan Review* XIII (Winter, 1946), 121-123.

S. John, "The Characters of Albert Camus," *University of Toronto Quarterly* XXIII (July, 1954), 366-368.

S. John, "Image and Symbol in the Work of Albert Camus," *French Studies* IX (January, 1955), 45-47, 50.

B. Renée Lang, "Two Books, Two Creeds," *Books Abroad* XXI (1947), 385-386.

Kermit Lansner, "Albert Camus," *Kenyon Review* XIV (Autumn, 1952), 569-572.

Nathan Leites, "Trends in Affectlessness," *American Imago* IV, No. 2 (April, 1947), 89-112. — reprinted, titled "The Stranger," in Williams Phillips, *Art and Psychoanalysis*, 247-267.

Max Lerner, *Actions and Passions*, 46-49.

Albert Maquet, *Albert Camus: The Invincible Summer*, 48-61.

Gabriel Marcel, "The Refusal of Salvation and the Exaltation of the Man of Absurdity," in Marcel, *Homo Viator*, 203-206.

H. A. Mason, "M. Camus and the Tragic Hero," *Scrutiny* XIV (December, 1946), 82-89.

Justin O'Brien, "Presenting a New French Writer," *New York Herald Tribune Book Review* (April 14, 1946), 4.

Henri Peyre, *The Contemporary French Novel*, 243-246.

Richard Plant, "Benign Indifference," *Saturday Review of Literature* XXIX (May 18, 1946), 10.

Norman Podhoretz, "Books," *New Yorker* XXXIV (March 29, 1958), 115.

C. J. Rolo, "Albert Camus: A Good Man," *Atlantic Monthly* CCI (May, 1958), 30.

Louis R. Rossi, "Albert Camus: The Plague of Absurdity," *Kenyon Review* XX (Summer, 1958), 399-422.

Leon Roth, "A Contemporary Moralist: Albert Camus," *Philosophy* XXX (October, 1955), 292-293.

L. S. Roudiez, "Disagreement on Camus," *French Review* XXIX (February, 1956), 332.

L. S. Roudiez and Herbert S. Gershman, "Disagreement on Camus," *French Review* XXIX (May, 1956), 491-493.

Jean-Paul Sartre, "Camus' 'The Outsider,'" in Sartre, *Literary and Philosophical Essays*, (1955), 24-41. — reprinted in Sartre, *Literary Essays* (Wisdom Library, 1957), 24-41.

Lurline V. Simpson, "Tensions in the Works of Albert Camus," *Modern Language Journal* XXXVIII (April, 1954), 186-187.

F. C. St. Aubyn, "Albert Camus: Dialogue or Monologue?" *Books Abroad* XXXI (Spring, 1957), 122-123.

Philip Thody, *Albert Camus*, 1-9, 111-120.

Carl A. Viggiani, "Camus' L'Étranger," *PMLA* LXXI (December, 1956), 865-887.

Edmund Wilson, Review in *New Yorker* XXII (April 13, 1946), 113-114.

CANFIELD, DOROTHY

1. FLINT AND FIRE
   Dorothy Canfield, "How 'Flint and Fire' Started and Grew," in Stegner, Scowcroft, and Ilyin, *The Writer's Art*, 289-298. — reprinted in Douglas Bement and Ross M. Taylor, *The Fabric of Fiction*, 599-606. — reprinted from Benjamin A. Heydrick, *Americans All* (Harcourt, 1920).

CAPOTE, TRUMAN

1. CHILDREN ON THEIR BIRTHDAYS
   James B. Hall and Joseph Langland, *The Short Story*, 235-236.
2. THE HEADLESS HAWK
   Paul Levine, "Truman Capote: The Revelation of the Broken Image," *Virginia Quarterly Review* XXXIV (Autumn, 1958), 606-608.
3. MASTER MISERY
   John W. Aldridge, "The Metaphorical World of Truman Capote," *Western Review* XV (Summer, 1951), 248-249.
   Paul Levine, "Truman Capote: The Revelation of the Broken Image," *Virginia Quarterly Review* XXXIV (Autumn, 1958), 605-606.
4. MIRIAM
   Paul Levine, "Truman Capote: The Revelation of the Broken Image," *Virginia Quarterly Review* XXXIV (Autumn, 1958), 606.
5. A TREE OF NIGHT
   Paul Levine, "Truman Capote: The Revelation of the Broken Image," *Virginia Quarterly Review* XXXIV (Autumn, 1958), 608-609.

CASSILL, R. V.

1. LARCHMOOR IS NOT THE WORLD
   Kenneth Kempton, *Short Stories for Study*, 300-303.

CATHER, WILLA

1. THE AFFAIR AT GROVER STATION
   Mildred R. Bennett, *Early Stories of Willa Cather*, 239-256, passim.
2. BEFORE BREAKFAST
   David Daiches, *Willa Cather*, 171-173.

3. THE BEST YEARS
   David Daiches, *Willa Cather,* 170-171.
4. THE BOHEMIAN GIRL
   E. K. Brown and Leon Edel, *Willa Cather: A Critical Biography,* 161-166.
5. THE CLEMENCY OF THE COURT
   Mildred R. Bennett, *Early Stories of Willa Cather,* 33-34, passim.
   E. K. Brown and Leon Edel, *Willa Cather: A Critical Biography,* 59-61.
6. COMING, APHRODITE!
   David Daiches, *Willa Cather,* 153-154.
   Howard Mumford Jones, *The Bright Medusa,* 17-21.
7. THE CONVERSION OF SUM LOO
   Mildred R. Bennett, *The Early Stories of Willa Cather,* 263, 268.
8. THE COUNT OF CROW'S NEST
   Mildred R. Bennett, *Early Stories of Willa Cather,* 115-145, passim.
9. THE DANCE AT CHEVALIER'S
   Mildred R. Bennett, *Early Stories of Willa Cather,* 217-229, passim.
10. A DEATH IN THE DESERT
    David Daiches, *Willa Cather,* 149-152.
11. THE DIAMOND MINE
    David Daiches, *Willa Cather,* 154-157.
12. ELEANOR'S HOUSE
    E. K. Brown and Leon Edel, *Willa Cather: A Critical Biography,* 143-144.
13. THE ENCHANTED BLUFF
    E. K. Brown and Leon Edel, *Willa Cather: A Critical Biography,* 149-150.
    Philip L. Gerber, "Willa Cather and the Big Red Rock," *College English* XIX (January, 1958), 152-153, 156.
14. ERIC HERMANNSON'S SOUL
    Mildred R. Bennett, *Early Stories of Willa Cather,* 187-215, passim.
15. THE FEAR THAT WALKS BY NOONDAY
    Mildred R. Bennett, *Early Stories of Willa Cather,* 45.
16. FLAVIA AND HER ARTISTS
    E. K. Brown and Leon Edel, *Willa Cather: A Critical Biography,* 115-116.
17. LOU, THE PROPHET
    Mildred R. Bennett, *Early Stories of Willa Cather,* 9-17, passim.
18. THE MARRIAGE OF PHAEDRA
    E. K. Brown and Leon Edel, *Willa Cather: A Critical Biography,* 117-118.

CATHER WILLA, Continued

19. THE NAMESAKE
E. K. Brown and Leon Edel, *Willa Cather: A Critical Biography*, 141-143.

20. NANETTE: AN ASIDE
Mildred R. Bennett, *Early Stories of Willa Cather*, 93-102, passim.

21. NEIGHBOUR ROSICKY
Mary Orvis, *The Art of Writing Fiction*, 223-224.

22. A NIGHT AT GREENWAY COURT
Mildred R. Bennett, *Early Stories of Willa Cather*, 77-91, passim.

23. THE OLD BEAUTY
David Daiches, *Willa Cather*, 168-170.

24. OLD MRS. HARRIS
David Daiches, *Willa Cather*, 158-166.

25. ON THE DIVIDE
Mildred R. Bennett, *Early Stories of Willa Cather*, 59-75, passim.

26. PAUL'S CASE
E. K. Brown and Leon Edel, *Willa Cather: A Critical Biography*, 121-122.
David Daiches, *Willa Cather*, 145-146.
Winifred Lynskey, *Reading Modern Fiction* (Second Edition, 1957), 81-83.

27. PETER SADELACK, FATHER OF ANTON
Mildred R. Bennett, *Early Stories of Willa Cather*, 1-8, passim.

28. THE PRODIGIES
Mildred R. Bennett, *Early Stories of Willa Cather*, 169-185, passim.

29. A RESURRECTION
Mildred R. Bennett, *Early Stories of Willa Cather*, 147-165, passim.

30. THE SCULPTOR'S FUNERAL
David Daiches, *Willa Cather*, 144-145.
Howard Mumford Jones, *The Bright Medusa*, 15-17.

31. A SINGER'S ROMANCE
Mildred R. Bennett, *Early Stories of Willa Cather*, 257, 263.

32. A SON OF THE CELESTIAL: A CHARACTER
Mildred R. Bennett, *Early Stories of Willa Cather*, 25-32, passim.

33. A TALE OF THE WHITE PYRAMID
Mildred R. Bennett, *Early Stories of Willa Cather*, 19.

34. TOMMY, THE UNSENTIMENTAL
Mildred R. Bennett, *Early Stories of Willa Cather*, 103-113, passim.

35. A WAGNER MATINÉE
David Daiches, *Willa Cather*, 147-149.

CHEEVER, JOHN

1. THE ENORMOUS RADIO
   James B. Hall and Joseph Langland, *The Short Story*, 175-176.

CHEKHOV, ANTON

1. AN ACQUAINTANCE
   (see "A Gentleman Friend")
2. AFTER THE THEATRE
   Robert G. Davis, *Instructor's Manual for "Ten Modern Masters,"* 22-23.
3. AGAFYA
   W. H. Bruford, *Anton Chekhov*, 18.
4. AN ANONYMOUS STORY
   W. H. Bruford, *Chekhov and His Russia*, 100-103.
5. ANYUTA
   Renato Poggioli, *The Phoenix and the Spider*, 122-124.
6. THE BET
   J. Rives Childs, "Chekhov's 'The Bet': Its Source in Lord Cecil's Wager," *South Atlantic Quarterly* XL (October, 1941), 397-400.
7. THE BETROTHED
   Edmund Wilson, "Seeing Chekhov Plain," *New Yorker* XXVIII (November 22, 1952), 194, 197.
8. THE BISHOP
   W. H. Bruford, *Chekhov and His Russia*, 137-139.
9. THE BLACK MONK
   Edward J. O'Brien, *The Short Story Case Book*, 113-179.
10. A BORING STORY
    (see "A Dreary Story")
11. THE BURBOT
    (see "The Fish")
12. THE CHORUS GIRL
    Herbert Barrows, *Suggestions for Teaching "15 Stories,"* 13-14.
    Séan O'Faoláin, *The Short Story*, 184-186.
    Renato Poggioli, *The Phoenix and the Spider*, 113-115.
13. LA CIGALE
    (see "The Grasshopper")
14. THE DARLING
    Renato Poggioli, *The Phoenix and the Spider*, 124-130.
15. A DOCTOR'S VISIT
    W. H. Bruford, *Chekhov and His Russia*, 185-186.

CHEKHOV, ANTON, Continued

Ronald Hingley, *Chekhov: A Biographical and Critical Study,* 156-158.

16. A DREARY STORY
W. H. Bruford, *Anton Chekhov,* 34-35.
Ronald Hingley, *Chekhov: A Biographical and Critical Study,* 100-103.
Thomas Mann, "The Stature of Anton Chekhov," *New Republic* CXXXII (May 16, 1955), 24-25.

17. THE DUEL
W. H. Bruford, *Chekhov and His Russia,* 166-167, 206-208.
Frank O'Connor, *The Mirror in the Roadway,* 259-262.
Gilbert Phelps, " 'Indifference' in the Letters and Tales of Chekhov," *Cambridge Journal* VII (January, 1954), 214-216.

18. THE ENEMIES
Dorothy Brewster and Angus Burrell, *Modern Fiction,* 364-365.
W. H. Bruford, *Chekhov and His Russia,* 157-158.

19. THE FISH
W. H. Bruford, *Anton Chekhov,* 17.

20. THE GAMEKEEPER
(see "The Huntsman")

21. A GENTLEMAN FRIEND
Renato Poggioli, *The Phoenix and the Spider,* 115-117.

22. GOOSEBERRIES
Séan O'Faoláin, *The Short Story,* 173-175.
Mark Schorer, *The Story,* 62-64.
Raymond W. Short and Richard B. Sewall, *A Manual of Suggestions for Teachers Using "Short Stories for Study,"* 31-33.
V. Yermilov, "Chekhov the Realist," *Masses and Mainstream* VII (July, 1954), 32.

23. THE GRASSHOPPER
Séan O'Faoláin, *The Short Story,* 90-91.
West and Stallman, *The Art of Modern Fiction,* 95-98.
V. Yermilov, "Chekhov the Realist," *Masses and Mainstream* VII (July, 1954), 27.

24. HEARTACHE
Renato Poggioli, *The Phoenix and the Spider,* 118-119.

25. THE HUNTSMAN
W. H. Bruford, *Anton Chekhov,* 17-18.

26. IN EXILE
Stegner, Scowcroft, and Ilyin, *The Writer's Art,* 18-20.

27. IN THE CART
(see "The Schoolmistress")

CHEKHOV, ANTON, Continued

28. THE KISS
Sylvia Berkman, *Katherine Mansfield*, 153.
Ronald Hingley, *Chekhov: A Biographical and Critical Study*, 73-76.
29. THE LADY WITH A LAPDOG
(see "The Lady with the Dog")
30. THE LADY WITH THE DOG
Royal A. Gettmann and Bruce Harkness, *Teacher's Manual for "A Book of Stories,"* 4-7.
Gilbert Phelps, " 'Indifference' in the Letters and Tales of Chekhov," *Cambridge Journal* VII (January, 1954), 211-213.
31. THE LAMENT
Brooks and Warren, *Understanding Fiction*, 247-250.
32. LIGHTS
W. H. Bruford, *Chekhov and His Russia*, 204-206.
33. THE LOTTERY TICKET
Dorothy Brewster and Angus Burrell, *Modern Fiction*, 359.
34. THE MAN IN A CASE
V. Yermilov, "Chekhov the Realist," *Masses and Mainstream* VII (July, 1954), 33.
35. MISERY
(see "Heartache")
36. MY LIFE
Ronald Hingley, *Chekhov: A Biographical and Critical Study*, 161-164.
37. NAME-DAY
(see "The Party")
38. ON THE ROAD
Alfred Dashiell, *Editor's Choice*, 232.
Caroline Gordon, "Notes on Chekhov and Maugham," *Sewanee Review* LVII (Summer, 1949), 405-410. — reprinted, revised, in Gordon and Tate, *The House of Fiction*, 175-178.
Simon O. Lesser, *Fiction and the Unconscious*, 153, 156-159.
Stegner, Scowcroft, and Ilyin, *The Writer's Art*, 37-40.
39. ON THE WAY
(see "On the Road")
40. THE PARTY
W. H. Bruford, *Anton Chekhov*, 27-29.
41. PEASANTS
W. H. Bruford, *Chekhov and His Russia*, 38-75.
42. POLINKA
Renato Poggioli, *The Phoenix and the Spider*, 111-113.

CHEKHOV, ANTON, Continued

43. ROTHSCHILD'S FIDDLE
   Frank O'Connor, *The Mirror in the Roadway*, 256.
44. THE SCHOOLMISTRESS
   Herbert Barrows, *Suggestions for Teaching "15 Stories,"* 10-12.
   H. E. Bates, *The Modern Short Story*, 87-89.
45. SERGEANT PRISHIBEYEV
   (see "Under-officer Prishibeyev")
46. THE SERVICE OF THE DEAD
   Renato Poggioli, *The Phoenix and the Spider*, 120-122.
47. SLEEPYHEAD
   Elisabeth Schneider, "Katherine Mansfield and Chekhov," *Modern Language Notes* L (June, 1935), 394-397.
48. SMALL FRY
   Dorothy Brewster and Angus Burrell, *Modern Fiction*, 362-363.
49. THE STEPPE
   Dorothy Brewster and Angus Burrell, *Modern Fiction*, 365-368.
   W. H. Bruford, *Anton Chekhov*, 33.
   Ronald Hingley, *Chekhov: A Biographical and Critical Study*, 77-81.
50. THE STORY OF AN UNKNOWN PERSON
   William Gerhardi, *Anton Chekhov*, 116-120.
51. THE STUDENT
   W. H. Bruford, *Chekhov and His Russia*, 209-210.
52. THE TEACHER OF LITERATURE
   Ronald Hingley, *Chekhov: A Biographical and Critical Study*, 206-209.
53. A TEDIOUS TALE
   (see "A Dreary Story")
54. THREE YEARS
   W. H. Bruford, *Chekhov and His Russia*, 180-183.
   V. Yermilov, "Chekhov the Realist," *Masses and Mainstream* VII (July, 1954), 31.
55. UNDER-OFFICER PRISHIBEYEV
   V. Yermilov, "Chekhov the Realist," *Masses and Mainstream* VII (July, 1954), 25.
56. VANKA
   Renato Poggioli, *The Phoenix and the Spider*, 110-111.
57. VEROTCHKA
   Dorothy Brewster and Angus Burrell, *Modern Fiction*, 372-373.
   Séan O'Faoláin, "On a Story by Tchekov," *Life and Letters To-Day* XVII (Autumn, 1937), 60-65.
   Séan O'Faoláin, *The Short Story*, 76-78.

CHEKHOV, ANTON, Continued

58. WARD NO. 6
Montgomery Belgion, "Tchekov and Dostoievsky," *Criterion* XVI (October, 1936), 17-23.
W. H. Bruford, *Anton Chekhov*, 35-36.
W. H. Bruford, *Chekhov and His Russia*, 159-160.
Ronald Hingley, *Chekhov: A Biographical and Critical Study*, 151-156.
Charles Neider, *Short Novels of the Masters*, 36.
Marc Slonim, *Modern Russian Literature*, 69-70.
V. Yermilov, "Chekhov the Realist," *Masses and Mainstream* VII (July, 1954), 28-31.
59. THE WITCH
W. H. Bruford, *Anton Chekhov*, 18-19.
60. A WOMAN'S KINGDOM
W. H. Bruford, *Chekhov and His Russia*, 186-188.

CLARK, WALTER VAN TILBURG

1. HOOK
Herbert Wilner, "Walter Van Tilburg Clark," *Western Review* XX (Winter, 1956), 104-106.
2. THE PORTABLE PHONOGRAPH
Walter Van Tilburg Clark, "The Ghost of an Apprehension," *Pacific Spectator* III (Summer, 1949), 254-263. — reprinted in Stegner, et al., *The Writer's Art*, 264-273. — reprinted in Locke, Gibson, and Arms, *Introduction to Literature* (Second Edition, 1952), 486-493. — reprinted in Stallman and Watters, *The Creative Reader*, 269-274. — reprinted in Mark Schorer, *The Story*, 278-287.
Vernon Young, "Gods Without Heroes: The Tentative Myth of Van Tilburg Clark," *Arizona Quarterly* VII (Summer, 1951), 114-116.
3. THE RAPIDS
James B. Hall and Joseph Langland, *The Short Story*, 390-391.
4. THE WATCHFUL GODS
John Portz, "Idea and Symbol in Walter Van Tilburg Clark," *Accent* XVII (Spring, 1957), 125-128.
5. THE WIND AND THE SNOW OF WINTER
Mary Orvis, *The Art of Writing Fiction*, 76-77, 127-128.

COMFORT, ALEX

1. THE MARTYRDOM OF THE HOUSE
   Felheim, Newman, and Steinhoff, *Study Aids for Teachers for "Modern Short Stories,"* 46-48.

CONRAD, JOSEPH

1. AMY FOSTER
   Albert J. Guerard, *Conrad: The Novelist,* 49-51.
   Albert J. Guerard, *Joseph Conrad* (1947), 69-70.
   Gustav Morf, *The Polish Heritage of Joseph Conrad,* 167-176.
   Thomas Moser, *Joseph Conrad,* 86-87.
   Marvin Mudrick, "Conrad and the Terms of Modern Criticism," *Hudson Review* VII (Autumn, 1954), 422-424.
   Mark Schorer, *The Story,* 243-246.
   Stallman and Watters, *Creative Reader,* 326-328.
   Edward Wasiolek, "Yanko Gooral, A Note on Name Symbolism in Conrad's 'Amy Foster,'" *Modern Language Notes* LXII (June, 1956), 418-419.
   Walter F. Wright, *Romance and Tragedy in Joseph Conrad,* 165-166.
2. THE ANARCHIST
   R. L. Mégroz, *Joseph Conrad's Mind and Method,* 202-204.
3. BECAUSE OF THE DOLLARS
   Walter F. Wright, *Romance and Tragedy in Joseph Conrad,* 162-163.
4. THE BLACK MATE
   R. L. Mégroz, *Joseph Conrad's Mind and Method,* 77-78.
5. THE DUEL
   Conrad's Prefaces to His Works, 118-119.
   J. DeLancey Ferguson, "The Plot of Conrad's 'The Duel,'" *Modern Language Notes* L (June, 1935), 385-390.
   Paul L. Wiley, *Conrad's Measure of Man,* 92-94.
   Walter F. Wright, *Romance and Tragedy in Joseph Conrad,* 31-32.
6. THE END OF THE TETHER
   W. W. Bancroft, *Joseph Conrad: His Philosophy of Life,* 84-87.
   Douglas Hewitt, *Conrad: A Reassessment,* 28-30.
   William T. Moynihan, "Conrad's 'The End of the Tether': A New Reading," *Modern Fiction Studies* IV (Summer, 1958), 173-177.
   Paul L. Wiley, *Conrad's Measure of Man,* 64-69.
   Walter F. Wright, *Romance and Tragedy in Joseph Conrad,* 96-97.
7. FALK
   Conrad's Prefaces to His Works, 79-80.

CONRAD, JOSEPH, Continued

Edward Crankshaw, *Joseph Conrad,* 92-95.
Albert J. Guerard, *Conrad: The Novelist,* 20-21.
Douglas Hewitt, *Joseph Conrad: A Reassessment,* 40-45.
Thomas Moser, *Joseph Conrad,* 99-100.
Edward Visiak, *The Mirror of Conrad,* 35-36.
H. T. Webster, "Conrad's Changes in Narrative Conception in the Manuscripts of *Typhoon and Other Stories* and *Victory,*" *PMLA* LXIV (December, 1949), 954-955.
H. T. Webster, "Conrad's 'Falk,'" *Explicator* VII (June, 1949), item 56.
Paul L. Wiley, *Conrad's Measure of Man,* 74-77.
8. FREYA OF THE SEVEN ISLES
W. W. Bancroft, *Joseph Conrad: His Philosophy of Life,* 53-55.
Thomas Moser, *Joseph Conrad,* 100-101.
Paul L. Wiley, *Conrad's Measure of Man,* 139-141.
Walter F. Wright, *Romance and Tragedy in Joseph Conrad,* 163-165.
9. GASPAR RUIZ
Conrad's Prefaces to His Works, 116-117.
Walter F. Wright, *Romance and Tragedy in Joseph Conrad,* 91-92.
10. HEART OF DARKNESS
G. H. Bantock, "The Two 'Moralities' of Joseph Conrad," *Essays in Criticism* III (April, 1953), 134-136.
Sam S. Baskett, "Jack London's Heart of Darkness," *American Quarterly* X (Spring, 1958), 72-76.
Joseph Warren Beach, *The Twentieth Century Novel,* 342-344.
M. C. Bradbrook, *Joseph Conrad: Poland's English Genius,* 27-31.
Harold R. Collins, "Kurtz, the Cannibals, and the Second-rate Helmsman," *Western Humanities Review* VIII (Autumn, 1954), 299-310.
Edward Crankshaw, *Joseph Conrad,* 133-134.
Richard Curle, "Conrad's Diary," *Yale Review* XV (January, 1926), 254-266.
Leonard F. Dean, "Tragic Pattern in Conrad's 'Heart of Darkness,'" *College English* VI (November, 1944), 100-104.
Wilfred S. Dowden, "The Light and the Dark: Imagery and Thematic Development in Conrad's 'Heart of Darkness,'" *Rice Institute Pamphlets* XLIV, i (1957), 33-51.
Robert O. Evans, "Conrad's Underworld," *Modern Fiction Studies* II (May, 1956), 56-62.
Robert O. Evans, "Further Comment on 'The Heart of Darkness,'" *Modern Fiction Studies* III (Winter, 1957-1958), 358-361.

CONRAD, JOSEPH, Continued

Lillian Feder, "Marlow's Descent into Hell," *Nineteenth-Century Fiction* IX (March, 1955), 280-292.

Ford Madox Ford, *Portraits from Life,* 59-63; or *Mightier Than the Sword* (English Edition), 86-91.

G. S. Fraser, *The Modern Writer and His World,* 63-64.

Edward Garnett, "Introductory Essay," in *Conrad's Prefaces to His Works,* 13-16.

Seymour L. Gross, "A Further Note on the Function of the Frame in 'Heart of Darkness,' " *Modern Fiction Studies* III (Summer, 1957), 167-170.

Albert J. Guerard, *Conrad: The Novelist,* 33-48.

Louis J. Halle, Jr., "Joseph Conrad: An Enigma Decoded," *Saturday Review of Literature* XXXI (May 22, 1948), 7-8, 32-34.

L. Hamalian and E. L. Volpe, *Ten Modern Short Novels,* 194-195.

Robert F. Haugh, *Joseph Conrad,* 35-55.

Douglas Hewitt, *Joseph Conrad,* 16-27.

Douglas Hewitt, "Joseph Conrad's Hero: 'Fidelity' or 'The Choice of Nightmares,' " *Cambridge Journal* II (August, 1949), 685-687.

Dorothy M. Hoare, *Some Studies in the Modern Novel,* 121-123.

Alan M. Hollingsworth, "Freud, Conrad, and 'The Future of an Illusion,' " *Literature and Psychology* V (November, 1955), 82.

Gérard Jean-Aubry, *The Sea Dreamer: Joseph Conrad,* 152-153. 159-160, 163-171.

Arnold Kettle, "The Greatness of Joseph Conrad," *Modern Quarterly* III, n.s. (Summer, 1948), 64-70.

F. R. Leavis, "Joseph Conrad," *Scrutiny* X (June, 1941), 23-32. — reprinted in F. R. Leavis, *The Great Tradition,* 174-182. — reprinted in J. W. Aldridge, *Critiques and Essays on Modern Fiction,* 107-113.

J. B. Ludwig and W. R. Poirier, *Instructor's Manual to Accompany "Stories: British and American,"* 20-24.

R. M. Ludwig and M. B. Perry, *Nine Short Novels,* xxxvii-xliii.

Robert L. Morris, "The Classical Reference in Conrad's Fiction," *College English* VII (March, 1946), 313-315.

Thomas Moser, *Joseph Conrad,* 78-81.

Guy Owen, Jr., "A Note on 'Heart of Darkness,' " *Nineteenth Century Fiction* XII (September, 1957), 168-169.

R. J. Owen, "Joseph Conrad: Two Books," *Notes and Queries* V (June, 1958), 260.

R. W. Short and R. B. Sewall, *A Manual of Suggestions for Teachers Using "Short Stories for Study,"* 58-64.

CONRAD, JOSEPH, Continued

William Bysshe Stein, "Buddhism and 'The Heart of Darkness,' " *Western Humanities Review* XI (Summer, 1957), 281-285.

William Bysshe Stein, "The Lotus Posture and 'The Heart of Darkness,' " *Modern Fiction Studies* II (Winter, 1956-1957), 235-237.

Jerome Thale, "Marlow's Quest," *University of Toronto Quarterly* XXIV (July, 1955), 351-358.

Jerome Thale, "The Narrator as Hero," *Twentieth Century Literature* III (July, 1957), 69-73.

[William York Tindall, "The Symbolic Novel," *A.D. 52,* III (Winter, 1952), 56-68.]

William Y. Tindall, *The Literary Symbol,* 86-91.

Leonard Unger, *The Man in the Name,* 195-200, 207-211, 216-218.

Paul L. Wiley, *Conrad's Measure of Man,* 61-64.

Walter F. Wright, *Romance and Tragedy in Joseph Conrad,* 30-31, 143-160.

11. THE IDIOTS

Milton Chaikin, "Zola and Conrad's 'The Idiots,' " *Studies in Philology* LII (July, 1955), 502-507.

Albert J. Guerard, *Conrad: The Novelist,* 94-96.

Walter F. Wright, *Romance and Tragedy in Joseph Conrad,* 169-171.

12. IL CONDE

W. W. Bancroft, *Joseph Conrad, His Philosophy of Life,* 36-38.

Paul L. Wiley, *Conrad's Measure of Man,* 89-90.

John H. Wills, "Adam, Axel, and 'Il Conde,' " *Modern Fiction Studies* I (February, 1955), 22-25.

Walter F. Wright, *Romance and Tragedy in Joseph Conrad,* 167-168.

13. THE INFORMER

W. W. Bancroft, *Joseph Conrad: His Philosophy of Life,* 18-19.

Irving Howe, *Politics and the Novel* (Meridian Books), 85.

Paul L. Wiley, *Conrad's Measure of Man,* 88-89.

14. KARAIN

Albert J. Guerard, *Conrad: The Novelist,* 90-92.

Gustav Morf, *The Polish Heritage of Joseph Conrad,* 113-114.

Walter F. Wright, *Romance and Tragedy in Joseph Conrad,* 25-27.

15. THE LAGOON

F. A. D., "Conrad's 'The Lagoon,' " *Explicator* IX (1951), item 7.

Robert F. Gleckner, "Conrad's 'The Lagoon,' " *Explicator* XVI, No. 6 (March, 1958), item 33.

Albert J. Guerard, *Conrad: The Novelist,* 65-68.

CONRAD, JOSEPH, Continued

Thomas A. Gullason, "Conrad's 'The Lagoon,'" *Explicator* XIV, No. 4 (January, 1956), item 23.

Eleanor M. Sickels, "Conrad's 'The Lagoon,'" *Explicator* XV, No. 3 (December, 1956), item 17.

Walter F. Wright, *Romance and Tragedy in Joseph Conrad*, 92-93.

16. AN OUTPOST OF PROGRESS

W. W. Bancroft, *Joseph Conrad: His Philosophy of Life*, 80-83.

Sam S. Baskett, "Jack London's Heart of Darkness," *American Quarterly* X (Spring, 1958), 67-70.

Albert J. Guerard, *Conrad: The Novelist*, 64-65.

Leonard Unger, *The Man in the Name*, 232-234.

Walter F. Wright, *Romance and Tragedy in Joseph Conrad*, 131-134.

17. THE PARTNER

W. W. Bancroft, *Joseph Conrad: His Philosophy of Life*, 56-57.

18. THE PLANTER OF MALATA

Conrad's Prefaces to His Works, 155-157.

Albert J. Guerard, *Joseph Conrad* (1947), 46-47.

Thomas Moser, *Joseph Conrad*, 144-145.

Paul L. Wiley, *Conrad's Measure of Man*, 158-162.

19. PRINCE ROMAN

Gustave Morf, *The Polish Heritage of Joseph Conrad*, 192-199.

20. THE RETURN

Edward Crankshaw, *Joseph Conrad*, 84-85.

Albert J. Guerard, *Conrad: The Novelist*, 96-99.

Thomas Moser, *Joseph Conrad*, 71-78.

Paul L. Wiley, *Conrad's Measure of Man*, 25-28.

21. THE SECRET SHARER

Beardsley, Daniel, and Leggett, *Aids to Study for "Theme and Form: An Introduction to Literature,"* 96-97.

Carl Benson, "Conrad's Two Stories of Initiation," *PMLA* LXIX (March, 1954), 46-56.

Robert G. Davis, *Instructor's Manual for "Ten Modern Masters,"* 34-35.

Robert O. Evans, "Conrad: A Nautical Image," *Modern Language Notes* LXXII (February, 1957), 98-99.

Albert J. Guerard, *Conrad: The Novelist* (1958), 21-29.

Albert J. Guerard, *Joseph Conrad* (1947), 38-42.

Robert F. Haugh, *Joseph Conrad*, 78-82.

Douglas Hewitt, *Conrad: A Reassessment*, 70-79.

Winifred Lynskey, *Reading Modern Fiction* (Second Edition, 1957), 147-149.

CONRAD, JOSEPH, Continued

F. R. Leavis, "Joseph Conrad," *Sewanee Review* LXVI (Spring, 1958), 185-187.

Alfred C. Ward, *Aspects of the Modern Short Story*, 148-157.

H. T. Webster, "Conrad's Changes in Narrative Conception in the Manuscripts of *Typhoon and Other Stories* and *Victory*," *PMLA* LXIV (December, 1949), 953-954.

Paul L. Wiley, *Conrad's Measure of Man*, 69-74.

Walter F. Wright, *Romance and Tragedy in Joseph Conrad*, 12-17, 44-45, 62-65.

25. THE WARRIOR'S SOUL
Walter F. Wright, *Romance and Tragedy in Joseph Conrad*, 168-169.

26. YOUTH
Robert G. Davis, *Instructor's Manual for "Ten Modern Masters,"* 33-34.

Albert J. Guerard, *Conrad: The Novelist*, 16-18.

Robert F. Haugh, *Joseph Conrad*, 20-24.

Douglas Hewitt, *Conrad: A Reassessment*, 27-28.

Gérard Jean-Aubry, *The Sea Dreamer: Joseph Conrad*, 93-99.

Thomas Moser, *Joseph Conrad*, 43-49, 128-129.

V. S. Pritchett, *The Living Novel*, 144-145.

Leonard Unger, *The Man in the Name*, 240-242.

Walter F. Wright, *Romance and Tragedy in Joseph Conrad*, 9-12.

COPPARD, A. E.

1. ADAM AND EVE AND PINCH ME
Jaffe and Scott, *Studies in the Modern Short Story*, 400-403.

2. FIFTY POUNDS
R. B. Heilman, *Modern Short Stories*, 38-39.

3. THE HIGGLER
Edward J. O'Brien, *The Short Story Case Book*, 543-599.

4. WILLIE WAUGH
Royal A. Gettmann and Bruce Harkness, *Teacher's Manual for "A Book of Stories,"* 39-40.

CRANE, STEPHEN

1. THE BLUE HOTEL
John Berryman, *Stephen Crane*, 208-214.

James Trammell Cox, "Stephen Crane as Symbolic Naturalist:

CRANE, STEPHEN, Continued

An Analysis of 'The Blue Hotel,' " *Modern Fiction Studies* III (Summer, 1957) , 147-158.

William M. Gibson, "Introduction," in Crane, *Selected Prose and Poetry* (Rinehart Editions, 1950) , xiii-xiv.

Stanley B. Greenfield, "The Unmistakable Stephen Crane," *PMLA* LXXIII (December, 1958) , 565-568.

Winifred Lynskey, *Reading Modern Fiction* (Second Edition, 1957) , 173-175.

Russell Roth, "A Tree in Winter: The Short Fiction of Stephen Crane," *New Mexico Quarterly* XXIII (Summer, 1953) , 194-195.

Joseph N. Satterwhite, "Stephen Crane's 'The Blue Hotel': The Failure of Understanding," *Modern Fiction Studies* II (Winter, 1956-1957) , 238-241.

Robert W. Stallman, *Stephen Crane: An Omnibus*, 482-483.

Vincent Starrett, "Stephen Crane: An Estimate," *Sewanee Review* XXVIII (July, 1920) , 407-408.

Walter Sutton, "Pity and Fear in 'The Blue Hotel,' " *American Quarterly* IV (Spring, 1952) , 73-76.

C. C. Walcutt, *American Literary Naturalism*, 72-74.

2. THE BRIDE COMES TO YELLOW SKY
   Robert Barnes, "Crane's 'The Bride Comes to Yellow Sky,' " *Explicator* XVI, No. 7 (April, 1958) , item 39.

   Thomas Beer, *Stephen Crane*, 217.

   Russell Roth, "A Tree in Winter: The Short Fiction of Stephen Crane," *New Mexico Quarterly* XXIII (Summer, 1953) , 191-193.

   Robert W. Stallman, *Stephen Crane: An Omnibus*, 483-485.

   Carl Van Doren, "Introduction," in *Twenty Stories by Stephen Crane* (World Publishing, 1945) , xiii-xiv.

   Eudora Welty, "The Reading and Writing of Short Stories," *Atlantic Monthly* CLXXXIII (February, 1949) 57-58. — reprinted in William Van O'Connor, *Modern Prose: Form and Style*, 434-435.

3. THE CHARGE OF WILLIAM B. PERKINS
   E. R. Hagemann, "Crane's 'Real' War in His Short Stories," *American Quarterly* VIII (Winter, 1956) , 359.

4. THE CLAN OF NO-NAME
   John Berryman, *Stephen Crane*, 253-256.

   E. R. Hagemann, "Crane's 'Real' War in His Short Stories," *American Quarterly* VIII (Winter, 1956) , 363-364.

5. THE CRY OF A HUCKLEBERRY PUDDING
   Melvin Schoberlin, "Introduction," in *The Sullivan County Sketches of Stephen Crane* (1949) , 16-17.

6. DEATH AND THE CHILD
   John W. Schroeder, "Stephen Crane Embattled," *University of Kansas City Review* XVII (Winter, 1950), 120-121.
7. AN EPISODE OF WAR
   Robert W. Stallman, *Stephen Crane: An Omnibus*, 376-377.
8. THE FIVE WHITE MICE
   John Berryman, *Stephen Crane*, 108-110.
9. GEORGE'S MOTHER
   Robert W. Stallman, *Stephen Crane: An Omnibus*, 19-20.
10. GOD REST YE, MERRY GENTLEMEN
    E. R. Hagemann, "Crane's 'Real' War in His Short Stories," *American Quarterly* VIII (Winter, 1956), 360.
11. HORSES—ONE DASH
    Thomas Beer, *Stephen Crane*, 116-117.
    John Berryman, *Stephen Crane*, 104-107.
12. THE LITTLE REGIMENT
    E. R. Hagemann, "Crane's 'Real' War in His Short Stories," *American Quarterly* VIII (Winter, 1956), 358, 365, 366.
13. MAGGIE: A GIRL OF THE STREETS
    Marcus Cunliffe, "Stephen Crane and the American Background of *Maggie*," *American Quarterly* VII (Spring, 1955), 31-44.
    William M. Gibson, "Introduction," in Crane, *Selected Prose and Poetry* (Rinehart Editions, 1950), vii-viii.
    D. Heiney, *Recent American Literature*, 55-56.
    R. W. Stallman, "Stephen Crane's Primrose Path," *New Republic* CXXXIII (September 19, 1955), 17-18.
    R. W. Stallman, "Stephen Crane's Revision of *Maggie: A Girl of the Streets*," *American Literature* XXVI (January, 1955), 528-536.
    William Bysshe Stein, "New Testament Inversions in Crane's 'Maggie,'" *Modern Language Notes* LXXIII (April, 1958), 268-272.
    C. C. Walcutt, *American Literary Naturalism*, 67-72.
14. MARINES SIGNALLING UNDER FIRE AT GUANTANAMO
    E. R. Hagemann, "Crane's 'Real' War in His Short Stories," *American Quarterly* VIII (Winter, 1956), 365.
15. THE MONSTER
    Thomas Beer, *Stephen Crane*, 162-164.
    John Berryman, *Stephen Crane*, 191-196.
    Wilson Follett, "Introduction," in *The Work of Stephen Crane*, Vol. 3, ix-xi, xv-xvii.
    John W. Schroeder, "Stephen Crane Embattled," *University of Kansas City Review* XVII (Winter, 1950), 127-129.

CRANE, STEPHEN, Continued

C. C. Walcutt, *American Literary Naturalism,* 82-84.

16. A MYSTERY OF HEROISM
E. R. Hagemann, "Crane's 'Real' War in His Short Stories," *American Quarterly* VIII (Winter, 1956), 362.

17. THE OPEN BOAT
Richard P. Adams, "Naturalistic Fiction: 'The Open Boat,'" *Tulane Studies in English* IV (1954), 137-146.
Herbert Barrows, *Suggestions for Teaching "15 Stories,"* 5-7.
Thomas Beer, *Stephen Crane,* 143-146.
Joseph Conrad, "Introduction," in Thomas Beer, *Stephen Crane,* 13-14.
Cyrus Day, "Stephen Crane and the Ten-foot Dinghy," *Boston University Studies in English* III (Winter, 1957), 193-213.
William M. Gibson, "Introduction," in Crane, *Selected Prose and Poetry* (Rinehart Editions, 1950), xi-xii.
Caroline Gordon, "Stephen Crane," *Accent* IX (Spring, 1949), 153-157. — reprinted in Gordon and Tate, *The House of Fiction,* 308-312.
Stanley B. Greenfield, "The Unmistakable Stephen Crane," *PMLA* LXXIII (December, 1958), 563-565.
D. Heiney, *Recent American Literature,* 58.
Daniel G. Hoffman, *The Poetry of Stephen Crane,* 271-278.
Edd Winfield Parks, "Crane's 'The Open Boat,'" *Nineteenth-Century Fiction* VIII (June, 1953), 77.
Russell Roth, "A Tree in Winter: The Short Fiction of Stephen Crane," *New Mexico Quarterly* XXIII (Summer, 1953), 193-194.
John W. Schroeder, "Stephen Crane Embattled," *University of Kansas City Review* XVII (Winter, 1950), 127-129.
Robert W. Stallman, *Stephen Crane: An Omnibus,* 416-420.
R. W. Stallman, "Stephen Crane: A Revaluation," in John W. Aldridge, *Critiques and Essays on Modern Fiction,* 247, 259-262.
Randall Stewart, "Dreiser and the Naturalistic Heresy," *Virginia Quarterly Review* XXXIV (Winter, 1958), 102-103. — reprinted in Stewart, *American Literature and Christian Doctrine,* 109-110.
Carl Van Doren, "Introduction," in *Twenty Stories by Stephen Crane* (World Publishing, 1945), x-xi.
West and Stallman, *Art of Modern Fiction,* 53-57.

18. THE PRICE OF THE HARNESS
E. R. Hagemann, "Crane's 'Real' War in His Short Stories," *American Quarterly* VIII (Winter, 1956), 360-361.

19. THE UPTURNED FACE
Robert W. Stallman, *Stephen Crane: An Omnibus,* 375-376.

CRANE, STEPHEN, Continued

20. VIRTUE IN WAR
E. R. Hagemann, "Crane's 'Real' War in His Short Stories,"
American Quarterly VIII (Winter, 1956), 363.

DAUDET, ALPHONSE

1. FATHER GAUCHER'S ELIXIR
James B. Hall and Joseph Langland, *The Short Story*, 47-48.
2. THE GIRL IN ARLES
Beardsley, Daniel, and Leggett, *Aids to Study for "Theme and Form: An Introduction to Literature,"* 14.

DE LA MARE, WALTER

1. OUT OF THE DEEP
Peter Penzoldt, *The Supernatural in Fiction*, 212-223.
2. A RECLUSE
Peter Penzoldt, *The Supernatural in Fiction*, 206-212.

DONAHOE, EDWARD

1. HEAD BY SCOPAS
James C. Freeman, "Donahoe's 'Head by Scopas,'" *Explicator* IX
(December, 1950), item 19.
Robert W. Stallman, "The Critical Reader," *College English* IX
(April, 1948), 362-369. — reprinted in West and Stallman, *Art of Modern Fiction*, 443-452.

DOSTOEVSKY, FYODOR

1. ANOTHER MAN'S WIFE AND THE HUSBAND UNDER THE BED
Charles E. Passage, *Dostoevski the Adapter*, 64-65.
2. A CHRISTMAS TREE AND A WEDDING
Charles E. Passage, *Dostoevski the Adapter*, 69-72.
3. THE CRAWLER
(see "Polzunkov")
4. THE CROCODILE
Charles E. Passage, *Dostoevski the Adapter*, 141-142.

DOSTOEVSKY, FYODOR, Continued

5. THE DOUBLE

E. H. Carr, *Dostoevsky, 1821-1881: A New Biography*, 42-44.

Stanley M. Coleman, "The Phantom Double: Its Psychological Significance," *British Journal of Medical Psychology* XIV (1934), 254-273.

Erik Krag, "The Riddle of the Other Goljadkin: Some Observations on Dostoevskij's 'Double,'" in Morris Halle, *For Roman Jakobson*, 265-272.

Clarence A. Manning, "The Double of Dostoevsky," *Modern Language Notes* LIX (May, 1944), 317-321.

Charles E. Passage, *Dostoevski the Adapter*, 14-37.

Vladimir Seduro, *Dostoyevski in Russian Literary Criticism*, 6-7, 11-12, 14-15, 16, 17.

Ernest J. Simmons, *Dostoevski: The Making of a Novelist*, 38-43; (London, 1950 Edition), 37-41.

Marc Slonim, *The Epic of Russian Literature*, 280-281.

Ralph Tymms, *Doubles in Literary Psychology*, 103-105.

6. THE DREAM OF A RIDICULOUS MAN

Demetrios Capetanakis, *The Shores of Darkness*, 112-114.

David Magarshack, *The Best Short Stories of Dostoevsky*, xv-xviii, xxii-xxiii.

Avrahm Yarmolinsky, *Dostoevsky: His Life and Art*, 345-347.

7. THE ETERNAL HUSBAND

André Gide, *Dostoevsky* (New Directions, 1949), 114-125.

J. A. T. Lloyd, *Fyodor Dostoevsky*, 170-176.

Helen Muchnic, *Dostoevsky's English Reputation (1881-1936)*, 172-175.

Frank O'Connor, "Dostoevsky and the Unnatural Triangle," in O'Connor, *The Mirror in the Roadway*, 205-210.

Charles E. Passage, *Dostoevski the Adapter*, 146-149.

V. S. Pritchett, *The Living Novel*, 239-240.

Philip Rahv, "Introduction," in Rahv, *Great Russian Short Novels*, xiii-xv.

Ernest J. Simmons, *Dostoevski: The Making of a Novelist*, 235-239; (London, 1950 Edition), 185-188.

8. A FAINT HEART

Charles E. Passage, *Dostoevski the Adapter*, 65-68.

Ernest J. Simmons, *Dostoevski: The Making of a Novelist*, 46-48.

9. THE FRIEND OF THE FAMILY

Stanislaw Mackiewicz, *Dostoyevsky*, 73-78.

V. S. Pritchett, *Books in General*, 141-145.

Ernest J. Simmons, *Dostoevski: The Making of a Novelist*, 84-89; (London, 1950 Edition), 71-75.

DOSTOEVSKY, FYODOR, Continued

    Avrahm Yarmolinsky, *Dostoevsky: His Life and Art*, 144-145.
10. THE GAMBLER
    E. H. Carr, *Dostoevsky, 1821-1881: A New Biography,* 109-111.
    D. S. Savage, "Dostoevski: The Idea of 'The Gambler,' " *Sewanee Review* LVIII (Spring, 1950), 281-298.
    Ernest J. Simmons, *Dostoevsky: The Making of a Novelist,* 185-192; (London, 1950 Edition), 147-153.
    Marc Slonim, *The Epic of Russian Literature,* 283-284.
    Avrahm Yarmolinsky, *Dostoevsky: His Life and Art,* 217-220.
11. A GENTLE CREATURE
    David Magarshack, *The Best Short Stories of Dostoevsky,* xxi.
12. THE GRAND INQUISITOR
    Nicholas Berdyaev, *Dostoevsky,* 188-212.
    Royal A. Gettmann and Bruce Harkness, *Teacher's Manual for "A Book of Stories,"* 64-68.
    Romani Guardini, "The Legend of the Grand Inquisitor," *Cross Currents* III (Fall, 1952), 58-86.
    Mischa H. Fayer, *Gide, Freedom and Dostoevsky,* 104-105.
    René Fueloep-Miller, *Fyodor Dostoevsky: Insight, Faith, and Prophecy,* 55-57, 109-111.
    Janko Lavrin, *Dostoevsky: A Study,* 130-138.
    D. H. Lawrence, " 'The Grand Inquisitor,' " in Lawrence, *Selected Literary Criticism* (London: Heinemann, 1955), 233-241.
    Waclaw Lednicki, "Dostoevsky and Belinsky," in Lednicki, *Russia, Poland, and the West,* 254-261.
    Clarence A. Manning, "The Grand Inquisitor," *American Theological Review* XV (January, 1933), 16-26.
    Philip Rahv, "The Legend of the Grand Inquisitor," *Partisan Review* XXI (May-June, 1954), 249-271.
    Neal Riemer, "Some Reflections on 'The Grand Inquisitor' and Modern Democratic Theory," *Ethics* LXVII (July, 1957), 249-256.
    Vladimir Seduro, *Dostoyevski in Russian Literary Criticism,* 49-51.
    Melvin Seiden, "The Classroom as Underground: Notes on 'The Grand Inquisitor,' " *Journal of General Education* X (October, 1957), 217-222.
    Marc Slonim, *The Epic of Russian Literature,* 289-291.
    James C. S. Wernham, "Guardini, Berdyaev and the Legend of the Grand Inquisitor," *Hibbert Journal* LIII (January, 1955), 157-164.
    V. V. Zenkovskii, *Russian Thinkers and Europe,* 166-167, 170.
13. AN HONEST THIEF
    [Mildred A. Martin, "The Last Shall Be First: A Study of Three Russian Short Stories," *Bucknell Review* VI (March, 1956), 13-23.]
    Charles E. Passage, *Dostoevski the Adapter,* 68-69.

DOSTOEVSKY, FYODOR, Continued

14. THE LANDLADY
   Dominique Arban, "Dostoevsky and the Old Man's Murder,"
   London Magazine V (October, 1958) , 50-59.
   George Gibian, "Dostoevskij's Use of Russian Folklore," *Journal
   of American Folklore* LXIX (Summer, 1956) , 245-248.
   Stanislaw Mackiewicz, *Dostoyevsky,* 34-35.
   Julius Meier-Graefe, *Dostoevsky: The Man and His Work,* 74-75.
   Charles E. Passage, *Dostoevski the Adapter,* 41-62.
   Vladimir Seduro, *Dostoevski in Russian Literary Criticism,* 8-9.
   Ernest J. Simmons, *Dostoevski: The Making of a Novelist,* 44-46.
15. THE LEGEND OF THE GRAND INQUISITOR
   (see "The Grand Inquisitor")
16. A LITTLE HERO
   Charles E. Passage, *Dostoevski the Adapter,* 106-111.
17. THE MISTRESS OF THE HOUSE
   (see "The Landlady")
18. NOTES FROM THE UNDERGROUND
   William Barrett, "Existentialism as a Symptom of Man's Contemporary Crisis," in Stanley R. Hopper, *Spiritual Problems in Contemporary Literature,* 148-149.
   Monroe C. Beardsley, "Dostoevsky's Metaphor of the 'Underground,'" *Journal of the History of Ideas* III (June, 1942) , 265-
   268.
   Nicholas Berdyaev, *Dostoievsky,* 50-54.
   E. H. Carr, *Dostoevsky, 1821-1881: A New Biography,* 118-122.
   [Anne Freemantle, Ernest J. Simmons, and Lyman Bryson, "Notes
   from Underground," in *Invitation to Learning Reader* VI (1957) ,
   137-144.]
   René Fueloep-Miller, *Fyodor Dostoevsky: Insight, Faith, and
   Prophecy,* 111-113.
   Vyacheslav Ivanov, *Freedom and the Tragic Life: A Study in
   Dostoevsky,* 134-141.
   Walter Kaufmann, *Existentialism from Dostoevsky to Sartre*
   (Meridian Books) , 12-14, 52-53.
   Janko Lavrin, *Russian Writers: Their Lives and Literature,* 181-
   184.
   Waclaw Lednicki, "Dostoevsky—The Man from Underground," in
   Lednicki, *Russia, Poland, and the West,* 180-248.
   Thomas Mann, "Dostoevsky—in Moderation," in *The Short Novels
   of Dostoevsky* (Dial Press, 1945) , xviii-xix.
   Ralph E. Matlaw, "Structure and Integration in 'Notes From the
   Underground,'" *PMLA* LXXIII (March, 1958) , 101-109.

J. Middleton Murry, *Fyodor Dostoevsky: A Critical Study,* 90-96.

Charles Neider, *Short Novels of the Masters,* 18-21.

Karl Pfleger, "Dostoevsky, the Man from the Underworld," in Pfleger, *Wrestlers with Christ,* 191-206.

William Phillips, "Dostoevsky's Underground Man," *Partisan Review* XIII (November-December, 1946), 551-561. — reprinted in Phillips, *The Short Stories of Dostoevsky* (Dial, 1946), vii-xx.

John Cowper Powys, *Dostoievsky: A Study,* 82-87.

Philip Rahv, *Image and Idea,* 126.

Nathan A. Scott, "Dostoevski—Tragedian of Excursion into Unbelief," in Scott, *Tragic Vision and the Christian Faith,* 194-198.

Vladimir Seduro, *Dostoyevski in Russian Literary Criticism,* 89-91.

Ernest J. Simmons, *Dostoevski: The Making of a Novelist,* 129-138; (London, 1950 Edition), 98-111.

Marc Slonim, *The Epic of Russian Literature,* 282-283.

George Steiner, *Tolstoy or Dostoevsky,* 220-230.

I. Traschen, "Dostoevsky's 'Notes from Underground,'" *Accent* XVI (Autumn, 1956), 255-264.

Avrahm Yarmolinsky, *Dostoevsky: His Life and Art,* 187-192.

Avrahm Yarmolinsky, *Dostoievsky: A Study in His Ideology* (Ph. D. Dissertation, Columbia University), 31-32.

Avrahm Yarmolinsky, "Introduction," in Yarmolinsky, *A Treasury of Great Russian Short Stories,* ix-x.

V. V. Zenkovskii, *Russian Thinkers and Europe,* 163-164.

19. A NOVEL IN NINE LETTERS

Charles E. Passage, *Dostoevski the Adapter,* 38-40.

20. THE PEASANT MAREY

Robert A. Durr, "Dostoevsky's 'The Peasant Marey,'" *Explicator* X (March, 1952), item 35.

Mark Kanzer, "Dostoevsky's 'The Peasant Marey,'" *American Imago* IV (April, 1947), 78-87.

David Magarshack, *The Best Short Stories of Dostoevsky,* xiii-xiv.

Raymond W. Short and Richard B. Sewall, *A Manual of Suggestions for Teachers Using "Short Stories for Study,"* 2-3.

21. POLZUNKOV

Charles E. Passage, *Dostoevski the Adapter,* 63-64.

22. POOR FOLK

E. H. Carr, *Dostoevsky, 1821-1881: A New Biography,* 40-44.

Ernest J. Simmons, *Dostoevski: The Making of a Novelist,* 23-35.

23. THE UNCLE'S DREAM

V. S. Pritchett, *The Living Novel,* 236-237.

Ernest J. Simmons, *Dostoevski: The Making of a Novelist,* 80-84; (London, 1950 Edition), 69-71.

DOSTOEVSKY, FYODOR, Continued

24. AN UNPLEASANT PREDICAMENT
Katherine Mansfield, *Novels and Novelists,* 112-113.
Charles E. Passage, *Dostoevski the Adapter,* 126-131.
V. S. Pritchett, *The Living Novel,* 237-238.
25. THE VILLAGE OF STEPANCHIKOVO AND ITS
INHABITANTS
(see "The Friend of the Family")
26. WHITE NIGHTS
Charles E. Passage, *Dostoevski the Adapter,* 73-81.

DREISER, THEODORE

1. THE LOST PHOEBE
R. B. West, Jr., *The Short Story in America, 1900-1950,* 41-42.
2. TYPHOON
R. B. West, Jr., *The Short Story in America, 1900-1950,* 37-41.

EDMONDS, WALTER D.

1. DEATH OF RED PERIL
Kenneth Kempton, *Short Stories for Study,* 108-114.

ENRIGHT, ELIZABETH

1. THE SARDILLION
Kenneth Kempton, *Short Studies for Study,* 53-59.

FARRELL, JAMES T.

1. THE BENEFITS OF AMERICAN LIFE
James B. Hall and Joseph Langland, *The Short Story,* 94-95.
Frank O'Malley, "James T. Farrell: The Twilight Images," in
Harold C. Gardiner, *Fifty Years of the American Novel,* 242.
2. CLYDE
Frank O'Malley, "James T. Farrell: The Twilight Images," in
Harold C. Gardiner, *Fifty Years of the American Novel,* 242-243.
3. STUDS
James T. Farrell, Comment in Whit Burnett, *This Is My Best,* 440.

FARRELL, JAMES T., Continued

4. TWO SISTERS
   Frank O'Malley, "James T. Farrell: The Twilight Images," in
   Harold C. Gardiner, *Fifty Years of the American Novel*, 249-250.

FAULKNER, WILLIAM

1. AD ASTRA
   Campbell and Foster, *William Faulkner*, 23-24.
2. ALL THE DEAD PILOTS
   James B. Hall and Joseph Langland, *The Short Story*, 64-66.
3. BARN BURNING
   Walter Havighurst: *Instructor's Manual: "Masters of the Modern
   Short Story,"* 7-8.
   D. Heiney, *Recent American Literature*, 225-226.
   Irving Malin, *William Faulkner*, 81.
4. THE BEAR
   John Arthos, "Ritual and Humor in the Writing of William
   Faulkner," *Accent* IX (Autumn, 1948), 18.
   Irving D. Blum, "The Parallel Philosophy of Emerson's 'Nature'
   and Faulkner's 'The Bear,'" *Emerson Society Quarterly*, No. 13
   (IV Quarter, 1958), 22-25.
   Ursula Brumm, "Wilderness and Civilization: A Note on William
   Faulkner," *Partisan Review* XXII (Summer, 1955), 349-350.
   John F. Butler, *Exercises in Literary Understanding*, 45-47.
   Harry M. Campbell, "Structural Devices in the Works of William
   Faulkner," *Perspective* III (Autumn, 1950), 215-218. — reprinted
   in Campbell and Foster, *William Faulkner*, 75-79.
   Carvel Collins, "Are These Mandalas?" *Literature and Psychology*
   III, No. 5 (November, 1953), 3-6.
   Carvel Collins, "Faulkner and Certain Earlier Southern Fiction,"
   College English XVI (November, 1954), 96-97.
   Carvel Collins, "A Note on the Conclusion of 'The Bear,'"
   Faulkner Studies II (Winter, 1954), 58-60.
   Malcolm Cowley, "William Faulkner's Legend of the South,"
   Sewanee Review LIII (Summer, 1945), 349-351, 360-361. — re-
   printed in Allen Tate, *A Southern Vanguard*, 18-19, 26-27. — re-
   printed in *The Wind and the Rain* (Spring, 1949), 248-249, 255.
   — reprinted in Ray B. West, *Essays in Modern Literary Criticism*,
   518-519, 525-526. — reprinted in John W. Aldridge, *Critiques and
   Essays on Modern Fiction*, 436-437, 441-442.*

---

*Note: The essay in Aldridge combines the materials in Cowley's
Sewanee article and his introduction to *The Portable Faulkner*.

Ralph Ellison, Irving Howe, and Lyman Bryson, Discussion of "The Bear," *Invitation to Learning Reader,* No. 9 (1953), 40-46.

R. W. Flint, "Faulkner as Elegist," *Hudson Review* VII (Summer, 1954), 253-254.

Ruel E. Foster, "A Further Note on the Conclusion of 'The Bear' " *Faulkner Studies* III (Spring, 1954), 4-5.

Ruel E. Foster, "Primitivism," in Campbell and Foster, *William Faulkner,* 146-158.

Barbara Giles, "The South of William Faulkner," *Masses and Mainstream* III (February, 1950), 33-36.

Walter Havighurst, *Masters of the Modern Short Story,* xii.

D. Heiney, *Recent American Literature,* 226-227.

Blaise Hettich, "A Bedroom Scene in Faulkner," *Renascence* VIII (Spring, 1956), 121-126.

Irving Howe, *William Faulkner,* 66-70, 186-189.

Robert A. Jelliffe, *Faulkner at Nagano,* 50-51, 92-93.

Phyllis Jobe, " 'The Bear': A Critical Study," *Nimrod* II (Winter, 1958), 27-30.

Alfred Kazin, "Faulkner in His Fury," in Kazin, *The Inmost Leaf,* 266-267.

Dayton Kohler, "William Faulkner and the Social Conscience," *College English* XI (December, 1949), 124-125.

Kenneth LaBudde, "Cultural Primitivism in William Faulkner's ' The Bear,' " *American Quarterly* II (Winter, 1950), 322-328.

R. W. B. Lewis, "The Hero in the New World: William Faulkner's 'The Bear,' " *Kenyon Review* XIII (Autumn, 1951), 641-660.

Walton Litz, "Genealogy As Symbol in *Go Down, Moses,*" *Faulkner Studies* I (Winter, 1952), 49-50.

Walton Litz, "William Faulkner's Moral Vision," *Southwest Review* XXXVII (Summer, 1952), 205-207.

R. M. Ludwig and M. B. Perry, *Nine Short Novels,* xxxiii-xxxvii.

John Lydenberg, "Nature Myth in William Faulkner's 'The Bear,' " *American Literature* XXIV (March, 1952), 62-72.

Andrew Lytle, "The Son of Man: He Will Prevail," *Sewanee Review* LXIII (Winter, 1955), 127-128.

Hugh Maclean, "Conservatism in Modern American Fiction," *College English* XV (March, 1954), 322-325.

Irving Malin, *William Faulkner,* 26-28, 70-73, 85-86.

Ward L. Miner, *The World of William Faulkner,* 149-151.

W. R. Moses, "Where History Crosses Myth: Another Reading of 'The Bear,' " *Accent* XIII (Winter, 1953), 21-33.

William Van O'Connor, "The Wilderness Theme in Faulkner's

FAULKNER, WILLIAM, Continued

'The Bear,' " *Accent* XIII (Winter, 1953), 12-20. — reprinted in O'Connor, *The Tangled Fire of William Faulkner,* 125-134.

Russell Roth, "William Faulkner: The Pattern of Pilgrimage," *Perspective* II (Summer, 1949), 251-254.

Raymond W. Short and Richard B. Sewall, *A Manual of Suggestions for Teachers Using "Short Stories for Study,"* 36-38.

George Snell, "The Fury of William Faulkner," *Western Review* XI (Autumn, 1946), 39-40. — reprinted in Snell, *Shapers of American Fiction,* 102-103.

Stallman and Watters, *Creative Reader,* 332.

Randall Stewart, *American Literature and Christian Doctrine,* 136-139.

Randall Stewart, "Hawthorne and Faulkner," *College English* XVII (February, 1956), 260.

Randall Stewart and Dorothy Bethurum, *Modern American Narration (Living Masterpieces of American Literature,* Vol. 3), 106-110.

William Y. Tindall, *The Literary Symbol,* 164-166.

R. P. Warren, "William Faulkner," *New Republic* CXV (August 12, 1946), 176-180; CXV (August 26, 1946), 234-237.* — reprinted in William Van O'Connor, *Forms of Modern Fiction,* 125-143. — reprinted in Hoffman and Vickery, *Faulkner: Two Decades of Criticism,* 82-101. — reprinted in M. D. Zabel, *Literary Opinion in America,* 464-477. — reprinted, considerably revised, in R. P. Warren, *Selected Essays,* 59-79.

Eudora Welty, "The Reading and Writing of Short Stories," *Atlantic Monthly* CLXXXIII (March, 1949), 48. — reprinted in William Van O'Connor, *Modern Prose: Form and Style,* 440-442.

R. B. West, Jr., *The Short Story in America: 1900-1950,* 101-105.

5. A BEAR HUNT
Dale G. Breaden, "William Faulkner and the Land," *American Quarterly* X (Fall, 1958), 354-355.

6. BLACK MUSIC
David Garnett, "Books in General," *New Statesman and Nation* VIII, n.s. (September 29, 1934), 396.

7. THE COURTSHIP
Jose Yglesias, "Neurotic Visions," *Masses and Mainstream* II (December, 1949), 76.

8. DELTA AUTUMN
Walton Litz, "Genealogy As Symbol in *Go Down, Moses,*" *Faulkner Studies* I (Winter, 1952), 50-51.

---

* Note: Since "The Bear" is used intermittently throughout the article as a central reference, the listed pages include the entire article.

FAULKNER, WILLIAM, Continued

Ward L. Miner, *The World of William Faulkner*, 154-156.

William Van O'Connor, "The Wilderness Theme in Faulkner's 'The Bear,'" *Accent* XIII (Winter, 1953), 19-20. — reprinted in O'Connor, *The Tangled Fire of William Faulkner*, 133-134.

R. P. Warren, "William Faulkner," *New Republic* CXV (August, 12, 1946), 176-180; CXV (August 26, 1946), 234-237.* — reprinted in William Van O'Connor, *Forms of Modern Fiction* 125-143. — reprinted in Hoffman and Vickery, *Faulkner: Two Decades of Criticism*, 82-101. — reprinted in M. D. Zabel, *Literary Opinion in America*, 464-477. — reprinted, considerably revised, in R. P. Warren, *Selected Essays*, 59-79.

9. DR. MARTINO
   Irving Malin, *William Faulkner*, 82.
10. DRY SEPTEMBER
    William B. Bache, "Moral Awareness in 'Dry September,'" *Faulkner Studies* III (Winter, 1954), 53-57.
    Robert G. Davis, *Instructor's Manual for "Ten Modern Masters,"* 44.
    William J. Griffin, "How to Read Faulkner: A Powerful Plea for Ignorance," *Tennessee Studies in Literature* I (1956), 28-30.
11. ELLY
    Irving Malin, *William Faulkner*, 34-35.
12. THE FIRE AND THE HEARTH
    John Arthos, "Ritual and Humor in the Writing of William Faulkner," *Accent* IX (Autumn, 1948), 19.
    Irene C. Edmonds, "Faulkner and the Black Shadow," in Rubin and Jacobs, *Southern Renascence*, 201-202.
    Horace Gregory, Review of *Go Down, Moses, New York Times Book Review* (May 10, 1942), 4.
    Walton Litz, "Genealogy As Symbol in *Go Down, Moses*," *Faulkner Studies* I (Winter, 1952), 49-50.
    Ernest Sandeen, "William Faulkner: Tragedian of Yoknapatawpha," in Harold C. Gardiner, *Fifty Years of the American Novel*, 170.
13. FOX HUNT
    Dale G. Breaden, "William Faulkner and the Land," *American Quarterly* X (Fall, 1958), 354-355.
14. GO DOWN, MOSES
    Irving Malin, *William Faulkner*, 74.

---

* Note: Since "Delta Autumn" is used intermittently throughout the article as a central reference, the listed pages include the entire article.

Arthur Mizener, "The Thin Intelligent Face of American Fiction," *Kenyon Review* XVII (Autumn, 1955) , 507-519.

15. THE HOUND
Leonidas M. Jones, "Faulkner's 'The Hound,' " *Explicator* XV, No. 6 (March, 1957) , item 37.

16. KNIGHT'S GAMBIT
William Van O'Connor, *The Tangled Fire of William Faulkner,* 145.

17. LION
William Van O'Connor, "The Wilderness Theme in Faulkner's 'The Bear,' " *Accent* XIII (Winter, 1953) , 17-18. — reprinted in O'Connor, *The Tangled Fire of William Faulkner,* 131-132.

18. MONK
Albert Guerard, "Justice in Yoknapatawpha County: Some Symbolic Motifs in Faulkner's Later Writing," *Faulkner Studies* II (Winter, 1954) , 50-52.
William Van O'Connor, *The Tangled Fire of William Faulkner,* 143-144.

19. AN ODOR OF VERBENA
Irving Malin, *William Faulkner,* 37, 75, 78.

20. THE OLD PEOPLE
Robert G. Davis, *Instructor's Manual for "Ten Modern Masters,"* 46-47.
Walton Litz, "William Faulkner's Moral Vision," *Southwest Review* XXXVII (Summer, 1952) , 204-205.
Ernest Sandeen, "William Faulkner: Tragedian of Yoknapatawpha," in Harold C. Gardiner, *Fifty Years of the American Novel,* 181.
Mark Schorer, *The Story,* 418-419.

21. RED LEAVES
William Van O'Connor, *The Tangled Fire of William Faulkner,* 69.

22. A ROSE FOR EMILY
Beardsley, Daniel, and Leggett, *Aids to Study for "Theme and Form: An Introduction to Literature,"* 41-42.
Brooks and Warren, *Understanding Fiction,* 409-414. — reprinted in Locke, Gibson, and Arms, *Introduction to Literature* (First Edition, 1948) , 187-191; (Second Edition, 1952) , 451-455; (Third Edition, 1957) , 443-446.
Campbell and Foster, *William Faulkner,* 99-100.
William T. Going, "Chronology in Teaching 'A Rose for Emily,' " *Exercise Exchange* (Rinehart) V (February, 1958) , 8-11.

FAULKNER, WILLIAM, Continued

William T. Going, "Faulkner's 'A Rose for Emily,'" *Explicator* XVI, No. 5 (February, 1958), item 27.

D. Heiney, *Recent American Literature*, 224-225.

C. W. M. Johnson, "Faulkner's 'A Rose for Emily,'" *Explicator* VI (May, 1948), item 45.

Kenneth Kempton, *The Short Story*, 104-106.

Irving Malin, *William Faulkner*, 37-38.

William Van O'Connor, "The State of Faulkner Criticism," *Sewanee Review* LX (Winter, 1952), 183-184.

William Van O'Connor, *The Tangled Fire of William Faulkner*, n. 68-69.

Sale, Hall, and Steinmann, *Critical Discussions for Teachers Using "Short Stories: Tradition and Direction,"* 37-40.

George Snell, "The Fury of William Faulkner," *Western Review* XI (Autumn, 1946), 35-37. — reprinted in Snell, *Shapers of American Fiction*, 96-99.

Floyd C. Watkins, "The Structure of 'A Rose for Emily,'" *Modern Language Notes* LXIX (November, 1954), 508-510.

Ray B. West, Jr., "Atmosphere and Theme in Faulkner's 'A Rose for Emily,'" *Perspective* II (Summer, 1949), 239-245. — reprinted in Hoffman and Vickery, *William Faulkner: Two Decades of Criticism*, 259-267.

Ray B. West, Jr., "Faulkner's 'A Rose for Emily,'" *Explicator* VII (October, 1948), item 8.

Ray B. West, Jr., *The Short Story in America, 1900-1950*, 93-94.

West and Stallman, *Art of Modern Fiction*, 270-275.

23. SHINGLES FOR THE LORD

Dale G. Breaden, "William Faulkner and the Land," *American Quarterly* X (Fall, 1958), 353-354.

24. SMOKE

William Van O'Connor, *The Tangled Fire of William Faulkner*, 142-143.

25. SPOTTED HORSES

Beardsley, Daniel, and Leggett, *Aids to Study for "Theme and Form: An Introduction to Literature,"* 66.

Harry M. Campbell, "Mr. Roth's Centaur and Faulkner's Symbolism," *Western Review* XVI (Summer, 1952), 320-321.

Alfred Dashiell, *Editor's Choice*, 153-154.

Felheim, Newman, and Steinhoff, *Study Aids for Teachers for "Modern Short Stories,"* 17-19.

Caroline Gordon, "Faulkner and Flaubert," *Hudson Review* I

(Summer, 1948), 226-231. — reprinted, revised, in Gordon and Tate, *The House of Fiction,* 531-534.

Jack Barry Ludwig and W. Richard Poirier, *Instructor's Manual to Accompany "Stories: British and American,"* 10-11.

William Van O'Connor, *The Tangled Fire of William Faulkner,* 122-124.

Russell Roth, "The Centaur and the Pear Tree," *Western Review* XVI (Spring, 1952), 199-205.

26. THAT EVENING SUN

Robert Cantwell, "Faulkner's Thirteen Stories," *New Republic* LXVIII (October 21, 1931), 271.

Leonard H. Frey, "Irony and Point of View in 'That Evening Sun,'" *Faulkner Studies* II (Autumn, 1953), 33-40.

Evans B. Harrington, "Technical Aspects of William Faulkner's 'That Evening Sun,'" *Faulkner Studies* I (Winter, 1952), 54-59.

R. B. Heilman, *Modern Short Stories,* 80-81.

Kenneth Kempton, *The Short Story,* 8-10.

Claude-Edmonde Magny, "Faulkner's Inverse Theology," *Cross Currents* IV (Spring-Summer, 1954), 218.

Edwin Muir, Review of *These Thirteen, Listener* X (October-December, 1933), 519.

Edward J. O'Brien, *The Short Story Case Book,* 325-361.

Mary Orvis, *The Art of Writing Fiction,* 104-105.

Norman Holmes Pearson, "Faulkner's Three 'Evening Suns,'" *Yale University Library Gazette* XXIX (October, 1954), 61-70.

George Snell, "The Fury of William Faulkner," *Western Review* XI (Autumn, 1946), 37-39. — reprinted in Snell, *Shapers of American Fiction,* 99-102.

R. B. West, Jr., *The Short Story in America, 1900-1950,* 98-99.

Stephen E. Whicher, "The Compsons' Nancies—A Note on *The Sound and the Fury* and 'That Evening Sun,'" *American Literature* XXVI (May, 1954), 253-255.

27. THERE WAS A QUEEN

Irving Malin, *William Faulkner,* 39.

George Marion O'Donnell, "Faulkner's Mythology," *Kenyon Review* I (Summer, 1939), 287-288. — reprinted in Hoffman and Vickery, *William Faulkner: Two Decades of Criticism,* 51-52.

28. UNCLE WILLY

William Van O'Connor, "Protestantism in Yoknapatawpha County," in Rubin and Jacobs, *Southern Renascence,* 153-154.

29. WAS

Robert G. Davis, *Instructor's Manual for "Ten Modern Masters,"* 45-46.

Russell Roth, "The Brennan Papers: Faulkner in Manuscript," *Perspective* II (Summer, 1949), 219-224.

30. WASH

Dale G. Breaden, "William Faulkner and the Land," *American Quarterly* X (Fall, 1958), 355-356.

Royal A. Gettmann and Bruce Harkness, *Teacher's Manual for "A Book of Stories,"* 13-16.

Ward L. Miner, *The World of William Faulkner,* 134.

FIEDLER, LESLIE

1. LET NOTHING YOU DISMAY

Judah Goldin, "The Contemporary Jew and His Judaism," in S. R. Hopper, *Spiritual Problems in Contemporary Literature,* 220-221.

FITZGERALD, F. SCOTT

1. ABSOLUTION

James E. Miller, Jr., *The Fictional Technique of Scott Fitzgerald,* 88-89.

2. BABYLON REVISITED

D. Heiney, *Recent American Literature,* 147-148.

James M. Harrison, "Fitzgerald's 'Babylon Revisited,'" *Explicator* XVI, No. 4 (January, 1958), item 20.

D. S. Savage, "The Significance of F. Scott Fitzgerald," *Arizona Quarterly* VIII (Autumn, 1952), 208-209.

Ray B. West, Jr., *The Short Story in America: 1900-1950,* 68.

3. THE BABY PARTY

Alfred Dashiell, *Editor's Choice,* 190.

4. THE DIAMOND AS BIG AS THE RITZ

Maxwell Geismar, *Last of the Provincials,* 310-312.

Charles S. Holmes, "Fitzgerald: The American Theme," *Pacific Spectator* VI (Spring, 1952), 248-249.

James E. Miller, Jr., *The Fictional Technique of Scott Fitzgerald,* 48-50.

5. THE LAST OF THE BELLES

Winifred Lynskey, *Reading Modern Fiction* (Second Edition, 1957), 200-202.

6. MAY DAY

Edwin S. Fussell, "Fitzgerald's Brave New World," *ELH* XIX (December, 1952), 293-294.

Maxwell Geismar, *Last of the Provincials*, 308-309.

James E. Miller, Jr., *The Fictional Technique of Scott Fitzgerald*, 46-48.

Ray B. West, Jr., *The Short Story in America: 1900-1950*, 65-66.

7. THE RICH BOY

Aerol Arnold, "Why Structure in Fiction: A Note to Social Scientists," *American Quarterly* X (Fall, 1958), 332-336.

Brooks, Purser, and Warren, *An Approach to Literature*, 240-241.

Weller Embler, "F. Scott Fitzgerald and the Future," *Chimera* IV (Autumn, 1945), 48-55.

Arthur Mizener, *The Far Side of Paradise*, 193-195; (Vintage Books, 1959), 210-212.

8. "THE SENSIBLE THING"

James E. Miller, Jr., *The Fictional Technique of Scott Fitzgerald*, 87-88.

9. WINTER DREAMS

James E. Miller, Jr., *The Fictional Technique of Scott Fitzgerald*, 83-87.

Arthur Mizener, *The Far Side of Paradise*, 192-193; (Vintage Books, 1959), 209-210.

FLAUBERT, GUSTAVE

1. HÉRODIAS

C. A. Burns, "The Manuscripts of Flaubert's 'Trois Contes,'" *French Studies* VIII (October, 1954), 311-314, 319-324.

Lionel Trilling, "Flaubert's Last Testament," *Partisan Review* XX (November-December, 1953), 627-630. — reprinted as introduction to Flaubert, *Bouvard and Pécuchet* (New Directions, 1954), xxxiii-xxxvii. — reprinted in Trilling, *The Opposing Self*, 201-205.

2. THE LEGEND OF ST. JULIAN

(see "St. Julian")

3. A SIMPLE HEART

C. A. Burns, "The Manuscripts of Flaubert's 'Trois Contes,'" *French Studies* VIII (October, 1954), 299-306, 315-317.

Gordon and Tate, *House of Fiction*, 24-26.

Börge Gedsö Madsen, "Realism, Irony and Compassion in Flaubert's 'Un Coeur Simple,'" *French Review* XXVII (February, 1954), 253-258.

J. Middleton Murry, *Countries of the Mind* (First and Second Series, Oxford University Press, 1937), 168-170. — reprinted in

Murry, *John Clare and Other Studies* (Peter Nevill, 1950), 140-141.

Charles Neider, *Short Novels of the Masters,* 28-33.

Anthony Thorlby, *Gustave Flaubert and the Art of Realism,* 57-59.

Lionel Trilling, "Flaubert's Last Testament," *Partisan Review* XX (November-December, 1953), 627-630. — reprinted as introduction to Flaubert, *Bouvard and Pécuchet* (New Directions, 1954), xxxiii-xxxvii. — reprinted in Trilling, *The Opposing Self,* 201-205.

Martin Turnell, "Flaubert (II)," *Scrutiny* XIII (Spring, 1946), 286-288. — reprinted in Turnell, *The Novel in France* (Vintage Books, 1958), 321-324.

4. ST. JULIAN

B. F. Bart, "The Moral of Flaubert's 'Saint-Julien,'" *Romanic Review* XXXVIII (February, 1947), 23-33.

C. A. Burns, "The Manuscripts of Flaubert's 'Trois Contes,'" *French Studies* VIII (October, 1954), 306-311, 317-319.

Lionell Trilling, "Flaubert's Last Testament," *Partisan Review* XX (November-December, 1953), 627-630. — reprinted as introduction to Flaubert, *Bouvard and Pécuchet* (New Directions, 1954), xxxiii-xxxvii. — reprinted in Trilling, *The Opposing Self,* 201-205.

FOLEY, MARTHA

1. ONE WITH SHAKESPEARE

Edward J. O'Brien, *The Short Story Case Book,* 509-523.

FORSTER, E. M.

1. ALBERGO EMPEDOCLE

Lionel Trilling, *E. M. Forster,* 36-54.

2. THE CELESTIAL OMNIBUS

James McConkey, *The Novels of E. M. Forster,* 49.

Lionel Trilling, *E. M. Forster,* 55.

Austin Warren, "The Novels of E. M. Forster," *American Review* IX (Summer, 1937), 233-234. — reprinted, revised, in Warren, *Rage for Order,* 125. — reprinted in J. W. Aldridge, *Critiques and Essays on Modern Fiction,* 478.

Stewart C. Wilcox, "The Allegory of Forster's 'The Celestial

FORSTER, E. M., Continued

Omnibus,' " *Modern Fiction Studies* II (Winter, 1956-1957) , 191-196.
3. THE CURATE'S FRIEND
J. K. Johnstone, *The Bloomsbury Group,* 101-102.
Rose Macaulay, *The Writings of E. M. Forster,* 29-30.
Lionel Trilling, *E. M. Forster,* 50, 52.
4. THE ETERNAL MOMENT
Cyril Connolly, *The Condemned Playground,* 257-258.
Rose Macaulay, *The Writings of E. M. Forster,* 31, 276.
James McConkey, *The Novels of E. M. Forster,* 28, 49.
Lionel Trilling, *E. M. Forster,* 44-46.
Austin Warren, "The Novels of E. M. Forster," *American Review* IX (Summer, 1937) , 243-244. — reprinted, revised, in Warren, *Rage for Order,* 133-134. — reprinted in J. W. Aldridge, *Critiques and Essays on Modern Fiction,* 482-483.
5. THE MACHINE STOPS
Felheim, Newman, and Steinhoff, *Study Aids for Teachers for "Modern Short Stories,"* 11-12.
Rose Macaulay, *The Writings of E. M. Forster,* 31.
Lionel Trilling, *E. M. Forster,* 47-48.
Rex Warner, *E. M. Forster,* 23.
6. MR. ANDREWS
Robert B. Heilman, *Modern Short Stories,* 310-311.
7. THE OTHER KINGDOM
Dorothy M. Hoare, *Some Studies in the Modern Novel,* 70-71.
Rose Macaulay, *The Writings of E. M. Forster,* 30.
Lionel Trilling, *E. M. Forster,* 49.
8. THE OTHER SIDE OF THE HEDGE
Winifred Lynskey, *Reading Modern Fiction,* (Second Edition, 1957) , 208.
Rose Macaulay, *The Writings of E. M. Forster,* 32-33.
Austin Warren, "The Novels of E. M. Forster," *American Review* IX (Summer, 1937) , 243. — reprinted, revised, in Warren, *Rage for Order,* 134. — reprinted in J. W. Aldridge *Critiques and Essays on Modern Fiction,* 483.
9. THE POINT OF IT
Lionel Trilling, *E. M. Forster,* 43.
10. THE ROAD FROM COLONUS
Montgomery Belgion, "The Diabolism of Mr. E. M. Forster," *Criterion* XIV (October, 1934) , 65.
Walter Havighurst, "Symbolism and the Students," *College English* XVI (April, 1955) , 429-434.

FORSTER, E. M., Continued

James McConkey, *The Novels of E. M. Forster,* 50-52, 75.
J. K. Johnstone, *The Bloomsbury Group,* 104-105.
Sale, Hall, and Steinmann, *Critical Discussions for Teachers Using "Short Stories: Tradition and Direction,"* 30-33.
Lionel Trilling, *E. M. Forster,* 38-44.
Austin Warren, "The Novels of E. M. Forster," *American Review* IX (Summer, 1937), 243-244. — reprinted, revised, in Warren, *Rage for Order,* 133-134. — reprinted in J. W. Aldridge, *Critiques and Essays on Modern Fiction,* 482-483.

11. THE STORY OF A PANIC
Dorothy M. Hoare, *Some Studies in the Modern Novel,* 70-71.
J. K. Johnstone, *The Bloomsbury Group,* 101-102.
Lionel Trilling, *E. M. Forster,* 50, 52, 55.

12. THE STORY OF THE SIREN
Dorothy M. Hoare, *Some Studies in the Modern Novel,* 71-72.
Rose Macaulay, *The Writings of E. M. Forster,* 31-32.
Katherine Mansfield, *Novels and Novelists,* 238-239.
James McConkey, *The Novels of E. M. Forster,* 49.
Lionel Trilling, *E. M. Forster,* 43-44, 52.

FREEMAN, MARY E. WILKINS

1. A CONFLICT ENDED
Edward Foster, *Mary E. Wilkins Freeman,* 76-79.

2. A GALA DRESS
Edward Foster, *Mary E. Wilkins Freeman,* 93-99.

3. THE GENTIAN
Edward Foster, *Mary E. Wilkins Freeman,* 71-73.

4. TWO OLD LOVERS
Edward Foster, *Mary E. Wilkins Freeman,* 54-55.

5. A VILLAGE LEAR
Edward Foster, *Mary E. Wilkins Freeman,* 99-102.

GALSWORTHY, JOHN

1. MANNA
Raymond W. Short and Richard B. Sewall, *A Manual of Suggestions for Teachers Using "Short Stories for Study,"* 27-29.

GERRY, BILL

1. UNDERSTAND WHAT I MEAN?
   Mary Orvis, *The Art of Writing Fiction,* 81-83.

GIDE, ANDRÉ

1. EL HADJ
   Edmund L. Loughnan, "Thirteenth Apostle: A Study of M. André Gide," *Sewanee Review* XXXIX (July, 1931), 298-299.
   Harold March, *Gide and the Hound of Heaven,* 105-106.
   Justin O'Brien, *Portrait of André Gide,* 141-142.
   Enid Starkie, *André Gide,* 24.
   Lawrence Thomas, *André Gide: The Ethic of the Artist,* 91-96.
2. GENEVIÈVE
   Van Meter Ames, *André Gide,* 253-254.
   Albert J. Guerard, *André Gide,* 146-148.
   Klaus Mann, *André Gide and the Crisis of Modern Thought,* 219-222.
   George D. Painter, *André Gide,* 153-155.
   Enid Starkie, *André Gide,* 46.
3. THE IMMORALIST
   Van Meter Ames, *André Gide,* 47-56, 63-64, 226-228.
   Ernest Boyd, "The Protestant Barres," *New Republic* XXXIX (July 23, 1924), 247-248.
   G. Brée and M. Guiton, *An Age of Fiction,* 27-29.
   Thomas Cordle, "Gide and the Novel of the Egoist," *Yale French Studies,* No. 7 (1951), 92-93.
   Mischa H. Fayer, *Gide, Freedom and Dostoevsky,* 28-31.
   Wallace Fowlie, *Clowns and Angels,* 33-41.
   Albert J. Guerard, *André Gide,* 99-118.
   Henry Hazlitt, "Gide's First Novel," *Nation* CXXX (April 23, 1930), 491.
   Louis Kronenberger, "Man's Ethical Dilemma in André Gide's 'Immoralist,' " *New York Times Book Review* (April 20, 1930), 9.
   Klaus Mann, *André Gide and the Crisis of Modern Thought,* 100-105.
   Harold March, *Gide and the Hound of Heaven,* 117-123.
   Justin O'Brien, "Gide's Fictional Technique," *Yale French Studies,* No. 7 (1951), 81-83.
   Justin O'Brien, *Portrait of André Gide,* 169-177, 277-280.
   George D. Painter, *André Gide,* 64-70.
   Henri Peyre, *The Contemporary French Novel,* 88-90.

J. D. Scott, "Novelists-Philosophers: André Gide," *Horizon* XI (April, 1945), 272-278.

Enid Starkie, *André Gide*, 29-30.

Lawrence Thomas, *André Gide: The Ethic of the Artist*, 125-139.

4. ISABELLE

G. Brée and M. Guiton, *An Age of Fiction*, 17-18.

Albert J. Guerard, *André Gide*, 124-128.

Louis Kronenberger, "André Gide's Contrasting Aspects in Two Novelettes," *New York Times Book Review* (May 24, 1931), 2.

Klaus Mann, *André Gide and the Crisis of Modern Thought*, 142-144.

Harold March, *Gide and the Hound of Heaven*, 188-189.

George D. Painter, *André Gide*, 92-95.

Léon Pierre-Quint, *André Gide*, 173-174.

Enid Starkie, *André Gide*, 32-33.

Geoffrey Stone, Review of *Two Symphonies, Bookman* LXXIV (October, 1931), 196.

Gerald Sykes, "For Connoisseurs," *New Republic* LXVII (July 29, 1931), 295.

Gerald Sykes, "The Sins of a Critic," *Nation* CXXXIII (September 9, 1931), 260-261.

Lawrence Thomas, *André Gide: The Ethic of the Artist*, 152-155.

5. MARSHLANDS

Van Meter Ames, *André Gide* 40-41, 234-235.

G. Brée and M. Guiton, *An Age of Fiction*, 24-25.

Albert J. Guerard, *André Gide*, 69-71.

Harold March, *Gide and the Hound of Heaven*, 111-112, 114.

Justin O'Brien, *Portrait of André Gide*, 106-117.

George D. Painter, *André Gide*, 41-44.

Henri Peyre, "With Gidean Irony," *New York Times Book Review* (November 29, 1953), 4, 32.

Lawrence Thomas, *André Gide: The Ethic of the Artist*, 63-81.

6. PALUDES

(see "Marshlands")

7. THE PASTORAL SYMPHONY

Van Meter Ames, *André Gide*, 110.

Germaine Brée, "Form and Content in André Gide," *French Review* XXX (May, 1957), 424.

Thomas Cordle, "Gide and the Novel of the Egoist," *Yale French Studies*, No. 7 (1951), 94-95.

John Cruickshank, "Gide's Treatment of Time in 'La Symphonie Pastorale,'" *Essays in Criticism* VII (April, 1957), 134-143.

GIDE, ANDRÉ, Continued

John Cruickshank, "Note on Gide's 'Symphonie Pastorale,'"
Modern Language Review XLIX (October, 1954), 475-478.

Ralph Freedman, "Imagination and Form in André Gide: 'La
Porte etroite' and 'La Symphonie pastorale,'" *Accent* XVII
(Autumn, 1957), 217-228.

E. W. Gosse, "Psychology of the Blind," in Gosse, *Books on the
Table*, 286-290.

Albert J. Guerard, *André Gide*, 139-144.

L. Hamalian and E. L. Volpe, *Ten Modern Short Novels*, 423-427.

Lawrence E. Harvey, "The Utopia of Blindness in Gide's 'Symphonie pastorale,'" *Modern Philology* LV (February, 1958), 188-
197.

Louis Kronenberger, "André Gide's Contrasting Aspects in Two
Novelettes," *New York Times Book Review* (May 24, 1931), 2.

Edmund L. Loughnan, "Thirteenth Apostle: A Study of M. André
Gide," *Sewanee Review* XXXIX (July, 1931), 300-301.

Klaus Mann, *André Gide and the Crisis of Modern Thought*,
152-156.

Harold March, *Gide and the Hound of Heaven*, 253-357.

W. G. Moore, "André Gide's 'Symphonie Pastorale,'" *French
Studies* IV (January, 1950), 16-26.

Justin O'Brien, "Gide's Fictional Technique," *Yale French Studies*,
No. 7 (1951), 84-85.

Justin O'Brien, *Portrait of André Gide*, 221-224.

George D. Painter, *André Gide*, 120-125.

Charles Parnell, "André Gide and his 'Symphonie Pastorale,'"
Yale French Studies, No. 7 (1951), 60-71.

Henri Peyre, *The Contemporary French Novel*, 87-88.

Léon Pierre-Quint, *André Gide*, 104-106.

Enid Starkie, *André Gide*, 37-38.

Geoffrey Stone, Review of *Two Symphonies, Bookman* LXXIV
(October, 1931), 196-197.

Gerald Sykes, "For Connoisseurs," *New Republic* LXVII (July 29,
1931), 295.

Gerald Sykes, "The Sins of a Critic," *Nation* CXXXIII (September 9, 1931), 260-261.

Lawrence Thomas, *André Gide: The Ethic of the Artist*, 102-104.

Martin Turnell, "André Gide and the Disintegration of the Protestant Cell," *Yale French Studies*, No. 7 (1951), 25-31.

8. PROMETHEUS MISBOUND

Van Meter Ames, *André Gide*, 43-46.

G. Brée and M. Guiton, *An Age of Fiction*, 25-27.

Albert J. Guerard, *André Gide,* 77-78.

Harold March, *Gide and the Hound of Heaven,* 108-115.

Justin O'Brien, *Portrait of André Gide,* 150-160.

George D. Painter, *André Gide,* 57-60.

Henri Peyre, "With Gidean Irony," *New York Times Book Review* (November 29, 1953) , 32.

Enid Starkie, *André Gide,* 25-26.

Lawrence Thomas, *André Gide: The Ethic of the Artist,* 110-120.

9. THE RETURN OF THE PRODIGAL SON

Van Meter Ames, *André Gide,* 65, 226-227.

Albert J. Guerard, *André Gide,* 82.

Edmund L. Loughnan, "Thirteenth Apostle: A Study of M. André Gide," *Sewanee Review* XXXIX (July, 1931) , 297.

Klaus Mann, *André Gide and the Crisis of Modern Thought,* 106-110, 255.

Harold March, *Gide and the Hound of Heaven,* 145-148.

Justin O'Brien, *Portrait of André Gide,* 207-211.

George D. Painter, *André Gide,* 83-85.

Lawrence Thomas, *André Gide: The Ethic of the Artist,* 139-144.

Martin Turnell, "André Gide and the Disintegration of the Protestant Cell," *Yale French Studies,* No. 7 (1951) , 21.

10. ROBERT

George D. Painter, *André Gide,* 151-153.

Léon Pierre-Quint, *André Gide,* 126-130.

Lawrence Thomas, *André Gide: The Ethic of the Artist,* 214-217.

11. SCHOOL FOR WIVES

Van Meter Ames, *André Gide,* 108-110.

Mischa H. Fayer, *Gide, Freedom and Dostoevsky,* 110-111.

Albert J. Guerard, *André Gide,* 145-146.

George D. Painter, *André Gide,* 149-151.

Léon Pierre-Quint, *André Gide,* 235-236.

12. STRAIT IS THE GATE

Van Meter Ames, *André Gide,* 18-21, 55-64, 225-228.

Anon., Review of *Strait Is the Gate, Times Literary Supplement* (December 4, 1924) , 820.

Ernest Boyd, "The Protestant Barres," *New Republic* XXXIX (July 23, 1924) , 248.

Thomas Cordle, "Gide and the Novel of the Egoist," *Yale French Studies,* No. 7, (1951) , 93-94.

Wallace Fowlie, "The Fountain and the Thirst: an Interpretation of Gide," *Accent* VI (Winter, 1946) , 71-73. — reprinted in Ray B. West, *Essays in Modern Literary Criticism,* 494-497.

GIDE, ANDRE, Continued

Ralph Freedman, "Imagination and Form in André Gide: 'La Porte etroit' and 'La Symphonie pastorale,' " *Accent* XVII Autumn 1957) , 217-228.

Albert J. Guerard, *André Gide*, 118-124.

Joseph Wood Krutch, "The Ecstasy That Refrains," *Nation* CXVIII (April 16, 1924) , 447-448.

Klaus Mann, *André Gide and the Crisis of Modern Thought*, 117-125, 247.

Harold March, *Gide and the Hound of Heaven*, 149-165.

Justin O'Brien, "Gide's Fictional Technique," *Yale French Studies*, No. 7 (1951) , 81-84.

Justin O'Brien, *Portrait of André Gide*, 213-220, 341-346.

George D. Painter, *André Gide*, 86-90.

Henri Peyre, *The Contemporary French Novel*, 90-94.

Enid Starkie, *André Gide*, 30-32.

Lawrence Thomas, *André Gide: The Ethic of the Artist*, 145-151.

Martin Turnell, "André Gide and the Disintegration of the Protestant Cell," *Yale French Studies*, No. 7 (1951) , 21-25.

13. THESEUS

Van Meter Ames, *André Gide*, 42, 116-117.

G. Brée and M. Guiton, *An Age of Fiction*, 29-30.

Albert J. Guerard, *André Gide*, 90-92.

B. Renée Lang, "Two Books, Two Creeds," *Books Abroad* XXI (1947) , 383-384.

J. R. Loy, "Prometheus, Theseus, the Uncommon Man and an Eagle," *Yale French Studies*, No. 7 (1951) , 32-43.

Harold March, *Gide and the Hound of Heaven*, 355-362.

Justin O'Brien, *Portrait of André Gide*, 201-206, 239, 242, 244, 339-340.

George D. Painter, *André Gide*, 179-183.

V. S. Pritchett, "Books in General," *New Statesman and Nation* XL (August 26, 1950) , 231-232.

John Russell, "The Old Age of André Gide," *Horizon* XVI (December, 1947) , 346-349.

Harry Slochower, "André Gide's 'Theseus' and the French Myth," *Yale French Studies* No. 4 (Autumn-Winter, 1949) , 34-43.

Enid Starkie, *André Gide*, 53-54.

Irvin Stock, "André Gide: Apostle of Progress," *Accent* IX (Summer, 1949) , 202-214.

Lawrence Thomas, *André Gide: The Ethic of the Artist*, 220.

14. THE TREATISE OF THE NARCISSUS

Van Meter Ames, *André Gide*, 185-186.

GIDE, ANDRÉ, Continued

Mischa H. Fayer, *Gide, Freedom and Dostoevsky,* 19-20.
Klaus Mann, *André Gide and the Crisis of Modern Thought,* 60-61.
Harold March, *Gide and the Hound of Heaven,* 52-54.
Justin O'Brien, *Portrait of André Gide,* 38-39, 72-76, 338-339.
George D. Painter, *André Gide,* 32.
Enid Starkie, *André Gide,* 17.
Lawrence Thomas, *André Gide: The Ethic of the Artist,* 49-54.

GIONO, JEAN

1. THE CORN DIES
Raymond W. Short and Richard B. Sewall, *A Manual of Suggestions for Teachers Using "Short Stories for Study,"* 12-15.

GLATSTEIN, JACOB

1. CITIZEN GOD
Judah Goldin, "The Contemporary Jew and His Judaism," in S. R. Hopper, *Spiritual Problems in Contemporary Literature,* 213-214.

GOGOL, NIKOLAI

1. THE CLOAK
(see "The Overcoat")
2. THE DIARY OF A MADMAN
Janko Lavrin, *Gogol,* 110-115.
David Magarshack, *Gogol: A Life,* 119-121.
3. THE GREATCOAT
(see "The Overcoat")
4. HOW THE TWO IVANS QUARRELLED
(see "The Quarrel between Ivan Ivanovitch and Ivan Niforovitch")
5. A MADMAN'S DIARY
(see "The Diary of a Madman")
6. THE NEVSKY PROSPECT
Janko Lavrin, *Gogol,* 107-110.
Marc Slonim, *The Epic of Russian Literature,* 164-165.

GOGOL, NIKOLAI, Continued

7. THE NOSE
[Herbert E. Bowman, "The Nose," *Slavonic and East European Review* XXXI (1953), 204-211.]
Victor Erlich, "Gogol and Kafka: Note on 'Realism' and 'Surrealism,'" in Morris Halle, *For Roman Jakobson*, 102-104.
Janko Lavrin, *Gogol*, 115-116.
Janko Lavrin, *Nikolai Gogol: A Centenary Survey*, 71-74.
David Magarshack, *Gogol: A Life*, 125.
Marc Slonim, *The Epic of Russian Literature*, 165.
8. THE OLD-WORLD LANDOWNERS
Janko Lavrin, *Gogol*, 59-66.
Janko Lavrin, *Nikolai Gogol: A Centenary Survey*, 45-48.
9. THE OVERCOAT
Janko Lavrin, *Gogol*, 117-127.
Janko Lavrin, *Nikolai Gogol: A Centenary Survey*, 74-77.
[Mildred A. Martin, "The Last Shall be First: A Study of Three Russian Short Stories," *Bucknell Review* VI (March, 1956), 13-23.]
Vladimir Nabokov, *Nikolai Gogol*, 140-149.
Marc Slonim, *The Epic of Russian Literature*, 167.
Leon Stilman, "Gogol's 'Overcoat' — Thematic Pattern and Origins," *American Slavic and East European Review* XI (April, 1952), 138-148.
10. THE PORTRAIT
Janko Lavrin, *Gogol*, 97-105.
Janko Lavrin, *Nikolai Gogol: A Centenary Survey*, 62-66.
David Magarshack, *Gogol: A Life*, 113-118.
11. THE QUARREL BETWEEN IVAN IVANOVITCH AND IVAN NIKIFOROVITCH
Janko Lavrin, *Gogol*, 82-92.
Janko Lavrin, *Nikolai Gogol: A Centenary Survey*, 56-59.
David Magarshack, *Gogol: A Life*, 122.
12. THE STORY OF A QUARREL BETWEEN IVAN INVANO-VICH AND IVAN NIKIFOROVICH
(see "The Quarrel Between Ivan Ivanovitch and Ivan Nikiforovitch")
13. VIY
Janko Lavrin, *Gogol*, 76-81.
Janko Lavrin, *Nikolai Gogol: A Centenary Survey*, 53-55.
David Magarshack, *Gogol: A Life*, 124-125.

GOODMAN, PAUL

1. A PRAYER FOR DEW
Judah Goldin, "The Contemporary Jew and His Judaism," in S. R. Hopper, *Spiritual Problems in Contemporary Literature,* 218.

GORDON, CAROLINE

1. THE BRILLIANT LEAVES
Louise Cowan, "Nature and Grace in Caroline Gordon," *Critique: Studies in Modern Fiction* I (Winter, 1956), 14-16.

Andrew Lytle, "Caroline Gordon and the Historic Image," *Sewanee Review* LVII (Autumn, 1949), 562-567.

2. THE CAPTIVE
Vivienne Koch, "The Forest of the South," *Sewanee Review* LIV (Summer, 1946), 545.

3. THE FOREST OF THE SOUTH
Vivienne Koch, "The Forest of the South," *Sewanee Review* LIV (Summer, 1946), 546-547.

Andrew Nelson Lytle, " 'The Forest of the South,' " *Critique: Studies in Modern Fiction* I (Winter, 1956), 5-6.

4. HEAR THE NIGHTINGALE SING
Andrew Nelson Lytle, " 'The Forest of the South,' " *Critique: Studies in Modern Fiction* I (Winter, 1956), 6-7.

5. THE ICE HOUSE
Andrew Nelson Lytle, " 'The Forest of the South,' " *Critique: Studies in Modern Fiction* I (Winter, 1956), 7-8.

6. THE LAST DAY IN THE FIELD
Beardsley, Daniel, and Leggett, *Aids to Study for "Theme and Form: An Introduction to Literature,"* 84-85.

R. B. Heilman, *Modern Short Stories,* 48-49.

7. THE LONG DAY
Vivienne Koch, "The Forest of the South," *Sewanee Review* LIV (Summer, 1946), 544-545.

8. OLD RED
Morgan Blum, "The Shifting Point of View: Joyce's 'The Dead' and Gordon's 'Old Road,' " *Critique: Studies in Modern Fiction* I (Winter, 1956), 58-66.

Brooks and Warren, *Understanding Fiction,* 82-87.

Vivienne Koch, "The Forest of the South," *Sewanee Review* LIV (Summer, 1946), 545-546. — reprinted, revised, in Rubin and Jacobs, *Southern Renascence,* 328-329.

9. SUMMER DUST
Vivienne Koch, "The Forest of the South," *Sewanee Review* **LIV** (Summer, 1946), 544. — reprinted, revised, in Rubin and Jacobs, *Southern Renascence,* 327.

GOSS, JOHN

1. BIRD SONG
Mary Orvis, *The Art of Writing Fiction,* 144-147.

GRANBERRY, EDWIN

1. A TRIP TO CZARDIS
Kenneth Kempton, *Short Stories for Study,* 225-231.
Kenneth Kempton, *The Short Story,* 197-200.
Mary Orvis, *The Art of Writing Fiction,* 89-90.

GREENE, GRAHAM

1. ACROSS THE BRIDGE
Walter Havighurst, *Instructor's Manual: "Masters of the Modern Short Story,"* 27-28.
2. THE BASEMENT ROOM
Sale, Hall, and Steinmann, *Critical Discussions for Teachers Using "Short Stories: Tradition and Direction,"* 62-64.
R. B. Heilman, *Modern Short Stories,* 264-266.
Mark Schorer, *The Story,* 183-185.
Gerald E. Silveira, "Graham Greene's 'The Basement Room,'" *Explicator* XV, No. 3 (December, 1956), item 13.
3. THE SECOND DEATH
Winifred Lynskey, *Reading Modern Fiction* (Second Edition, 1957), 245-246.

HARDY, THOMAS

1. THE ROMANTIC ADVENTURES OF A MILKMAID
Joseph Warren Beach, *The Technique of Thomas Hardy,* 124-127.
Albert J. Guerard, *Thomas Hardy: The Novels and Stories,* 93-96.

2. SQUIRE PETRICK'S LADY
   Albert J. Guerard, *Thomas Hardy: The Novels and Stories,* 26.
3. THE THREE STRANGERS
   Brooks, Purser, and Warren, *An Approach to Literature,* 99-101.
   William Van O'Connor, "Cosmic Irony in Hardy's 'The Three
   Strangers,'" *College English* XLVII (May, 1958), 248-254.
4. A TRADITION OF 1804
   Herbert Barrows, *Suggestions for Teaching "15 Stories,"* 3-5.
5. A TRAGEDY OF TWO AMBITIONS
   Felheim, Newman, and Steinhoff, *Study Aids for Teachers for
   "Modern Short Stories,"* 8-10.
   Helmut E. Gerber, "Hardy's 'A Tragedy of Two Ambitions,'"
   Explicator XIV, No. 9 (June, 1956), item 55.
6. THE WITHERED ARM
   Albert J. Guerard, *Thomas Hardy: The Novels and Stories,* 92-93.

HARTE, BRET

1. LUCK OF ROARING CAMP
   Brooks, Purser, and Warren, *An Approach to Literature,* 86-87.
2. TENNESSEE'S PARTNER
   Brooks and Warren, *Understanding Fiction,* 214-220.

HAWTHORNE, NATHANIEL

1. ALICE DOANE'S APPEAL
   Robert Cantwell, *Nathaniel Hawthorne: The American Years,*
   108-109.
   Seymour L. Gross, "Hawthorne's 'Alice Doane's Appeal,'" *Nine-
   teenth Century Fiction* X (December, 1955), 232-236.
   Roy Harvey Pearce, "Hawthorne and The Sense of the Past or,
   The Immortality of Major Molineux," *ELH* XXI (December,
   1954), 337-339.
   John W. Shroeder, "'That Inward Sphere': Notes on Haw-
   thorne's Heart Imagery and Symbolism," *PMLA* LXV (March,
   1950), 114-116.
   W. B. Stein, *Hawthorne's Faust,* 55-56.
   H. H. Waggoner, *Hawthorne: A Critical Study,* 38-45.
   H. H. Waggoner, "Hawthorne's Beginning: 'Alice Doane's Appeal,'" *University of Kansas City Review* XVI (Summer, 1950),
   254-260.

H. H. Waggoner, "Introduction," to Hawthorne, *Selected Tales and Sketches* (Rinehart Editions, 1950) , xi-xii.

2. THE AMBITIOUS GUEST
    B. Bernard Cohen, "The Sources of 'The Ambitious Guest,'" *Boston Public Library Quarterly* IV (October, 1952) , 221-224.
    C. H. Edgren, "Hawthorne's 'The Ambitious Guest': An Interpretation," *Nineteenth-Century Fiction* X (Sepember, 1955) , 151-156.
    W. B. Stein, *Hawthorne's Faust*, 71-72.

3. THE ARTIST OF THE BEAUTIFUL
    Richard Beale Davis, "Hawthorne, Fanny Kemble, and 'The Artist of the Beautiful,'" *Modern Language Notes* LXX (December, 1958) , 589-592.
    Henry G. Fairbanks, "Hawthorne amid the Alien Corn," *College English* XVII (February, 1956) , 266.
    Richard H. Fogle, "The World and the Artist: A Study of Hawthorne's 'The Artist of the Beautiful,'" *Tulane Studies in English* I (1949) , 31-52. — reprinted, revised, in Fogle, *Hawthorne's Fiction: The Light and the Dark,* 70-90.
    Hawthorne, *Passages from the American Note-Books,* 211.
    R. W. B. Lewis, *The American Adam,* 118-119.
    F. O. Matthiessen, *The American Renaissance,* 223-224.
    Patricia Moyer, "Time and the Artist in Kafka and Hawthorne," *Modern Fiction Studies* IV (Winter, 1958-1959) , 295-306.
    Donald A. Ringe, "Hawthorne's Psychology of the Head and Heart," *PMLA* LXV (March, 1950) , 123-124.
    W. B. Stein, *Hawthorne's Faust*, 93-96, 149.
    Randall Stewart, "Introduction," in *The American Notebooks by Nathaniel Hawthorne* (Yale, 1932) , xlvi.
    Rudolph Von Abele, "Baby and Butterfly," *Kenyon Review* XV (Spring, 1953) , 280-292. — reprinted, revised, in Von Abele, *The Death of the Artist: A Study of Hawthorne's Disintegration,* 32-43.
    Austin Warren, *Nathaniel Hawthorne,* 366.

4. THE BIRTHMARK
    Newton Arvin, "Introduction" to *Hawthorne's Short Stories* (Vintage Books, 1955) , x-xii.
    Brooks and Warren, *Understanding Fiction,* 103-106.
    Neal F. Doubleday, "Hawthorne's Use of Three Gothic Patterns," *College English* VII (February, 1946) , 261.
    Hawthorne, *Passages from the American Note-Books,* 106-210; *American Notebooks* (Yale, 1932) , 97.
    R. B. Heilman, "Hawthorne's 'The Birthmark': Science as Re-

ligion," *South Atlantic Quarterly* XLVIII (October, 1949), 575-583.

Kenneth Kempton, *The Short Story,* 74-78, 82-83.

Simon O. Lesser, "The Attitude of Fiction," *Modern Fiction Studies* II (May, 1956), 52-55. — reprinted in Lesser, *Fiction and the Unconscious,* 87-90; with additional materials, 94-98.

Roy R. Male, *Hawthorne's Tragic Vision,* 80-84.

F. O. Matthiessen, *The American Renaissance,* 253-254.

James E. Miller, Jr., "Hawthorne and Melville: The Unpardonable Sin," *PMLA* LXX (March, 1955), 92-93, 99, 101-102.

W. B. Stein, *Hawthorne's Faust,* 91-92, 148.

Randall Stewart, "Introduction," in *The American Notebooks by Nathaniel Hawthorne* (Yale, 1932), xxiv-xxv, xlv-xlvi.

Randall Stewart, "The Vision of Evil in Hawthorne and Melville," in Nathan Scott, *Tragic Vision and the Christian Faith,* 241-243. — reprinted in Randall Stewart, *American Literature and Christian Doctrine,* 79-81.

W. R. Thompson, "Aminadab in Hawthorne's 'The Birthmark,' " *Modern Language Notes* LXX (June, 1955), 413-415.

Mark Van Doren, *Nathaniel Hawthorne,* 130-131.

H. H. Waggoner, *Hawthorne: A Critical Study,* 113-114, 187-188.

Austin Warren, *Nathaniel Hawthorne,* 366-367.

5. THE CANTERBURY PILGRIMS

W. B. Stein, *Hawthorne's Faust,* 83-84.

H. H. Waggoner, "Hawthorne's 'Canterbury Pilgrims': Theme and Structure," *New England Quarterly* XXII (September, 1949), 373-387. — reprinted, revised, with additional material, in Waggoner, *Hawthorne: A Critical Study* 29-31, 64-78, 90-92.

H. H. Waggoner, "Introduction," in Hawthorne, *Selected Tales and Sketches,* xii-xiii.

6. THE CELESTIAL RAILROAD

Neal F. Doubleday, "Hawthorne's Satirical Allegory," *College English* III (January, 1942), 329-332.

Walter Havighurst, "Symbolism and the Student," *College English* XVI (April, 1955), 431.

F. O. Matthiessen, *The American Renaissance,* 198-199.

Mark Van Doren, *The Best of Hawthorne,* 422-423.

H. H. Waggoner, *Hawthorne: A Critical Study,* 16-20.

Austin Warren, *Nathaniel Hawthorne,* xxii-xxiv.

7. THE CHRISTMAS BANQUET

Neal F. Doubleday, "Hawthorne's Satirical Allegory," *College English* III (January, 1942), 326-329.

Hawthorne, *Passages from the American Note-Books,* 32, 33.

8. **THE DEVIL IN MANUSCRIPT**
 Marius Bewley, *The Complex Fate,* 58-59.
 W. B. Stein, *Hawthorne's Faust,* 57-59.

9. **DR. HEIDEGGER'S EXPERIMENT**
 Neal F. Doubleday, "Hawthorne's Use of Three Gothic Patterns,"
 College English VII (February, 1946), 260-261.
 V. E. Gibbens, "Hawthorne's Note to 'Dr. Heidegger's Experiment,'" *Modern Language Notes* LX (June, 1945), 408-409.
 W. B. Stein, *Hawthorne's Faust,* 82-83.
 Alfred C. Ward, *Aspects of the Modern Short Story,* 22-25.

10. **DROWNE'S WOODEN IMAGE**
 Alexander Cowie, *The Rise of the American Novel,* 351-352.
 W. B. Stein, *Hawthorne's Faust,* 96-97, 149.

11. **EARTH'S HOLOCAUST**
 Neal F. Doubleday, "Hawthorne's Satirical Allegory," *College English* III (January, 1942), 332-336.
 Hawthorne, *Passages from the American Note-Books,* 211; *American Notebooks* (Yale, 1932), 98.
 R. W. B. Lewis, *The American Adam,* 13-14.
 W. B. Stein, *Hawthorne's Faust,* 101-103.
 Randall Stewart, "Introduction," in *The American Notebooks by Nathaniel Hawthorne* (Yale, 1932), xxv-xxvi.
 H. H. Waggoner, *Hawthorne: A Critical Study,* 19-23.
 Austin Warren, *Nathaniel Hawthorne,* xlvi-xlvii.

12. **EDWARD RANDOLPH'S PORTRAIT**
 W. B. Stein, *Hawthorne's Faust,* 76-77.

13. **EGOTISM; OR, THE BOSOM SERPENT**
 W. C. Brownell, *American Prose Masters,* 79-80.
 Hawthorne, *Passages from the American Note-Books,* 34; *American Notebooks* (Yale, 1932), 93.
 James E. Miller, Jr., "Hawthorne and Melville: The Unpardonable Sin," *PMLA* LXX (March, 1955), 94, 102.
 Randall Stewart, "Introduction," in *The American Notebooks of Nathaniel Hawthorne* (Yale, 1932), xlvii-xlviii.
 Rudolph Von Abele, *The Death of the Artist: A Study of Hawthorne's Disintegration,* 18-30.

14. **ENDICOTT OF THE RED CROSS**
 Q. D. Leavis, "Hawthorne as Poet—Part II" *Sewanee Review* LIX (Summer, 1951), 426-430.

15. **ETHAN BRAND**
 Herbert Barrows, *Suggestions for Teaching "15 Stories,"* 17-19.

Marius Bewley, "James' Debt to Hawthorne (III) : The American Problem," *Scrutiny* XVII (Spring, 1950), 17-19. — reprinted in Bewley, *The Complex Fate,* 59-60.

Neal F. Doubleday, "Hawthorne's Use of Three Gothic Patterns," *College English* VII (February, 1946), 258-259.

Richard H. Fogle, "The Problem of Allegory in Hawthorne's 'Ethan Brand,' " *University of Toronto Quarterly* XVII (January, 1948), 191-203. — reprinted, revised, in Fogle, *Hawthorne's Fiction: The Light and the Dark,* 41-58.

Stanley Geist, "Fictitious Americans," *Hudson Review* V (Summer, 1952), 199-202.

Hawthorne, *American Notebooks* (Yale, 1932), 106.

Roy R. Male, *Hawthorne's Tragic Vision,* 85-89.

Leo Marx, "The Machine in the Garden," *New England Quarterly* XXIX (March, 1956), 27-42.

James E. Miller, Jr., "Hawthorne and Melville: The Unpardonable Sin," *PMLA* LXX (March, 1955), 92, 95-96, 98, 103.

Sherman Paul, "Hawthorne's Ahab," *Notes and Queries* CXCVI (June 9, 1951), 255-257.

Glenn Pedersen, "Blake's Urizen as Hawthorne's Ethan Brand," *Nineteenth Century Fiction* XII (March, 1958), 304-314.

George Reeves, Jr., "Hawthorne's 'Ethan Brand,' " *Explicator* XIV, No. 9 (June, 1956), item 56.

Cyril A. Reilly, "On the Dog's Chasing His Own Tail in 'Ethan Brand,' " *PMLA* LXVIII (December, 1953), 975-981.

B. A. Sokoloff, "Ethan Brand's Twin," *Modern Language Notes* LXXIII (June, 1958), 413-414.

Stallman and Watters, *Creative Reader,* 338-339.

W. B. Stein, *Hawthorne's Faust,* 97-100, 149-150.

Randall Stewart, *American Literature and Christian Doctrine,* 95-96.

Randall Stewart, "Ethan Brand," *Saturday Review of Literature* V (April 27, 1929), 967.

Wright Thomas and Stuart Gerry Brown, *Reading Prose: An Introduction to Critical Study,* 680-681.

Mark Van Doren, *Nathaniel Hawthorne,* 138-139.

Austin Warren, *Nathaniel Hawthorne,* xxxvi-xxxvii.

16. FANCY'S SHOW BOX

Neal F. Doubleday, "The Theme of Hawthorne's 'Fancy's Show Box,' " *American Literature* X (November, 1938), 341-343.

Henry G. Fairbanks, "Sin, Free Will, and Pessimism in Hawthorne," *American Association of University Professors Bulletin* LXXI (December, 1956) , 978-979, 986.

H. H. Waggoner, *Hawthorne: A Critical Study,* 12-16.

17. FEATHERTOP

Darrel Abel, "The Theme of Isolation in Hawthorne," *Personalist* XXXII (Winter, 1951) , 53-55.

Robert Allen Durr, "Feathertop's Unlikely Love Affair," *Modern Language Notes* LXXII (November, 1957) , 492-493.

Hawthorne, *Passages from the American Note-Books,* 211; *American Notebooks* (Yale, 1932) , 126.

Alfred A. Kern, "Hawthorne's 'Feathertop' and 'R. L. R.' " *PMLA* LII (June, 1937) , 503-510.

Randall Stewart, "Introduction," in *The American Notebooks by Nathaniel Hawthorne* (Yale, 1932) , xxvi.

18. FIRE WORSHIP

Millicent Bell, "Hawthorne's 'Fire Worship': Interpretation and Source," *American Literature* XXIV (March, 1952) , 31-39.

Roy R. Male, "Criticism of Bell's 'Hawthorne's "Fire Worship": Interpretation and Source,' " *American Literature* XXV (March, 1953) , 85-87.

19. FRAGMENTS FROM A JOURNAL OF A SOLITARY MAN

W. B. Stein, *Hawthorne's Faust,* 58-59.

20. THE GENTLE BOY

Louise Dauner, "The 'Case' of Tobias Pearson," *American Literature* XXI (January, 1950) , 464-472.

Seymour L. Gross, "Hawthorne's Revision of 'The Gentle Boy,' " *American Literature* XXVI (May, 1954) , 196-208.

Roy R. Male, *Hawthorne's Tragic Vision,* 45-48.

F. O. Matthiessen, *The American Renaissance,* 215-218.

G. Harrison Orians, "The Sources and Themes of Hawthorne's 'The Gentle Boy,' " *New England Quarterly* XIV (December, 1941) , 664-678.

Roy Harvey Pearce, "Hawthorne and The Sense of the Past or, The Immortality of Major Molineux," *ELH* XXI (December, 1954) , 335-337.

W. B. Stein, *Hawthorne's Faust,* 63-65.

Mark Van Doren, *Nathaniel Hawthorne,* 72-74.

21. THE GRAY CHAMPION

B. Bernard Cohen, " 'The Gray Champion,' " *Folio* (Indiana University) XIII (February, 1948) , 11-12.

Edward J. O'Brien, *The Short Story Case Book,* 213-227.

W. B. Stein, *Hawthorne's Faust,* 145-146.
Mark Van Doren, *The Best of Hawthorne,* 419-420.
22. THE GREAT CARBUNCLE
W. B. Stein, *Hawthorne's Faust,* 75-76.
23. THE GREAT STONE FACE
Hawthorne, *Passages from the American Note-Books,* 210.
James E. Miller, Jr., "Hawthorne and Melville: The Unpardonable Sin," *PMLA* LXX (March, 1955), 104-105.
24. THE HALL OF FANTASY
Neal F. Doubleday, "Hawthorne's Satirical Allegory," *College English* III (January, 1942), 326-329.
25. THE HAUNTED MIND
W. B. Stein, *Hawthorne's Faust,* 67-68.
H. H. Waggoner, *Hawthorne: A Critical Study,* 9-11.
26. THE HOLLOW OF THE THREE HILLS
Marius Bewley, "Hawthorne and 'The Deeper Psychology,'" *Mandrake* II (Autumn-Winter, 1955-1956), 370-373.
F. O. Matthiessen, *The American Renaissance,* 205-206.
W. B. Stein, *Hawthorne's Faust,* 55-58.
27. THE INTELLIGENCE OFFICE
Neal F. Doubleday, "Hawthorne's Satirical Allegory," *College English* III (January, 1942), 326-327.
W. B. Stein, *Hawthornes Faust,* 89-90.
28. JOHN INGLEFIELD'S THANKSGIVING
W. B. Stein, *Hawthorne's Faust,* 89-90.
29. LADY ELEANORE'S MANTLE
Seymour L. Gross, "Hawthorne's 'Lady Eleanore's Mantle' as History," *Journal of English and Germanic Philology* LIV (October, 1955), 549-554. — reprinted in University of Illinois English Department, *Studies in Memory of John Jay Parry,* 89-94.
James E. Miller, Jr., "Hawthorne and Melville: The Unpardonable Sin," *PMLA* LXX (March, 1955), 97, 99, 105
W. B. Stein, *Hawthorne's Faust,* 76-78.
30. THE LILY'S QUEST
Hawthorne, *Passages from the American Note-Books,* 37, 38.
31. THE MAN OF ADAMANT
Joseph X. Brennan and Seymour L. Gross, "The Origin of Hawthorne's Unpardonable Sin," *Boston University Studies in English* III (Summer, 1957), 126-129.
Hawthorne, *Passages from the American Note-Books,* 24.
Mark Van Doren, *Nathaniel Hawthorne,* 89.
H. H. Waggoner, *Hawthorne: A Critical Study,* 95-100.

32. THE MAYPOLE OF MERRY MOUNT
Richard P. Adams, "Hawthorne's Provincial Tales," *New England Quarterly* XXX (March, 1957), 44-45.
Richard H. Fogle, *Hawthorne's Fiction: The Light and the Dark*, 59-69.
Q. D. Leavis, "Hawthorne as Poet," *Sewanee Review* LIX (Spring, 1951), 185-195.
G. Harrison Orians, "Hawthorne and 'The Maypole of Merry-Mount,'" *Modern Language Notes* LIII (March, 1938), 159-167.
W. B. Stein, *Hawthorne's Faust*, 59-61.
John B. Vickery, "The Golden Bough at Merry Mount," *Nineteenth Century Fiction* XII (December, 1957), 203-214.

33. THE MINISTER'S BLACK VEIL
Richard H. Fogle, "An Ambiguity of Sin or Sorrow," *New England Quarterly* XXI (September, 1948), 342-349. — reprinted, revised, in Fogle, *Hawthorne's Fiction: The Light and the Dark*, 33-40.
Paul Goodman, *The Structure of Literature*, 253-257.
W. B. Stein, *Hawthorne's Faust*, 3-4, 80-81.
W. B. Stein, "The Parable of the Antichrist in 'The Minister's Black Veil,'" *American Literature* XXVII (November, 1955), 386-392.
Randall Stewart, "Introduction," in *The American Notebooks of Nathaniel Hawthorne* (Yale, 1932), xlvii.
Mark Van Doren, *The Best of Hawthorne*, 421.
Gilbert P. Voight, "The Meaning of 'The Minister's Black Veil,'" *College English* XIII (March, 1952), 337-338.

34. MONSIEUR DU MIROIR
W. B. Stein, *Hawthorne's Faust*, 68.

35. MRS. BULLFROG
W. B. Stein, *Hawthorne's Faust*, 70-71.

36. MY KINSMAN, MAJOR MOLINEUX
Richard P. Adams, "Hawthorne's Provincial Tales," *New England Quarterly* XXX (March, 1957), 45-48.
Quentin Anderson, "Henry James and the New Jerusalem," *Kenyon Review* VIII (Autumn, 1946), 565-566.
Marius Bewley, *The Complex Fate*, n. 81.
Richard Chase, "The Progressive Hawthorne," *Partisan Review* XVI (January, 1949), 98-99.
Seymour L. Gross, "Hawthorne's 'My Kinsman, Major Molineux': History as Moral Adventure," *Nineteenth Century Fiction* XII (September, 1957), 97-109.

HAWTHORNE, NATHANIEL, Continued

Q. D. Leavis, "Hawthorne as Poet," *Sewanee Review* LIX (Spring, 1951), 198-205.

Simon O. Lesser, "The Image of the Father," *Partisan Review* XXII (Summer, 1955), 372-381. — reprinted in William Phillips, *Art and Psychoanalysis,* 226-236. — reprinted in Lesser, *Fiction and the Unconscious,* 212-224.

Roy R. Male, *Hawthorne's Tragic Vision,* 48-53.

Franklin B. Newman, " 'My Kinsman, Major Molineux,' " *University of Kansas City Review* XXI (Spring, 1955), 203-212.

Roy Harvey Pearce, "Hawthorne and The Sense of the Past, or the Immortality of Major Molineux," *ELH* XXI (December, 1954), 327-334.

Mark Van Doren, *Nathaniel Hawthorne,* 75-76.

H. H. Waggoner, *Hawthorne: A Critical Study,* 46-53.

Stallman and Watters, *Creative Reader,* 331-332.

W. B. Stein, "Teaching Hawthorne's 'My Kinsman, Major Molineux,' " *College English* XX (November, 1958), 83-86.

37. THE NEW ADAM AND EVE

Marius Bewley, "Hawthorne and 'The Deeper Psychology,' " *Mandrake* II (Autumn-Winter, 1955-1956), 368-370.

Hawthorne, *Passages from the American Note-Books,* 33.

W. B. Stein, *Hawthorne's Faust,* 100-101.

38. PETER GOLDTHWAITE'S TREASURE

W. B. Stein, *Hawthorne's Faust,* 69-71.

39. THE PROCESSION OF LIFE

Hawthorne, *Passages from the American Note-Books,* 34, 35.

40. THE PROPHETIC PICTURES

Newton Arvin, "Introduction" to *Hawthorne's Short Stories* (Vintage Books, 1955), viii-x.

Marius Bewley, "Hawthorne and 'The Deeper Psychology,' " *Mandrake* II (Autumn-Winter, 1955-1956), 369-370.

Alice L. Cooke, "The Shadow of Martinus Scriblerus in Hawthorne's 'The Prophetic Pictures,' " *New England Quarterly* XVII (December, 1944), 598-604.

Mary E. Dichmann, "Hawthorne's 'Prophetic Pictures,' " *American Literature* XXIII (May, 1951), 188-202.

June Lundblad, *Nathaniel Hawthorne and the Tradition of Gothic Romance,* 41-43. — reprinted in Lundblad, *Nathaniel Hawthorne and European Literary Tradition,* 98-100.

W. B. Stein, *Hawthorne's Faust,* 73-75.

41. RAPPACCINI'S DAUGHTER

Charles Boewe, "Rappaccini's Garden," *American Literature* XXX (March, 1958), 37-49.

Frank Davidson, "Hawthorne's Hive of Honey," *Modern Language Notes* LXI (January, 1946), 18-21.

Neal F. Doubleday, "Hawthorne's Use of Three Gothic Patterns," *College English* VII (February, 1946), 259-260.

Richard H. Fogle, *Hawthorne's Fiction: The Light and the Dark*, 91-103, 205-206.

Frederick L. Gwynn, "Hawthorne's 'Rappaccini's Daughter,'" *Nineteenth Century Fiction* VII (December, 1952), 217-219.

Hawthorne, *Passages from the American Note-Books*, 209.

W. Stacy Johnson, "Sin and Salvation in Hawthorne," *Hibbert Journal* L (October, 1952), 46.

Kenneth Kempton, *The Short Story*, 83-86.

Roy R. Male, Jr., "The Dual Aspects of Evil in 'Rappaccini's Daughter,'" *PMLA* LXIX (March, 1954), 99-109. — reprinted, revised, in Male, *Hawthorne's Tragic Vision*, 55-70.

James E. Miller, Jr., "Hawthorne and Melville: The Unpardonable Sin," *PMLA* LXX (March, 1955), 93-94.

Sherwood R. Price, "The Heart, the Head, and 'Rappaccini's Daughter,'" *New England Quarterly* XXVII (September, 1954), 399-403.

Philip Rahv, "The Dark Lady of Salem," *Partisan Review* VIII (September-October, 1941), 370-372. — reprinted in Rahv, *Image and Idea*, 31-32.

Walter Rawls, "Hawthorne's 'Rappaccini's Daughter,'" *Explicator* XV, No. 7 (April, 1957), item 47.

Arthur L. Scott, "The Case of the Fatal Antidote," *Arizona Quarterly* XI (Spring, 1955), 38-43.

W. B. Stein, *Hawthorne's Faust*, 92-93, 148-149.

Randall Stewart, "Introduction," in *The American Notebooks by Nathaniel Hawthorne* (Yale, 1932), lxxi, lxxiv.

Mark Van Doren, *The Best of Hawthorne*, 423.

Mark Van Doren, *Nathaniel Hawthorne*, 131-132.

H. H. Waggoner, *Hawthorne: A Critical Study*, 101-116.

H. H. Waggoner, "Introduction," in Hawthorne, *Selected Tales and Sketches* (Rinehart Editions, 1950), xvi-xv.

West and Stallman, *Art of Modern Fiction*, 28-32.

42. ROGER MALVIN'S BURIAL

Richard P. Adams, "Hawthorne's Provincial Tales," *New England Quarterly* XXX (March, 1957), 48-50.

G. H. Orians, "The Source of Hawthorne's 'Roger Malvin's Burial,'" *American Literature* X (November, 1938), 313-318.

Roy Harvey Pearce, "Hawthorne and The Sense of the Past or,

HAWTHORNE, NATHANIEL, Continued

Richard H. Fogle, "Ambiguity and Clarity in Hawthorne's 'Young Goodman Brown,'" *New England Quarterly* XVIII (December, 1945), 448-465. — reprinted, revised, in Fogle, *Hawthorne's Fiction: The Light and the Dark*, 15-32. — reprinted in Locke, Gibson, and Arms, *Introduction to Literature* (Third Edition, 1957), 280-290.

Royal A. Gettmann and Bruce Harkness, *Teacher's Manual for "A Book of Stories,"* 53-56.

Gordon and Tate, *The House of Fiction,* 36-39.

Q. D. Leavis, "Hawthorne as Poet," *Sewanee Review* LIX (Spring, 1951), 195-198.

Jane Lundblad, *Nathaniel Hawthorne and the Tradition of Gothic Romance,* 35-37. — reprinted in Lundblad, *Nathaniel Hawthorne and European Literary Tradition,* 93-94.

Roy R. Male, *Hawthorne's Tragic Vision,* 76-80.

F. O. Matthiessen, *American Renaissance,* 282-284. — reprinted in Locke, Gibson, and Arms, *Introduction to Literature* (First Edition, 1948), 495-496; (Second Edition, 1952), 301-302.

D. M. McKeithan, "Hawthorne's 'Young Goodman Brown': An Interpretation," *Modern Language Notes* LXVII (February, 1952), 93-96.

Donald A. Ringe, "Hawthorne's Psychology of the Head and the Heart," *PMLA* LXV (March, 1950), 113-114.

John W. Schroeder, "'That Inward Sphere': Notes on Hawthorne's Heart Imagery and Symbolism," *PMLA* LXV (March, 1950), 113-114.

W. B. Stein, *Hawthorne's Faust,* 6-7, 61-63.

Randall Stewart, "The Vision of Evil in Hawthorne and Melville," in Nathan A. Scott, *The Tragic Vision and the Christian Faith,* 243-244. — reprinted in Stewart, *American Literature and Christian Doctrine,* 81-82.

Mark Van Doren, *The Best of Hawthorne,* 416-417.

Mark Van Doren, *Nathaniel Hawthorne,* 76-79.

Austin Warren, *Nathaniel Hawthorne,* 361-362.

HEGGEN, THOMAS

1. NIGHT WATCH
Stegner, Scowcroft, and Ilyin, *The Writer's Art,* 213-218.

HEMINGWAY, ERNEST

1. AFTER THE STORM
   Edmund Wilson, *The Wound and the Bow*, 224-225.
2. AN ALPINE IDYLL
   John Atkins, *Ernest Hemingway*, 207-208.
   Carlos Baker, *Hemingway*, 119-121.
   Edmund Wilson, "The Sportsman's Tragedy," *New Republic* LIII (December 14, 1927), 102. — reprinted in Wilson, *The Shores of Light*, 340-341.
   Philip Young, *Ernest Hemingway*, 31-32.
3. THE BATTLER
   William B. Bache, "Hemingway's 'The Battler,'" *Explicator* XIII, No. 1, (October, 1954), item 4.
   Randall Stewart and Dorothy Bethurum, *Modern American Narration (Living Masterpieces of American Literature*, Vol. 3), 68-70.
   Philip Young, *Ernest Hemingway*, 8-11, 205-207.
4. BIG TWO-HEARTED RIVER
   Charles A. Allen, "Ernest Hemingway's Clean, Well-Lighted Heroes," *Pacific Spectator* IX (Autumn, 1955), 383-384.
   Carlos Baker, *Hemingway*, 125-127.
   Malcolm Cowley, "Hemingway at Midnight," *New Republic* CXI (August 14, 1944), 190, 192.
   George Hemphill, "Hemingway and James," *Kenyon Review* XI (Winter, 1949), 54-55. — reprinted in John K. M. McCaffery, *Ernest Hemingway: The Man and His Work*, 334.
   Randall Stewart, *American Literature and Christian Doctrine*, 135-137.
   C. C. Walcutt, *American Literary Naturalism*, 271-272.
   Philip Young, *Ernest Hemingway*, 15-20.
5. A CANARY FOR ONE
   Carlos Baker, *Hemingway*, 137-138.
6. THE CAPITAL OF THE WORLD
   Delmore Schwartz, "The Fiction of Ernest Hemingway," *Perspectives USA*, No. 13 (Autumn, 1955), 85-86.
   Edmund Wilson, "Ernest Hemingway: Bourbon Gauge of Morale," *Atlantic Monthly* CLXIV (July, 1939), 45. — reprinted, revised, in Wilson, *The Wound and the Bow*, 236-237. — reprinted in Wilson, *Eight Essays*, 110. — reprinted in John K. M. McCaffery, *Ernest Hemingway: The Man and His Work*, 253.
7. CAT IN THE RAIN
   Carlos Baker, *Hemingway*, 135-136.

HEMINGWAY, ERNEST, Continued

Theodore Bardacke, "Hemingway's Women," in John K. M. Mc-Caffery, *Ernest Hemingway: The Man and His Work,* 344.

8. CHE TI DICE LA PATRIA?
Carlos Baker, *Hemingway,* 200-201.

9. A CLEAN WELL-LIGHTED PLACE
William B. Bache, "Craftsmanship in 'A Clean, Well-Lighted Place,'" *Personalist* XXXVII (Winter, 1956), 60-64.
Carlos Baker, *Hemingway,* 123-125.
William E. Colburn, "Confusion in 'A Clean, Well-Lighted Place,'" *College English* XX (February, 1959), 241-242.
R. B. Heilman, *Modern Short Stories,* 390-392.
F. P. Kroeger, "The Dialogue in 'A Clean, Well-Lighted Place,'" *College English* XX (February, 1959), 240-241.
Bernard S. Oldsey, "Hemingway's Old Men," *Modern Fiction Studies* I (August, 1955), 32.
Mark Schorer, *The Story,* 425-428.
Randall Stewart, *American Literature and Christian Doctrine,* 134-135.
Randall Stewart and Dorothy Bethurum, *Modern American Narration (Living Masterpieces of American Literature,* Vol. 3), 68-70.
R. P. Warren, "Hemingway," *Kenyon Review* IX (Winter, 1947), 5-6. — reprinted in *Horizon* XV (April, 1947), 159-160. — reprinted, revised, in J. W. Aldridge, *Critiques and Essays on Modern Fiction,* 454-455. — reprinted in M. D. Zabel, *Literary Opinion in America* (Revised Edition, 1951), 447-448. — reprinted in R. P. Warren, *Selected Essays,* 91-92.
Ray B. West, Jr., *The Short Story in America, 1900-1950,* 97-98.
Philip Young, *Ernest Hemingway,* 165-166.

10. CROSS-COUNTRY SNOW
Carlos Baker, *Hemingway,* 121, 133.
Demore Schwartz, "The Fiction of Ernest Hemingway," *Perspectives USA,* No. 13 (Autumn, 1955), 72-73.
Philip Young, *Ernest Hemingway,* 14-15.

11. THE DOCTOR AND THE DOCTOR'S WIFE
George Hemphill, "Hemingway and James," *Kenyon Review* XI (Winter, 1949), 57-58. — reprinted in John K. M. McCaffery, *Ernest Hemingway: The Man and His Work,* 336.
Philip Young, *Ernest Hemingway,* 4-5.

12. THE END OF SOMETHING
George Hemphill, "Hemingway and James," *Kenyon Review* XI (Winter, 1949), 54. — reprinted in John K. M. McCaffery, *Ernest Hemingway: The Man and His Work,* 333.

HEMINGWAY, ERNEST, Continued

Alice Parker, "Hemingway's 'The End of Something,' " *Explicator* X (March, 1952), item 36.

Joseph Whitt, "Hemingway's 'The End of Something,' " *Explicator* IX (June, 1951), item 58.

Philip Young, *Ernest Hemingway*, 4-6.

13. FATHERS AND SONS

Carlos Baker, *Hemingway*, 129-131, 133-134.

Bernard S. Oldsey, "Hemingway's Old Men," *Modern Fiction Studies* I (August, 1955), 31-32.

Philip Young, *Ernest Hemingway*, 32-34.

14. FIFTY GRAND

Carlos Baker, *Hemingway*, 122.

Charles A. Fenton, "No Money for the King-bird: Hemingway's Prizefight Stories," *American Quarterly* IV (Winter, 1952), 342-347.

Richard Summers, *Craft of the Short Story*, 190-192.

Philip Young, *Ernest Hemingway*, 36-37.

15. THE GAMBLER, THE NUN, AND THE RADIO

Alfred Dashiell, *Editor's Choice*, 131-132.

Delmore Schwartz, "Ernest Hemingway's Literary Situation," *Southern Review* III (Spring, 1938), 775-776.

Delmore Schwartz, "The Fiction of Ernest Hemingway," *Perspectives USA*, No. 13 (Autumn, 1955), 75, 79.

Philip Young, *Ernest Hemingway*, 38-41.

16. HILLS LIKE WHITE ELEPHANTS

H. E. Bates, *The Modern Short Story*, 172-173.

Norman Friedman, "What Makes a Short Story Short?" *Modern Fiction Studies* IV (Summer, 1958), 107-108.

17. HOMAGE TO SWITZERLAND

Carlos Baker, *Hemingway*, 138-139.

18. IN ANOTHER COUNTRY

Carlos Baker, *Hemingway*, 137.

Brooks, Purser, and Warren, *An Approach to Literature*, 104-106.

Robert G. Davis, *Instructor's Manual for "Ten Modern Masters,"* 26-27.

James B. Hall and Joseph Langland, *The Short Story*, 456-457.

J. B. Ludwig and W. R. Poirer, *Instructor's Manual to Accompany "Stories: British and American,"* 12-13.

R. W. Short and R. B. Sewall, *A Manual of Suggestions for Teachers Using "Short Stories for Study,"* (Revised Edition, 1950), 22-24.

Philip Young, *Ernest Hemingway*, 30-31.

19. INDIAN CAMP

George Hemphill, "Hemingway and James," *Kenyon Review* XI (Winter, 1949), 56.

Harry Levin, "Observations on the Style of Ernest Hemingway," *Kenyon Rewiev* XIII (Autumn, 1951), 606-607. — reprinted in Levin, *Contexts of Criticism*, 164.

Delmore Schwartz, "The Fiction of Ernest Hemingway," *Perspectives USA*, No. 13 (Autumn, 1955), 84-85.

Philip Young, *Ernest Hemingway*, 3-4.

20. THE KILLERS

Carlos Baker, *Hemingway*, 122-123.

Cleanth Brooks and Robert Penn Warren, " 'The Killers,' " *American Prefaces* VII (Spring, 1942), 195-209. — reprinted in Brooks and Warren, *Understanding Fiction*, 316-324.

Robert Daniel, "Hemingway and His Heroes," *Queen's Quarterly* LIV (Winter, 1947-48), 471-477.

Leonard H. Frey, "Irony and Point of View in 'That Evening Sun,' " *Faulkner Studies* II (Autumn, 1953), 39-40.

Leo Gurko, "The Achievement of Ernest Hemingway," *College English* XIII (April, 1952), 370. — reprinted in *English Journal* XLI (June, 1952), 292-293.

Adrian H. Jaffe and Virgil Scott, "Analysis," in Jaffe and Scott, *Studies in the Short Story*, 208-210.

Kenneth Kempton, *The Short Story*, 39-41, 110-112, 126.

Robert Littell, "Notes on Hemingway," *New Republic* LI (August 10, 1927), 305.

Michael F. Moloney, "Ernest Hemingway: The Missing Third Dimension," in Harold C. Gardiner, *Fifty Years of the American Novel*, 188.

Edward C. Sampson, "Hemingway's 'The Killers,' " *Explicator* XI (October, 1952), item 2.

R. W. Short and R. B. Sewall, *A Manual of Suggestions for Teachers Using "Short Stories for Study,"* 24-26.

Robert P. Weeks, "Hemingway's 'The Killers,' " *Explicator* XV. No. 8 (May, 1957), item 53.

Philip Young, *Ernest Hemingway*, 20-22.

21. THE LIGHT OF THE WORLD

Carlos Baker, *Hemingway*, 140-141.

Séan O'Faoláin, *The Short Story*, 215-216.

Philip Young, *Ernest Hemingway*, 22-23.

HEMINGWAY, ERNEST, Continued

22. MY OLD MAN

Robert G. Davis, *Instructor's Manual for "Ten Modern Masters,"* 25-26.

Philip Young, *Ernest Hemingway,* 149.

23. A NATURAL HSTORY OF THE DEAD

R. P. Warren, "Hemingway," *Kenyon Review* IX (Winter, 1947), 4-5. — reprinted in *Horizon* XV (April, 1947), 158-159. — reprinted, revised, in J. W. Aldridge, *Critiques and Essays on Modern Fiction,* 454-455. — reprinted in M. D. Zabel, *Literary Opinion in America* (Revised Edition, 1951), 446-447. — reprinted in R. P. Warren, *Selected Essays,* 90-91.

24. NOW I LAY ME

Herbert Barrows, *Suggestions for Teaching "Fifteen Stories,"* 7-9.

Royal A. Gettmann and Bruce Harkness, *Teacher's Manual for "A Book of Stories,"* 34-35.

Philip Young, *Ernest Hemingway,* 29-30.

25. THE OLD MAN AND THE SEA

John W. Aldridge, "Hemingway: The Etiquette of the Berserk," *Mandrake* II (Autumn-Winter, 1954-1955), 331-333. — reprinted in Aldridge, *In Search of Heresy,* 149-152.

Charles A. Allen, "Ernest Hemingway's Clean, Well-Lighted Heroes," *Pacific Spectator* IX (Autumn, 1955), 387-389.

John Atkins, *Ernest Hemingway,* 227-230.

Melvin Bachman, "Hemingway: The Matador and the Crucified," *Modern Fiction Studies* I (August, 1955), 9-11.

Carlos Baker, *Hemingway* (Second Edition, 1956), 289-328.

Carlos Baker, "Marvel Who Must Die," *Saturday Review* XXXV (September 6, 1952), 10-11. — reprinted in Edward Wagenknecht, *A Preface to Literature,* 341-344.

Lois L. Barnes, "The Helpless Hero of Ernest Hemingway," *Science & Society* XVII (Winter, 1953), 1-8.

Joseph Beaver, " 'Technique' in Hemingway," *College English* XIV (March, 1953), 325-328.

Harvey Breit, "Hemingway's 'Old Man,' " *Nation* CLXXV (September 6, 1952), 194.

L. Cotten, "Hemingway's 'The Old Man and the Sea,' " *Explicator* XI (March, 1953), item 38.

Malcolm Cowley, "Hemingway's Novel Has the Rich Simplicity of a Classic," *New York Herald Tribune Book Review* (September 7, 1952), 1, 17.

Robert G. Davis, "Hemingway's Tragic Fisherman," *New York Times Book Review* (September 7, 1952), 1, 20.

F. W. Dupee, "Hemingway Revealed," *Kenyon Review* XV (Winter, 1953), 150-155. — reprinted in *Perspectives USA*, No. 3 (Spring, 1953), 127-130.

W. M. Frohock, "Mr. Hemingway's Truly Tragic Bones," *Southwest Review* XXXVIII (Winter, 1953), 74-77.

Brendan Gill, "Not to Die," *New Yorker* XXVIII (September 6, 1952), 104.

Leo Gurko, " 'The Old Man and the Sea,' " *College English* XVII (October, 1955), 11-15. — reprinted in *English Journal* XLIV (1955), 377-382.

D. Heiney, *Recent American Literature*, 161-162.

Milton Howard, "Hemingway and Heroism," *Masses and Mainstream* V (October, 1952), 1-8.

Seymour Krim, "Ernest Hemingway: Valor and Defeat," *Commonweal* LVI (September 19, 1952), 584-586.

R. W. B. Lewis, "Eccentrics' Pilgrimage," *Hudson Review* VI (Spring, 1953), 146-148.

Bernard S. Oldsey, "Hemingway's Old Men," *Modern Fiction Studies* I (August, 1955), 34-35.

William Phillips, "Male-ism and Moralism," *American Mercury* LXXV (October, 1952), 93-96.

José Antonio Portuondo, "The Old Man and Society," *Américas* IV (December, 1952), 43-44.

Philip Rahv, "Latest Hemingway and Steinbeck," *Commenary* XIV (October, 1952), 390-391.

Mark Schorer, "With Grace Under Pressure," *New Republic* CXXVII (October 6, 1952), 19-20.

Delmore Schwartz, "The Fiction of Ernest Hemingway," *Perspectives USA*, No. 13 (Autumn, 1955), 82-84.

J. D. Scott, "New Novels," *New Statesman and Nation* XLIV (September 13, 1952), 297-298.

Robert D. Spector, "Hemingway's 'The Old Man and the Sea,' " *Explicator* XI, No. 5 (March, 1953), item 38.

William Y. Tindall, *The Literary Symbol*, 163.

Ray B. West, Jr., "The Sham Battle Over Ernest Hemingway," *Western Review* XVII (Spring, 1953), 238-240.

Philip Young, *Ernest Hemingway*, 93-105.

Morton D. Zabel, *Craft and Character in American Fiction*, 321-326.

HEMINGWAY, ERNEST, Continued

26. OUT OF SEASON
Carlos Baker, *Hemingway*, 121.
Philip Young, *Ernest Hemingway*, 149-150.

27. A PURSUIT RACE
Edmund Wilson, "The Sportsman's Tragedy," *New Republic* LIII (December 14, 1927), 102. — reprinted in Wilson, *Shores of Light*, 341.

28. THE SHORT HAPPY LIFE OF FRANCIS MACOMBER
John Atkins, *Ernest Hemingway*, 15-16, 43, 128-129, 132-133.
Carlos Baker, *Hemingway*, 186-191.
Warren Beck, "The Shorter Happy Life of Mrs. Macomber," *Modern Fiction Studies* I (November, 1955), 28-37.
Tom Burnam, "Primitivism and Masculinity in the Work of Hemingway," *Modern Fiction Studies* I (August, 1955), 23-24.
[Ronald S. Crane, "Observations on a Story by Hemingway," *English "A" Analyst* (English Department, Northwestern University), No. 16.] — reprinted, revised, in Locke, Gibson, and Arms, *Introduction to Literature* (Third Edition, 1957), 470-479.
Robert G. Davis, *Instructor's Manual for "Ten Modern Masters,"* 27-29.
[Lambert Ennis, "The Short Happy Life of Francis Macomber," *English "A" Analyst* (English Department, Northwestern University), No. 9.]
Harry Levin, "Observations On the Style of Ernest Hemingway," *Kenyon Review* XIII (Autumn, 1951), 607. — reprinted in Levin, *Contexts of Criticism*, 164-165.
[Merril M. May, "Macomber as a Hero," *English "A" Analyst* (English Department, Northwestern University), No. 10.]
Mary Orvis, *The Art of Writing Fiction*, 99-101, 129-132.
Sale, Hall, and Steinmann, *Critical Discussions for Teachers Using "Short Stories: Tradition and Direction,"* 40-44.
[M. J. Wagner, "A Note on the Ending of the Story," *English "A" Analyst* (English Department, Northwestern University), No. 9.]
Ray B. West, Jr., "Analysis," in West and Stallman, *The Art of Modern Fiction*, 259-262. — reprinted as part of Ray B. West, Jr., "Three Methods of Modern Fiction: Ernest Hemingway, Eudora Welty, Thomas Mann," *College English* XII (January, 1951), 194-196. — reprinted in Locke, Gibson, and Arms, *Introduction to Literature* (Second Edition, 1952), 479-481.
Ray B. West, Jr., "Ernest Hemingway: The Failure of Sensibility," *Sewanee Review* LIII (Winter, 1945), 131.

HEMINGWAY, ERNEST, Continued

Ray B. West, Jr., *The Short Story in America, 1900-1950,* 99-101.
Edmund Wilson, "Ernest Hemingway: Bourbon Gauge of Morale," *Atlantic Monthly* CLXIV (July, 1939), 46. — reprinted, revised, in Wilson, *The Wound and the Bow,* 239-240. — reprinted in Wilson, *Eight Essays,* 112-113. — reprinted in John K. M. McCaffery, *Ernest Hemingway: The Man and His Work,* 255.
Philip Young, *Ernest Hemingway,* 41-46, 168.

29. A SIMPLE INQUIRY
Edmund Wilson, "The Sportsman's Tragedy," *New Republic* LIII (December 14, 1927), 102. — reprinted in Wilson, *Shores of Light,* 341.

30. THE SNOWS OF KILIMANJARO
Alfred Angstrom, "Dante, Flaubert, and 'The Snows of Kilimanjaro,'" *Modern Language Notes* LXV (March, 1950), 203-205.
William B. Bache, "*Nostromo* and 'The Snows of Kilimanjaro,'" *Modern Language Notes* LXXII (January, 1957), 32-34.
Carlos Baker, *Hemingway,* 164-165, 186-187, 191-196.
Tom Burnam, "Primitivism and Masculinity in the Work of Hemingway," *Modern Fiction Studies* I (August, 1955) 23.
Martin S. Dworkin, "A Dead Leopard and an Empty Grail," *Humanist* XIII (July-August, 1953), 164-165.
Gordon and Tate, *The House of Fiction,* 419-423.
D. Heiney, *Recent American Literature,* 163-164.
Winifred Lynskey, *Reading Modern Fiction,* (Second Edition, 1957), 266-268.
Michael F. Moloney, "Ernest Hemingway: The Missing Third Dimension," in Harold C. Gardiner, *Fifty Years of the American Novel,* 186.
Douglas H. Orrok, "Hemingway, Hugo, and Revelation," *Modern Language Notes* LXVI (November, 1951), 441-445.
E. W. Tedlock, Jr., "Hemingway's 'The Snows of Kilimanjaro,'" *Explicator* VIII (October, 1949), item 7.
Charles C. Walcutt, "Hemingway's 'The Snow of Kilimanjaro,'" *Explicator* VII (April, 1949), item 43.
Edmund Wilson, "Ernest Hemingway: Bourbon Gauge of Morale," *Atlantic Monthly* CLXIV (July, 1939), 46. — reprinted, revised, in Wilson, *The Wound and the Bow,* 239. — reprinted in Wilson, *Eight Essays,* 112. — reprinted in John K. M. McCaffery, *Ernest Hemingway: The Man and His Work,* 255.
Philip Young, *Ernest Hemingway,* 46-50.

31. SOLDIER'S HOME

Charles A. Allen, "Ernest Hemingway's Clean, Well-Lighted Heroes," *Pacific Spectator* IX (Autumn, 1955), 384-385.

John Atkins, *Ernest Hemingway*, 205-206.

James B. Colvert, "Ernest Hemingway's Morality in Action," *American Literature* XXVII (November, 1955), 374-375.

32. TEN INDIANS

John Atkins, *Ernest Hemingway*, 204.

Carlos Baker, *Hemingway*, 129.

Norman Friedman, "What Makes a Short Story Short?," *Modern Fiction Studies* IV (Summer, 1958), 108.

Jarvis Thurston, *Reading Modern Short Stories*, 15-16, 22, 171-176.

33. THE THREE-DAY BLOW

Carlos Baker, *Hemingway*, 136.

Fred B. Millett, *Reading Fiction*, 65-66, 261-262.

Phillip Young, *Ernest Hemingway*, 6-7.

34. THE UNDEFEATED

Carlos Baker, *Hemingway*, 122.

Michael F. Moloney, "Ernest Hemingway: The Missing Third Dimension," in Harold C. Gardiner, *Fifty Years of the American Novel*, 186.

Edward J. O'Brien, *The Short Story Case Book*, 263-323.

Randall Stewart and Dorothy Bethurum, *Modern American Narration (Living Masterpieces of American Literature,* Vol. 3), 68-70.

Ray B. West, Jr., *The Short Story in America, 1900-1950,* 91-95.

35. UP IN MICHIGAN

Carlos Baker, *Hemingway*, 135.

Philip Young, *Ernest Hemingway*, 150.

36. A VERY SHORT STORY

George Hemphill, "Hemingway and James," *Kenyon Review* XI (Winter, 1949), 53. — reprinted in John K. M. McCaffery, *Ernest Hemingway: The Man and His Work*, 332.

37. A WAY YOU'LL NEVER BE

Philip Young, *Ernest Hemingway*, 23-26.

HESSE, HERMANN

1. A CHILD'S SOUL

Oskar Seidlin, "Hermann Hesse: The Exorcism of the Demon," in *New Directions in Prose and Poetry, No. 14,* 112, 115.

HESSE, HERMAN, Continued

2. DIARY FROM A HEALTH RESORT
   Oskar Seidlin, "Hermann Hesse: The Exorcism of the Demon,"
   in *New Directions in Prose and Poetry, No. 14*, 125-126.
3. JOURNEY TO THE EAST
   Claude Hill, "The Journey to the East," *Saturday Review* XL
   (June 1, 1957), 12-13.
   J. C. Middleton, "Hermann Hesse's 'Morgenlandfahrt,'" *Germanic
   Review* XXXII (December, 1957), 299-310.
4. KING YU
   Ernst Rose, "The Beauty from Pao: Heine—Bierbaum—Hesse,"
   Germanic Review XXXII February, 1957), 17-18.
5. SIDDHARTHA
   Bernard Landis, "The Philosophical Fiction of Hermann Hesse,"
   Accent XIII (Winter, 1953), 59-63.
   Johannes Malthaner, "Hermann Hesse's 'Siddhartha,'" *German
   Quarterly* XXV (March, 1952), 103-109.
   Oskar Seidlin, "Hermann Hesse: The Exorcism of the Demon,"
   in *New Directions in Prose and Poetry, No. 14*, 127-128.

HUGHES, LANGSTON

1. SLAVE ON THE BLOCK
   Alfred Dashiell, *Editor's Choice*, 168-169.

HUNT, HAMLEN

1. TONIGHT WE EAT LEANING
   Judah Goldin, "The Contemporary Jew and His Judaism," in
   S. R. Hopper, *Spiritual Problems in Contemporary Literature*,
   215-216.

HUXLEY, ALDOUS

1. THE GIACONDA SMILE
   Wallace Douglas, *The Critical Reader*, 274-280.
   R. B. Heilman, *Modern Short Stories*, 238-239.
2. NUNS AT LUNCHEON
   Kenneth Kempton, *Short Stories for Study*, 273-277.
   Stegner, Scowcroft, and Ilyin, *The Writer's Art*, 110-114.

HUXLEY, ALDOUS, Continued

3. YOUNG ARCHIMEDES

Raymond W. Short and Richard B. Sewall, *A Manual of Suggestions for Teachers Using "Short Stories for Study,"* 45-47.

IRVING, WASHINGTON

1. THE ADVENTURE OF THE GERMAN STUDENT
   Walter A. Reichart, *Washington Irving and Germany,* 149-151.
2. THE ADVENTURE OF THE MYSTERIOUS PICTURE
   Walter A. Reichart, *Washington Irving and Germany,* 149-151.
3. THE ADVENTURE OF MY UNCLE
   Walter A. Reichart, *Washington Irving and Germany,* 145-147.
4. BUCKTHORNE AND HIS FRIENDS
   Walter A. Reichart, *Washington Irving and Germany,* 139-140, 151-153.
5. THE LEGEND OF SLEEPY HOLLOW
   Elmer L. Brooks, "A Note on Irving's Source," *American Literature* XXV (May, 1953), 229-230.
   Daniel G. Hoffman, "Irving's Use of American Folklore in 'The Legand of Sleepy Hollow,' " *PMLA* LXVIII (June, 1953), 425-435.
   Kenneth Kempton, *The Short Story,* 79-81.
   Henry A. Pochmann, "Irving's German Sources in *The Sketch Book,*" *Studies in Philology* XXVII (July, 1930), 498-504.
   Walter A. Reichart, *Washington Irving and Germany,* 30-32.
   Sara Puryear Rodes, "Washington Irving's Use of Traditional Folklore," *Southern Folklore Quarterly* XX (September, 1956), 147-149.
   Raymond W. Short and Richard B. Sewall, *A Manual of Suggestions for Teachers Using "Short Stories for Study,"* 4-7.
6. RIP VAN WINKLE
   Elmer L. Brooks, "A Note on the Source of 'Rip Van Winkle,' " *American Literature* XXV (January, 1954), 495-496.
   A. Grove Day, *The Greatest American Short Stories* (1953), 349-359.
   John T. Krumpelmann, "Revealing the Source of Irving's 'Rip Van Winkle,' " *Monatshefte* XLVII (November, 1955), 361-362.
   Francis V. Lloyd, "Irving's 'Rip Van Winkle,' " *Explicator* IV (February, 1946), item 26.
   Henry A. Pochmann, "Irving's German Sources in *The Sketch Book,*" *Studies in Philology* XXVII (July, 1930), 477-478, 489-498.

Arthur H. Quinn, *The Literature of the American People,* 214.

Walter A. Reichart, "Concerning the Sources of Irving's 'Rip Van Winkle,'" *Monatshefte* XLVIII (February, 1956), 94-95.

Walter A. Reichart, *Washington Irving and Germany,* 22-30.

Sara Puryear Rodes, "Washington Irving's Use of Traditional Folklore," *Southern Folklore Quarterly* XX (September, 1956), 149-153.

John B. Thompson, "The Genesis of the Rip Van Winkle Legend," *Harper's Magazine* LXVII (September, 1883), 617-622.

W. Silas Vance, "Mrs. Rip Van Winkle," *American Mercury* LXXXVI (April, 1958), 118-121.

George Wetzel, "Irving's Rip Van Winkle,'" *Explicator* X (June, 1952), item 54.

Stanley T. Williams, *The Life of Washington Irving* I, 183-187.

7. THE SPECTRE BRIDEGROOM

Walter A. Reichart, *Washington Irving and Germany,* 32-35.

Henry A. Pochmann, "Irving's German Sources in *The Sketch Books,*" *Studies in Philology* XXVII (July, 1930), 504-506.

8. THE STORY OF THE YOUNG ITALIAN

Walter A. Reichart, *Washington Irving and Germany,* 149-151.

ISHERWOOD, CHRISTOPHER

1. PRATER VIOLET

G. H. Bantock, "The Novels of Christopher Isherwood," in B. Rajan, *The Novelist As Thinker,* 55-57.

Isaac Rosenfeld, "Isherwood's Master Theme," *Kenyon Review* VIII (Summer, 1946), 487-492.

IVANOV, VSEVOLOD

1. THE KID

James B. Hall and Joseph Langland, *The Short Story,* 108-109.

JACKSON, SHIRLEY

1. THE LOTTERY

R. B. Heilman, *Modern Short Stories,* 384-385.

JACKSON, SHIRLEY, Continued

Seymour Lainoff, "Jackson's 'The Lottery,'" *Explicator* XII, No. 5 (March, 1954), item 34.

JAMES, HENRY

1. THE ABASEMENT OF THE NORTHMORES
   Henry James, *Art of the Novel*, 234-235; *Notebooks*, 296-297.
2. ADINA
   Quentin Anderson, *The American Henry James*, 153-156.
   Cornelia P. Kelley, *The Early Development of Henry James*, 156-157.
3. THE ALTAR OF THE DEAD
   R. P. Blackmur, "The Sacred Fount," *Kenyon Review* IV (Autumn 1942), 338-340.
   Leon Edel, *The Ghostly Tales of Henry James*, 353-356.
   Pelham Edgar, *Henry James*, 103-105.
   Clifton Fadiman, *Short Stories of Henry James*, 358-360.
   Graham Greene, "Henry James: The Religious Aspect," in Greene, *The Lost Childhood*, 34-36.
   Charles G. Hoffmann, *The Sh rt Novels of Henry James*, 54-55.
   Edwin Honig, "The Merciful Fra'd in Three Stories of Henry James," *Tiger's Eye* No. 9 (October, 1949), 91-95.
   Henry James, *The Art of the Novel*, 241-245; *Notebooks*, 164-167.
   Wright Thomas and Stuart Gerry Brown, *Reading Prose: An Introduction to Critical Study*, 682-683.
   William Troy, "The Altar of Henry James," *New Republic* CVIII (February 15, 1943), 228-230. — reprinted in F. W. Dupee, *The Question of Henry James*, 270-272.
   M. D. Zabel, "Introduction" to *Henry James' In the Cage and Other Tales* (Anchor Books, 1958), 20-21.
4. THE ASPERN PAPERS
   Henry S. Canby, *Turn·West, Turn East*, 232-233.
   F. W. Dupee, *Henry James*, 146-148; (Anchor Books), 126-128.
   Leon Edel, "The Aspern Papers: Great Aunt Wyckoff and Juliana Bordereau," *Modern Language Notes* LXVII (June, 1952), 392-395.
   Leon Edel, *Henry James: Selected Fiction*, 416-419.
   Charles G. Hoffmann, *The Short Novels of Henry James*, 45-47.
   Henry James, *The Art of the Novel*, 159-169; *Notebooks*, 71-73. — reprinted in Leon Edel, *Henry James: Selected Fiction*, 406-416.

John Lehmann, "A Question of Covering One's Tracks," in Lehmann, *The Open Night*, 45-53.

Charles Neider, *Short Novels of the Masters*, 15-16.

Philip Rahv, *The Great Short Novels of Henry James*, 465-467.

Irving Wallace, "The Real Juliana Bordereau," in Wallace, *The Fabulous Originals*, 52-55.

[Thomas Wilcox, "A Way into 'The Aspern Papers,'" *Exercise Exchange* (Rinehart) III (December, 1955), 5-6]

5. AT ISELLA

John R. Adams, "'At Isella': Some Horrible Printing Corrected," *Mark Twain Quarterly* V (Spring, 1942), 10, 23.

Cornelia P. Kelley, *The Early Development of Henry James*, 115-117.

6. THE AUTHOR OF BELTRAFFIO

Quentin Anderson, *The American Henry James*, 143-146, 147, 149.

Quentin Anderson, "Henry James and the New Jerusalem," *Kenyon Review* VIII (Autumn, 1946), 538-540.

G. S. Hellman, "Stevenson and Henry James: The Rare Friendship Between Two Stylists," *Century Magazine* CXI (January, 1926), 340-345.

Henry James, *The Art of the Novel*, 235-236; *Notebooks*, 57-59.

F. O. Matthiessen, "Henry James' Portrait of the Artist," *Partisan Review* XI (Winter, 1944), 72-73. — reprinted in Matthiessen, *Stories of Writers and Artists*, 2-3.

John C. Neff, "Henry James the Reporter," *The New Mexico Quarterly* VIII (February, 1938), 14.

Ezra Pound, *Literary Essays of Ezra Pound*, 314-316.

Philip Rahv, *The Great Short Novels of Henry James*, 415-416.

Rebecca West, *Henry James*, 78-80.

7. THE BEAST IN THE JUNGLE

Joseph Warren Beach, *The Method of Henry James* (Revised Edition, Saifer, 1954), xcix-ci.

Beardsley, Daniel, and Leggett, *Aids to Study for "Theme and Form: An Introduction to Literature,"* 97-98.

Louise Dauner, "Henry James and the Garden of Death," *University of Kansas City Review* XIX (Winter, 1952), 140-141.

F. W. Dupee, *Henry James*, 180-182; (Anchor Books), 155-157.

Leon Edel, *The Ghostly Tales of Henry James*, 667-670.

Leon Edel, *Henry James: Selected Fiction*, xvii.

Pelham Edgar, *Henry James*, 151-152.

Clifton Fadiman, *Short Stories of Henry James*, 598-602.

JAMES, HENRY, Continued

L. Hamalian and E. L. Volpe, *Ten Modern Short Novels,* 103-107.
Charles G. Hoffmann, *The Short Novels of Henry James,* 98-104.
Edwin Honig, "The Merciful Fraud in Three Stories of Henry James," *Tiger's Eye* No. 9 (October, 1949), 87-91.
Henry James, *The Art of the Novel,* 245-248; *Notebooks,* 311-312.
— both items reprinted in Leon Edel, *Henry James: Selected Fiction,* 536-542.
David Kerner, "A Note on 'The Beast in the Jungle,'" *University of Kansas City Review* XVII (Winter, 1950), 109-118.
L. C. Knights, "Henry James and the Trapped Spectator," *Southern Review* IV (Winter, 1939), 611-613. — reprinted in Knights, *Explorations* (George W. Stewart, 1947), 185-189.
J. R. Lucke, "The Inception of 'The Beast in the Jungle,'" *New England Quarterly* XXVI (December, 1953), 529-532.
Betty Miller, "Miss Savage and Miss Bartram," *Nineteenth Century* CXLIV (November, 1948), 285-292.
Séan O'Faoláin, *The Short Story,* 210.
Philip Rahv, *The Great Short Novels of Henry James,* 751-752.
John W. Shroeder, "The Mothers of Henry James," *American Literature* XXII (January, 1951), 430-431.
Francis E. Smith, "'The Beast in the Jungle': The Limits of Method," *Perspective* I (Autumn, 1947), 33-40.
Randall Stewart, *American Literature and Christian Doctrine,* 104-106.
Edward Stone, "James' 'Jungle': The Seasons," *University of Kansas City Review* XXI (Winter, 1954), 142-144.
John L. Sweeney, "The Demuth Pictures," *Kenyon Review* V (Autumn, 1943), 522-532.
Allen Tate, "Three Commentaries: Poe, James, and Joyce," *Sewanee Review* LVIII (Winter, 1950), 5-10. — reprinted in Gordon and Tate, *House of Fiction,* 228-231.
M. D. Zabel, "Introduction" to *Henry James' In the Cage and Other Tales* (Anchor Books, 1958), 21-22.

8. THE BELDONALD HOLBEIN
Henry James, *Notebooks,* 290-291.
Christof Wegelin, *The Image of Europe in Henry James,* 52-53.

9. THE BENCH OF DESOLATION
Charles G. Hoffmann, *The Short Novels of Henry James,* 111-117.
Henry James, *Notebooks,* 330-332.
Winifred Lynskey, *Reading Modern Fiction* (Second Edition, 1957), 306-310.

JAMES, HENRY, Continued

10. BENVOLIO
Quentin Anderson, *The American Henry James,* 38-39.
Cornelia P. Kelley, *The Early Development of Henry James,* 233-234.

11. THE BIRTHPLACE
Quentin Anderson, "Introduction," in James, *Selected Short Stories* (Rinehart Editions, 1950), ix-xiv.
Clifton Fadiman, *Short Stories of Henry James,* 546-547.
Henry James, *The Art of the Novel,* 248-249; *Notebooks,* 306-307.

12. BROKEN WINGS
Henry James, *The Art of the Novel,* 236-237; *Notebooks,* 282.

13. BROOKSMITH
Clifton Fadiman, *Short Stories of Henry James,* 291-292.
Henry James, *The Art of the Novel,* 282-283; *Notebooks,* 64-65.

14. A BUNDLE OF LETTERS
Clifton Fadiman, *Short Stories of Henry James,* 78-81.
Henry James, *The Art of the Novel,* 212-213; *Notebooks,* 11-12.
Cornelia P. Kelley, *The Early Development of Henry James,* 273-275.

15. THE CHAPERON
Henry James, *The Art of the Novel,* 138-139; *Notebooks,* 106-109.

16. COVERING END
Henry James, *Notebooks,* 185-187.
B. M. Levy, " 'The High Bid' and the Forbes-Robertsons," *College English* VIII (March, 1947), 284-292.

17. THE COXON FUND
Henry James, *The Art of the Novel,* 229-231; *Notebooks,* 152-155, 160-164.

18. CRAPY CORNELIA
Marius Bewley, *The Complex Fate,* n. 76-77.
Marius Bewley, "Henry James and 'Life,' " *Hudson Review* XI (Summer, 1958), 183-184.
John W. Shroeder, "The Mothers of Henry James," *American Literature* XXII (January, 1951), 424-431.

19. CRAWFORD'S CONSISTENCY
Cornelia P. Kelley, *The Early Development of Henry James,* 129-130, 239.
Edna Kenton, *Eight Uncollected Tales of Henry James,* 6-7, 16.
B. R. McElderry, Jr., "The Uncollected Stories of Henry James," *American Literature* XXI (November, 1949), 285-286.

20. DAISY MILLER

Henry S. Canby, *Turn West, Turn East,* 123-125.

Viola R. Dunbar, "A Note on the Genesis of 'Daisy Miller,'" *Philological Quarterly* XXVII (April, 1948), 184-186.

Viola R. Dunbar, "The Revision of 'Daisy Miller,'" *Modern Language Notes* LXV (May, 1950), 311-317.

F. W. Dupee, *Henry James,* 107-113; (Anchor Books), 91-97.

Pelham Edgar, *Henry James,* 25-27.

Stanley Geist, "Fictitious Americans," *Hudson Review* V (Summer, 1952), 203-206.

Edgar Goodspeed, "A Footnote to 'Daisy Miller,'" *Atlantic Monthly* CLIII (February, 1934), 252-253.

Charles G. Hoffmann, *The Short Novels of Henry James,* 16-25, 29-30.

Henry James, *The Art of the Novel,* 267-270; *Letters* (Lubbock), I, 66; *Selected Letters* (Edel), 138-140. − the first of these items is reprinted in Leon Edel, *Henry James: Selected Fiction,* 75-78.

Annette Kar, "Archetypes of American Innocence: Lydia Blood and Daisy Miller," *American Quarterly* V (Spring, 1953), 31-38.

B. R. McElderry, Jr., "The 'Shy, Incongruous Charm' of 'Daisy Miller,'" *Nineteenth Century Fiction* X (September, 1955), 162-165.

Philip Rahv, *The Great Short Novels of Henry James,* 87-88.

George Stevens, "The Return of Henry James," *Saturday Review of Literature* XXVIII (March 3, 1945), 8.

Edward Stone, "A Further Note on 'Daisy Miller' and Cherbuliez," *Philological Quarterly* XXIX (April, 1950), 213-216.

Christof Wegelin, *The Image of Europe in Henry James,* 61-64.

Rebecca West, *Henry James,* 44-48.

21. A DAY OF DAYS

Cornelia P. Kelley, *The Early Development of Henry James,* 57.

Robert C. LeClair, *Young Henry James, 1843-1870,* 382-383.

22. THE DEATH OF THE LION

R. P. Blackmur, "In the Country of the Blue," *Kenyon Review* V (Autumn, 1943), 610-612. − reprinted in F. W. Dupee, *The Question of Henry James,* 205-207. − reprinted in John W. Aldridge, *Critiques and Essays on Modern Fiction,* 314-315.

Pelham Edgar, *Henry James,* 164-165.

James Grossman, "The Face in the Mountain," *Nation* CLXI (September 8, 1945), 230-232.

Henry James, *The Art of the Novel,* 217-220; *Notebooks,* 147-150.

JAMES, HENRY, Continued

F. O. Matthiessen, "Henry James' Portrait of the Artist," *Partisan Review* XI (Winter, 1944), 74. — reprinted in Matthiessen, *Stories of Writers and Artists*, 4.

23. DE GREY: A ROMANCE
Joseph Warren Beach, *The Method of Henry James*, 184-185.
Leon Edel, *The Ghostly Tales of Henry James*, 26-28.
Cornelia P. Kelley, *The Early Development of Henry James*, 87-88.
Robert C. LeClair, *Young Henry James, 1843-1870*, 405.

24. THE DIARY OF A MAN OF FIFTY
Henry James, *Notebooks*, 8-9.
Q. D. Leavis, "Henry James: The Stories," *Scrutiny* XIV (Spring, 1947), 226.

25. EUGENE PICKERING
W. D. Howells, Review of *The Passionate Pilgrim and Other Tales*, *Atlantic Monthly* XXXV (April, 1875), 493-494.
Cornelia P. Kelley, *The Early Development of Henry James*, 165-168.

26. EUROPE
Marius Bewley, "Henry James and 'Life,'" *Hudson Review* XI (Summer, 1958), 177-179.
Clifton Fadiman, *Short Stories of Henry James*, 382-384.
Royal A. Gettmann and Bruce Harkness, *Teacher's Manual for "A Book of Stories,"* 36-39.
Henry James, *The Art of the Novel*, 238-240; *Notebooks*, 190-191.

27. THE FIGURE IN THE CARPET
Quentin Anderson, *The American Henry James*, 146-149.
Quentin Anderson, "Henry James and the New Jerusalem," *Kenyon Review* VIII (Autumn, 1946), 540-541.
Joseph Warren Beach, *The Method of Henry James*, 145-148, 152-155.
Beardsley, Daniel, and Leggett, *Aids to Study for "Theme and Form: An Introduction to Literature,"* 57.
R. P. Blackmur, "In the Country of the Blue," *Kenyon Review* (Autumn, 1943), 608-609. — reprinted in F. W. Dupee, *The Question of Henry James*, 203-204. — reprinted in John W. Aldridge, *Critiques and Essays on Modern Fiction*, 312-313.
Pelham Edgar, *Henry James*, 115-117, 166-168.
James Grossman, "The Face in the Mountain," *Nation* CLXI (September 8, 1945), 230-232.
Henry James, *The Art of the Novel*, 227-229; *Notebooks*, 220-224, 229-230.

JAMES, HENRY, Continued

Robert Lynd, *Books and Authors,* 113-117.

F. O. Matthiessen, "Henry James' Portrait of the Artist," *Partisan Review* XI (Winter, 1944), 76-77. — reprinted in Matthiessen, *Stories of Writers and Artists,* 6-7.

F. O. Matthiessen, *Henry James: The Major Phase,* 42.

Edouard Roditi, "Oscar Wilde and Henry James," *University of Kansas City Review,* XV (Autumn, 1949), 52-56.

Perry D. Westbrook, "The Supersubtle Fry," *Nineteenth Century Fiction* VIII (September, 1953), 137-140.

M. D. Zabel, "Introduction" to *Henry James' In the Cage and Other Tales* (Anchor Books, 1958), 19-20.

28. FLICKERBRIDGE

Henry James, *The Art of the Novel,* 284-285; *Notebooks,* 286-288.

S. Gorley Putt, "The Passionate Pilgrim: An Aspect of Henry James," *The Wind and the Rain* IV (Spring, 1948), 232-233.

29. FORDHAM CASTLE

Henry James, *The Art of the Novel,* 276-280; *Notebooks,* 267-268, 274-275, 292, 293-294.

30. FOUR MEETINGS

Clifton Fadiman, *Short Stories of Henry James,* 37-38.

Felheim, Newman, and Steinhoff, *Study Aids for Teachers for "Modern Short Stories,"* 39-42.

Cornelia P. Kelley, *The Early Development of Henry James,* 259-261.

Sale, Hall, and Steinmann, *Critical Discussions for Teachers Using "Short Stories: Tradition and Direction,"* 11-14.

31. THE FRIENDS OF THE FRIENDS

R. P. Blackmur, "The Sacred Fount," *Kenyon Review* IV (Autumn, 1942), 336-337.

Leon Edel, *The Ghostly Tales of Henry James,* 395-396.

Henry James, *Notebooks,* 231, 241-245.

32. GABRIELLE DE BERGERAC

Cornelia P. Kelley, *The Early Development of Henry James,* 88-91.

Edna Kenton, *Eight Uncollected Tales of Henry James,* 7-9, 185-186.

Robert C. LeClair, *Young Henry James, 1843-1870,* 424-427.

John C. Neff, "Henry James the Reporter," *The New Mexico Quarterly* VIII (February, 1938), 13-14.

33. GEORGIANA'S REASONS

Henry James, *Notebooks,* 59-61.

34. THE GHOSTLY RENTAL
    Leon Edel, *The Ghostly Tales of Henry James,* 103-105.
    Edna Kenton, *Eight Uncollected Tales of Henry James,* 14, 17.
    B. R. McElderry, Jr., "The Uncollected Stories of Henry James,"
    American Literature XXI (November, 1949), 289.
35. THE GIVEN CASE
    Henry James, *Notebooks,* 164, 234, 235.
36. GLASSES
    Henry James, *Notebooks,* 205-206.
37. THE GREAT CONDITION
    Henry James, *Notebooks,* 269-273.
38. THE GREAT GOOD PLACE
    Osborne Andreas, *Henry James and the Expanding Horizon,*
    127-128.
    Joseph M. DeFalco, " 'The Great Good Place': A Journey into the
    Psyche," *Literature and Psychology* VIII (Spring, 1958), 18-20.
    Leon Edel, *The Ghostly Tales of Henry James,* 567-570.
    Clifton Fadiman, *Short Stories of Henry James,* 413-415.
    Ford Madox Ford, *Portraits from Life,* 11; or *Mightier Than the
    Sword* (English Edition), 25.
    F. O. Matthiessen, *Henry James: The Major Phase,* 143-144.
    John W. Shroeder, "The Mothers of Henry James," *American
    Literature* XXII (January, 1951), 426-429.
    M. D. Zabel, "Introduction" to *Henry James' In the Cage and
    Other Tales* (Anchor Books, 1958), 22-24.
39. GREVILLE FANE
    James Grossman, "The Face in the Mountain," *Nation,* CLXI
    (September 8, 1945), 230-232.
    Henry James, *The Art of the Novel,* 234; *Notebooks,* 10-11, 93-95.
    F. O. Matthiessen, "Henry James' Portrait of the Artist," *Partisan
    Review* XI (Winter, 1944), 74-75. — reprinted in Matthiessen,
    Stories of Writers and Artists, 4-5.
40. THE IMPRESSIONS OF A COUSIN
    Raymond D. Havens, "Henry James' 'The Impressions of a
    Cousin,'" *Modern Language Notes* LXV (May, 1950), 317-319.
    Henry James, *Notebooks,* 19-20, 52-53.
41. AN INTERNATIONAL EPISODE
    Pelham Edgar, *Henry James,* 28-29.
    Charles G. Hoffmann, *The Short Novels of Henry James,* 16-19.
    Henry James, *Selected Letters* (Edel), 73-78.
    Cornelia P. Kelley, *The Early Development of Henry James,*
    264-266.

JAMES, HENRY, Continued

Philip Rahv, *The Great Short Novels of Henry James,* 147-149.
George Stevens, "The Return of Henry James," *Saturday Review of Literature* XXVIII (March 3, 1945), 8.
Christof Wegelin, *The Image of Europe in Henry James,* 48-52.

42. IN THE CAGE
Pelham Edgar, *Henry James,* 130.
Albert C. Friend, "A Forgotten Story by Henry James," *South Atlantic Quarterly* LIII (January, 1954), 100-108.
Henry James, *The Art of the Novel,* 154-158.
L. C. Knights, "Henry James and the Trapped Spectator," *Southern Review* IV (Winter, 1939), 607-611. — reprinted in Knights, *Explorations* (George W. Stewart, 1947), 182-185.
M. D. Zabel, "Introduction" to *Henry James' In the Cage and Other Tales* (Anchor Books, 1958), 6-12.

43. JOHN DELAVOY
Henry James, *Notebooks,* 245-247.

44. THE JOLLY CORNER
Miriam Allott, "Symbol and Image in the Later Work of Henry James," *Essays in Criticism* III (July, 1953), 330-332.
Quentin Anderson, *The American Henry James,* 175-182.
Maurice Beebe, "The Turned Back of Henry James," *South Atlantic Quarterly* LIII (October, 1954), 535-537.
R. P. Blackmur, "The Sacred Fount," *Kenyon Review* IV (Autumn, 1942), 340-343.
Van Wyck Brooks, "Henry James: The American Scene," *Dial* LXXV (July, 1923), 29-30. — reprinted in Brooks, *The Pilgrimage of Henry James,* 27-29.
Leon Edel, *The Ghostly Tales of Henry James,* 720-725.
Leon Edel, *Henry James: The Untried Years,* 75-79.
Clifton Fadiman, *Short Stories of Henry James,* 641-644.
Graham Greene, "Henry James," in D. Verschoyle, *The English Novelists,* 243-244.
Edwin Honig, "The Merciful Fraud in Three Stories of Henry James," *Tiger's Eye* No. 9 (October, 1949), 84-87.
Henry James, *The Art of the Novel,* 252-258; *Notebooks,* 364, 367.
F. O. Matthiessen, *The American Novels and Stories of Henry James,* xxiii.
F. O. Matthiessen, *Henry James: The Major Phase,* 136-137.
[Robert Rogers, "The Beast in Henry James," *American Imago* XIII (Winter, 1956), 427-453.]
Saul Rosenzweig, "The Ghost of Henry James: A Study in

Thematic Apperception," *Partisan Review* XI (Fall, 1944), 448-449.

John W. Shroeder, "The Mothers of Henry James," *American Literature* XXII (January, 1951), 424-431.

Floyd Stovall, "Henry James' 'The Jolly Corner,'" *Nineteenth Century Fiction* XII (June, 1957), 72-84.

Christof Wegelin, *The Image of Europe in Henry James*, 155-156.

M. D. Zabel, "Introduction" to *Henry James' In the Cage and Other Tales* (Anchor Books, 1958), 24-26.

45. JULIA BRIDE

Charles G. Hoffmann, *The Short Novels of Henry James*, 110-111.

Henry James, *The Art of the Novel*, 262-266.

Frank O'Connor, "Transition: Henry James," in O'Connor, *The Mirror in the Roadway*, 234.

Christof Wegelin, *The Image of Europe in Henry James*, 159-160.

46. LADY BARBERINA

Henry James, *The Art of the Novel*, 198-206; *Notebooks*, 49-51; *Letters* (Lubbock), I, 103.

Philip Rahv, *The Great Short Novels of Henry James*, 317-319.

47. A LANDSCAPE PAINTER

Miriam Allott, "'The Lord of Burleigh' and Henry James's 'A Landscape Painter," *Notes and Queries* V, n.s. (May, 1955), 220-221.

Cornelia P. Kelley, *The Early Development of Henry James*, 55-56.

Robert C. LeClair, *Young Henry James, 1843-1870*, 381-382.

48. THE LAST OF THE VALERII

Joseph Warren Beach, *The Method of Henry James*, 189-190.

Leon Edel, *The Ghostly Tales of Henry James*, 69-70.

Cornelia P. Kelley, *The Early Development of Henry James*, 153-156.

Christof Wegelin, *The Image of Europe in Henry James*, 32-33.

49. THE LESSON OF THE MASTER

R. P. Blackmur, "Henry James," in Spiller, *Literary History of the United States*, II, 1050.

R. P. Blackmur, "In the Country of the Blue," *Kenyon Review* V (Autumn, 1943), 604-605, 614-615. — reprinted in F. W. Dupee, *The Question of Henry James*, 199-200, 208-210. — reprinted in John W. Aldridge, *Critiques and Essays on Modern Fiction*, 309-310, 316-317.

Henry James, *The Art of the Novel*, 223-226; *Notebooks*, 87; *Letters* (Lubbock), I, 192-193.

Q. D. Leavis, "Henry James: The Short Stories," *Scrutiny* XIV (Spring, 1947), 225-226.

F. O. Matthiessen, "Henry James' Portrait of the Artist," *Partisan Review* XI (Winter, 1944), 71-72. — reprinted in Matthiessen, *Stories of Writers and Artists,* 1-2.

Lyon N. Richardson, *Henry James: Representative Selections,* 487-488.

Parker Tyler, "The Child as 'The Figure in the Carpet,'" *Chicago Review* II (Winter, 1957), 31-42.

50. THE LIAR

Marius Bewley, "Appearance and Reality in Henry James," *Scrutiny* XVII (Sumer, 1950), 93-96. — reprinted in Bewley, *The Complex Fate,* 84-88.

Clifton Fadiman, *Short Stories of Henry James,* 183-186.

Henry James, *The Art of the Novel,* 178-179; *Notebooks,* 61-62.

R. J. Kane, "Hawthorne's 'The Prophetic Pictures' and James' 'The Liar,'" *Modern Language Notes* LXV (April, 1950), 257-258.

West and Stallman, *Art of Modern Fiction,* 209-216.

51. A LIGHT MAN

Robert Cantwell, "A Little Reality," *Hound and Horn* VI (April-June, 1934), 503.

Leon Edel, *Henry James: The Untried Years,* 250-251.

Robert C. LeClair, *Young Henry James, 1843-1870,* 423-424.

52. LONGSTAFF'S MARRIAGE

Leon Edel, *Henry James: The Untried Years,* 54-55, 327-330.

53. LORD BEAUPRÉ

Henry James, *Notebooks,* 114-116.

54. LOUISA PALLANT

Clifton Fadiman, *Short Stories of Henry James,* 123-125.

Henry James, *Notebooks,* 73-75; *Selected Letters* (Edel), 182-183.

55. MADAME DE MAUVES

G. H. Bantock, "Morals and Civilization in Henry James," *Camridge Journal* VII (December, 1953), 172-173.

Marius Bewley, "Henry James and 'Life,'" *Hudson Review* XI (Summer, 1958), 167-174.

Henry S. Canby, *Turn West, Turn East,* 107-108.

Louise Dauner, "Henry James and the Garden of Death," *University of Kansas City Review* XIX (Winter, 1952), 139-140.

Charles G. Hoffmann, *The Short Novels of Henry James,* 9-16.

W. D. Howells, Review of *The Passionate Pilgrim and Other Tales, Atlantic Monthly* XXXV (April, 1875), 492-493.

Henry James, *The Art of the Novel,* 196-197.

JAMES, HENRY, Continued

Cornelia P. Kelley, *The Early Development of Henry James,* 160-165.

R. M. Ludwig and M. B. Perry, *Nine Short Novels,* xxvii-xxix.

S. Gorley Putt, "The Passionate Pilgrim: An Aspect of Henry James," *The Wind and the Rain* IV (Spring, 1948) , 234.

Philip Rahv, *The Great Short Novels of Henry James,* 3-5.

Lyon N. Richardson, *Henry James: Representative Selections,* 486-487.

Stephen Spender, "The School of Experience in the Early Novels," *Hound and Horn* VI (April-June, 1934) , 425-426. — reprinted in Spender, *The Destructive Element,* 32-34.

George Stevens, "The Return of Henry James," *Saturday Review of Literature* XXVIII (March 3, 1945) , 30, 32.

Christof Wegelin, *The Image of Europe in Henry James,* 38-39, 43-46.

Rebecca West, *Henry James,* 28-30.

56. THE MADONNA OF THE FUTURE

Walter Havighurst, *Instructor's Manual: "Masters of the Modern Short Story,"* 15-16.

W. D. Howells, Review of *The Passionate Pilgrim and Other Tales, Atlantic Monthly* XXXV (April, 1875) , 493.

Cornelia P. Kelley, *The Early Development of Henry James,* 149-152.

F. O. Matthiessen, "Henry James' Portrait of the Artist," *Partisan Review* XI (Winter, 1944) , 82-83. — reprinted in Matthiessen, *Stories of Writers and Artists,* 12-13.

Robert J. Niess, "Henry James and Zola: A Parallel," *Revue de Littérature Comparée* XXX (January-March, 1956) , 93-98.

Christof Wegelin, *The Image of Europe in Henry James,* 33.

57. THE MARRIAGES

Henry James, *The Art of the Novel,* 281-282; *Notebooks,* 70-71.

58. MASTER EUSTACE

Cornelia P. Kelley, *The Early Development of Henry James,* 127-129.

59. MAUD-EVELYN

Joseph Warren Beach, *The Method of Henry James,* 40-41.

R. P. Blackmur, "Henry James," in Spiller, *Literary History of the United States,* II, 1052.

R. P. Blackmur, "The Sacred Fount," *Kenyon Review* IV (Autumn, 1942) , 337-338.

Leon Edel, *The Ghostly Tales of Henry James,* 598-600.

Henry James, *Notebooks,* 265.

Question of Henry James, 207-208. — reprinted in John W. Aldridge, *Critiques and Essays on Modern Fiction,* 315.

Henry James, *The Art of the Novel,* 226-227; *Notebooks,* 180-181, 200-205.

Ilse Dusoir Lind, "The Inadequate Vulgarity of Henry James," *PMLA* LXVI (December, 1951), 904-910.

F. O. Matthiessen, "Henry James' Portrait of the Artist," *Partisan Review* XI (Winter, 1944), 75. — reprinted in Matthiessen, *Stories of Writers and Artists,* 5.

Lyon N. Richardson, *Henry James: Representative Selections,* 489-490.

69. NONA VINCENT
Leon Edel, *The Ghostly Tales of Henry James,* 174-176.

70. OSBORNE'S REVENGE
Leon Edel, *Henry James: The Untried Years,* 257-258.

Cornelia P. Kelley, *The Early Development of Henry James,* 84.

Robert C. LeClair, *Young Henry James, 1843-1870,* 406-408.

B. R. McElderry, Jr., "The Uncollected Stories of Henry James," *American Literature* XXI (November, 1949), 284-285.

71. OWEN WINGRAVE
R. P. Blackmur, "The Sacred Fount," *Kenyon Review* IV (Autumn, 1942), 332-335.

Leon Edel, *The Ghostly Tales of Henry James,* 311-315.

Henry James, *The Art of the Novel,* 258-260; *Notebooks,* 118-121.

72. PANDORA
Charles R. Anderson, "Henry James's Fable of Carolina," *South Atlantic Quarterly* LIV (April, 1954), 249-250.

Henry James, *The Art of the Novel,* 270-274; *Notebooks,* 56-57.

F. O. Matthiessen, *The American Novels and Stories of Henry James,* xiv-xv.

73. THE PAPERS
Henry James, *Notebooks,* 313-314.

74. A PASSIONATE PILGRIM
Pelham Edgar, *Henry James,* 17-18.

Albert F. Gegenheimer, "Early and Late Revisions in Henry James's 'A Passionate Pilgrim,'" *American Literature* XXIII (May, 1951), 233-242.

W. D. Howells, Review of *The Passionate Pilgrim and Other Tales, Atlantic Monthly* XXXV (April, 1875), 491-492.

Henry James, *The Art of the Novel,* 193-196.

Cornelia P. Kelley, *The Early Development of Henry James,* 117-120.

JAMES, HENRY, Continued

S. Gorley Putt, "The Passionate Pilgrim: An Aspect of Henry James," *The Wind and the Rain* IV (Spring, 1948) , 230-232.
Christof Wegelin, *The Image of Europe in Henry James,* 34-35, 37-38.

75. PASTE
Robert G. Davis, *Instructor's Manual for "Ten Modern Masters,"* 38-39.
Gilbert Highet, *People, Places, and Books,* 189-190.
Henry James, *The Art of the Novel,* 237-238; *Notebooks,* 177-178, 196-198.

76. THE PATAGONIA
Henry James, *Notebooks,* 86-90.

77. PATH OF DUTY
Marius Bewley, "Appearance and Reality in Henry James," *Scrutiny* XVII (Summer, 1950) , 92-93. — reprinted in Bewley, *The Complex Fate,* 82-84.
Henry James, *Notebooks,* 54-56.
Leo B. Levy, *Versions of Melodrama,* 52-54.

78. THE PENSION BEAUREPAS
Henry James, *The Art of the Novel,* 216.
Cornelia P. Kelley, *The Early Development of Henry James,* 273-275.

79. THE POINT OF VIEW
Henry James, *The Art of the Novel,* 214-216; *Notebooks,* 15.
F. O. Matthiessen, *The American Novels and Stories of Henry James,* xiii-xiv.

80. POOR RICHARD
Joseph Warren Beach, *The Method of Henry James,* 175-176.
Leon Edel, *Henry James: The Untried Years,* 236-238.
Cornelia P. Kelley, *The Early Development of Henry James,* 70-72.
Robert C. LeClair, *Young Henry James, 1843-1870,* 394-397.

81. THE PRIVATE LIFE
R. P. Blackmur, "In the Country of the Blue," *Kenyon Review* V (Autumn, 1943) , 609-610. — reprinted in F. W. Dupee, *The Question of Henry James,* 205-207. — reprinted in John W. Aldridge, *Critiques and Essays on Modern Fiction,* 315-316.
Leon Edel, *The Ghostly Tales of Henry James,* 210-212.
Henry James, *The Art of the Novel,* 249-252; *Notebooks,* 109-110, 143, 144.
Sidney E. Lind, "James's 'The Private Life' and Browning," *American Literature* XXIII (November, 1951) , 315-322.

JAMES, HENRY, Continued

82. A PROBLEM
Cornelia P. Kelley, *The Early Development of Henry James,* 83-84.
Robert C. LeClair, *Young Henry James, 1843-1870,* 405-406.
B. R. McElderry, Jr., "The Uncollected Stories of Henry James," *American Literature* XXI (November, 1949), 282-283.

83. PROFESSOR FARGO
Cornelia P. Kelley, *The Early Development of Henry James.* 168-169.

84. THE PUPIL
Leon Edel, *Henry James: Selected Fiction,* 480-481.
Clifton Fadiman, *Short Stories of Henry James,* 268-272.
Charles G. Hoffmann, *The Short Novels of Henry James,* 52.
Henry James, *The Art of the Novel,* 150-154. — reprinted in Leon Edel, *Henry James: Selected Fiction,* 476-480.
Terence Martin, "James's 'The Pupil': The Art of Seeing Through," *Modern Fiction Studies* IV (Winter, 1958-1959), 335-345.
Ferner Nuhn, *The Wind Blew from the East,* 139-140.
Philip Rahv, *The Great Short Novels of Henry James,* 567-569.
Raymond W. Short and Richard B. Sewall, *A Manual of Suggestions for Teachers Using "Short Stories for Study,"* 48-51.

85. THE REAL RIGHT THING
Leon Edel, *The Ghostly Tales of Henry James,* 551-552.
Henry James, *Notebooks,* 265, 266.

86. THE REAL THING
Quentin Anderson, *The American Henry James,* 142, 146.
Quentin Anderson, "Henry James and the New Jerusalem," *Kenyon Review* VIII (Autumn, 1946), 539.
Quentin Anderson, "Introduction," in James, *Selected Short Stories* (Rinehart Editions, 1950), vii-viii.
Quentin Anderson, "The Two Henry Jameses," *Scrutiny* XIV (September, 1947), 248-249.
Clifton Fadiman, "A Note," in Fadiman, *The Short Stories of Henry James,* 216-27. — reprinted in Locke, Gibson, and Arms, *Introduction to Literature* (First Edition, 1948), 333-334; (Second Edition, 1952, and Third Edition, 1957), 330-331.
Ford Madox Ford, *Portraits from Life,* 8-10; or *Mightier Than the Sword* (English Edition), 22-25.
Henry James, *The Art of the Novel,* 283-284; *Notebooks,* 102-105.
Seymour Lainoff, "A Note on Henry James's 'The Real Thing,' " *Modern Language Notes* LXXI (March, 1956), 192-193.
[William F. Marquardt, "A Practical Approach to 'The Real

Thing,' " *English "A" Analyst* (Northwestern University) , No. 14 (1949) .]

F. O. Matthiessen, "Henry James' Portrait of the Artist," *Partisan Review* XI (Winter, 1944) , 83-84. — reprinted in Matthiessen, *Stories of Writers and Artists,* 13-14.

Gorham Munson, "The Real Thing: A Parable for Writers of Fiction," *University of Kansas City Review* XVI (Summer, 1950) , 261-264.

Séan O'Faoláin, *The Short Story,* 181-182, 211-215.

[Claire Raeth, "The Real Approach to 'The Real Thing,' " *English "A" Analyst* (Northwestern University) , No. 15 (1949) .]

Lyon N. Richardson, *Henry James: Representative Selections,* 489.

Edouard Roditi, *Oscar Wilde,* 104-105.

Walter F. Wright, " 'The Real Thing,' " *Research Studies of the State College of Washington* XXV (1957) , 85-90.

87. THE ROMANCE OF CERTAIN OLD CLOTHES

Miriam Allott, "James Russell Lowell: A Link Between Tennyson and Henry James," *Review of English Studies* VI, n.s. (October, 1955) , 399-401.

Leon Edel, *The Ghostly Tales of Henry James,* 3-4.

Raymond D. Havens, "Henry James on One of His Early Stories," *American Literature* XXIII (March, 1951) , 131-133.

W. D. Howells, Review of *The Passionate Pilgrim and Other Tales, Atlantic Monthly* XXXV (April, 1875) , 494.

Cornelia P. Kelley, *The Early Development of Henry James,* 81-83.

Robert C. LeClair, *Young Henry James, 1843-1870,* 400-402.

F. O. Matthiessen, *The James Family,* 316-317.

88. A ROUND OF VISITS

Marius Bewley, "Henry James and 'Life,' " *Hudson Review* XI (Summer, 1958) , 182-183.

Henry James, *Notebooks,* 158-160, 280-282.

F. O. Matthiessen, *The American Novels and Stories of Henry James,* xxiii-xxiv.

F. O. Matthiessen, *Henry James: The Major Phase,* 113-117.

Christof Wegelin, *The Image of Europe in Henry James,* 156-157.

89. THE SIEGE OF LONDON

Henry James, *The Art of the Novel,* 209-212.

Philip Rahv, *The Great Short Novels of Henry James,* 225-226.

90. SIR DOMINICK FERRAND

Leon Edel, *The Ghostly Tales of Henry James,* 250-251.

Henry James, *Notebooks,* 117-118.

91. SIR EDMUND ORME
    Leon Edel, *The Ghostly Tales of Henry James*, 141-142.
    Henry James, *The Art of the Novel*, 260-261; *Notebooks*, 9-10.
92. THE SOLUTION
    Henry James, *Notebooks*, 95-96.
93. THE SPECIAL TYPE
    Henry James, *Notebooks*, 232-233.
94. THE STORY IN IT
    Pelham Edgar, *Henry James*, 149-150.
    Henry James, *The Art of the Novel*, 285-286; *Notebooks*, 275-279.
    F. O. Matthiessen, "Henry James' Portrait of the Artist," *Partisan Review* XI (Winter, 1944) 84-85. — reprinted in Matthiessen, *Stories of Writers and Artists*, 14-15.
95. THE STORY OF A MASTERPIECE
    Cornelia P. Kelley, *The Early Development of Henry James*, 80-81.
    Edna Kenton, *Eight Uncollected Tales of Henry James*, 5, 12.
    Robert C. LeClair, *Young Henry James, 1843-1870*, 398-400.
    F. O. Matthiessen, *The James Family*, 316-317.
    B. R. McElderry, Jr., "The Uncollected Stories of Henry James," *American Literature* XXI (November, 1949), 283-284.
96. THE STORY OF A YEAR
    Maurice Beebe, "The Turned Back of Henry James," *South Atlantic Quarterly* LIII (October, 1954), 533-536.
    Leon Edel, *Henry James: The Untried Years*, 220-221.
    Cornelia P. Kelley, *The Early Development of Henry James*, 34-37.
    Edna Kenton, *Eight Uncollected Tales of Henry James*, 10-11.
    Robert C. LeClair, *Young Henry James, 1843-1870*, 377-379.
    F. O. Matthiessen, *The American Novels and Stories of Henry James*, viii.
    B. R. McElderry, Jr., "The Uncollected Stories of Henry James," *American Literature* XXI (November, 1949), 281-282.
    Saul Rosenzweig, "The Ghost of Henry James: A Study in Thematic Apperception," *Character and Personality* XII (December, 1943), 79-99. — reprinted in *Partisan Review* XI (Fall, 1944), 442-445. — reprinted, revised, in William Phillips, *Art and Psychoanalysis*, 89-111.
97. THE SWEETHEART OF M. BRISEUX
    Quentin Anderson, *The American Henry James*, 140.
    Cornelia P. Kelley, *The Early Development of Henry James*, 152-153.
98. THE THIRD PERSON
    Leon Edel, *The Ghostly Tales of Henry James*, 630-632.

JAMES, HENRY, Continued

99. THE TONE OF TIME
Clifton Fadiman, *Short Stories of Henry James*, 457-459.
Henry James, *Notebooks*, 265-266, 283-284.
Fred B. Millett, *Reading Fiction*, 199-200.

100. A TRAGEDY OF ERROR
Leon Edel, *Henry James: The Untried Years*, 215-218.
Leon Edel, "'A Tragedy of Error': James's First Story," *New England Quarterly* XXIX (September, 1956), 291-295.
Robert L. Gale, "A Note on Henry James's First Short Story," *Modern Language Notes* LXXII (February, 1957), 103-107.

101. TRAVELLING COMPANIONS
Quentin Anderson, *The American Henry James*, 134-141.
Quentin Anderson, "Henry James and the New Jerusalem," *Kenyon Review* VIII (Autumn, 1946), 536-538.
Joseph Warren Beach, *The Method of Henry James*, 187-189.
Cornelia P. Kelley, *The Early Development of Henry James*, 113-115.
Robert C. LeClair, *Young Henry James, 1843-1870*, 435-437.
Leo B. Levy, *Versions of Melodrama*, 27-28.

102. THE TREE OF KNOWLEDGE
Robert G. Davis, *Instructor's Manual for "Ten Modern Masters,"* 37-38.
Clifton Fadiman, *Short Stories of Henry James*, 432-434.
Henry James, *The Art of the Novel*, 234-236; *Notebooks*, 289-290.

103. THE TURN OF THE SCREW
Osborn Andreas, *Henry James and the Expanding Horizon*, 46-47.
Marius Bewley, "Appearance and Reality in Henry James," *Scrutiny* XVII (Summer, 1950), 102-114. — reprinted in Bewley, *The Complex Fate*, 114-131.
Marius Bewley, "Maisie, Miles, and Flora, The Jamesian Innocents: A Rejoinder," *Scrutiny* XVII (Autumn, 1950), 255-259. — reprinted in Bewley, *The Complex Fate*, 132-143.
Heywood Broun, "Introduction" to James, *The Turn of the Screw* (Modern Library, 1930), vii-ix.
Kenneth Burke, *A Rhetoric of Motives*, 116-117.
Oscar Cargill, "Henry James As Freudian Pioneer," *Chicago Review* X (Summer, 1956), 13-29.
Richard Chase, *The American Novel and Its Tradition*, 239-241.
Carvel Collins, "James' 'The Turn of the Screw,'" *Explicator* XIII, No. 8 (June, 1955), item 49.
Peter Coveney, *Poor Monkey: The Child in Literature*, 164-168.

George N. Dove, "The 'Haunted Personality' in Henry James," *Tennessee Studies in Literature* III (1958), 99-106.

F. W. Dupee, *Henry James*, 183-184; (Anchor Books), 159-160.

Leon Edel, *The Ghostly Tales of Henry James*, 425-435.

Leon Edel, "Hugh Walpole and Henry James: The Fantasy of the 'Killer and the Slain,'" *American Imago* VIII (December, 1951), 358-359.

Leon Edel, *The Psychological Novel, 1900-1950*, 57-68.

Leon Edel and Gordon N. Ray, *Henry James and H. G. Wells*, 56.

Oliver Evans, "James' Air of Evil: 'The Turn of the Screw,'" *Partisan Review* XVI (February, 1949), 175-187.

N. Bryllion Fagin, "Another Reading of 'The Turn of the Screw,'" *Modern Language Notes* LVI (March, 1941), 196-202.

Joseph Firebaugh, "Inadequacy in Eden: Knowledge and 'The Turn of the Screw,'" *Modern Fiction Studies* III (Spring, 1957), 57-63.

Ford Madox Ford, *Portraits from Life*, 11-12; or *Mightier Than the Sword* (English Edition), 26-27.

Harold C. Goddard, "A Pre-Freudian Reading of 'The Turn of the Screw,'" *Nineteenth Century Fiction* XII (June, 1957), 5-36.

Carl H. Grabo, *The Technique of the Novel*, 204-214.

R. B. Heilman, "The Freudian Reading of 'The Turn of the Screw,'" *Modern Language Notes* LXIII (November, 1947), 433-445.

R. B. Heilman, "'The Turn of the Screw' As Poem," *University of Kansas City Review* XIV (Summer, 1948), 277-289. — reprinted in Mark Schorer, *The Story*, 586-606. — reprinted in W. Van O'Connor, *Forms of Modern Fiction*, 211-228.

Charles G. Hoffmann, "Innocence and Evil in James' 'The Turn of the Screw,'" *University of Kansas City Review* XX (Winter, 1953), 97-105. — reprinted, considerably revised, in Hoffmann, *The Short Novels of Henry James*, 70-96.

Henry James, *The Art of the Novel*, 169-177; *Notebooks*, 178-179. — reprinted in Mark Schorer, *The Story: A Critical Anthology*, 563-572; n. 565.

Henry James, *Letters* (Lubbock), I, 279, 296-297, 298-299, 300-301; *Selected Letters* (Edel), 150-151.

Alexander E. Jones, "Point of View in 'The Turn of the Screw,'" *PMLA* LXXIV (March, 1959), 112-122.

Edna Kenton, "Henry James to the Ruminant Reader: 'The Turn of the Screw,'" *Arts* VI (November, 1924), 245-255.

F. R. Leavis, "Comment," in Marius Bewley, *The Complex Fate,* 144.

F. R. Leavis, "James's 'What Maisie Knew', A Disagreement," *Scrutiny* XVII (Summer, 1950), 115-119. — reprinted in Marius Bewley, *The Complex Fate,* 114-119.

Leo B. Levy, " 'The Turn of the Screw' as Retaliation," *College English* XVII (February, 1956), 286-288.

Robert Liddell, "The 'Hallucination' Theory of the 'Turn of the Screw,' " in Liddell, *A Treatise on the Novel,* 138-145.

John Lydenberg, "The Governess Turns the Screws," *Nineteenth Century Fiction* XII (June, 1957), 37-58.

Robert Lynd, *Books and Writers,* 9-10.

Earl R. Miner, "Henry James's Metaphysical Romances," *Nineteenth Century Fiction* IX (June, 1954), 9-21.

Ferner Nuhn, *The Wind Blew from the East,* 140-141.

Frank O'Connor, "Transition: Henry James," in O'Connor, *The Mirror in the Roadway,* 226-228.

Peter Penzoldt, *The Supernatural in Fiction,* 218-223.

K. A. Porter, Allen Tate, and Mark Van Doren, Discussion in Mark Van Doren, *The New Invitation to Learning,* 221-235.

Philip Rahv, *The Great Short Novels of Henry James,* 623-625.

Glenn Reed, "Another Turn on James's 'The Turn of the Screw,' " *American Literature* XX (January, 1949), 413-423.

Lyon N. Richardson, *Henry James: Representative Selections,* lxxxiv-lxxxvii.

Francis X. Roellinger, Jr., "Psychical Research and 'The Turn of the Screw,' " *American Literature* XX (January, 1949), 401-412.

John Silver, "A Note on the Freudian Reading of 'The Turn of the Screw,' " *American Literature* XXIX (May, 1957), 207-211.

E. E. Stoll, "Symbolism in Coleridge," *PMLA* LXII (March, 1948), 229-233.

A. J. A. Waldock, "Mr. Edmund Wilson and 'The Turn of the Screw,' " *Modern Language Notes* LXII (May, 1947), 331-334.

Alfred C. Ward, *Aspects of the Modern Short Story,* 89-101.

Edmund Wilson, "The Ambiguity of Henry James," *Hound and Horn* VII (April-June, 1934), 385-393. — reprinted in Edmund Wilson, *The Triple Thinkers,* 122-133. — reprinted, revised, in F. W. Dupee, *The Question of Henry James,* 160-168.

Yvor Winters, *Maule's Curse,* 186-187, 197. — reprinted in Winters, *In Defense of Reason,* 316-317, 326.

Robert Lee Wolff, "The Genesis of the 'Turn of the Screw,' " *American Literature* XIII (March, 1941), 1-8.

JAMES, HENRY, Continued

104. THE TWO FACES
Richard E. Amacher, "James' 'The Two Faces,'" *Explicator* XII,
No. 3 (December, 1953), item 20.
Henry James, *The Art of the Novel*, 177-179; *Notebooks*, 284-286.
Henry R. Rupp, "James' 'The Two Faces,'" *Explicator* XVI, No.
5 (February, 1956), item 30.
105. THE WHEEL OF TIME
Henry James, *Notebooks*, 123-124.

JAMES, M. R.

1. THE ASHTREE
Peter Penzoldt, *The Supernatural in Fiction*, 198-200.
2. THE DIARY OF MR. POYNTER
Peter Penzoldt, *The Supernatural in Fiction*, 193-198.

JEWETT, SARAH ORNE

1. A WHITE HERON
Herbert Barrows, *Suggestions for Teaching "15 Stories,"* 26-27.

JOYCE, JAMES

1. AFTER THE RACE
Brewster Ghiselin, "The Unity of Joyce's 'Dubliners,'" *Accent*
XVI (Summer, 1956), 200.
R. Levin and C. Shattuck, "First Flight to Ithaca," *Accent* IV
(Winter, 1944), 85-86. — reprinted in Givens, *James Joyce*, 66-67.
2. ARABY
Brooks and Warren, *Understanding Fiction*, 420-423.
Brewster Ghiselin, "The Unity of Joyce's 'Dubliners,'" *Accent*
XVI (Summer, 1956), 199.
R. Levin and C. Shattuck, "First Flight to Ithaca," *Accent* IV
(Winter, 1944), 82. — reprinted in Givens, *James Joyce*, 58-60.
Magalaner and Kain, *Joyce*, 77-79.
3. THE BOARDING HOUSE
Brewster Ghiselin, "The Unity of Joyce's 'Dubliners,'" *Accent*
XVI (Summer, 1956), 201-202.
Hugh Kenner, *Dublin's Joyce*, 49-50.

R. Levin and C. Shattuck, "First Flight to Ithaca," *Accent* IV (Winter, 1944), 86-87. — reprinted in Givens, *James Joyce*, 68-69.

4. CLAY

Sylvia Berkman, *Katherine Mansfield,* 161-162.

Brooks, Purser, and Warren, *An Approach to Literature,* 137-140.

Francis Connolly, *The Types of Literature,* 709-711.

Brewster Ghiselin, "The Unity of Joyce's 'Dubliners,'" *Accent* XVI (Summer, 1956), 203-204.

Richard B. Hudson, "Joyce's 'Clay,'" *Explicator* VI (March, 1948), item 30.

R. Levin and C. Shattuck, "First Flight to Ithaca," *Accent* IV (Winter, 1944), 90-91. — reprinted in Givens, *James Joyce*, 76-77.

Marvin Magalaner, "The Other Side of James Joyce," *Arizona Quarterly* IX (Spring, 1953), 7-16. — reprinted, revised, with additional material, in Magalaner and Kain, *Joyce*, 84-91, 99-101.

W. T. Noon, S.J., "Joyce's 'Clay': An Interpretation," *College English* XVII (November, 1955), 93-95.

Norman Holmes Pearson, "Joyce's 'Clay,'" *Explicator* VII (October, 1948), item 9.

Raymond W. Short and Richard B. Sewall, *A Manual of Suggestions for Teachers Using "Short Stories for Study,"* 4-5.

5. COUNTERPARTS

Brewster Ghiselin, "The Unity of Joyce's 'Dubliners,'" *Accent* XVI (Summer, 1956), 202-203.

R. Levin and C. Shattuck, "First Flight to Ithaca," *Accent* IV (Winter, 1944), 89-90. — reprinted in Givens, *James Joyce*, 73-76.

6. THE DEAD

H. E. Bates, *The Modern Short Story: A Critical Survey,* 154-156.

Sylvia Berkman, *Katherine Mansfield,* 164-165.

Morgan Blum, "The Shifting Point of View: Joyce's 'The Dead' and Gordon's 'Old Red,'" *Critique: Studies in Modern Fiction* I (Winter, 1956), 45-58.

Kenneth Burke, "Three Definitions," *Kenyon Review* XIII (Spring, 1951), 186-192.

David Daiches, *The Novel and the Modern World,* 91-100.

T. S. Eliot, *After Strange Gods,* 37-38.

Richard Ellmann, "The Backgrounds of 'The Dead,'" *Kenyon Review* XX (Autumn, 1958), 507-528.

Richard Ellmann, "The Limits of Joyce's Naturalism," *Sewanee Review* LXIII (Autumn, 1955), 570-571.

Felheim, Newman, and Steinhoff, *Study Aids for Teachers for "Modern Short Stories,"* 55-57.

JOYCE, JAMES, Continued

Gerhard Friedrich, "Bret Harte as a Source for James Joyce's 'The Dead,' " *Philological Quarterly* XXXIII (October, 1954), 442-444.

Brewster Ghiselin, "The Unity of Joyce's 'Dubliners,' " *Accent* XVI (Summer, 1956), 207-210.

Herbert Gorman, *James Joyce: His First Forty Years*, 56-58.

William Powell Jones, *James Joyce and the Common Reader*, 17.

Stanislaus Joyce, *My Brother's Keeper*, 152.

Julian B. Kaye, "The Wings of Daedalus: Two Stories in 'Dubliners,' " *Modern Fiction Studies* IV (Spring, 1958), 37-41.

Hugh Kenner, *Dublin's Joyce*, 62-68.

Harry Levin, *James Joyce*, 35-37.

R. Levin and C. Shattuck, "First Flight to Ithaca," *Accent* IV (Winter, 1944), 96-99. — reprinted in Givens, *James Joyce*, 87-92.

Ludwig and Poirier, *Stories: British and American*, 387-391.

Magalaner and Kain, *Joyce*, 92-98.

Milton Miller, "Definition by Comparison: Chaucer, Lawrence, and Joyce," *Essays in Criticism* III (October, 1953), 377-381.

Charles Neider, *Short Novels of the Masters*, 37-39.

William T. Noon, *Joyce and Aquinas*, 84-85.

Frank O'Connor, "And It's a Lonely, Personal Art," in Francis Brown, *Highlights of Modern Literature* (New American Library), 78.

Frank O'Connor, "Joyce and Dissociated Metaphor," in O'Connor, *The Mirror in the Roadway*, 299-301.

Brendan P. O Hehir, "Structural Symbol in Joyce's 'The Dead,' " *Twentieth Century Literature* III (April, 1957), 3-13.

Sale, Hall, and Steinmann, *Critical Discussions for Teachers Using "Short Stories: Tradition and Direction,"* 33-37.

D. S. Savage, *The Withered Branch*, 186-187.

William M. Schutte, *Joyce and Shakespeare*, 137.

Stephen Spender, *The Destructive Element*, 169-172.

J. I. M. Stewart, *James Joyce*, 14-15.

Allen Tate, "Three Commentaries: Poe, James, and Joyce," *Sewanee Review* LVIII (Winter, 1950), 10-15. — reprinted in Gordon and Tate, *The House of Fiction*, 279-282.

William Y. Tindall, *The Literary Symbol*, 224-228.

Rebecca West, *Strange Necessity*, 26-28.

7. AN ENCOUNTER

Brewster Ghiselin, "The Unity of Joyce's 'Dubliners,' " *Accent* XVI (Summer, 1956), 198.

Stanislaus Joyce, *My Brother's Keeper*, 62-63.

117

Julian B. Kaye, "The Wings of Daedalus: Two Stories in 'Dubliners,'" *Modern Fiction Studies* IV (Spring, 1958), 31-37.

R. Levin and C. Shattuck, "First Flight to Ithaca," *Accent* IV (Winter, 1944), 81. — reprinted in Givens, *James Joyce*, 57-58.

Magalaner and Kain, *Joyce*, 75-77.

Stephen Spender, *The Destructive Element*, 170.

8. EVELINE

Brewster Ghiselin, "The Unity of Joyce's 'Dubliners,'" *Accent* XVI (Summer, 1956), 199-200.

Herbert Gorman, *James Joyce: His First Forty Years*, 49-51.

R. Levin and C. Shattuck, "First Flight to Ithaca," *Accent* IV (Winter, 1944), 83-84. — reprinted in Givens, *James Joyce*, 61-63.

9. GRACE

Brewster Ghiselin, "The Unity of Joyce's 'Dubliners,'" *Accent* XVI (Summer, 1956), 206-207.

Stanislaus Joyce, *My Brother's Keeper*, 225-228.

Julian B. Kaye, "Simony, the Three Simons, and Joycean Myth," in Marvin Magalaner, *A James Joyce Miscellany*, 23-24.

R. Levin and C. Shattuck, "First Flight to Ithaca," *Accent* IV (Winter, 1944), 94-95. — reprinted in Givens, *James Joyce*, 84-86.

Marvin Magalaner, "Leopold Bloom before *Ulysses*," *Modern Language Notes* LXVIII (February, 1953), 110-112.

J. Mitchell Morse, "The Disobedient Artist: Joyce and Loyola," *PMLA* LXXII (December, 1957), 1023-1025.

Frank O'Connor, "Joyce and Dissociated Metaphor," in O'Connor, *The Mirror in the Roadway*, 298-299.

10. IVY DAY IN THE COMMITTEE ROOM

Joseph L. Blotner, "'Ivy Day in the Committee Room': Death Without Resurrection," *Perspective* IX (Summer, 1957), 210-217.

David Daiches, *The Novel and the Modern World*, 89-90.

Brewster Ghiselin, "The Unity of Joyce's 'Dubliners,'" *Accent* XVI (Summer, 1956), 205-206.

Stanislaus Joyce, *My Brother's Keeper*, 206.

R. Levin and C. Shattuck, "First Flight to Ithaca," *Accent* IV (Winter, 1944), 93-94. — reprinted in Givens, *James Joyce*, 81-83.

Magalaner and Kain, *Joyce*, 79-84.

Frank O'Connor, "Joyce and Dissociated Metaphor," in O'Connor, *The Mirror in the Roadway*, 296-298.

Stegner, Scowcroft, and Ilyin, *The Writer's Art*, 92-95.

J. I. M. Stewart, *James Joyce*, 13.

11. A LITTLE CLOUD

Brewster Ghiselin, "The Unity of Joyce's 'Dubliners,'" *Accent* XVI (Summer, 1956), 202.

James B. Hall and Joseph Langland, *The Short Story*, 264.

R. B. Heilman, *Modern Short Stories*, 146-147.

Hugh Kenner, *Dublin's Joyce*, 56-57.

R. Levin and C. Shattuck, "First Flight to Ithaca," *Accent* IV (Winter, 1944), 87-89. — reprinted in Givens, *James Joyce*, 70-72.

James Ruoff, " 'A Little Cloud': Joyce's Portrait of the Would-Be Artist," *Research Studies of the State College of Washington*, XXV (1957), 256-271.

Mark Schorer, *The Story*, 304-305.

Clarice Short, "Joyce's 'A Little Cloud,' " *Modern Language Notes* LXXII (April, 1957), 275-278.

12. A MOTHER

Brewster Ghiselin, "The Unity of Joyce's 'Dubliners,' " *Accent* XVI (Summer, 1956), 206.

R. Levin and C. Shattuck, "First Flight to Ithaca," *Accent* IV (Winter, 1944), 94. — reprinted in Givens, *James Joyce*, 83-84.

13. A PAINFUL CASE

Herbert Barrows, *Suggestions for Teaching "15 Stories,"* 19-22.

[A. Bronson Feldman, "James Joyce's 'A Painful Case' (1905). A Portrait of Obsessional Narcissism." *Psychoanalysis* III and IV (Winter, 1957), 3-12.]

Royal A. Gettmann and Bruce Harkness, *Teacher's Manual for "A Book of Stories,"* 7-9.

Brewster Ghiselin, "The Unity of Joyce's 'Dubliners,' " *Accent* XVI (Summer, 1956), 204.

Stanislaus Joyce, *My Brother's Keeper*, 158-160.

Hugh Kenner, *Dublin's Joyce*, 46-47, 58-61.

R. Levin and C. Shattuck, "First Flight to Ithaca," *Accent* IV (Winter, 1944), 91-92. — reprinted in Givens, *James Joyce*, 78-79.

Marvin Magalaner, "Joyce, Nietzsche, and Hauptmann in James Joyce's 'A Painful Case,' " *PMLA* LXVIII (March, 1953), 95-102.

Rebecca West, *Strange Necessity*, 24-26.

14. THE SISTERS

William A. Fahey, "Joyce's 'The Sisters,' " *Explicator* XVII, No. 4, (January, 1959), item 26.

Gerhard Friedrich, "The Gnomonic Clue to James Joyce's 'Dubliners,' " *Modern Language Notes* LXXII (June, 1957), 421-423.

Brewster Ghiselin, "The Unity of Joyce's 'Dubliners,' " *Accent* XVI (Summer, 1956), 196-198.

Julian B. Kaye, "Simony, the Three Simons, and Joycean Myth," in Marvin Magalaner, *A James Joyce Miscellany*, 21-23.

Hugh Kenner, *Dublin's Joyce*, 50-53.

R. Levin and C. Shattuck, "First Flight to Ithaca," *Accent* IV (Winter, 1944), 80-81. — reprinted in Givens' *James Joyce*, 55-57. Ludwig and Poirier, *Stories: British and American*, 385-386.

Marvin Magalaner, " 'The Sisters' of Joyce," *University of Kansas City Review* XVIII (Summer, 1952), 255-261. — reprinted, considerably revised, in Magalaner and Kain, *Joyce*, 71-75.

15. TWO GALLANTS

Brewster Ghiselin, "The Unity of Joyce's 'Dubliners,' " *Accent* XVI (Summer, 1956), 200-201.

R. Levin and C. Shattuck, "First Flight to Ithaca," *Accent* IV (Winter, 1944), 84-85. — reprinted in Givens, *James Joyce*, 63-66.

William T. Noon, *Joyce and Aquinas*, 83-84.

KAFKA, FRANZ

1. BEFORE THE LAW

Herbert Tauber, *Franz Kafka*, 68.

2. BLUMFELD, AN ELDERLY BACHELOR

Lienhard Bergel, "Blumfeld, An Elderly Bachelor," in Angel Flores, *The Kafka Problem*, 172-178.

Herbert Tauber, *Franz Kafka*, 122-123.

3. THE BURROW

Lienhard Bergel, "The Burrow," in Angel Flores, *The Kafka Problem*, 199-206.

Edwin Berry Burgum, "Franz Kafka and the Bankruptcy of Faith," *Accent* III (Spring, 1943), 154-157. — reprinted in Quinn and Shattuck, *Accent Anthology*, 511-514.

Selma Fraiberg, "Dream and Creation in Kafka," *Partisan Review* XXIII (Winter, 1956), 57. — reprinted, revised, in William Phillips, *Art and Psychoanalysis*, 31-32.

Paul Goodman, *Kafka's Prayer*, 222-227.

J. P. Hodin, "Memories of Franz Kafka," *Horizon* XVII (January, 1948), 38. — reprinted in Hoden, *The Dilemma of Being Modern*, 15-16.

H. S. Reiss, "Franz Kafka," *German Life and Letters*, I, n.s. (April, 1948), 187-188.

D. S. Savage, "Franz Kafka: Faith and Vocation," *Sewanee Review* LIV (April-June, 1946), 239. — reprinted in Flores, *The Kafka Problem*, 334.

Herbert Tauber, *Franz Kafka*, 211-213.

William Y. Tindall, *The Literary Symbol*, 136.

KAFKA, FRANZ, Continued

Augusta Walker, "Allegory: A Light Conceit," *Partisan Review* XXII. (Fall, 1955), 484-490.

4. THE CARES OF A FAMILY MAN
Herbert Tauber, *Franz Kafka,* 72.

5. CHILDREN ON A COUNTRY ROAD
Herbert Tauber, *Franz Kafka,* 10-11.

6. A COMMON CONFUSION
Hannah Arendt, "Franz Kafka: A Revaluation," *Partisan Review* XI (Fall, 1944), 418-420.

7. A COUNTRY DOCTOR
Basil Busacca, "A Country Doctor," in Flores and Swander, *Kafka Today,* 45-54.
Margaret Church, "Kafka's 'A Country Doctor,'" *Explicator* XVI, No. 8 (May, 1958), item 45.
Stanley Cooperman, "Kafka's 'A Country Doctor,'" *University of Kansas City Review* XXIV (Autumn, 1957), 75-80.
Ronald Gray, *Kafka's Castle,* 19-21.
Frederick J. Hoffman, *Freudianism and the Literary Mind* (2nd edit., 1957), 201-202.
Richard H. Lawson, "Kafka's Landarzt," *Monatshefte* XLIX (October, 1957), 265-271.
Herbert Tauber, *Franz Kafka,* 74-76.

8. DESCRIPTION OF A STRUGGLE
Hannah Arendt, "The Jews as Pariah: A Hidden Tradition," *Jewish Social Studies* VI (April, 1944), 113-115.
Herbert Tauber, *Franz Kafka,* 1-11.

9. A DREAM
Herbert Tauber, *Franz Kafka,* 71.

10. ELEVEN SONS
Herbert Tauber, *Franz Kafka,* 74.

11. FIRST SORROW
Herbert Tauber, *Franz Kafka,* 190.

12. A FRATRICIDE
Herbert Tauber, *Franz Kafka,* 71.

13. THE GIANT MOLE
Guenther Anders, "Kafka: Ritual Without Religion," *Commentary* VIII (December, 1949), 568-569.
Philip Rahv, "Exegetical Notes" in Kafka, *Great Wall of China* (trans. by Edwin and Willa Muir), 314-315.
Herbert Tauber, *Franz Kafka,* 199-201.

14. GIVE IT UP!
Heinz Politzer, "Give It Up!" in Angel Flores, *The Kafka Problem,* 117-121.

15. THE GREAT WALL OF CHINA

Jean Collignon, "Kafka's Humor," *Yale French Studies,* No. 16 (1956), 55-61, passim.

Paul Goodman, *Kafka's Prayer,* 235-240.

Clement Greenberg, "At the Building of the Great Wall of China," in Flores and Swander, *Kafka Today,* 77-81.

Philip Rahv, "Exegetical Notes" in Kafka, *Great Wall of China* (trans. by Edwin and Willa Muir), 312-314.

Philip Rahv, "Introduction" to *Selected Stories of Franz Kafka* (Modern Library, 1952), xii-xiii.

Harry Slochower, "Franz Kafka—Pre-Fascist Exile," in *A Franz Kafka Miscellany* (2nd edit., 1946), 28.

Harry Slochower, *No Voice is Wholly Lost,* 123.

Herbert Tauber, *Franz Kafka,* 123-129.

16. THE HUNGER ARTIST

Kate Flores, "The Judgment," in Flores and Swander, *Kafka Today,* 19-20.

Claude-Edmonde Magny, "The Objective Depiction of Absurdity," *Quarterly Review of Literature* II, No. 3 (1945), 224-225. — reprinted in Angel Flores, *The Kafka Problem,* 92-94.

Patricia Moyer, "Time and the Artist in Kafka and Hawthorne," *Modern Fiction Studies* IV (Winter, 1958-1959), 295-306.

Charles Neider, *The Frozen Sea,* 82.

William C. Rubinstein, "Franz Kafka: A Hunger Artist," *Monatshefte* XLIV (January, 1952), 13-19.

Harry Slochower, "Franz Kafka—Pre-Fascist Exile," in *A Franz Kafka Miscellany* (2nd edit., 1946), 29.

Robert W. Stallman, "Kakfa's Cage," *Accent* VIII (Winter, 1948), 117-125. — reprinted, revised, in West and Stallman, *Art of Modern Fiction,* 366-372. — reprinted, revised, in Stallman and Watters, *Creative Reader,* 318-323. — reprinted, revised, in Flores and Swander, *Kafka Today,* 61-70.

Stallman and Watters, *Creative Reader,* 343.

Herbert Tauber, *Franz Kafka,* 190-193.

17. THE HUNTER GRACCHUS

Caroline Gordon, "Notes on Hemingway and Kafka," *Sewanee Review* LVII (Spring, 1949), 220-226. — reprinted, revised, in Gordon and Tate, *The House of Fiction,* 286-289.

Frederick J. Hoffman, *Freudianism and the Literary Mind* (2nd edit., 1957), 206-207.

Bernard Knieger, "Kafka's 'The Hunter Gracchus,'" *Explicator* XVII, No. 6 (March, 1959), item 39.

Charles Neider, *The Frozen Sea*, 84-85.
18. AN IMPERIAL MESSAGE
Hans Joachim Schoeps, "The Tragedy of Faithlessness," in Flores, *The Kafka Problem*, 294-296.
Rebecca West, "Kafka and the Mystery of Bureaucracy," *Yale Review* XLVII (Autumn, 1957), 33-35. — reprinted in R. West, *The Court and the Castle*, 301-305.
19. IN THE GALLERY
Herbert Tauber, *Franz Kafka*, 66-67, 69.
20. IN THE PENAL COLONY
Brooks and Warren, *Understanding Fiction*, 467-472.
Wayne Burns, " 'In the Penal Colony': Variations on a Theme by Octave Mirbeau," *Accent* XVII (Winter, 1957), 45-51.
Wayne Burns, "Kafka and Alex Comfort: The Penal Colony Revisited," *Arizona Quarterly* VIII (Summer, 1952), 103-104.
Ronald Gray, *Kafka's Castle*, 21-24.
James B. Hall and Joseph Langland, *The Short Story*, 201-202.
Frederick J. Hoffman, *Freudianism and the Literary Mind* (2nd edit., 1957), 204-205.
Adrian H. Jaffe and Virgil Scott, "Analysis of 'In the Penal Colony,' " in Jaffe and Scott, *Studies in the Short Story*, 468-470.
Charles Neider, *The Frozen Sea*, 78-80.
Herbert Tauber, *Franz Kafka*, 58-64.
Austin Warren, "An Exegetical Note on 'The Penal Colony,' " *Southern Review* VII (Autumn, 1941), 363-365. — reprinted in Angel Flores, *The Kafka Problem*, 140-142.
Rebecca West, "Kafka and the Mystery of Bureaucracy," *Yale Review* XLVII (Autumn, 1957), 30-32. — reprinted in R. West, *The Court and the Castle*, 299-301.
21. IN OUR SYNAGOGUE
Herbert Tauber, *Franz Kafka*, 73.
22. INVESTIGATIONS OF A DOG
Paul Goodmans, *Kafka's Prayer*, 231-235; 242-253.
J. Hillis Miller, Jr., "Franz Kafka and the Metaphysics of Alienation," in Nathan A. Scott, *The Tragic Vision and the Christian Faith*, 285-286.
Charles Neider, "The Cabalists," in Angel Flores, *The Kafka Problem*, 430-432. — reprinted in Neider, *The Frozen Sea*, 41-44.
Philip Rahv, "Exegetical Notes" in Kafka, *Great Wall of China* (trans. by Edwin and Willa Muir), 309-312.
Nathan A. Scott, Jr., *Rehearsals of Discomposure*, 43-44.
Herbert Tauber, *Franz Kafka*, 201-211.

KAFKA, FRANZ, Continued

Edmund Wilson, "A Dissenting Opinion on Kafka," *New Yorker* XXIII (July 26, 1947), 62-63. — reprinted in Wilson, *Classics and Commercials*, 389-390.

23. JACKALS AND ARABS
Herbert Tauber, *Franz Kafka*, 69-70.

24. JOSEPHINE, THE SINGER
Charles Neider, *Frozen Sea*, 82-83.
Herbert Tauber, *Franz Kafka*, 193-198.
Charles R. Woodring, "Josephine the Singer, or the Mouse Folk," in Flores and Swander, *Kafka Today*, 71-75.

25. THE JUDGMENT
Felheim, Newman, and Steinhoff, *Study Aids for Teachers for "Modern Short Stories,"* 36-39.
Kate Flores, "Franz Kafka and the Nameless Guilt: An Analysis of 'The Judgment,' " *Quarterly Review of Literature* III, No. 4 (1947), 382-405. — reprinted, revised, in Flores and Swander, *Kafka Today*, 5-23.
Selma Fraiberg, "Dream and Creation in Kafka," *Partisan Review* XXIII (Winter, 1956), 58. — reprinted, revised, in William Phillips, *Art and Psychoanalysis*, 33.
Royal A. Gettmann and Bruce Harkness, *Teacher's Manual for "A Book of Stories,"* 62-64.
George Gibian, *"Dichtung und Wahrheit*: Three Versions of Reality in Franz Kafka," *German Quarterly* XXX (January, 1957), 24-28.
Frederick J. Hoffman, *Freudianism and the Literary Mind* (2nd edit., 1957), 179-180.
Claude-Edmonde Magny, "The Objective Depiction of Absurdity," *Quarterly Review of Literature* II, No. 3 (1945), 214-218. — reprinted in Angel Flores, *The Kafka Problem*, 81-85.
Charles Neider, *The Frozen Sea*, 73-78.
Philip Rahv, "Introduction" to *Selected Stories of Franz Kafka* (Modern Library, 1952), xiii-xv.
Francis Russell, *Three Studies in Twentieth Century Obscurity*, 55-57.
Nathan A. Scott, Jr., *Rehearsals of Discomposure*, 35-36, 39-42.
Herbert Tauber, *Franz Kafka*, 12-17.

26. THE LEVY OF TROOPS
Herbert Tauber, *Franz Kafka*, 129-130.

27. A LITTLE WOMAN
Herbert Tauber, *Franz Kafka*, 189-190.

28. THE MARRIED COUPLE
Charles Neider, *Frozen Sea*, 83.
Nathan A. Scott, Jr., *Rehearsals of Discomposure*, 27-28.
Jarvis Thurston, *Reading Modern Short Stories*, 371-376. — reprinted, considerably revised, in Flores and Swander, *Franz Kafka Today*, 83-91.

29. MEMOIRS OF THE KALDA RAILROAD
Selma Fraiberg, "Dream and Creation in Kafka," *Partisan Review* XXIII (Winter, 1956)`, 50-51. — reprinted, revised, in William Phillips, *Art and Psychoanalysis*, 24-25.

30. THE MERCHANT MESSNER
Selma Fraiberg, "Dream and Creation in Kafka," *Partisan Review* XXIII (Winter, 1956), 59-66. — reprinted, revised, in William Phillips, *Art and Psychoanalysis*, 42-49.

31. METAMORPHOSIS
Douglas Angus, "Kafka's 'Metamorphosis' and 'The Beauty and the Beast' Tale," *Journal of English and Germanic Philology* LIII (January, 1954), 69-71.
Basil Busacca, "A Country Doctor," in Flores and Swander, *Kafka Today*, 49.
Victor Erlich, "Gogol and Kafka: Note on 'Realism' and 'Surrealism,' " in Morris Halle, *For Roman Jakobson*, 102-104.
George Gibian, *"Dichtung und Wahrheit*: Three Versions of Reality in Franz Kafka," *German Quarterly* XXX (January, 1957), 28-31.
Paul Goodman, "Preface" to Kafka's *Metamorphosis* (trans. by A. L. Lloyd, 1946), 5-8.
A. Desmond Hawkins, "Fiction Chronicle," *Criterion* XVII (April, 1938), 506-508.
Frederick J. Hoffman, *Freudianism and the Literary Mind* (2nd edit., 1957), 184-185.
Norman N. Holland, "Kafka's 'Metamorphosis': Realism and Unrealism," *Modern Fiction Studies* IV (Summer, 1958), 143-150.
Paul L. Landsberg, "Kafka and 'The Metamorphosis,' " *Quarterly Review of Literature* II, No. 3, (1945), 228-236. — reprinted in Angel Flores, *The Kafka Problem*, 122-133.
Henry Loeblowitz-Lennard, "Some Leitmotifs in Franz Kafka's Work Psychoanalytically Explored," *University of Kansas City Review* XIII (Winter, 1946), 115-118.
R. M. Ludwig and M. B. Perry, *Nine Short Novels*, xlv-xlvii.
F. D. Luke, "Kafka's 'Die Verwandlung,' " *Modern Language*

KAFKA, FRANZ, Continued

Review XLVI (April, 1951), 232-245. — reprinted in Flores and Swander, *Kafka Today*, 25-43.

William A. Madden, "A Myth of Mediation: Kafka's 'Metamorphosis,' " *Thought* XXVI (Summer, 1951), 246-266.

Charles Neider, *The Frozen Sea*, 77-78.

Charles Neider, *Short Novels of the Masters*, 45-47.

I. F. Parry, "Kafka and Gogol," *German Life and Letters* VI, No. 2, n.s. (January, 1953), 143-144.

Renato Poggioli, "Kafka and Dostoevsky," in Angel Flores, *The Kafka Problem*, 102-104.

Heinz Politzer, "Franz Kafka's Letter to His Father," *Germanic Review* XXVIII (October, 1953), 173-175.

Philip Rahv, "Franz Kafka: The Hero as Lonely Man," *Kenyon Review* I (Winter, 1939), 67-68.

Philip Rahv, "Introduction" to *Selected Stories of Franz Kafka* (Modern Library, 1952), xi-xii, xix-xx.

Francis Russell, *Three Studies in Twentieth Century Obscurity*, 52-54.

Nathan A. Scott, Jr., *Rehearsals of Discomposure*, 37-39.

Joachim H. Seyppel, "The Animal Theme and Totemism in Franz Kafka," *Literature and Psychology* IV (September, 1954), 59-60.

Harry Slochower, *No Voice Is Wholly Lost*, 105.

Walter H. Sokel, "Kafka's 'Metamorphosis': Rebellion and Punishment," *Monatshefte* XLVIII (April-May, 1956), 203-214.

Herbert Tauber, *Franz Kafka*, 18-26.

32. MY NEIGHBOR
Herbert Tauber, *Franz Kafka*, 69.

33. THE NEXT VILLAGE
Herbert Tauber, *Franz Kafka*, 73-74.

34. AN OLD PAGE
Winifred Lynskey, *Reading Modern Fiction*, (Second Edition, 1957), 320-322.
Herbert Tauber, *Franz Kafka*, 68.

35. ON A LITTLE RAILWAY IN RUSSIA
Herbert Tauber, *Franz Kafka*, 121-122.

36. PROMETHEUS
Herbert Tauber, *Franz Kafka*, 73.

37. THE REFUSAL
Herbert Tauber, *Franz Kafka*, 130.

38. A REPORT TO AN ACADEMY
Robert Kauf, "Once Again: Kafka's 'A Report to an Academy,' " *Modern Language Quarterly* XV (December, 1954), 359-365.

Claude-Edmonde Magny, "The Objective Depiction of Absurdity," *Quarterly Review of Literature* II, No. 3 (1945), 222-224. — reprinted in Angel Flores, *The Kafka Problem*, 89-92.

William C. Rubinstein, "Franz Kafka's 'A Report to an Academy,'" *Modern Language Quarterly* XIII (December, 1952), 372-376. — reprinted in Flores and Swander, *Kafka Today*, 55-60.

Herbert Tauber, *Franz Kafka*, 67, 70-71.

39. THE STOKER

H. E. Jacob, "Truth for Truth's Sake," in Angel Flores, *The Kafka Problem*, 59.

Robert Donald Spector, "Kafka's 'The Stoker' As Short Story," *Modern Fiction Studies* II (May, 1956), 80-81.

Guy Stern, "'Explication de Texte' at the Fourth Semester Level," *Modern Language Journal* XLI (January, 1957), 37-38.

Herbert Tauber, *Franz Kafka*, 30-32.

40. THE WHITE HORSE

Selma Fraiberg, "Kafka and the Dream," in William Phillips, *Art and Psychoanalysis*, 34-42.

KIPLING, RUDYARD

1. AS EASY AS A. B. C.

J. M. S. Tompkins, "Kipling's Later Tales: The Theme of Healing," *Modern Language Review* XLV (January, 1950), 31-32.

2. BROTHER SQUARE-TOES

Ann M. Weygandt, "A Study of Kipling's Use of Historical Materials in 'Brother Square-Toes' and 'A Priest in Spite of Himself,'" *Delaware Notes* XXVII (1954), 83-106.

3. THE BRUSHWOOD BOY

Walter Morris Hart, *Kipling: The Story Writer*, 181-191.

4. THE CHILDREN OF THE ZODIAC

J. M. S. Tompkins, "Kipling's Later Tales: The Theme of Healing," *Modern Language Review* XLV (January, 1950), 22-23.

5. THE CONVERSION OF AURELIAN McGOGGIN

John Palmer, *Rudyard Kipling* (Third Edition, 1928), 44-46.

6. DAYSPRING MISHANDLED

Esther Kaufman, "Kipling and the Technique of Action," *Nineteenth Century Fiction* VI (September, 1951), 109-111.

Edward Shanks, *Rudyard Kipling*, 246-250.

7. THE ENEMIES TO EACH OTHER

J. M. S. Tompkins, "Kipling's Later Tales: The Theme of Heal-

KIPLING, RUDYARD, Continued

ing," *Modern Language Review* XLV (January, 1950) , 29-30.

8. THE EYE OF ALLAH
Bonamy Dobrée, *Rudyard Kipling,* 14-15.
J. M. S. Tompkins, "Kipling's Later Tales: The Theme of Healing," *Modern Language Review* XLV (January, 1950), 20-21.

9. FALSE DAWN
C. E. Carrington, *The Life of Rudyard Kipling,* 71-73.

10. FRIENDLY BROOK
Edward Shanks, *Rudyard Kipling,* 206-208.

11. AN HABITATION ENFORCED
Edward Shanks, *Rudyard Kipling,* 198-204.

12. THE HEAD OF THE DISTRICT
John Palmer, *Rudyard Kipling* (Third Edition, 1928) , 47-50.
Alfred C. Ward, *Aspects of the Modern Short Story,* 119-122.

13. KAA'S HUNTING
Edward Shanks, *Rudyard Kipling,* 160-164.

14. THE KING'S ANKUS
Walter Morris Hart, *Kipling: The Story Writer,* 144-152.

15. LOVE-O'-WOMEN
Edward Shanks, *Rudyard Kipling,* 60-63.

16. A MADONNA OF THE TRENCHES
J. M. S. Tompkins, "Kipling's Later Tales: The Themes of Healing," *Modern Language Review* XLV (January, 1950) , 23-25.

17. THE MAN WHO WOULD BE KING
Brooks and Warren, *Understanding Fiction,* 61-64.
Paul Russell, Jr., "Irony, Freemasonry, and Humane Ethics in Kipling's 'The Man Who Would Be King," *ELH* XXV (September, 1958) , 216-233.

18. THE MARK OF THE BEAST
Boris Ford, "A Case for Kipling?" in Eric Bentley, *Importance of Scrutiny,* 334.
Alfred C. Ward, *Aspects of the Modern Short Sory,* 124-125.

19. MARY POSTGATE
Noel Annan, "Kipling the Conservative," *Listener* LII, No. 1333 (1954) , 439.
Boris Ford, "A Case for Kipling?" in Eric Bentley, *Importance of Scrutiny,* 334-336.

20. MY SON'S WIFE
T. S. Eliot, *A Choice of Kipling's Verse,* 33.

21. ON GREENHOW HILL
Gordon and Tate, *The House of Fiction,* 244-247.

128

KIPLING, RUDYARD, Continued

22. THE PHANTOM RICKSHAW
Peter Penzoldt, *The Supernatural in Fiction*, 127-132.
23. 'A PRIEST IN SPITE OF HIMSELF'
Ann M. Weygandt, "A Study of Kipling's Use of Historical Materials in 'Brother Square-Toes' and 'A Priest in Spite of Himself,'" *Delaware Notes* XXVII (1954), 83-106.
24. THE RESCUE OF PLUFFLES
Esther Kaufman, "Kipling and the Technique of Action," *Nineteenth Century Fiction* VI (September, 1951), 117-118.
25. THE TENDER ACHILLES
J. M. S. Tompkins, "Kipling's Later Tales: The Theme of Healing," *Modern Language Review* XLV (January, 1950), 27-28.
26. 'THEY'
Walter Morris Hart, *Kipling: The Story Writer*, 194-202.
R. Thurston Hopkins, *Rudyard Kipling: A Literary Appreciation*, 67-71.
Peter Penzoldt, *The Supernatural in Fiction*, 134-142.
Edward Shanks, *Rudyard Kipling*, 252-256.
27. TODS' AMENDMENT
John Palmer, *Rudyard Kipling* (Third Edition, 1928), 41-44.
28. UNPROFESSIONAL
J. M. S. Tompkins, "Kipling's Later Tales: The Theme of Healing," *Modern Language Review* XLV (January, 1950), 21-22.
29. THE WISH HOUSE
J. M. S. Tompkins, "Kipling's Later Tales: The Theme of Healing," *Modern Language Review* XLV (January, 1950), 23-24.
30. WITHOUT BENEFIT OF CLERGY
Walter Morris Hart, *Kipling: The Story Writer*, 69-80.

KOMROFF, MANUEL

1. HAMLET'S DAGGER
Edward J. O'Brien, *The Short Story Case Book*, 389-403.

LAGERKVIST, PÄR

1. FATHER AND I
Royal A. Gettmann and Bruce Harkness, *Teacher's Manual for "A Book of Stories,"* 30-33.

LARDNER, RING

1. ALABI IKE
   Gilbert Seldes, "Introduction" to Seldes, *Portable Ring Lardner*, 6.
2. A CADDY'S DIARY
   James T. Farrell, *The League of Frightened Philistines*, 33-34.
3. EX PARTE
   Jarvis Thurston, *Reading Modern Short Stories*, 42-51.
4. GOLDEN HONEYMOON
   Douglas Bement, *Weaving the Short Story*, 253-281.
   Donald Elder, *Ring Lardner: A Biography*, 209-211.
   Clifton Fadiman, "Ring Lardner and the Triangle of Hate," *Nation* CXXXVI (March 22, 1933), 316.
   James T. Farrell, *The League of Frightened Philistines*, 34-35.
5. HAIRCUT
   Donald Elder, *Ring Lardner: A Biography*, 237-238.
   Margaret C. Kasten, "The Satire of Ring Lardner," *English Journal* XXXVI (April, 1947), 194-195.
   Gorham Munson, "The Recapture of the Storyable," *University Review* X (Autumn, 1943), 42.
6. HORSESHOES
   Delmore Schwartz, "Ring Lardner, Highbrow in Hiding," *Reporter* XV (August 9, 1956), 52.
7. LOVE NEST
   John Berryman, "The Case of Ring Lardner: Art and Entertainment," *Commentary* XXII (November, 1956), 420-421.
8. MY ROOMY
   Donald Elder, *Ring Lardner: A Biography*, 207-208.
9. SOME LIKE THEM COLD
   Stegner, Scowcroft, and Ilyin, *The Writer's Art*, 133-135.

LAWRENCE, D. H.

1. THE BLIND MAN
   Beardsley, Daniel, and Leggett, *Aids to Study for "Themes and Form: An Introduction to Literature,"* 96.
   Harry T. Moore, *The Life and Works of D. H. Lawrence*, 204-205.
   Mark Spilka, "Was D. H. Lawrence a Symbolist," *Accent* XV (Winter, 1955), 56-59. — reprinted, with additions, in Mark Spilka, *The Love Ethic of D. H. Lawrence*, 25-30, 151-153.
   Richard B. Vowles, "Lawrence's 'The Blind Man,'" *Explicator* XI (December, 1952), item 14.

LAWRENCE, D. H., Continued

2. BLUE MOCCASINS
   Harry T. Moore, *The Life and Works of D. H. Lawrence,* 271-272.
   Kingsley Widmer, "Birds of Passion and Birds of Marriage in D. H. Lawrence," *University of Kansas City Review* XXV (Autumn, 1958), 74.
3. THE BORDER LINE
   Graham Hough, *The Dark Sun,* 187-188.
   Harry T. Moore, *The Life and Works of D. H. Lawrence,* 245-246.
   Anthony West, "The Short Stories," in Hoffman and Moore, *The Achievement of D. H. Lawrence,* 216-221.
4. THE CAPTAIN'S DOLL
   Monroe Engel, "The Continuity of Lawrence's Short Novels," *Hudson Review* XI (Summer, 1958), 203-204.
   Dorothy M. Hoare, *Some Studies in the Modern Novel,* 108-109.
   Graham Hough, *The Dark Sun,* 177-179.
   F. R. Leavis, " 'The Captain's Doll,' " *Scrutiny* XIX (October, 1953), 273-296. — reprinted, with additional material, in Leavis, *D. H. Lawrence: Novelist,* 48-52, 242-278.
   Anthony West, "The Short Stories," in Hoffman and Moore, *The Achievement of D. H. Lawrence,* 216.
5. DAUGHTERS OF THE VICAR
   Graham Hough, *The Dark Sun,* 170.
   F. R. Leavis, "Lawrence and Class," *Sewanee Review* LXII (Autumn, 1954), 535-562. — reprinted, with additions, in. F. R. Leavis, *D. H. Lawrence: Novelist,* 55-56, 77-95, 100-107, 122.
   Mark Spilka, *The Love Ethic of D. H. Lawrence,* 203.
   Eliseo Vivas, "Mr. Leavis on D. H. Lawrence," *Sewanee Review* LXV (Winter, 1957), 124-126.
6. ENGLAND, MY ENGLAND
   Graham Hough, *The Dark Sun,* 172-173.
   F. R. Leavis, *D. H. Lawrence: Novelist,* 332-335.
   Harry T. Moore, *The Intelligent Heart,* 224-225.
   Harry T. Moore, *The Life and Works of D. H. Lawrence,* 200-201.
   Anthony West, "The Short Stories," in Hoffman and Moore, *The Achievement of D. H. Lawrence.* 212.
7. THE ESCAPED COCK
   (see "The Man Who Died")
8. FANNIE AND ANNIE
   F. R. Leavis, "Lawrence and Class," *Sewanee Review* LXII (Autumn, 1954), 552-556. — reprinted in F. R. Leavis, *D. H. Lawrence: Novelist,* 95-100.

LAWRENCE, D. H., Continued

9. THE FOX
Monroe Engel, "The Continuity of Lawrence's Short Novels,"
Hudson Review XI (Summer, 1958), 201-203.
Graham Hough, *The Dark Sun*, 176-177.
F. R. Leavis, *D. H. Lawrence: Novelist*, 320-332.
Charles Neider, *Short Novels of the Masters*, 43-44.
10. GLAD GHOSTS
Harry T. Moore, *The Life and Works of D. H. Lawrence*, 252-254.
11. THE HORSE DEALER'S DAUGHTER
Brooks, Purser, and Warren, *An Approach to Literature*, 186-188.
F. R. Leavis, *D. H. Lawrence: Novelist*, 311-315.
Mark Schorer, *The Story*, 326-329.
12. JIMMY AND THE DESPERATE WOMAN
Harry T. Moore, *The Life and Works of D. H. Lawrence*, 247.
13. THE LAST LAUGH
Harry T. Moore, *The Intelligent Heart*, 332.
Harry T. Moore, *The Life and Works of D. H. Lawrence*, 248-250.
14. THE LADYBIRD
Monroe Engel, "The Continuity of Lawrence's Short Novels,"
Hudson Review XI (Summer, 1958), 204-206.
Graham Hough, *The Dark Sun*, 175-176.
F. R. Leavis, *D. H. Lawrence: Novelist*, 55-66.
Harry T. Moore, *The Life and Works of D. H. Lawrence*, 208.
Father William Tiverton, *D. H. Lawrence and Human Existence*,
45-46.
Anthony West, "The Short Stories," in Hoffman and Moore, *The
Achievement of D. H. Lawrence*, 212-213.
15. THE LOVELY LADY
Harry T. Moore, *The Life and Works of D. H. Lawrence*, 272-275.
16. THE MAN WHO DIED
Monroe Engel, "The Continuity of Lawrence's Short Novels,"
Hudson Review XI (Summer, 1958), 208-209.
Mary Freeman, *D. H. Lawrence*, 208-209.
Gilbert Highet, *People, Places, and Books*, 41-42.
Frederick J. Hoffman, *Freudianism and the Literary Mind* (2nd
edition, 1957), 159. — reprinted, revised, from Hoffman, *Freudian-
ism* (1st edition, 1945), in Hoffman and Moore, *The Achievement
of D. H. Lawrence*, 114-115.
Graham Hough, *The Dark Sun*, 189-190, 246-252.
Milton Miller, "Definition by Comparison: Chaucer, Lawrence,
and Joyce," *Essays in Criticism* III (October, 1953), 374-377.
Harry T. Moore, *The Intelligent Heart*, 364-365.

Harry T. Moore, *The Life and Works of D. H. Lawrence*, 286-288.

Edwin Muir, Review of *The Tales of D. H. Lawrence, Listener* XI, No. 273 (1934), 596.

J. M. Murry, "The Escaped Cock," *Criterion* X (October, 1930), 183-188.

J. M. Murry, *Love, Freedom and Society*, 77-78, 93-94, 103-104, 119-121.

Mark Spilka, *The Love Ethic of D. H. Lawrence*, 219-231.

H. Steinhauer, "Eros and Psyche: A Nietzschean Motif in Anglo-American Literature," *Modern Language Notes* LXIV (April, 1949), 223-225.

William Y. Tindall, *The Later D. H. Lawrence*, 397-398.

Diana Trilling, "Introduction" to *The Portable D. H. Lawrence*, 29.

17. THE MAN WHO LOVED ISLANDS

F. R. Leavis, *D. H. Lawrence: Novelist*, 337-339.

Harry T. Moore, *The Life and Works of D. H. Lawrence*, 252.

Anthony West, "The Short Stories," in Hoffman and Moore, *The Achievement of D. H. Lawrence*, 204-206.

Kingsley Widmer, "D. H. Lawrence and the Art of Nihilism," *Kenyon Review* XX (Autumn, 1958), 610-615.

18. MOTHER AND DAUGHTER

F. R. Leavis, *D. H. Lawrence: Novelist*, 346-351.

Harry T. Moore, *The Life and Works of D. H. Lawrence*, 269-271.

19. NONE OF THAT

Harry T. Moore, *The Life and Works of D. H. Lawrence*, 254-255.

Richard Rees, *Brave Men*, 68-69.

20. THE ODOUR OF CHRYSANTHEMUMS

Frank Amon, "D. H. Lawrence and the Short Story," in Hoffman and Moore, *The Achievement of D. H. Lawrence*, 223-226.

Ford Madox Ford, *Portraits from Life*, 70-74; or *Mightier Than the Sword* (English Edition), 98-103.

Royal A. Gettmann and Bruce Harkness, *Teacher's Manual for "A Book of Stories,"* 18-21.

W. Havighurst, "Symbolism and the Student," *College English* XVI (April, 1955), 429-434.

21. THE OVERTONE

Harry T. Moore, *The Life and Works of D. H. Lawrence*, 275-276.

22. THE PRIMROSE PATH

Harry T. Moore, *The Life and Works of D. H. Lawrence*, 203.

23. THE PRINCESS

Graham Hough, *The Dark Sun*, 179-180.

LAWRENCE, D. H., Continued

F. R. Leavis, *D. H. Lawrence: Novelist,* 336-337, 339-342.
Harry T. Moore, *The Intelligent Heart,* 331-332.
Harry T. Moore, *The Life and Works of D. H. Lawrence,* 228-230.
Anaïs Nin, *D. H. Lawrence,* 139-140.

24. THE PRUSSIAN OFFICER
Frank Amon, "D. H. Lawrence and the Short Story," in Hoffman and Moore, *The Achievement of D. H. Lawrence,* 226-231.
Philip Appleman, "D. H. Lawrence and the Intrusive Knock," *Modern Fiction Studies* III (Winter, 1957-1958), 328-329.
Robert G. Davis, *Instructor's Manual for "Ten Modern Masters,"* 47-48.
Harry T. Moore, *The Intelligent Heart,* 147-149.
Mark Spilka, *The Love Ethic of D. H. Lawrence,* 172.
Anthony West, "The Short Stories," in Hoffman and Moore, *The Achievement of D. H. Lawrence,* 215-216.
Kingsley Widmer, "D. H. Lawrence and the Art of Nihilism," *Kenyon Review* XX (Autumn, 1958), 604-610.

25. THE ROCKING-HORSE WINNER
Frank Amon, "D. H. Lawrence and the Short Story," in Hoffman and Moore, *The Achievement of D. H. Lawrence,* 231–233.
Robert G. Davis, *Instructor's Manual for "Ten Modern Masters,"* 50.
Wallace Douglas, *The Critical Reader,* 274-280.
Gordon and Tate, *House of Fiction,* 348-351.
Graham Hough, *The Dark Sun,* 188.
Harry T. Moore, *The Life and Works of D. H. Lawrence,* 277-279.
Richard Rees, *Brave Men,* 94.
W. D. Snodgrass, "A Rocking-Horse: The Symbol, the Pattern, the Way to Live," *Hudson Review* XI (Summer, 1958), 191-200.

26. SAMSON AND DELILAH
F. R. Leavis, *D. H. Lawrence: Novelist,* 310-311.

27. SECOND BEST
Harry T. Moore, *The Life and Works of D. H. Lawrence,* 114-115.

28. THE SHADES OF SPRING
Philip Appleman, "One of D. H. Lawrence's 'Autobiographical' Characters," *Modern Fiction Studies* II (Winter, 1956-1957), 237-238.
Robert G. Davis, *Instructor's Manual for "Ten Modern Masters,"* 49.

29. THE SHADOW IN THE ROSE GARDEN
Herbert Barrows, *Suggestions for Teaching "15 Stories,"* 29-31.
T. S. Eliot, *After Strange Gods,* 36-37.

LAWRENCE, D. H., Continued

Harry T. Moore, *The Life and Works of D. H. Lawrence*, 117-118.
Sale, Hall, and Steinmann, *Critical Discussions for Teachers Using "Short Stories: Tradition and Direction,"* 28-30.
Stephen Spender, *The Destructive Element*, 168-169.
30. SMILE
Harry T. Moore, *The Life and Works of D. H. Lawrence*, 250-251.
31. ST. MAWR
David Craig, "Mr. Liddell and Dr. Leavis," *Essays in Criticism* V (January, 1955), 64-67.
Monroe Engel, "The Continuity of Lawrence's Short Novels," *Hudson Review* XI (Summer, 1958), 206-208.
Gilbert Highet, *People, Places, and Books*, 39-41.
Graham Hough, *The Dark Sun*, 179-186.
F. R. Leavis, "The Novel As Dramatic Poem (IV) : 'St. Mawr,' " *Scrutiny* XVII (Spring, 1950), 38-53. — reprinted, with additions, in Leavis, *D. H. Lawrence: Novelist*, 48-49, 279-306, 346-347.
Robert Liddell, "Lawrence and Dr. Leavis: The Case of 'St. Mawr,' " *Essays in Criticism* IV (July, 1954), 322-327.
Harry T. Moore, *The Intelligent Heart*, 330-331.
Harry T. Moore, *The Life and Works of D. H. Lawrence*, 225-228.
J. M. Murry, *Love, Freedom and Society*, 24-28, 34-38.
Richard Rees, *Brave Men*, 118-119.
Mark Roberts, "Mr. Liddell and Dr. Leavis," *Essays in Criticism* V (January, 1955), 68-75.
T. W. Thomas, "Mr. Liddell and Dr. Leavis," *Essays in Criticism* V (January, 1955), 76-80.
William Y. Tindall, *The Later D. H. Lawrence*, 3-4.
Eliseo Vivas, "Mr. Leavis on D. H. Lawrence," *Sewanee Review* LXV (Winter, 1957), 126-127.
32. SUN
F. R. Leavis, *D. H. Lawrence: Novelist*, 355-357.
Harry T. Moore, *The Life and Works of D. H. Lawrence*, 256-258.
Anaïs Nin, *D. H. Lawrence*, 10.
Mark Spilka, *The Love Ethic of D. H. Lawrence*, 41-42.
William Y. Tindall, *The Later D. H. Lawrence*, xv, 299.
John Wain, "The Teaching of D. H. Lawrence," *Twentieth Century* CLVII (May, 1955), 464-465.
33. THINGS
F. R. Leavis, *D. H. Lawrence: Novelist*, 357-362.
Harry T. Moore, *The Life and Works of D. H. Lawrence*, 279-281.
Anthony West, "The Short Stories," in Hoffman and Moore, *The Achievement of D. H. Lawrence*, 211-212.

LAWRENCE, D. H., Continued

34. THE THORN IN THE FLESH
Anthony West, "The Short Stories," in Hoffman and Moore, *The Achievement of D. H. Lawrence*, 215.

35. TWO BLUE BIRDS
F. R. Leavis, *D. H. Lawrence: Novelist*, 351-355.
Kingsley Widmer, "Birds of Passion and Birds of Marriage in D. H. Lawrence," *University of Kansas City Review* XXV (Autumn, 1958), 77-79.

36. WHITE STOCKINGS
F. R. Leavis, *D. H. Lawrence: Novelist*, 308-310.

37. THE WINTRY PEACOCK
James B. Hall and Joseph Langland, *The Short Story*, 250-251.
Kingsley Widmer, "Birds of Passion and Birds of Marriage in D. H. Lawrence," *University of Kansas City Review* XXV (Autumn, 1958), 74-77.

38. THE WOMAN WHO RODE AWAY
Graham Hough, *The Dark Sun*, 138-146.
F. R. Leavis, *D. H. Lawrence: Novelist*, 342-346.
John Heywood Thomas, "The Perversity of D. H. Lawrence," *Criterion* X (October, 1930), 12-13.
William Y. Tindall, *The Later D. H. Lawrence*, 299-300.
Anthony West, "The Short Stories," in Hoffman and Moore, *The Achievement of D. H. Lawrence*, 214-215.

39. YOU TOUCHED ME
Graham Hough, *The Dark Sun*, 173-174.
F. R. Leavis, *D. H. Lawrence: Novelist*, 315-321.

LE FANU, J. SHERIDAN

1. GREEN TEA
Peter Penzoldt, *The Supernatural in Fiction*, 77.
V. S. Pritchett, *The Living Novel*, 105-106.

LESKOV, NICHOLAS

1. THE ENCHANTED WANDERER
Marc Slonim, *Modern Russian Literature*, 47-48.

LE SUEUR, MERIDEL

1. ANUNCIATION
   Mary Orvis, *The Art of Writing Fiction*, 233-234.
2. BREATHE UPON THESE SLAIN
   Mary Orvis, *The Art of Writing Fiction*, 149-151.

LEWIS, ALUN

1 THE RAID
  Herbert Barrows, *Suggestions for Teaching "15 Stories,"* 27-28.

LEWIS, WYNDHAM

1. CANTELMAN'S SPRING-MATE
   Hugh Kenner, "The Revenge of the Void," *Hudson Review* VI
   (Autumn, 1953), 390-392.

LIASHKO, N.

1. THE SONG OF THE CHAINS
   Alfred Dashiell, *Editor's Choice*, 259-260.

LIVESAY, DOROTHY

1. THE GLASS HOUSE
   Kenneth Kempton, *Short Stories for Study*, 182-187.

LONDON, JACK

1. IN A FAR COUNTRY
   Sam S. Baskett, "Jack London's Heart of Darkness," *American
   Quarterly* X (Spring, 1958), 67-70.

LOVECRAFT, H. P.

1. THE MUSIC OF ERICH ZANN
   James B. Hall and Joseph Langland, *The Short Story*, 157-159.

MACAULEY, ROBIE

1. THE INVADERS
Kenneth Kempton, *Short Stories for Study*, 204-211.

MALAMUD, BERNARD

1. ANGEL LEVINE
Dan Jacobson, "Magic and Morality," *Commentary* XXVI (October, 1958), 360.
2. THE PRISON
Kenneth Kempton, *Short Stories for Study*, 316-321.

MANHEIM, RALPH

1. THE GIRL WHO LOVED SEDERS
Judah Goldin, "The Contemporary Jew and His Judaism," in S. R. Hopper, *Spiritual Problems in Contemporary Literature*, 221-222.

MANN, THOMAS

1. AT THE PROPHET'S
Henry Hatfield, *Thomas Mann*, 27-28.
2. BASHAN AND I
(see "A Man and His Dog")
3. THE BLACK SWAN
Anon., "Unhappy Widow," *Times (London) Literary Supplement* (April 9, 1954), 229.
Carlos Baker, "Facts of Life—and Death," *Nation* CLXXVIII (June 19, 1954), 526-527.
Joseph Frank, "Mann—Death and Transfiguration," *New Republic* CXXXI (July 5, 1954), 18-19.
Brendan Gill, "Lean Years," *New Yorker* XXX (July 10, 1954), 70-71.
Gilbert Highet, "Life and Health, Disease and Death," *Harper's Magazine* CCIX (July, 1954), 93.
F. D. Hirschbach, *The Arrow and the Lyre*, 24-26.
J. M. Lindsay, *Thomas Mann*, 25-26, 54--55.
George D. Painter, "A Review of 'The Black Swan,' by Thomas Mann," *Listener* LII, No. 1343 (1954), 927.

Idris Parry, "Thomas Mann's Latest Phase," *German Life and Letters* VIII, n.s. (July, 1955), 241-246.

Virgilia Peterson, "A Nocturne in Mann Minor, *New York Herald Tribune Books* (June 6, 1954), 2.

Richard Plant, "The Late Sorrow," *New York Times Book Review* (June 6, 1954), 6.

Patrick Quinn, "Fiction Chronicle," *Hudson Review* VII (Autumn, 1954), 462-463.

Philip Rahv, "The Triumph of Decay," *Commentary* XVIII (July, 1954), 82-84.

Charles J. Rolo, "Of Love and Death," *Atlantic Monthly* CXCIV (July, 1954), 83.

4. THE BLOOD OF THE WALSUNGS

James A. Fuller, "The Humanism of Thomas Mann, *CEA Critic* XX (October, 1958), 7.

Henry Hatfield, *Thomas Mann*, 28-29.

F. D. Hirschbach, *The Arrow and the Lyre*, 9-10.

5. DEATH

Lydia Baer, *The Concept and the Function of Death in the Works of Thomas Mann*, 11.

6. DEATH IN VENICE

Lydia Baer, *The Concept and the Function of Death in the Works of Thomas Mann*, 33-39.

Berthold Biermann, "Thomas Mann and Goethe," in Charles Neider, *The Stature of Thomas Mann*, 245.

R. P. Blackmur, "In the Country of the Blue," *Kenyon Review* V (Autumn, 1943), 602-603. – reprinted in John W. Aldridge, *Critiques and Essays on Modern Fiction*, 308. – reprinted in F. W. Dupee, *The Question of Henry James*, 197-198.

John Bovey, "Death in Venice: Structure and Image," *Twice a Year* 5 and 6 (Fall-Winter, 1940), (Spring-Summer, 1940), 238-246.

Joseph Brennan, *Thomas Mann's World*, 46-48, 127-129.

Edwin Berry Burgum, "The Sense of the Present in Thomas Mann," *Antioch Review* II (Fall, 1942), 400-401.

Kenneth Burke, *Counter-Statement*, 92-95. – reprinted in Charles Neider, *The Stature of Thomas Mann*, 255-258. – reprinted in Zabel, *Literary Opinion in America* (Revised Edition, 1951), 243-245.

Cyril Connolly, *The Condemned Playground*, 66-67.

Malcolm Cowley, "The Last Great European," *New Republic* LXXXVII (June 24, 1936), 213.

MANN, THOMAS, Continued

H. Eichner, "Aspects of Parody in the Works of Thomas Mann," *Modern Language Review* XLVII (January, 1952), 34.

Arthur Eloesser, *Modern German Literature,* 233-234. — reprinted in Neider, *The Stature of Thomas Mann,* 424-425.

D. J. Enright, "Thomas Mann and the Abyss," *Scrutiny* XI (Summer, 1943), 317-318.

Bruno Frank, "Death in Venice," in Neider, *The Stature of Thomas Mann,* 120-123.

André von Gronicka, " 'Myth Plus Psychology': A Style Analysis of 'Death in Venice,' " *Germanic Review* XXXI (October, 1956), 191-205.

Albert J. Guerard, *André Gide,* 113-116.

Lorraine Gustafson, "Xenophon and *Der Tod in Venedig,*" *Germanic Review* XXI (October, 1946), 209-214.

Henry Hatfield, *Thomas Mann,* 61-63.

Erich Heller, *The Ironic German,* 98-115.

F. D. Hirschbach, *The Arrow and the Lyre,* 17-21.

Frederick J. Hoffman, *Freudianism and the Literary Mind* (Second Edition, 1957), 212.

Heinz Kohut, " 'Death in Venice' by Thomas Mann: A Story About the Disintegration of Artistic Sublimation," *Psychoanalytic Quarterly* XXVI (1957), 206-228.

Louis Kronenberger, "Finely Wrought Fiction," *Saturday Review of Literature* I (June 27, 1925), 851.

Joseph Wood Krutch, "Swan Song," *Nation* CXX (May 25, 1925), 330.

Ludwig Lewisohn, "Preface," in Mann's *Death in Venice* (Knopf, 1930), v-xv. — reprinted in Charles Neider, *The Stature of Thomas Mann,* 124-128.

J. M. Lindsay, *Thomas Mann,* 41-43, 50-51.

George Lupacs, "The Stature of Thomas Mann," *Masses and Mainstream* VIII (September, 1955), 24.

George March, "Thomas Mann and the Novel of Decadence," *Sewanee Review* XXXVII (October, 1927), 497-499.

Charles Neider, *Short Novels of the Masters,* 48-51.

Charles Neider, *The Stature of Thomas Mann,* 354-356.

R. A. Nicholls, *Nietzsche in the Early Work of Thomas Mann* 77-91.

W. H. Rey, "Tragic Aspects of the Artist in Thomas Mann's Work," *Modern Language Quarterly* XIX (September, 1958), 197-203.

M. L. Rosenthal, "The Corruption of Aschenbach," *University of Kansas City Review* XIV (Autumn, 1947), 49-56.

Joachim H. Seyppel, "Two Variations on a Theme: Dying in Venice," *Literature and Psychology* VII (February, 1957), 8-12.

George N. Shuster, "Art at War with the Good," in R. M. MacIver, *Great Moral Dilemmas in Literature, Past and Present*, 25-36.

R. Hinton Thomas, *Thomas Mann*, 59-84.

William Y. Tindall, *The Literary Symbol*, 222-224.

William Troy, "Thomas Mann: Myth and Reason," *Partisan Review* V (June, 1938), 28.

Constance Urdang, "Faust in Venice: The Artist and the Legend in 'Death in Venice,'" *Accent* XVIII (Autumn, 1958), 253-267.

Vernon Venable, "Poetic Reason in Thomas Mann," *Virginia Quarterly Review* XIV (Winter, 1938), 61-76. — reprinted in Neider, *The Stature of Thomas Mann*, 129-141.

Cuthbert Wright, "Eros," *Dial* LXXVIII (May, 1925), 420-425.

7. THE DILETTANTE

F. D. Hirschbach, *The Arrow and the Lyre*, 8-9.

Charles Neider, "Thomas Mann: The Artist as Bourgeois," *Rocky Mountain Review* IX (Summer, 1945), 172. — reprinted, revised, in Neider, *The Stature of Thomas Mann*, 334-335.

R. A. Nicholls, *Nietzsche in the Early Work of Thomas Mann*, 12.

R. Hinton Thomas, *Thomas Mann*, 26-29.

8. DISILLUSIONMENT

R. A. Nicholls, *Nietzsche in the Early Work of Thomas Mann*, 13-14.

R. Hinton Thomas, *Thomas Mann*, 20-21.

9. DISORDER AND EARLY SORROW

Walter Brooks, "The Leisure Arts," *Outlook* CLIV (February 26, 1930), 348.

Robert G. Davis, *Instructor's Manual for "Ten Modern Masters,"* 42-43.

Henry Hatfield, *Thomas Mann*, 87-88.

Jarvis Thurston, *Reading Modern Short Stories*, 7-8, 9-10, 20, 21, 27-28.

Petrie Townshend, "Short Stories," *Life and Letters of Today* XV (Winter, 1936-1937), 201.

Felix Wittmer, "Introduction," in Mann's *Unordnung und frühes Leid*, (German Edition, Prentice-Hall, 1930), 3-5.

10. FALLEN

F. D. Hirschbach, *The Arrow and the Lyre*, 3-5.

MANN, THOMAS, Continued

11. THE FIGHT BETWEEN JAPPE AND DO ESCOBAR
Robert G. Davis, *Instructor's Manual for "Ten Modern Masters,"* 41-42.

12. GLADIUS DEI
James A. Fuller, "The Humanism of Thomas Mann," *CEA Critic* XX (October, 1958), 6.
Henry Hatfield, *Thomas Mann,* 22-23.

13. A GLEAM
James B. Hall and Joseph Langland, *The Short Story,* 370.
Henry Hatfield, *Thomas Mann,* 27.

14. LITTLE HERR FRIEDEMANN
Lydia Baer, *The Concept and the Function of Death in the Works of Thomas Mann,* 12.
Robert G. Davis, *Instructor's Manual for "Ten Modern Masters,"* 40-41.
James A. Fuller, "The Humanism of Thomas Mann," *CEA Critic,* XX (October, 1958), 1, 6.
Henry Hatfield, *Thomas Mann,* 17-18.
F. D. Hirschbach, *The Arrow and the Lyre,* 5-8.
Charles Neider, "Thomas Mann: The Artist as Bourgeois," *Rocky Mountain Review* IX (Summer, 1945), 171-172. – reprinted, revised, in Neider, *The Stature of Thomas Mann,* 334.
R. A. Nicholls, *Nietzsche in the Early Work of Thomas Mann,* 10-12.
R. Hinton Thomas, *Thomas Mann,* 21-26.
Ray B. West, Jr., "Three Methods of Modern Fiction," *College English* XII (January, 1951), 197-198. – reprinted in West and Stallman, *Art of Modern Fiction,* 316-319.

15. LITTLE LIZZY
Lydia Baer, *The Concept and the Function of Death in the Works of Thomas Mann,* 12.
Thomas A. Fuller, "The Humanism of Thomas Mann," *CEA Critic* XX (October, 1958), 6.
Henry Hatfield, *Thomas Mann,* 19-20.
Charles Neider, "Thomas Mann: The Artist as Bourgeois," *Rocky Mountain Review* IX (Summer, 1945), 172-173. – reprinted, revised, in Charles Neider, *The Stature of Thomas Mann,* 335.

16. A MAN AND HIS DOG
Anon., "Bashan and I," *Times Literary Supplement* XXII (August 9, 1923), 532.
Jenny Ballou, "A Man's Best Friend," *New York Herald Tribune Books* (November 2, 1930), 17.

MANN, THOMAS, Continued

Frank X. Braun, "Thomas Mann's Canine Idyll," *Monatshefte* XLIX (April-May, 1957), 207-211.

Howard Coxe, "An Artist with a Bad Conscience," *New Republic* LXV (Decmber 3, 1930), 79-80.

Henry Hatfield, *Thomas Mann*, 88-89.

17. MARIO AND THE MAGICIAN

Anon., Review in *Times Literary Supplement* XXIX (August 28, 1930), 29.

Joseph Brennan, *Thomas Mann's World*, 150-152.

Malcolm Cowley, "The Last Great European," *New Republic* LXXXVII (June 24, 1936), 213-214.

Clifton Fadiman, *Reading I've Liked*, 31-32.

Clifton Fadiman, "Thomas Mann's Obsession," *Nation* CXXXII (February 11, 1931), 156.

Felheim, Newman, and Steinhoff, *Study Aids for Teachers for "Modern Short Stories,"* 48-51.

L. Hamalian and E. L. Volpe, *Ten Modern Short Novels*, 473-474.

Henry C. Hatfield, "Thomas Mann's 'Mario und der Zauberer': An Interpretation," *Germanic Review* XXI (December, 1946), 306-312. — reprinted, revised, in Charles Neider, *The Stature of Thomas Mann*, 168-173.

Henry Hatfield, *Thomas Mann*, 90-94.

Fritz Kaufmann, *Thomas Mann, The World as Will and Representation*, 217-218.

Louis Kronenberger, "Thomas Mann's Novelette of Hypnotism," *New York Times Book Review* (January 4, 1931), 8.

J. M. Lindsay, *Thomas Mann*, 30-31.

Winifred Lynskey, *Reading Modern Fiction* (Second Edition, 1957), 367-373.

George Lukacs, "The Stature of Thomas Mann," *Masses and Mainstream* VIII (September, 1955), 24.

Percy Matenko, "The Prototype of Cipolla in 'Mario und der Zauberer,'" *Italica* XXXI (September, 1954), 133-135.

Ferner Nuhn, "Three Decades of Thomas Mann's Work," *New York Herald Tribune Books* (June 7, 1936), 1.

William Van O'Connor, "Thomas Mann: The Politics of the Artist," *Meanjin Papers* V (Spring, 1946), 201-202.

Harry Slochower, *No Voice Is Wholly Lost*, 335.

William Leon Smyser, "Mood, Magic, and Murder," *Saturday Review of Literature* VII (February 21, 1931), 616.

Gerald Sykes, *"A Sketch of My Life. Mario and the Magician,"* *Bookman* (New York) LXXII (February, 1931), 640.

MANN, THOMAS, Continued

18. RAILWAY ACCIDENT
Seymour Lainoff, "A Note on Mann's 'Railway Accident,'" *College English* XVIII (October, 1956), 104-105.
Mark Schorer, *The Story*, 16-20.

19. THE TABLES OF THE LAW
Dorothy Donnelly, "Pulling the Lion's Teeth," *Commonweal* XLII (September 7, 1945), 503-504.
Henry Hatfield, *Thomas Mann*, 120-121.
Harold Rosenberg, "The Creation of an Identity," *Commentary* I (November, 1945), 92-94.
D. S. Savage, Review in *Spectator* CLXXVIII (May 30, 1947), 632, 634.

20. TOBIAS MINDERNICKEL
James A. Fuller, "The Humanism of Thomas Mann," *CEA Critic* XX (October, 1958), 6.
Royal A. Gettmann and Bruce Harkness, *Teacher's Manual for "A Book of Stories,"* 9-11.
R. A. Nicholls, *Nietzsche in the Early Work of Thomas Mann*, 13.
R. Hinton Thomas, *Thomas Mann*, 30-32.

21. TONIO KRÖGER
H. A. Basilius, "Thomas Mann's Use of Musical Structure and Techniques in 'Tonio Kröger,'" *Germanic Review* XIX (December, 1944), 284-308.
Joseph Brennan, *Thomas Mann's World*, 11-13, 19-26.
Calvin S. Brown, *Music and Literature*, 213-217.
Arthur Burkhard, "Thomas Mann's Treatment of the Marked Man," *PMLA* XLIII (June, 1928), 561-563.
Harold G. Carlson, "An Artistic Motif," *German Quarterly* XI (November, 1938), 198.
A. F. B. Clark, "The Dialectical Humanism of Thomas Mann," *University of Toronto Quarterly* VIII (October, 1938), 93-94. — reprinted in Charles Neider, *The Stature of Thomas Mann*, 295.
Malcolm Cowley, "The Last Great European," *New Republic* LXXXVII (June 24, 1936), 213.
Henry Hatfield, *Thomas Mann*, 52-56.
Erich Heller, *The Ironic German*, 68-85.
F. D. Hirschbach, *The Arrow and the Lyre*, 14-17.
J. M. Lindsay, *Thomas Mann*, 18, 31, 33-35.
R. M. Ludwig and M. B. Perry, *Nine Short Novels*, xxix-xxxii.
George March, "Thomas Mann and the Novel of Decadence," *Sewanee Review* XXXVII (October, 1927), 494-495.

K. W. Maurer, "Tonio Kröger and Hamlet," *Modern Language Review* XLIII (October, 1948), 520.

Charles Neider, "Thomas Mann: The Artist as Bourgeois," *Rocky Mountain Review* (Summer, 1945), 173-174. — reprinted, revised, in Neider, *The Stature of Thomas Mann*, 336-337; additional material, 353-354.

R. A. Nicholls, *Nietzsche in the Early Work of Thomas Mann*, 21-39.

R. Hinton Thomas, *Thomas Mann*, 1-3.

William Y. Tindall, *The Literary Symbol*, 221-222.

Kenneth G. Wilson, "The Dance as Symbol and Leitmotiv in Thomas Mann's 'Tonio Kröger,'" *Germanic Review* XXIX (December, 1954), 282-287.

22. THE TRANSPOSED HEADS

Anon., Review in *Times Literary Supplement* XL (August 16, 1941), 393.

Curtis Bradford, "Mann's New Excursions," *Sewanee Review* L (Winter, 1942), 142-143.

Joseph Brennan, *Thomas Mann*, 184-187.

Malcolm Cowley, "Finger Exercise," *New Republic* CIV (June 23, 1941), 104.

Else M. Fleissner, "Stylistic Confusion in Thomas Mann's Indian Legend, 'The Transposed Heads,'" *Germanic Review* XVIII (October, 1943), 209-212.

Henry Hatfield, *Thomas Mann*, 126-127.

F. D. Hirschbach, *The Arrow and the Lyre*, 22-24.

Marjorie Lawson, "The Transposed Heads of Goethe and of Mann," *Monatshefte* XXXIV (February, 1942), 87-92.

F. O. Matthiessen, "Thomas Mann's 'Transposed Heads,'" *New Yorker* XVII (June 7, 1941), 74.

Theodore Maynard, Review in *Commonweal* XXXIV (June 20, 1941), 211-212.

Agnes E. Meyer, "Thomas Mann's Fable for Today: 'The Transposed Heads,'" *New York Times Book Review* (June 8, 1941), 1, 15-16.

[F. L. Pfeiffer, "The Transposed Heads," *Interpreter* (University of Minnesota) XVI (November, 1941), 1-2, 4.]

Charles Poore, "Books of the Times," *New York Times* (June 6, 1941), 19.

Philip Blair Rice, "Hindu Tangle," *Kenyon Review* III (Autumn, 1941), 508-510.

N. L. Rothman, "Legend Out of India," *Saturday Review of Literature* XXIV (June 7, 1941), 7.

Krishnalal Shridharani, "Thomas Mann Spins a Fable of Brahmin India," *New York Herald Tribune Books* (June 8, 1941), 3.

Harry Slochower, "Mann's Latest Novels," *Accent* IV (Autumn, 1943), 6-8.

Harry Slochower, *No Voice Is Wholly Lost*, 355-358. — reprinted in Charles Neider, *The Stature of Thomas Mann*, 382-384.

[Lionel Trilling, "Thomas Mann's New Work Is a Comedy Ending in a Funeral," *PM's Weekly* (June 8, 1941), 3.]

Anthony West, "The Transposed Heads," *New Statesman and Nation* XXII, n.s. (November 15, 1941), 427.

A. Leslie Willson, "Thomas Mann's 'Die vertauschten Köpfe': The Catalyst of Creation," *Monatshefte* XLIX (November, 1957), 313-321.

23. TRISTAN

Lydia Baer, *The Concept and the Function of Death in the Works of Thomas Mann*, 23-27.

A. F. B. Clark, "The Dialectical Humanism of Thomas Mann," *University of Toronto Quarterly* VIII (October, 1938), 93. — reprinted in Charles Neider, *The Stature of Thomas Mann*, 294.

Henry Hatfield, *Thomas Mann*, 24-26.

F. D. Hirschbach, *The Arrow and the Lyre*, 10-14.

R. A. Nicholls, *Nietzsche in the Early Work of Thomas Mann*, 40-48.

24. THE WARDROBE

Henry Hatfield, *Thomas Mann*, 20-21.

25. THE WAY TO THE CHURCHYARD

Lydia Baer, *The Concept and the Function of Death in the Works of Thomas Mann*, 13.

Henry Hatfield, *Thomas Mann*, 22.

26. A WEARY HOUR

Joseph Brennan, *Thomas Mann*, 45.

Henry Hatfield, *Thomas Mann*, 56-57.

27. THE WILL TO HAPPINESS

Lydia Baer, *The Concept and the Function of Death in the Works of Thomas Mann*, 11-12.

R. A. Nicholls, *Nietzsche in the Early Work of Thomas Mann*, 7-10.

MANSFIELD, KATHERINE

1. THE ALOE
(see "Prelude")
2. AT THE BAY
Antony Alpers, *Katherine Mansfield*, 316-322.
Sylvia Berkman, *Katherine Mansfield*, 168-169.
Dorothy Brewster and Angus Burrell, *Modern Fiction*, 368-369.
George S. Hubbell, "Katherine Mansfield and Kezia," *Sewanee Review* XXXV (July, 1927), 332-333.
Kenneth Kempton, *Short Stories for Study*, 280-282.
Stegner, Scowcroft, and Ilyin, *The Writer's Art* 74-77.
3. BLISS
Sylvia Berkman, *Katherine Mansfield*, 107, 180, 192.
Dorothy Brewster and Angus Burrell, *Modern Fiction*, 374-377.
Chester Eisinger, "Mansfield's 'Bliss' " *Explicator* VII (May, 1949), item 48.
T. S. Eliot, *After Strange Gods*, 35-36.
R. B. Heilman, *Modern Short Stories*, 207-209.
A. G. van Kranendonk, "Katherine Mansfield," *English Studies* XII (April, 1930), 56-57.
Winifred Lynskey, *Reading Modern Fiction* (Second Edition, 1957), 384-385.
J. Middleton Murry, *Katherine Mansfield and Other Literary Portraits*, 9.
Edward Shanks, "Katherine Mansfield," *London Mercury* XVII (January, 1928), 289, 291-292.
Alfred C. Ward, *Aspects of the Modern Short Story*, 287-289.
4. THE-CHILD-WHO-WAS-TIRED
Antony Alpers, *Katherine Mansfield*, 129-132.
Sylvia Berkman, *Katherine Mansfield*, 43, 45.
Sam Hynes, "Katherine Mansfield: The Defeat of the Personal," *South Atlantic Quarterly* LII (October, 1953), 557.
Elisabeth Schneider, "Katherine Mansfield and Chekhov," *Modern Language Notes* L (June, 1935), 394-396.
5. THE COMMON ROUND
Sylvia Berkman, *Katherine Mansfield*, 82-83.
6. A CUP OF TEA
Sylvia Berkman, *Katherine Mansfield*, 179-180.
Edward J. O'Brien, *The Short Story Case Book*, 525-541.
Mary Orvis, *The Art of Writing Fiction*, 155.
7. THE DAUGHTERS OF THE LATE COLONEL
Sylvia Berkman, *Katherine Mansfield*, 169-170, 174, 184-185.
Walter Havighurst, *Masters of the Modern Short Story*, ix-x.

MANSFIELD, KATHERINE, Continued

[Arthur Nelson, "Katherine Mansfield: Artist in Miniature," *Yale Literary Magazine* (April, 1941) .] — reprinted in West and Stallman, *Art of Modern Fiction,* 155-160. — reprinted in Stallman and Watters, *Creative Reader,* 308-312.

Sale, Hall, and Steinmann, *Critical Discussions for Teachers Using "Short Stories: Tradition and Direction,"* 17-20.

Helen Shaw, "Katherine Mansfield," *Meanjin Papers* X (Summer, 1951) , 380-381.

West and Stallman, *Art of Modern Fiction,* 151-154.

8. A DILL PICKLE

Sylvia Berkman, *Katherine Mansfield,* 170-171.

9. THE DOLL'S HOUSE

George S. Hubbell, "Katherine Mansfield and Kezia," *Sewanee Review* XXXV (July, 1927) , 334-335.

10. THE ESCAPE

Sylvia Berkman, *Katherine Mansfield,* 192.

11. THE FLY

Thomas J. Assad, "Mansfield's 'The Fly,' " *Explicator* XIV, No. 2 (November, 1955) , item 10.

Sylvia Berkman, *Katherine Mansfield,* 137-140, 194-196.

Thomas A. Bledsoe, "Mansfield's 'The Fly,' " *Explicator* V (May, 1947) , item 53. — reprinted in Locke, Gibson, Arms, *Introduction to Literature* (Second Edition, 1952) , 412-413.

Dorothy Brewster and Angus Burrell, *Modern Fiction,* 362-364.

Stanley B. Greenfield, "Mansfield's 'The Fly,' " *Explicator* XVII (October, 1958) , item 2.

Willis D. Jacobs, "Mansfield's 'The Fly,' " *Explicator* V (February, 1947) , item 32. — reprinted in Locke, Gibson, Arms, *Introduction to Literature* (Second Edition, 1952) , 411-412.

R. W. Stallman, "Mansfield's 'The Fly,' " *Explicator* III (April, 1945) , item 49. — reprinted in Locke, Gibson, Arms, *Introduction to Literature* (Second Edition, 1952) , 410.

Stallman and Watters, *The Creative Reader,* 333.

Celeste Turner Wright, "Genesis of a Short Story," *Philological Quarterly* XXXIV (January, 1955) , 91-96.

Celeste Turner Wright, "Mansfield's 'The Fly,' " *Explicator* XII, No. 4 (February, 1954) , item 27.

12. THE GARDEN PARTY

Dorothy Brewster and Angus Burrell, *Modern Fiction,* 361-362.

Anne Friis, *Katherine Mansfield,* 105-106.

Mary Orvis, *The Art of Writing Fiction,* 16.

Warren S. Walker, "The Unresolved Conflict in 'The Garden

MANSFIELD, KATHERINE, Continued

Party,'" *Modern Fiction Studies* III (Winter, 1957-1958), 354-358.

13. HER FIRST BALL
Beardsley, Daniel, and Leggett, *Aids to Study for "Theme and Form: An Introduction to Literature,"* 4.
Felheim, Newman, and Steinhoff, *Study Aids for Teachers for "Modern Short Stories,"* 5-7.

14. THE HONEYMOON
Mary Orvis, *The Art of Writing Fiction,* 44-45.

15. AN INDISCREET JOURNEY
Sylvia Berkman, *Katherine Mansfield,* 63, 78-79.

16. JE NE PARLE PAS FRANCAIS
Sylvia Berkman, *Katherine Mansfield,* 63, 106, 167-168, 174, 181, 186.
J. M. Murry, *Between Two Worlds,* 463-465.

17. THE MAN WITHOUT A TEMPERAMENT
Robert G. Davis, *Instructor's Manual for "Ten Modern Masters,"* 24.

18. MARRIAGE A LA MODE
J. Middleton Murry, *Katherine Mansfield and Other Literary Portraits,* 9.

19. MISS BRILL
Sylvia Berkman, *Katherine Mansfield,* 162-163, 175.
Eudora Welty, "The Reading and Writing of Short Stories," *Atlantic Monthly* CLXXXIII (February, 1949), 58. — reprinted in William Van O'Connor, *Modern Prose: Form and Style,* 435-436.

20. MR. REGINALD PEACOCK'S DAY
Mary Orvis, *The Art of Writing Fiction,* 156.

21. PICTURES
Sylvia Berkman, *Katherine Mansfield,* 82-83, 191.
Dorothy Brewster and Angus Burrell, *Modern Fiction,* 374.

22. POISON
Sylvia Berkman, *Katherine Mansfield,* 171-172.

23. PRELUDE
Antony Alpers, *Katherine Mansfield,* 213-219.
Sylvia Berkman, *Katherine Mansfield,* 83-102, 192-193.
Anne Friis, *Katherine Mansfield,* 124-125.
George S. Hubbell, "Katherine Mansfield and Kezia," *Sewanee Review* XXXV (July, 1927), 329-331.
J. Middleton Murry, *Katherine Mansfield and Other Literary Portraits,* 12-14.

MANSFIELD, KATHERINE, Continued

24. PSYCHOLOGY
Sylvia Berkman, *Katherine Mansfield*, 164, 190-191.
Dorothy Brewster and Angus Burrell, *Modern Fiction*, 370-372.
25. REVELATIONS
Royal A. Gettmann and Bruce Harkness, *Teacher's Manual for "A Book of Stories,"* 11-13.
26. THE SINGING LESSON
Sylvia Berkman, *Katherine Mansfield*, 175.
27. SOMETHING CHILDISH BUT VERY NATURAL
Sylvia Berkman, *Katherine Manfield*, 77-78.
28. THE STRANGER
Sylvia Berkman, *Katherine Mansfield*, 165-167.
29. THE TIREDNESS OF ROSABEL
Antony Alpers, *Katherine Mansfield*, 106-108, 130-132.
30. A WEDDING
Sam Hynes, "Katherine Mansfield: The Defeat of the Personal," *South Atlantic Quarterly* LII (October, 1953), 556.
31. THE WIND BLOWS
Robert G. Davis, *Instructor's Manual for "Ten Modern Masters,"* 21-22.

MARCH, WILLIAM

1. A HAIRCUT IN TOULOUSE
Arno L. Bader, "The Structure of the Modern Short Story," *College English* VII (November, 1945), 88-90.
2. THE LITTLE WIFE
Edward J. O'Brien, *The Short Story Case Book*, 363-387.
3. PERSONAL LETTER
R. B. Heilman, *Modern Short Stories*, 178-179.
4. A SUM IN ADDITION
Brooks and Heilman, *Understanding Drama*, 15-18.

MARQUAND, JOHN P.

1. DEEP WATER
Harlan Hatcher, "John Phillips Marquand," *College English* I (November, 1939), 112-113.
2. GOOD MORNING, MAJOR
Edward J. O'Brien, *The Short Story Case Book*, 405-459.

MAUGHAM, W. SOMERSET

1. THE DOOR OF OPPORTUNITY
   Edwin Muir, "A Review of *Ah King,*" *Listener* X (October-December, 1933), 519.
2. THE FACTS OF LIFE
   R. B. Heilman, *Modern Short Stories,* 21-22.
3. THE FALL OF EDWARD BARNARD
   Leslie A. Marchand, "The Exoticism of Somerset Maugham," *Revue Anglo-Américaine* X (April, 1933), 326-327. — reprinted in Klaus W. Jonas, *The Maugham Enigma,* 68.
4. THE LION'S SKIN
   John Brophy, *Somerset Maugham,* 26-29.
5. MR. KNOW-ALL
   Robert G. Davis, *Instructor's Manual for "Ten Modern Masters,"* 39-40.
6. RAIN
   Richard A. Cordell, "The Trembling of a Leaf," in Klaus W. Jonas, *The Maugham Enigma,* 174-176.
   Caroline Gordon, "Notes on Chekhov and Maugham," *Sewanee Review* LVII (Summer, 1949), 401-405. — reprinted, slightly revised, in Gordon and Tate, *The House of Fiction,* 382-385.

MAUPASSANT, GUY DE

1. THE APPARITION
   Ernest George Atkin, "The Supernaturalism of Maupassant," *PMLA* XLII (March, 1927), 202-204.
   Otis Fellows, "Maupassant's 'Apparition': A Source and A Creative Process," *Romanic Review* XXXIII (February, 1942), 58-71.
2. BALL-OF-FAT
   (see "Tallow Ball")
3. BOULE DE SUIF
   (see "Tallow Ball")
4. THE DEVIL
   Séan O'Faoláin, *The Short Story,* 123-125.
5. LE DIABLE
   (see "The Devil")
6. EN FAMILLE
   (see "A Family Affair")
7. THE FALSE GEMS
   Francis Steegmuller, *Maupassant: A Lion in the Path,* 207-208.

MAUPASSANT, GUY DE, Continued

8. A FAMILY AFFAIR
G. Hainsworth, "Pattern and Symbol in the Work of Maupassant,"
French Studies V (January, 1951), 4.

9. FATHER AND SON
(see "Hautot, Father and Son")

10. FEAR
Ernest George Atkin, "The Supernaturalism of Maupassant,"
PMLA XLII (March, 1927), 194-195. 199-201.

11. HAPPINESS
Herbert Barrows, *Suggestions for Teaching "Fifteen Stories,"* 22-23.

12. HAUTOT, FATHER AND SON
Séan O'Faoláin, *The Short Story*, 126-131.

13. HIM
Ernest George Atkin, "The Supernaturalism of Maupassant,"
PMLA XLII (March, 1927), 204-207.

14. HISTOIRE D'UNE FILLE DE FERME
(see "Story of a Farm Girl")

15. THE HORLA
Ernest George Atkin, "The Supernaturalism of Maupassant,"
PMLA XLII (March, 1927), 205-208.
Francis Steegmuller, *Maupassant: A Lion in the Path*, 251-260.

16. THE INN
Ernest George Atkin, "The Supernaturalism of Maupassant,"
PMLA XLII (March, 1927), 201-202.

17. MADAME TELLIER'S ESTABLISHMENT
(see "La Maison Tellier")

18. LA MAISON TELLIER
G. Hainsworth, "Pattern and Symbol in the Work of Maupassant,"
French Studies V (January, 1951), 4.
V. S. Pritchett, *Books in General*, 100-103.
Francis Steegmuller, *Maupassant: A Lion in the Path*, 151-152.

19. LA MERE SAUVAGE
West and Stallman, *Art of Modern Fiction*, 74-77.

20. MISS HARRIET
Séan O'Faoláin, *The Short Story*, 135-143.

21. MOONLIGHT
Mary Orvis, *The Art of Writing Fiction*, 64-66.

22. THE NECKLACE
H. E. Bates, *The Modern Short Story*, 61-62.
Beardsley, Daniel, and Leggett, *Aids to Study for "Theme and Form: An Introduction to Literature,"* 21-22.
Douglas Bement, *Weaving the Short Story*, 72-74.

MAUPASSANT, GUY, DE, Continued

Brooks and Warren, *Understanding Fiction,* 126-127.
Robert G. Davis, *Instructor's Manual for "Ten Modern Masters,"* 38-39.
Séan O'Faoláin, *The Short Story,* 176-179.
Francis Steegmuller, *Maupassant: A Lion in the Path,* 203-210.
23. ON THE WATER
Ernest George Atkin, "The Supernaturalism of Maupassant," *PMLA* XLII (March, 1927), 197-199.
24. LE PAPA DE SIMON
(see "Simon's Papa")
25. A PIECE OF STRING
Douglas Bement, *Weaving the Short Story,* 54-60.
Kenneth Kempton, *The Short Story,* 107-109.
26. SIMON'S PAPA
Francis Steegmuller, *Maupassant: A Lion in the Path,* 71-72.
27. THE SKINNED HAND
Ernest George Atkin, "The Supernaturalism of Maupassant," *PMLA* XLII (March, 1927), 213-216.
28. UNE SOIRÉE
Séan O'Faoláin, *The Short Story,* 118-123.
29. STORY OF A FARM GIRL
Gordon and Tate, *The House of Fiction,* 192-194.
V. S. Pritchett, *Books in General,* 100-103.
30. TALLOW BALL
Brooks and Warren, *Understanding Fiction,* 397-400.
G. Hainsworth, "Pattern and Symbol in the Work of Maupassant," *French Studies* V (January, 1951), 3-4.
Séan O'Faoláin, *The Short Story,* 122-123.
Francis Steegmuller, *Maupassant: A Lion in the Path,* 106-111.
31. THE TELLIER HOUSE
(see "La Maison Tellier")
32. TWO LITTLE SOLDIERS
Brooks and Warren, *Understanding Fiction,* 263-264.
33. WHO KNOWS?
Ernest George Atkin, "The Supernaturalism of Maupassant," *PMLA* XLII (March, 1927), 218-219.
34. YVETTE
Francis Steegmuller, *Maupassant: A Lion in the Path,* 221-223.

MAXWELL, WILLIAM

1. THE ABSENT-MINDED HEART
   Kenneth Kempton, *Short Stories for Study*, 244-249.

McCARTHY, MARY

1. THE UNSPOILED REACTION
   Felheim, Newman, and Steinhoff, *Study Aids for Teachers for "Modern Short Stories,"* 31-34.

McCLEARY, DOROTHY

1. SOMETHING JOLLY
   Mary Orvis, *The Art of Writing Fiction*, 92-96.

McCULLERS, CARSON

1. THE BALLAD OF THE SAD CAFE
   Oliver Evans, "The Theme of Spiritual Isolation in Carson Mc-Cullers," *New World Writing*, No. 1 (April, 1952), 304-310.
   Dayton Kohler, "Carson McCullers: Variations on a Theme," *English Journal* XL (October, 1951), 418-419. — also in *College English* XIII (October, 1951), 4-5.

MELVILLE, HERMAN

1. THE APPLE-TREE TABLE
   Frank Davidson, "Melville, Thoreau, and 'The Apple-Tree Table,'" *American Literature* XXV (January, 1954), 479-488.
   Jay Leyda, "Notes on Sources, etc.," in *The Complete Stories of Herman Melville* (Random House, 1949), 470-471.
   Edward H. Rosenberry, *Melville and the Comic Spirit*, 182-183.
   Douglas Sackman, "The Original of Melville's 'Apple-Tree Table,'" *American Literature* XI (January, 1940), 448-451.
2. BARTLEBY THE SCRIVENER
   Newton Arvin, *Herman Melville*, 242-244.
   Richard Chase, *Herman Melville: A Critical Study*, 143-149.
   Richard Chase, "Introduction," in Melville, *Selected Tales and Poems* (Rinehart Editions, 1950), vii-viii.

MELVILLE, HERMAN, Continued

Alexander Eliot, "Melville and Bartleby," *Furioso* III (Fall, 1947), 11-23.

Richard H. Fogle, "Melville's 'Bartleby': Absolutism, Predestination, and Free Will," *Tulane Studies in English* IV (1954), 125-135.

Charles G. Hoffmann, "The Shorter Fiction of Herman Melville," *South Atlantic Quarterly* LII (July, 1953), 418-421.

Leon Howard, *Herman Melville: A Biography*, 208-209.

Alfred Kazin, "Ishmael in His Academic Heaven," *New Yorker* XXIV (February 12, 1949), 84, 87.

Patricia Lacy, "The Agatha Theme in Melville's Stories," *University of Texas Studies in English* XXXV (1956), 98-100.

Leo Marx, "Melville's Parable of the Walls," *Sewanee Review* LXI (Autumn, 1953), 602-627.

Ronald Mason, *The Spirit Above the Dust*, 190-192.

Lewis Mumford, *Herman Melville*, 236-239.

Egbert S. Oliver, "Explanatory Notes," in *Piazza Tales* (Hendricks House, 1948), 229-230.

Egbert S. Oliver, "A Second Look at 'Bartleby,' " *College English* VI (May, 1945), 431-439.

Edward H. Rosenberry, *Melville and the Comic Spirit*, 145-146.

3. THE BELL-TOWER

James Baird, *Ishmael*, 396-400.

Richard Chase, *Herman Melville: A Critical Study*, 122-125.

Richard Chase, "Introduction," in Melville, *Selected Tales and Poems*, (Rinehart Editions, 1950), xi-xii.

Charles A. Fenton, " 'The Bell-Tower': Melville and Technology," *American Literature* XXIII (May, 1951), 219-232.

Leon Howard, *Herman Melville: A Biography*, 222-223.

Egbert S. Oliver, "Explanatory Notes," in *Piazza Tales* (Hendricks House, 1948), 247-250.

4. BENITO CERENO

Newton Arvin, *Herman Melville*, 238-240.

Guy A. Cardwell, "Melville's Gray Story: Symbols and Meaning in 'Benito Cereno,' " *Bucknell Review* VIII (May, 1959), 154-167.

Richard Chase, *Herman Melville: A Critical Study*, 149-159.

Richard Chase, "Introduction," in Melville, *Selected Tales and Poems* (Rinehart Editions, 1950), v-vii.

Thomas E. Connolly, "A Note on Name Symbolism in Melville," *American Literature* XXV (January, 1954), 489-490.

Alexander Cowie, *The Rise of the American Novel*, 391-392.

[Warren D'Azevedo, "Revolt on the San Dominick," *Phylon* XVII (1956), 129-140.]

Rosalie Feltenstein, "Melville's 'Benito Cereno,'" *American Literature* XIX (November, 1947), 245-255.

Richard H. Fogle, "The Monk and the Bachelor: Melville's 'Benito Cereno,'" *Tulane Studies in English* III (1952), 155-178.

Tom Burns Haber, "A Note on Melville's 'Benito Cereno,'" *Nineteenth Century Fiction* VI (September, 1951), 146-147.

Charles G. Hoffmann, "The Shorter Fiction of Herman Melville," *South Atlantic Quarterly* LII (July, 1953), 425-430.

Leon Howard, *Herman Melville: A Biography*, 218-223.

Sidney Kaplan, "Herman Melville and the American National Sin: The Meaning of 'Benito Cereno,'" *Journal of Negro History* XLI (October, 1956), 311-338; XLII (January, 1957), 11-37.

Jay Leyda, "Introduction," in *The Complete Stories of Herman Melville* (Random House, 1949), xxii-xxiii.

Ronald Mason, *The Spirit Above the Dust*, 184-188.

F. O. Matthiessen, *The American Renaissance*, 476-477.

Lewis Mumford, *Herman Melville*, 244-246.

Charles Neider, *Short Novels of the Masters*, 8-11.

William Van O'Connor, "Melville on the Nature of Hope," *University of Kansas City Review* XXII (Winter, 1955), 127.

Ward Pafford and Floyd C. Watkins, " 'Benito Cereno': A Note in Rebuttal," *Nineteenth Century Fiction* VII (June, 1952), 68-71.

Joseph Schiffman, "Critical Problems in Melville's 'Benito Cereno,'" *Modern Language Quarterly* XI (September, 1950), 317-324.

H. H. Scudder, "Melville's 'Benito Cereno' and Captain Delano's Voyages," *PMLA* XLIII (June, 1928), 502-532.

William Bysshe Stein, "The Moral Axis of 'Benito Cereno,'" *Accent* XV (Summer, 1955), 221-233.

Randall Stewart and Dorothy Bethurum, *Classic American Fiction* (*Living Masterpieces of American Literature*, Vol. 2), 180-183.

Geoffrey Stone, *Melville*, 217-221.

Arthur L. Vogelback, "Shakespeare and Melville's 'Benito Cereno,'" *Modern Language Notes* LXVII (February, 1952), 113-116.

Stanley T. Williams, " 'Follow Your Leader': Melville's 'Benito Cereno,'" *Virginia Quarterly Review* XXIII (Winter, 1947), 65-76.

Yvor Winters, *Maule's Curse*, 77. — reprinted in Winters, *In Defense of Reason*, 222.

5. **BILLY BUDD, FORETOPMAN**

Charles Roberts Anderson, "The Genesis of Billy Budd," *American Literature* XII (November, 1940), 328-346.

Newton Arvin, *Herman Melville*, 292-299.

Newton Arvin, "A Note on the Background of 'Billy Budd,'" *American Literature* XX (March, 1948), 51-55.

W. H. Auden, *The Enchafèd Flood*, 144-149.

James Baird, *Ishmael*, 249-251, 272-273, 426-427.

William Braswell, "Melville's 'Billy Budd' as 'An Inside Narrative,'" *American Literature* XXIX (May, 1957), 133-146.

William Braswell, *Melville's Religious Thought*, 122-123.

[Kenneth W. Cameron, "'Billy Budd' and 'An Execution at Sea,'" *Emerson Society Quarterly*, No. 2 (First Quarter, 1956), 13-15.]

H. M. Campbell, "The Hanging Scene in Melville's 'Billy Budd, Foretopman,'" *Modern Language Notes* LXVI (June, 1951), 378-381.

H. M. Campbell, "The Hanging Scene in Melville's 'Billy Budd': A Reply to Mr. Giovannini," *Modern Language Notes* LXX (November, 1955), 497-500.

Frederic I. Carpenter, "Melville: The World in a Man-of-War," *University of Kansas City Review* XIX (Summer, 1953), 261-264.

Leonard Casper, "The Case Against Captain Vere," *Perspective* V (Summer, 1952), 146-152.

Richard Chase, *The American Novel and Its Tradition*, 113-115.

Richard Chase, "Dissent on Billy Budd," *Partisan Review* XV (November, 1948), 1212-1218.

Richard Chase, *Herman Melville: A Critical Study*, 258-277.

Richard Chase, "Introduction," in Melville, *Selected Tales and Poems* (Rinehart Editions, 1950), xiii-xvi.

Alexander Cowie, *The Rise of the American Novel*, 394-395.

Maurice B. Cramer, "'Billy Budd' and 'Billy Budd,'" *Journal of General Education* X (April, 1957), 78-91.

F. Barron Freeman, *Melville's Billy Budd*, 66-126.

John Freeman, *Herman Melville*, 131-135.

Vincent Freimarck, "Mainmast as Crucifix in 'Billy Budd,'" *Modern Language Notes* LXXII (November, 1957), 496-497.

Royal A. Gettmann and Bruce Harkness, *Teacher's Manual for "A Book of Stories,"* 71-74.

G. Giovannini, "The Hanging Scene in Melville's 'Billy Budd,'" *Modern Language Notes* LXX (November, 1955), 491-497.

Wendell Glick, "Expediency and Absolute Morality in 'Billy Budd,'" *PMLA* LXVIII (March, 1953), 103-110.

Richard and Rita Gollin, "Justice in an Earlier Treatment of the Billy Budd 'Theme,'" *American Literature* XXVIII (January, 1957), 513-515.

Tyrus Hillway, "Melville's 'Billy Budd,' " *Explicator* IV (November, 1945), item 12.

Tyrus Hillway, "Billy Budd: Melville's Human Sacrifice," *Pacific Spectator* VI (Summer, 1952), 342-347.

Leon Howard, *Herman Melville: A Biography* 324-328.

Alfred Kazin, "Ishmael in His Academic Heaven," *New Yorker* XXIV (February 12, 1949), 84, 87-89.

R. W. B. Lewis, *The American Adam,* 147-152.

Ronald Mason, *The Spirit Above the Dust,* 245-260.

F. O. Matthiessen, *The American Renaissance,* 500-514.

B. R. McElderry, Jr., "Three Earlier Treatments of the 'Billy Budd' Theme," *American Literature* XXVII (May, 1955), 251-257.

James E. Miller, Jr., " 'Billy Budd': The Catastrophe of Innocence," *Modern Language Notes* LXXIII (March, 1958), 168-176.

Lewis Mumford, *Herman Melville,* 353-356.

J. M. Murry, *John Clare and Other Studies,* 209-212.

John B. Noone, Jr., " 'Billy Budd,' Two Concepts of Nature," *American Literature* XXIX (November, 1957), 249-262.

Egbert S. Oliver, "Explanatory Notes," in *Piazza Tales* (Hendricks House, 1948), 230-238.

Norman Holmes Pearson, "Billy Budd: 'The King's Yarn,' " *American Quarterly* III (Summer, 1951), 99-114.

Henry F. Pommer, *Milton and Melville,* 87-90.

Herbert Reed, "Books in General," *New Statesman and Nation* XXXIII (May 31, 1947), 397.

M. L. Rosenthal and A. J. M. Smith, *Exploring Poetry,* 372-375.

Arthur Sale, "Captain Vere's Reasons," *Cambridge Journal* V (October, 1951), 3-18.

Joseph Schiffman, "Melville's Final Stage, Irony: A Re-examination of 'Billy Budd,' " *American Literature* XXII (May, 1950), 128-136.

William Ellery Sedgwick, *Herman Melville,* 231-249.

Oliver Snyder, "A Note on 'Billy Budd,' " *Accent* XI (Winter, 1951), 58-60.

Milton R. Stern, *The Fine Hammered Steel of Herman Melville,* 26-27, 206-239.

Milton R. Stern, "Introduction" and "A Note about the Text," in Melville, *Typee and Billy Budd* (Dutton Paperbacks, 1958), xx-xxv; 269-274.

Randall Stewart, "The Vision of Evil in Hawthorne and Melville," in Nathan Scott, *The Tragic Vision and the Christian Faith,*

MELVILLE, HERMAN, Continued

257-262. — reprinted in Randall Stewart, *American Literature and Christian Doctrine*, 98-102.

Geoffrey Stone, "Herman Melville: Loyalty to the Heart," in Harold C. Gardiner, *American Classics Reconsidered*, 227-228.

Geoffrey Stone, *Melville*, 306-319.

Lawrence Thompson, *Melville's Quarrel with God*, 355-414.

Willard Thorp, "Herman Melville," in Spiller, *Literary History of the United States*, I, 469-471.

William Y. Tindall, "The Ceremony of Innocence," in R. M. MacIver, *Great Moral Dilemmas in Literature, Past and Present*, 73-81.

Rudolph von Abele, "Melville and the Problem of Evil," *American Mercury* LXV (November, 1947), 597-598.

E. L. Grant Watson, "Melville's Testimony of Acceptance," *New England Quarterly* VI (June, 1933), 319-327.

R. E. Watters, "Melville's 'Sociality,' " *American Literature* XVII (March, 1945), 48-49.

Raymond Weaver, "Introduction," in *Shorter Novels of Herman Melville* (Liveright, 1928), xlix-li.

Charles Weir, Jr., "Malice Reconciled: A Note on Herman Melville's 'Billy Budd,' " *University of Toronto Quarterly* XIII (April, 1944), 276-285.

Ray B. West, Jr., "Primitivism in Melville," *Prairie Schooner* XXX (Winter, 1956), 379-385.

Ray B. West, Jr., "The Unity of 'Billy Budd,' " *Hudson Review* V (Spring, 1952), 120-128.

Yvor Winters, *Maule's Curse*, 86-87. — reprinted in Winters, *In Defense of Reason*, 230-231.

Nathalia Wright, *Melville's Use of the Bible*, 126-136.

Karl E. Zink, "Herman Melville and the Forms—Irony and Social Criticism in 'Billy Budd,' " *Accent* XII (Summer, 1952), 131-139.

6. COCK-A-DOODLE-DOO! OR
THE CROWING OF THE NOBLE COCK BENEVENTANO

Richard Chase, *Herman Melville: A Critical Study*, 163-167.

Charles G. Hoffmann, "The Shorter Fiction of Herman Melville," *South Atlantic Quarterly* LII (July, 1953), 421-422.

Leon Howard, *Herman Melville: A Biography*, 209.

Patricia Lacy, "The Agatha Theme in Melville's Stories," *University of Texas Studies in English* XXXV (1956), 100-102.

Egbert S. Oliver, " 'Cock-A-Doodle-Do!' and Transcendental Hocus-Pocus," *New England Quarterly* XXI (June, 1948), 204-216.

Edward H. Rosenberry, *Melville and the Comic Spirit*, 162-163.

MELVILLE, HERMAN, Continued

7. DANIEL ORME
William Braswell, *Melville's Religious Thought*, 124-126.
Richard Chase, *Herman Melville: A Critical Study*, 298-301.
F. Barron Freeman, "The Enigma of Melville's 'Daniel Orme,'"
American Literature XVI (November, 1944), 208-211.

8. THE ENCANTADAS OR ENCHANTED ISLES
James Baird, *Ishmael*, 313-314.
Richard Chase, *Herman Melville: A Critical Study*, 210-213.
Richard Chase, "Introduction," in Melville, *Selected Tales and Poems*, (Rinehart Editions, 1950), xii-xiii.
Richard H. Fogle, "The Unity of 'The Encantadas,'" *Nineteenth Century Fiction* X (June, 1955), 34-52.
Charles G. Hoffmann, "The Shorter Fiction of Herman Melville," *South Atlantic Quarterly* LII (July, 1953), 422-423.
Leon Howard, *Herman Melville: A Biography*, 209-213.
Leon Howard, "Melville and Spenser—A Note on Criticism," *Modern Language Notes* XLVI (May, 1931), 291-292.
Patricia Lacy, "The Agatha Theme in Melville's Stories," *University of Texas Studies in English* XXXV (1956), 102-103.
Jay Leyda, "Notes on Sources, etc.," in *The Complete Stories of Herman Melville* (Random House, 1949), 455-461.
Ronald Mason, *The Spirit Above the Dust*, 188-190.
Lewis Mumford, *Herman Melville*, 239-240.
Egbert S. Oliver, "Explanatory Notes," in *Piazza Tales* (Hendricks House, 1948), 241-247.
Russell Thomas, "Melville's Use of Some Sources in 'The Encantadas,'" *American Literature* III (January, 1932), 432-456.
Yvor Winters, *Maule's Curse*, 77-78. — reprinted in Winters, *In Defense of Reason*, 222-223.

9. THE FIDDLER
Richard Chase, *Herman Melville: A Critical Study*, 173-175.
Edward H. Rosenberry, *Melville and the Comic Spirit*, 144-145.

10. THE HAPPY FAILURE
Charles G. Hoffmann, "The Shorter Fiction of Herman Melville," *South Atlantic Quarterly* LII (July, 1953), 423-424.

11. I AND MY CHIMNEY
Richard Chase, *Herman Melville: A Critical Study*, 168-171.
Richard Chase, "Introduction," in Melville, *Selected Tales and Poems* (Rinehart Editions, 1950), x.
Leon Howard, *Herman Melville: A Biography*, 224-225.
Edward H. Rosenberry, *Melville and the Comic Spirit*, 180-182.

MELVILLE, HERMAN, Continued

Merton M. Sealts, "Herman Melville's 'I and My Chimney,'" *American Literature* XIII (May, 1941), 142-154.

William Ellery Sedgwick, *Herman Melville,* 193-197.

12. JIMMY ROSE
Richard Chase, *Herman Melville: A Critical Study,* 171-173.

Richard Chase, "Introduction," to Melville, *Selected Tales and Poems* (Rinehart Editions, 1950), viii-ix.

13. THE LIGHTNING-ROD MAN
Richard Chase, *Herman Melville: A Critical Study,* 167-168.

Richard Chase, "Introduction," in Melville, *Selected Tales and Poems* (Rinehart Editions, 1950), ix-x.

Charles G. Hoffmann, "The Shorter Fiction of Herman Melville," *South Atlantic Quarterly* LII (July, 1953), 423-424.

Jay Leyda, "Introduction," in *The Complete Stories of Herman Melville* (Random House, 1949), xxvi-xxvii.

Egbert S. Oliver, "Explanatory Notes," in *Piazza Tales* (Hendricks House, 1948), 238-241.

[Egbert S. Oliver, "Herman Melville's Lightning-Rod Man," *Philadelphia Forum* XXXV (June, 1956), 4-5, 17.]

14. THE PARADISE OF BACHELORS AND
THE TARTARUS OF MAIDS
Newton Arvin, *Herman Melville,* 236-237

Richard Chase, *Herman Melville: A Critical Study,* 159-163.

Richard Chase, "Introduction," in Melville, *Selected Tales and Poems* (Rinehart Editions, 1950), x-xi.

E. H. Eby, "Herman Melville's 'Tartarus of Maids,'" *Modern Language Quarterly* I (March, 1940), 95-100.

Charles G. Hoffmann, "The Shorter Fiction of Herman Melville," *South Atlantic Quarterly* LII (July, 1953), 424.

Jay Leyda, "Notes on Sources, etc.," in *The Complete Stories of Herman Melville* (Random House, 1949), 465-466.

W. R. Thompson, "'The Paradise of Bachelors and the Tartarus of Maids': A Reinterpretation," *American Quarterly* IX (Spring, 1957), 34-45.

15. THE PIAZZA
Leon Howard, *Herman Melville: A Biography,* 230.

Jay Leyda, "Notes on Sources, etc.," in *The Complete Stories of Herman Melville* (Random House, 1949), 472.

Ronald Mason, *The Spirit Above the Dust,* 182-184.

Egbert S. Oliver, "Explanatory Notes," in *Piazza Tales* (Hendricks House, 1948), 225-229.

MELVILLE, HERMAN, Continued

16. POOR MAN'S PUDDING AND RICH MAN'S CRUMBS
Charles G. Hoffmann, "The Shorter Fiction of Herman Melville,"
South Atlantic Quarterly LII (July, 1953) , 423-424.
Jay Leyda, "Notes on Sources, etc.,, in *The Complete Stories of
Herman Melville* (Random House, 1949) ,464-465.

MEREDITH, GEORGE

1. THE CASE OF GENERAL OPLE AND LADY CAMPER
Jack Lindsay, *George Meredith: His Life and Work,* 231-232.
Siegfried Sassoon, *Meredith,* 134-136.
Lionel Stevenson, *The Ordeal of George Meredith,* 214-215.
Alfred C. Ward, *Aspects of the Modern Short Story,* 79-83.
2. THE HOUSE ON THE BEACH
Jack Lindsay, *George Meredith: His Life and Work,* 230-231.
Lionel Stevenson, *The Ordeal of George Meredith,* 209-211.
Alfred C. Ward, *Aspects of the Modern Short Story,* 74-79.
3. THE TALE OF CHLOE
Siegfried Sassoon, *Meredith,* 137-138.
Lionel Stevenson, *The Ordeal of George Meredith,* 221-223.
Alfred C. Ward, *Aspects of the Modern Short Story,* 84-87.
Walter F. Wright, *Art and Substance in George Meredith,* 139-140.

MÉRIMÉE, PROSPER

1. THE BLUE ROOM
John C. Lapp, "The Denouement of Mérimée's 'La Chambre
bleue,' " *Modern Language Notes* LXVI (February, 1951) , 93-97.
2. MATEO FALCONE
Edward J. O'Brien, *The Short Story Case Book,* 69-95.
Harry Shaw and Douglas Bement, *Reading the Short Story,* 265.

MEYER, CORD, JR.

1. WAVES OF DARKNESS
Mary Orvis, *The Art of Writing Fiction,* 147-149.

MILBURN, GEORGE

1. THE WISH BOOK
Brooks, Purser, and Warren, *An Approach to Literature,* 60-61.

MORAVIA, ALBERTO

1. AGOSTINO
   L. Hamalian and E. L. Volpe, *Ten Modern Short Novels*, 717.

MOREAU, LOUIS

1. THE FACE
   Brooks and Warren, *Understanding Fiction*, 181-182.

MORRIS, A. G.

1. PANAHARD AND MR. SNAITH
   Edward J. O'Brien, *The Short Story Case Book*, 601-629.

O'CONNOR, FLANNERY

1. THE ARTIFICIAL NIGGER
   Walter Elder, "That Region," *Kenyon Review* XVII (Autumn, 1955), 668-669.
   Sister M. Bernetta Quinn, "View from a Rock: The Fiction of Flannery O'Connor and J. F. Powers," *Critique: Studies in Modern Fiction* II (Fall, 1958), 21-22.
2. THE DISPLACED PERSON
   Thomas H. Carter, "Rhetoric and Southern Landscapes," *Accent* XV (Autumn, 1955), 296.
   Walter Elder, "That Region," *Kenyon Review* XVII (Autumn, 1955), 669.
   Louis D. Rubin, Jr., "Flannery O'Connor: A Note on Literary Fashions," *Critique: Studies in Modern Fiction* II (Fall, 1958), 15-18.
   Louis D. Rubin, Jr., "Two Ladies of the South," *Sewanee Review* LXIII (Autumn, 1955), 680-681.
3. GOOD COUNTRY PEOPLE
   Thomas H. Carter, "Rhetoric and Southern Landscapes," *Accent* XV (Autumn, 1955), 296-297.
   Walter Elder, "That Region," *Kenyon Review* XVII (Autumn, 1955), 666, 668.
   Caroline Gordon, "With a Glitter of Evil," *New York Times Book Review* (June 12, 1955), 5.

O'CONNOR, FLANNERY, Continued

Louis D. Rubin, Jr., "Two Ladies of the South," *Sewanee Review* LXIII (Autumn, 1955), 679.
4. A GOOD MAN IS HARD TO FIND
Thomas H. Carter, "Rhetoric and Southern Landscapes," *Accent* XV (Autumn, 1955), 295-296.
5. A LATE ENCOUNTER WITH THE ENEMY
Walter Elder, "That Region," *Kenyon Review* XVII (Autumn, 1955), 670.
6. THE RIVER
Sylvia Stallings, "Flannery O'Connor: A New, Shining Talent Among Storytellers," *New York Herald Tribune Book Review* (June 5, 1955), 1.
7. A TEMPLE OF THE HOLY GHOST
Sister M. Bernetta Quinn, "View from a Rock: The Fiction of Flannery O'Connor and J. F. Powers," *Critique: Studies in Modern Fiction* II (Fall, 1958), 25.

O'CONNOR, FRANK

1. FIRST CONFESSION AND REPENTANCE
Royal A. Gettmann and Bruce Harkness, *Teacher's Manual for "A Book of Stories,"* 48-51.
2. GUESTS OF THE NATION
Gordon and Tate, *House of Fiction,* 441-444.
3. IN THE TRAIN
Séan O'Faoláin, *The Short Story,* 205-206.
4. JUDAS
Robert G. Davis, *Instructor's Manual for "Ten Modern Masters,"* 29-30.
5. THE MAJESTY OF THE LAW
Robert G. Davis, *Instructor's Manual for "Ten Modern Masters,"* 30-31.
6. MY OEDIPUS COMPLEX
James B. Hall and Joseph Langland, *The Short Story,* 217-218.
7. UPROOTED
Robert G. Davis, *Instructor's Manual for "Ten Modern Masters,"* 31-32.
Helmut E. Gerber, "O'Connor's 'Uprooted,'" *Explicator* XIV, No. 1 (October, 1955), item 7.

O'FAOLÁIN, SÉAN

1. THE MAN WHO INVENTED SIN
Felheim, Newman, and Steinhoff, *Study Aids for Teachers for "Modern Short Stories,"* 57-59.
James B. Hall and Joseph Langland, *The Short Story,* 78-79.
2. THE SMALL LADY
Donat O'Donnell, "The Parnellism of Séan O'Faoláin," *Irish Writing* No. 5 (July, 1948), 67-68.

O'HARA, JOHN

1. ARE WE LEAVING TOMORROW?
Arno L. Bader, "The Structure of the Modern Short Story," *College English* VII (November, 1945), 90-92.

O. HENRY

1. THE COMPLETE LIFE OF JOHN HOPKINS
Howard Baker, "The Contemporary Short Story," *Southern Review* III (Winter, 1938), 580-581.
2. THE FOOL-KILLER
Jay B. Hubbell, "Charles Napoleon Bonaparte Evans, Creator of Jesse Holmes the Fool-Killer," *South Atlantic Quarterly* XXXVI (October, 1937), 431-446.
3. THE FURNISHED ROOM
Brooks and Warren, *Understanding Fiction,* 114-118.
4. THE GIFT OF THE MAGI
Séan O'Faoláin, *The Short Story,* 171-172.
5. A MUNICIPAL REPORT
Kenneth Kempton, *The Short Story,* 94-98.
Edward J. O'Brien, *The Short Story Case Book,* 229-261.
6. THE PROOF OF THE PUDDING
James B. Hall and Joseph Langland, *The Short Story,* 28-29.
7. THE WHIRLIGIG OF LIFE
Gorham Munson, "The Recapture of the Storyable," *University Review* X (Autumn, 1943), 37-38.

ORWELL, GEORGE

1. ANIMAL FARM
Robert Fordyce Aickman, "Animal Farm," *Nineteenth Century*

CXXXVIII (December, 1945) , 255-261.

John Atkins, *George Orwell: A Literary Study,* 221-232.

Laurence Brander, *George Orwell,* 170-182.

Cyril Connolly, Review in *Horizon* XII (September, 1945) , 215-216.

Ernestine Evans, Review in *New York Herald Tribune Book Review* (August 25, 1946) , 4.

Northrop Frye, Review in *Canadian Forum* XXVI (December, 1946) , 211.

Charles Glicksberg, "The Literary Contribution of George Orwell," *Arizona Quarterly* X (Autumn, 1954) , 239.

Adam de Hegedus, "More Books of the Week," *Commonweal* XLIV (September 13, 1946) , 528-530.

Christopher Hollis, *A Study of George Orwell: The Man and His Works,* 139-153.

Tom Hopkinson, "Animal Farm," *World Review* (June, 1950) , 54-57.

Ellen Douglass Leyburn, *Satiric Allegory: Mirror of Man,* 68-70.

Kingsley Martin, "Soviet Satire," *New Statesman and Nation* XXX (September 8, 1945) , 165-166.

Isaac Rosenfeld, "A Barnyard History," *Nation* CLXIII (September 7, 1946) , 273-274.

Arthur M. Schlesinger, Jr., "Mr. Orwell and the Communists," *New York Times Book Review* (August 25, 1946) , 1, 28.

George Soule, "Orwell's Fables," *New Republic* CXV (September 2, 1946) , 266-267.

Richard J. Vorhees, "George Orwell: Rebellion and Responsibility," *South Atlantic Quarterly* LIII (October, 1954) , 557-558.

Frank W. Wadsworth, "Orwell's Later Work," *University of Kansas City Review* XXII (Summer, 1956) , 285.

PAGANO, JO

1. THE DISINHERITED
Alfred Dashiell, *Editor's Choice,* 326-327.

PARKER, DOROTHY

1. BIG BLONDE
Mary Orvis, *The Art of Writing Fiction,* 161-164.

PARKER, DOROTHY, Continued

2. MR. DURANT
   Mary Orvis, *The Art of Writing Fiction,* 159-161.
3. A TELEPHONE CALL
   Gorham Munson, "The Recapture of the Storyable," *University Review* X (Autumn, 1943), 43.

PATER, WALTER

1. SEBASTIAN VAN STORCK
   William W. Main, "Pater's 'Sebastian van Storck,'" *Explicator* XII, No. 7 (May, 1954), item 44.

PATTON, FRANCES GRAY

1. A PIECE OF BREAD
   Mary Orvis, *The Art of Writing Fiction,* 79-81.

PHILLIPS, THOMAS HAL

1. THE SHADOW OF AN ARM
   Kenneth Kempton, *Short Stories for Study,* 337-343.

PIRANDELLO, LUIGI

1. THE JAR
   Renato Poggioli, "Pirandello in Retrospect," *Italian Quarterly* I, No. 4 (1958), 23-26.
2. WAR
   Brooks and Warren, *Understanding Fiction,* 169-172.

PLOMER, WILLIAM

1. THY NEIGHBOUR'S CREED
   Royal A. Gettmann and Bruce Harkness, *Teacher's Manual for "A Book of Stories,"* 21-23.

1. THE ANGEL OF THE ODD: AN EXTRAVAGANZA
   Marie Bonaparte, *The Life and Works of Edgar Allan Poe: A Psycho-Analytic Interpretation,* 570-574.
2. THE ASSIGNATION
   Marie Bonaparte, *The Life and Works of Edgar Allan Poe: A Psycho-Analytic Interpretation,* 261-272.
3. THE BALLOON HOAX
   Harold H. Scudder, "Poe's 'Balloon Hoax,'" *American Literature* XXI (May, 1949), 179-190.
   W. K. Wimsatt, Jr., "A Further Note on Poe's 'Balloon Hoax,'" *American Literature* XXII (January, 1951), 491-492.
4. BERENICE
   Marie Bonaparte, *The Life and Works of Edgar Allan Poe: A Psycho-Analytic Interpretation,* 213-219.
   Frank Davidson, "A Note on Poe's 'Berenice,'" *American Literature* XI (May, 1939), 212-213.
   Arthur Hobson Quinn, *Edgar Allan Poe: A Critical Biography,* 213.
   Patrick F. Quinn, *The French Face of Poe,* 216-218, 267-268.
5. THE BLACK CAT
   Marie Bonaparte, "The Black Cat," *Partisan Review* XVII (November-December, 1950), 834-860. — reprinted in Bonaparte, *The Life and Works of Edgar Allan Poe: A Psycho-Analytic Interpretation,* 458-485.
   Edith S. Krappe, "A Possible Source for Poe's 'The Tell-Tale Heart,' and 'The Black Cat,'" *American Literature* XII (March, 1940), 84-88.
   Robert Penn Warren, "A Poem of Pure Imagination," *Kenyon Review* VIII (Summer, 1946), 399-400. — reprinted in Warren, *Selected Essays,* 230-231.
6. THE CASK OF AMONTILLADO
   Jacob H. Adler, "Are There Flaws in 'The Cask of Amontillado'?" *Notes and Queries* CXCIX (January, 1954), 32-34.
   Marie Bonaparte, *The Life and Works of Edgar Allan Poe: A Psycho-Analytic Interpretation,* 505-510.
   Edward H. Davidson, *Poe: A Critical Study,* 201-203.
   N. Bryllion Fagin, *The Histrionic Mr. Poe,* 169.
   Marvin Felheim, "'The Cask of Amontillado,'" *Notes and Queries* CXCIX (October, 1954), 447-448.
   Richard H. Fossum, "Poe's 'The Cask of Amontillado,'" *Explicator* XVII, No. 2 (November, 1958), item 16.

POE, EDGAR ALLAN, Continued

Howard M. Jones, "Poe, 'The Raven,' and the Anonymous Young Man," *Western Humanities Review* IX (Spring, 1955), 130.

Kenneth Kempton, *The Short Story*, 86-91.

Thomas O. Mabbott, "Poe's Vaults," *Notes and Queries* CXCVIII (December, 1953), 542-543.

Sam Moon, "The Cask of Amontillado," *Notes and Queries* CXCIX (October, 1954), 448.

Donald Pearce, "The Cask of Amontillado," *Notes and Queries* CXCIX (October, 1954), 448-449.

Joseph S. Schick, "The Origin of 'The Cask of Amontillado,'" *American Literature* VI (March, 1934), 18-21.

7. THE COLLOQUY OF MONOS AND UNA

Edward H. Davidson, *Poe: A Critical Study*, 133, 188-189.

Edward Hungerford, "Poe and Phrenology," *American Literature* II (November, 1930), 221-224.

Allen Tate, "The Angelic Imagination," *Kenyon Review* XIV (Summer, 1952), 462-468.

8. THE CONVERSATION OF EIROS AND CHARMION

Edward H. Davidson, *Poe: A Critical Study*, 132.

Allen Tate, "The Angelic Imagination," *Kenyon Review* XIV (Summer, 1952), 461-462.

9. A DESCENT INTO THE MAELSTROM

W. T. Bandy, "New Light on a Source of Poe's 'A Descent into the Maelstrom,'" *American Literature* XXIV (January, 1953), 534-537.

Patrick F. Quinn, *The French Face of Edgar Poe*, 59-60, 164.

Arlin Turner, "Sources of Poe's 'A Descent into the Maelstrom,'" *Journal of English and Germanic Philology* XLVI (July, 1947), 298-301.

10. THE DEVIL IN THE BELFRY

William Whipple, "Poe's Political Satire," *University of Texas Studies in English* XXXV (1956), 88-91.

11. ELEONORA

Sam S. Baskett, "A Damsel with a Dulcimer: An Interpretation of Poe's 'Eleonora,'" *Modern Language Notes* LXXIII (May, 1958), 332-338.

Marie Bonaparte, *The Life and Works of Edgar Allan Poe: A Psycho-Analytic Interpretation*, 251-257.

12. THE FACTS IN THE CASE OF M. VALDEMAR

Sidney E. Lind, "Poe and Mesmerism," *PMLA* LXII (December, 1947), 1090-1094.

13. THE FALL OF THE HOUSE OF USHER

Darrel Abel, "A Key to the House of Usher," *University of Toronto Quarterly* XVIII (January, 1949), 176-185.

Maurice Beebe, "The Fall of the House of Pyncheon," *Nineteenth Century Fiction* XI (June, 1956), 4-8.

Maurice Beebe, "The Universe of Roderick Usher," *Personalist* XXXVII (Spring, 1956), 147-160.

Marie Bonaparte, *The Life and Works of Edgar Allan Poe: A Psycho-Analytic Interpretation,* 237-250.

Brooks and Warren, *Understanding Fiction,* 202-205, 575.

James E. Cronin, "Poe's Vaults," *Notes and Queries* CXCVIII (September, 1953), 395-396.

Edward H. Davidson, *Poe: A Critical Study,* 196-198, 281.

Jeff Davis, "The Lady Madeleine as Symbol," *Annotator* (Purdue), No. 2 (April, 1954), 8-11.

N. Bryllion Fagin, *The Histrionic Mr. Poe,* 200-203.

Charles Feidelson, Jr., *Symbolism and American Literature,* 39-42.

Gordon and Tate, *The House of Fiction,* 114-117.

Robert Hamilton, "Poe and the Imagination," *Quarterly Review* CCLXXXVIII (October, 1950), 520-522.

Edward Hungerford, "Poe and Phrenology," *American Literature* II (November, 1930), 225-227.

Howard M. Jones, "Poe, 'The Raven,' and the Anonymous Young Man," *Western Humanities Review* IX (Spring, 1955), 130-131.

D. H. Lawrence, *Studies in Classic American Literature* (1923), 110-116. — reprinted in Edmund Wilson, *The Shock of Recognition,* 978-981.

Thomas O. Mabbott, "Poe's 'The Fall of the House of Usher,'" *Explicator* XV (November, 1956), item 7.

William L. Phillips, "Poe's 'The Fall of the House of Usher,'" *Explicator* IX (February, 1951), item 29.

Arthur Hobson Quinn, *Edgar Allan Poe: A Critical Biography,* 284-285.

Patrick F. Quinn, *The French Face of Edgar Poe,* 54-55, 237-252.

Edward Shanks, *Edgar Allan Poe,* 131-132, 136-137.

George Snell, *Shapers of American Fiction,* 55-56.

K. A. Spaulding, "Poe's 'The Fall of the House of Usher,'" *Explicator* X (June, 1952), item 52.

Leo Spitzer, "A Reinterpretation of 'The Fall of the House of Usher,'" *Comparative Literature* IV (Fall, 1952), 351-363.

Randall Stewart and Dorothy Bethurum, *Classic American Fiction* (*Living Masterpieces of American Literature,* Vol 2), 4-5.

POE, EDGAR ALLAN, Continued

Allen Tate, "Our Cousin, Mr. Poe," *Partisan Review* XVI (December, 1949), 1212-1214. — reprinted in William Phillips and Philip Rahv, *The New Partisan Reader, 1945-1953*, 337-339. — reprinted in Tate, *The Forlorn Demon*, 86-89.

Allen Tate, "Three Commentaries: Poe, James, and Joyce," *Sewanee Review* LVIII (Winter, 1950), 1-5. — reprinted in Gordon and Tate, *The House of Fiction*, 114-117.

Harry R. Warfel, "Poe's Dr. Percival: A Note on 'The Fall of the House of Usher,'" *Modern Language Notes* LIV (February, 1939), 129-131.

14. FOUR BEASTS IN ONE

William Whipple, "Poe's Political Satire," *University of Texas Studies in English* XXXV (1956), 82-84.

15. THE GOLD-BUG

Marie Bonaparte, *The Life and Works of Edgar Allan Poe: A Psycho-Analytic Interpretation*, 353-369.

J. Woodrow Hassell, "The Problem of Realism in 'The Gold Bug,'" *American Literature* XXV (May, 1953), 179-192.

Thomas O. Mabbott, "The Source of Poe's Motto for 'The Gold-Bug,'" *Notes and Queries* CXCVIII (February, 1953), 68.

16. HANS PFAALL

Meredith N. Posey, "Notes on Poe's 'Hans Pfaall,'" *Modern Language Notes* XLV (December, 1930), 501-507.

Edmund Reiss, "The Comic Setting of 'Hans Pfaall,'" *American Literature* XXIX (November, 1957), 306-309.

17. HOP-FROG

Marie Bonaparte, *The Life and Works of Edgar Allan Poe: A Psycho-Analytic Interpretation*, 510-514.

Killis Campbell, *The Mind of Poe*, 172.

18. HOW TO WRITE A BLACKWOOD ARTICLE

Clark Griffith, "Poe's 'Ligeia' and the English Romantics," *University of Toronto Quarterly* XXIV (October, 1954), 13-17.

Thomas H. McNeal, "Poe's 'Zenobia': An Early Satire on Margaret Fuller," *Modern Language Quarterly* XI (June, 1950), 205-216.

19. THE ISLAND OF THE FAY

Marie Bonaparte, *The Life and Works of Edgar Allan Poe: A Psycho-Analytic Interpretation*, 285-289.

F. DeWolfe Miller, "The Basis for Poe's 'The Island of the Fay,'" *American Literature* XIV (May, 1942), 135-140.

Patrick F. Quinn, *The French Face of Edgar Poe*, 262-266, 268.

20. KING PEST

Arthur Hobson Quinn, *Edgar Allan Poe: A Critical Biography*, 214.

William Whipple, "Poe's Political Satire," *University of Texas Studies in English* XXXV (1956), 84-88.

J. S. Wilson, "The Devil Was In It," *American Mercury* XXIV (October, 1931), 218.

21. LIGEIA

Roy P. Basler, "The Interpretation of 'Ligeia,' " *College English* V (April, 1944), 363-372. − reprinted in Stallman and Watters, *Creative Reader,* 286-294. − reprinted in Roy P. Basler, *Sex, Symbolism, and Psychology in Literature.*

Marie Bonaparte, *The Life and Works of Edgar Allan Poe: A Psycho-Analytic Interpretation,* 224-236.

Ethan Allen Cross, *A Book of the Short Story,* 1062-1063.

Clark Griffith, "Poe's 'Ligeia' and the English Romantics," *University of Toronto Quarterly* XXIV (October, 1954), 8-25.

Clayton Hamilton, *A Manual of the Art of Fiction,* 194-201.

Ruth Hudson, "Poe Recognizes 'Ligeia' as His Masterpiece," in *English Studies in Honor of James Southall Wilson* (University of Virginia Studies, Vol. IV, 1951), 36-44.

Edward Hungerford, "Poe and Phrenology," *American Literature* II (November, 1930), 228-231.

D. H. Lawrence, *Studies in Classic American Literature* (1923), 99-109. − reprinted in Edmund Wilson, *The Shock of Recognition,* 970-977.

Edgar Allan Poe and Philip P. Cooke, Letters in J. A. Harrison, *The Complete Works of Edgar Allan Poe,* XVII, 52-53, 49-50.

Arthur Hobson Quinn, *Edgar Allan Poe: A Critical Biography,* 269-271.

George Snell, *Shapers of American Fiction,* 54-55.

22. LIONIZING

Edward H. Davidson, *Poe: A Critical Study,* 146.

J. S. Wilson, "The Devil Was In It," *American Mercury* XXIV (October, 1931), 218-219.

23. LOSS OF BREATH

Marie Bonaparte, *The Life and Works of Edgar Allan Poe: A Psycho-Analytic Interpretation,* 373-410.

Walter F. Taylor, "Israfel in Motley, A Study of Poe's Humor," *Sewanee Review* XLII (July-September, 1934), 335-336.

Cornelia Varner, "Notes on Poe's Use of Contemporary Materials in Certain of His Stories," *Journal of English and Germanic Philology* XXXII (January, 1933), 77.

24. THE MAN OF THE CROWD

Marie Bonaparte, *The Life and Works of Edgar Allan Poe: A Psycho-Analytic Interpretation,* 413-426.

Edward H. Davidson, *Poe: A Critical Study,* 190-192.

Patrick F. Quinn, *The French Face of Edgar Poe,* 229-232.

25. THE MAN THAT WAS USED UP

Cornelia Varner, "Notes on Poe's Use of Contemporary Materials in Certain of His Stories," *Journal of English and Germanic Philology* XXXII (January, 1933), 77, 78.

George Wetzel, "The Source of Poe's 'Man That Was Used Up,' " *Notes and Queries* CXCVIII (January, 1953), 38.

William Whipple, "Poe's Political Satire," *University of Texas Studies in English* XXXV (1956), 91-94.

26. THE MASQUE OF THE RED DEATH

Walter Blair, "Poe's Conception of Incident and Tone in the Tale," *Modern Philology* XLI (May, 1944), 236-240. — reprinted in Locke, Gibson, and Arms, *Introduction to Literature* (First Edition, 1948), 429-433; (Second Edition, 1952), 306-311; (Third Edition, 1957), 295-299.

Marie Bonaparte, *The Life and Works of Edgar Allan Poe: A Psycho-Analytic Interpretation,* 514-521.

N. Bryllion Fagin, *The Histrionic Mr. Poe,* 215-216.

F. K. Mohr, "The Influence of Eichendorff's 'Ahnung und Gegenwart' on Poe's 'Masque of the Red Death,' " *Modern Language Quarterly* X (March, 1949), 3-15.

Patrick F. Quinn, *The French Face of Edgar Poe,* 119-121.

Randall Stewart and Dorothy Bethurum, *Classic American Fiction* (*Living Masterpieces of American Literature,* Vol. 2), 4-5.

27. MESMERIC REVELATION

Sidney E. Lind, "Poe and Mesmerism," *PMLA* LXII (December, 1947), 1086-1090.

28. METZENGERSTEIN

Marie Bonaparte, *The Life and Works of Edgar Allan Poe: A Psycho-Analytic Interpretation,* 273-282.

Grace P. Smith, "Poe's 'Metzengerstein,' " *Modern Language Notes* XLVIII (June, 1933), 356-359.

29. MORELLA

Marie Bonaparte, *The Life and Works of Edgar Allan Poe: A Psycho-Analytic Interpretation,* 220-223.

Thomas O. Mabbott, "The Source of the Title of Poe's 'Morella,' " *Notes and Queries* CLXXII (January 9, 1937), 26-27.

POE, EDGAR ALLAN, Continued

Walter G. Neale, Jr., "The Source of Poe's 'Morella,' " *American Literature* IX (May, 1937) , 237-239.

Arthur Hobson Quinn, *Edgar Allan Poe: A Critical Biography*, 213-214.

30. MS. FOUND IN A BOTTLE

Charles Feidelson, *Symbolism and American Literature*, 35-36.

George Snell, *Shapers of American Fiction*, 49-51.

J. S. Wilson, "The Devil Was In It," *American Mercury* XXIV (October, 1931) , 219.

31. THE MURDERS IN THE RUE MORGUE

Ernest Boll, "The Manuscript of 'The Murders in the Rue Morgue' and Poe's Revisions," *Modern Philology* XL (May, 1943) , 302-315.

Marie Bonaparte, *The Life and Works of Edgar Allan Poe: A Psycho-Analytic Interpretation*, 427-457.

John R. Moore, "Poe, Scott, and 'The Murders in the Rue Morgue,' " *American Literature* VIII (March, 1936) , 52-58.

Arthur Hobson Quinn, *Edgar Allan Poe: A Critical Biography*, 310-312.

32. THE MYSTERY OF MARIE ROGET

N. Bryllion Fagin, *The Histrionic Mr. Poe*, 172-173.

Edgar Allan Poe, Letter in J. A. Harrison, *The Complete Works of Edgar Allan Poe*, XVII, 112-113.

Arthur Hobson Quinn, *Edgar Allan Poe: A Critical Biography*, 355-358.

Irving Wallace, "The Real Marie Roget" in Wallace, *The Fabulous Originals*, 172-215.

W. K. Wimsatt, Jr., "Poe and the Mystery of Mary Rogers," *PMLA* LVI (March, 1941) , 230-248.

Samuel Copp Worthen, "Poe and the Beautiful Cigar Girl," *American Literature* XX (November, 1948) , 305-312.

33. NEVER BET THE DEVIL YOUR HEAD

Marie Bonaparte, *The Life and Works of Edgar Allan Poe: A Psycho-Analytic Interpretation*, 525-536.

34. THE OBLONG BOX

C. V. Carley, "A Source for Poe's 'Oblong Box,' " *American Literature* XXIX (November, 1957) , 310-312.

35. THE OVAL PORTRAIT

Patrick F. Quinn, *The French Face of Edgar Poe,* 259-262, 266, 269.

36. THE PIT AND THE PENDULUM

Margaret Alterton, "An Additional Source for Poe's 'The Pit and the Pendulum,' " *Modern Language Notes* XLVIII (June, 1933) , 349-356.

POE, EDGAR ALLAN, Continued

Marie Bonaparte, *The Life and Works of Edgar Allan Poe: A Psycho-Analytic Interpretation,* 575-593.

Boyd Carter, "Poe's Debt to Charles Brockden Brown," *Prairie Schooner* XXVII (Summer, 1953), 190-196.

D. L. Clark, "The Sources of Poe's 'The Pit and the Pendulum,'" *Modern Language Notes* XLIV (June, 1929), 349-356.

Edward J. O'Brien, *The Short Story Case Book,* 181-211.

Alfred C. Ward, *Aspects of the Modern Short Story,* 38-43.

37. THE POWER OF WORDS

Allen Tate, "The Angelic Imagination," *Kenyon Review* XIV (Summer, 1952), 468-472.

38. THE PREMATURE BURIAL

James B. Hall and Joseph Langland, *The Short Story,* 147-148.

39. PSYCHE ZENOBIA

(see "How to Write a Blackwood Article")

40. THE SIGNORA ZENOBIA

(see "How to Write a Blackwood Article")

41. SILENCE—A FABLE

Edward H. Davidson, *Poe: A Critical Study,* 130-132.

Clark Griffith, "Poe's 'Ligeia' and the English Romantics," *University of Toronto Quarterly* XXIV (October, 1954), 13-17.

J. S. Wilson, "The Devil Was In It," *American Mercury* XXIV (October, 1931), 215-216.

42. SIOPE—A FABLE

(see "Silence—A Fable")

43. SOME PASSAGES IN THE LIFE OF A LION

(see "Lionizing")

44. THE SPECTACLES

Cornelia Varner, "Notes on Poe's Use of Contemporary Materials in Certain of His Stories," *Journal of English and Germanic Philology* XXXII (January, 1933), 79-80.

45. A SUCCESSION OF SUNDAYS

(see "Three Sundays in a Week")

46. THE SYSTEM OF DR. TARR AND PROF. FETHER

William Whipple, "Poe's Two-Edged Satiric Tale," *Nineteenth Century Fiction* IX (September, 1954), 121-133.

47. A TALE OF JERUSALEM

Edward H. Davidson, *Poe: A Critical Study,* 147.

J. S. Wilson, "The Devil Was In It," *American Mercury* XXIV (October, 1931), 218.

POE, EDGAR ALLAN, Continued

48. A TALE OF THE RAGGED MOUNTAINS
    Marie Bonaparte, *The Life and Works of Edgar Allan Poe: A Psycho-Analytic Interpretation,* 559-568.
    N. Bryllion Fagin, *The Histrionic Mr. Poe,* 170-171.
    Sidney E. Lind, "Poe and Mesmerism," *PMLA* LXII (December, 1947), 1079-1085.

49. THE TELL-TALE HEART
    Marie Bonaparte, *The Life and Works of Edgar Allan Poe: A Psycho-Analytic Interpretation,* 491-504.
    Edward H. Davidson, *Poe: A Critical Study,* 189-190, 203, 210.
    Patrick F. Quinn, *The French Face of Edgar Poe,* 232-236.
    Alfred C. Ward, *Aspects of the Modern Short Story,* 35-37.

50. THE THOUSAND-AND-SECOND TALE OF SCHEHERAZADE
    Cornelia Varner, "Notes on Poe's Use of Contemporary Materials in Certain of His Stories," *Journal of English and Germanic Philology* XXXII (January, 1933), 78.

51. THREE SUNDAYS IN A WEEK
    Fannye N. Cherry, "The Source of Poe's 'Three Sundays in a Week,'" *American Literature* II (November, 1930), 232-235.
    Thomas O. Mabbott, "Poe and Dr. Lardner," *American Notes and Queries* III (November, 1943), 115-117.
    Archer Taylor, "Poe's Dr. Lardner, and 'Three Sundays in a Week,'" *American Notes and Queries* III (January, 1944), 153-155.

52. THE UNPARALLELED ADVENTURE OF ONE HANS PFAALL
    (see "Hans Pfaall")

53. THE VISIONARY
    (see "The Assignation")

54. WILLIAM WILSON
    Marie Bonaparte, *The Life and Works of Edgar Allan Poe: A Psycho-Analytic Interpretation,* 539-555.
    Edward H. Davidson, *Poe: A Critical Study,* 198-201, 282.
    Patrick F. Quinn, *The French Face of Edgar Poe,* 221-223.
    Edward Shanks, *Edgar Allan Poe,* 133-135.

PORTER, KATHERINE ANNE

1. CIRCUS
    S. H. Poss, "Variations on a Theme in Four Stories of Katherine

Anne Porter," *Twentieth Century Literature* IV (April-July, 1958) , 22.

2. THE CRACKED LOOKING-GLASS

Charles A. Allen, "Katherine Anne Porter: Psychology as Art," *Southwest Review* XLI (Summer, 1956) , 224-225.

H. J. Mooney, *Fiction and Criticism of Katherine Anne Porter*, 44-46.

R. P. Warren, "Irony With a Center: Katherine Anne Porter," *Kenyon Review* IV (Winter, 1942) , 41-42. — reprinted in R. P. Warren, *Selected Essays*, 148-149.

3. A DAY'S WORK

H. J. Mooney, *Fiction and Criticism of Katherine Anne Porter*, 50.

4. THE DOWNWARD PATH TO WISDOM

Charles A. Allen, "Katherine Anne Porter: Psychology as Art," *Southwest Review* XLI (Summer, 1956) , 223-224.

H. J. Mooney, *Fiction and Criticism of Katherine Anne Porter*, 51-54.

Mary Orvis, *The Art of Writing Fiction*, 27-28.

5. FLOWERING JUDAS

Charles A. Allen, "Katherine Anne Porter: Psychology as Art," *Southwest Review* XLI (Summer, 1956) , 227-229.

Charles Allen, "Southwestern Chronicle: Katherine Anne Porter," *Arizona Quarterly* II (Summer, 1946) , 90-92.

Louise Bogan, *Selected Criticism*, 34.

Lodwick Hartley, "Katherine Anne Porter," *Sewanee Review* XLVIII (April-June, 1940) , 212-213.

Robert B. Heilman, *Modern Short Stories*, 192-194.

D. Heiney, *Recent American Literature*, 320-321.

H. J. Mooney, *Fiction and Criticism of Katherine Anne Porter*, 47-48.

Katherine Anne Porter, Comment on 'Flowering Judas' in Whit Burnett, *This Is My Best*, 539-540.

R. P. Warren, "Irony With a Center: Katherine Anne Porter," *Kenyon Review* IV (Winter, 1942) , 32-35. — reprinted in R. P. Warren, *Selected Essays*, 140-143.

Ray B. West, Jr., "Katherine Anne Porter: Symbol and Theme in 'Flowering Judas,'" *Accent* VII (Spring, 1947) , 182-188. — reprinted, revised, in West and Stallman, *Art of Modern Fiction*, 287-292. — reprinted, revised, in Aldridge, *Critiques and Essays on Modern Fiction*, 217-230.

6. THE GRAVE

Beardsley, Daniel, and Leggett, *Aids to Study for "Theme and Form: An Introduction to Literature,"* 85-86.

S. H. Poss, "Variations on a Theme in Four Stories of Katherine Anne Porter," *Twentieth Century Literature* IV (April-July, 1958). 25-28.

Ray B. West, Jr., "Katherine Anne Porter and 'Historic Memory,' " in Rubin and Jacobs, *Southern Renascence,* 278-279.

7. HACIENDA

Charles A. Allen, "Katherine Anne Porter: Psychology as Art," *Southwest Review* XLI (Summer, 1956), 229-230.

Howard Baker, "Some Notes on New Fiction," *Southern Review* I (July, 1935), 188-189.

D. Heiney, *Recent American Literature,* 322-323.

H. J. Mooney, *Fiction and Criticism of Katherine Anne Porter,* 39-40.

8. HE

Howard Baker, "The Contemporary Short Story," *Southern Review* III (Winter, 1938), 595.

Mary Orvis, *The Art of Writing Fiction,* 66, 167.

9. THE JILTING OF GRANNY WEATHERALL

Charles A. Allen, "Katherine Anne Porter: Psychology as Art," *Southwest Review* XLI (Summer, 1956), 225-227.

H. J. Mooney, *Fiction and Criticism of Katherine Anne Porter,* 49-50.

10. THE LEANING TOWER

F. O. Matthiessen, Review of *The Leaning Tower, Accent* V (Winter, 1945), 122-123. — reprinted in Kerker Quinn and Charles Shattuck, *Accent Anthology,* 621-623.

H. J. Mooney, *Fiction and Criticism of Katherine Anne Porter,* 35-39.

Virgilia Sapieha, "Short Stories Distinguished for More Than Good Craftsmanship," *New York Herald Tribune Book Review* (September 17, 1944), 2.

Diana Trilling, "Fiction in Review," *Nation* CLIX (September, 1944), 359-360.

Vernon Young, "The Art of Katherine Anne Porter," *New Mexico Quarterly Review* XV (Autumn, 1945), 336-340. — reprinted in *American Thought—1947,* 234-237.

11. MARIA CONCEPCIÓN

Charles A. Allen, "Katherine Anne Porter: Psychology as Art," *Southwest Review* XLI (Summer, 1956), 225.

[Lillian B. Gilkes, "On Writing the Short Story," in Dorothy Brewster, *A Book of Contemporary Short Stories* (1936) , 703-705.]

D. Heiney, *Recent American Literature,* 319-320.

H. J. Mooney, *Fiction and Criticism of Katherine Anne Porter,* 48-49.

William Troy, "A Matter of Quality," *Nation* CXLI (October 30, 1935) , 517.

12. NOON WINE

Charles Allen, "Southwestern Chronicle: Katherine Anne Porter," *Arizona Quarterly* II (Summer, 1946) , 92-95.

Ben Belitt, "South Texas Primitive," *Nation* CXLIV (May 15, 1937) , 571.

Brooks, Purser, and Warren, *An Approach to Literature,* 218-219.

Royal A. Gettmann and Bruce Harkness, *Teacher's Manual for "A Book of Stories,"* 68-70.

Frederick J. Hoffman, "Katherine Anne Porter's 'Noon Wine,' " *CEA Critic* XVIII (November, 1956) , 1, 6-7.

R. M. Ludwig and M. B. Perry, *Nine Short Novels,* xx-xxiii.

H. J. Mooney, *Fiction and Criticism of Katherine Anne Porter,* 40-44.

Katherine Anne Porter, " 'Noon Wine': The Sources," *Yale Review* XLVI (Autumn, 1956) , 22-39.

Robert Penn Warren, "Introduction" to Edward Schwartz, *Katherine Anne Porter: A Critical Bibliography,* 7-9.

R. P. Warren, "Irony With a Center: Katherine Anne Porter," *Kenyon Review* IV (Winter, 1942) , 40-41. — reprinted, considerably expanded, in R. P. Warren, *Selected Essays,* 143-148.

Glenway Wescott, "Praise," *Southwestern Review* V (Summer, 1939) , 161-165.

Ray B. West, Jr., "Katherine Anne Porter and 'Historic Memory,' " in Rubin and Jacobs, *Southern Renascence,* 281-282. — reprinted from *Hopkins Review* VI (Fall, 1952) .

13. OLD MORTALITY

Brooks and Warren, *Understanding Fiction,* 529-534.

Lodwick Hartley, "Katherine Anne Porter," *Sewanee Review* XLVIII (April-June, 1940) , 210.

H. J. Mooney, *The Fiction and Criticism of Katherine Anne Porter,* 20-25.

S. H. Poss, "Variations on a Theme in Four Stories of Katherine Anne Porter," *Twentieth Century Literature* IV (April-July, 1958) , 22-23.

R. P. Warren, "Irony With a Center: Katherine Anne Porter,"

Kenyon Review IV (Winter, 1942), 35-40. — reprinted, considerably revised, in R. P. Warren, *Selected Essays,* 149-154.

Ray B. West, Jr., "Katherine Anne Porter and 'Historic Memory,' " in Rubin and Jacobs, *Southern Renascence,* 285-289. — reprinted from *Hopkins Review* VI (Fall, 1952).

14. THE OLD ORDER

H. J. Mooney, *The Fiction and the Criticism of Katherine Anne Porter,* 17-19.

Sale, Hall, and Steinmann, *Critical Discussions for Teachers Using "Short Stories: Tradition and Direction,"* 44-47.

15. PALE HORSE, PALE RIDER

H. J. Mooney, *Fiction and Criticism of Katherine Anne Porter,* 25-33.

William Phillips, *Great American Short Novels,* xiii.

S. H. Poss, "Variations on a Theme in Four Stories of Katherine Anne Porter," *Twentieth Century Literature* IV (April-July, 1958), 23-24.

Glenway Wescott, "Praise," *Southern Review* V (Summer, 1939), 165-166.

Ray B. West, Jr., *The Short Story in America: 1900-1950,* 74-75.

16. ROPE

Anon., Review of *Flowering Judas, New York Times Book Review* (September 28, 1930), 6.

Mary Orvis, *The Art of Writing Fiction,* 105-107.

17. THAT TREE

D. Heiney, *Recent American Literature,* 321-322.

H. J. Mooney, *Fiction and Criticism of Katherine Anne Porter,* 51.

18. THEFT

James B. Hall and Joseph Langland, *The Short Story,* 381-382

Mary Orvis, *The Art of Writing Fiction,* 123-125.

POWERS, J. F.

1. A COUPLE OF NIGHTS BEFORE CHRISTMAS

George Scouffas, "J. F. Powers: On the Vitality of Disorder," *Critique: Studies in Modern Fiction* II (Fall, 1958), 41-43, 57.

2. DEATH OF A FAVORITE

Naomi Lebowitz, "The Stories of J. F. Powers: The Sign of the Contradiction," *Kenyon Review* XX (Summer, 1958), 494-495.

3. THE FORKS

Royal A. Gettmann and Bruce Harkness, *Teacher's Manual for "A Book of Stories,"* 16-17.

POWERS, J. F., Continued

4. JAMESIE
   John P. Sisk, "The Complex Moral Vision of J. F. Powers,"
   Critique: Studies in Modern Fiction II (Fall, 1958), 38-39.
5. LIONS, HARTS, LEAPING DOES
   Naomi Lebowitz, "The Stories of J. F. Powers: The Sign of the
   Contradiction," *Kenyon Review* XX (Summer, 1958), 496-499.
   George Scouffas, "J. F. Powers: On the Vitality of Disorder,"
   Critique: Studies in Modern Fiction II (Fall, 1958), 43-51.
6. LOOK HOW THE FISH LIVE
   George Scouffas, "J. F. Powers: On the Vitality of Disorder,"
   Critique: Studies in Modern Fiction II (Fall, 1958), 51-55.
7. THE PRINCE OF DARKNESS
   Naomi Lebowitz, "The Stories of J. F. Powers: The Sign of the
   Contradiction," *Kenyon Review* XX (Summer, 1958), 494-496.
   James P. Shannon, "J. F. Powers on the Priesthood," *Catholic
   World* CLXXV (September, 1952), 432-437.
   John P. Sisk, "The Complex Moral Vision of J. F. Powers,"
   Critique: Studies in Modern Fiction II (Fall, 1958), 32-34.
8. THE VALIANT WOMAN
   Brooks, Purser, and Warren, *An Approach to Literature*, 117-118.
   James B. Hall and Joseph Langland, *The Short Story*, 299.
   Winifred Lynskey, *Reading Modern Fiction* (Second Edition,
   1957), 444-445.
9. ZEAL
   John P. Sisk, "The Complex Moral Vision of J. F. Powers,"
   Critique: Studies in Modern Fiction II (Fall, 1958), 28-30.

POWYS, T. F.

1. BOTTLE'S PATH
   Sale, Hall, and Steinmann, *Critical Discussions for Teachers for
   "Modern Short Stories,"* 25-28.

PRITCHETT, V. S.

1. THE APE
   R. B. Heilman, *Modern Short Stories,* 292-293.

PUSHKIN, ALEXANDER

1. AN AMATEUR PEASANT GIRL
   (see "The Peasant-Miss")
2. THE CAPTAIN'S DAUGHTER
   Janko Lavrin, *Pushkin and Russian Literature,* 189-193.
   V. Shklovski, "Pushkin's Prose," in *Pushkin: A Collection of Articles and Essays on the Great Russian Poet,* 109-115.
3. THE EGYPTIAN NIGHTS
   [Ralph E. Matlaw, "Poetry and the Poet in Romantic Society as Reflected in Pushkin's 'Egyptian Nights,'" *Slavonic and East European Review* XXXIII (1955), 102-119.]
4. HISTORY OF THE VILLAGE GORYUKHINO
   V. Shklovski, "Pushkin's Prose," in *Pushkin: A Collection of Articles and Essays on the Great Russian Poet,* 108.
5. THE LADY-RUSTIC
   (see "The Peasant-Miss")
6. MISTRESS INTO MAID
   (see "The Peasant-Miss")
7. THE PEASANT-MISS
   Waclaw Lednicki, *Bits of Table Talk on Pushkin, Mickiewicz, Goethe, Turgenev, and Sienkiewicz,* 11.
8. THE QUEEN OF SPADES
   V. Shklovski, "Pushkin's Prose," in *Pushkin: A Collection of Articles and Essays on the Great Russian Poet,* 108-109.
9. THE SHOT
   Waclaw Lednicki, *Bits of Table Talk on Pushkin, Mickiewicz, Goethe, Turgenev, and Sienkiewicz,* 14.
10. THE SNOWSTORM
    Waclaw Lednicki, "The Snowstorm," in Lednicki, *Bits of Table Talk on Pushkin, Mickiewicz, Goethe, Turgenev, and Sienkiewicz,* 33-59.
11. THE STATION-MASTER
    Waclaw Lednicki, *Bits of Table Talk on Pushkin, Mickiewicz, Goethe, Turgenev, and Sienkiewicz,* 12-13.
12. THE UNDERTAKER
    Waclaw Lednicki, *Bits of Table Talk on Pushkin, Mickiewicz, Goethe, Turgenev, and Sienkiewicz,* 13.

ROSENFELD, ISAAC

1. BAZAAR OF THE SENSES
   Judah Goldin, "The Contemporary Jew and His Judaism," in S. R. Hopper, *Spiritual Problems in Contemporary Literature,* 218.

RUSSELL, JOHN

1. THE PRICE OF THE HEAD
Adrian H. Jaffe and Virgil Scott, "Analysis," in Jaffe and Scott, *Studies in the Short Story*, 98-101.

SANSOM, WILLIAM

1. THE CLIFF
Howard Nemerov, "Sansom's Fictions," *Kenyon Review* XVII (Winter, 1955), 131-134.
2. HOW CLAEYS DIED
Herbert Barrows, *Suggestions for Teaching "Fifteen Stories,"* 14-16.

SAROYAN, WILLIAM

1. 1, 2, 3, 4, 5, 6, 7, 8
Edwin Berry Burgum, "The Lonesome Young Man on the Flying Trapeze," *Virginia Quarterly Review* XX (Summer, 1944), 394-395.
2. THE LIVING AND THE DEAD
Edmund Wilson, *The Boys in the Back Room*, 28-29.

SARTRE, JEAN-PAUL

1. INTIMACY
Edward Morris, "Intimacy," *Yale French Studies*, No. 1 (Spring-Summer, 1948), 73-79.
Henri Peyre, *The Contemporary French Novel*, 227.
2. THE MAKING OF A LEADER
Madeleine Smith, "'The Making of a Leader,'" *Yale French Studies*, No. 1 (Spring-Summer, 1948), 80-83.
3. THE WALL
James B. Hall and Joseph Langland, *The Short Story*, 128-129.
Henri Peyre, *The Contemporary French Novel*, 227.
West and Stallman, *Art of Modern Fiction*, 336-338.

SCHORER, MARK

1. THE FACE WITHIN THE FACE
James B. Hall and Joseph Langland, *The Short Story*, 276-277.

SCHORER, MARK, Continued

2. WHAT WE DON'T KNOW HURTS US
R. B. Heilman, *Modern Short Stories,* 96-97.

SCHWARTZ, DELMORE

1. AMERICA! AMERICA!
Morton Seif, "Fallen David and Goliath America: The Battle Report of Delmore Schwartz," *Jewish Social Studies* XIII (October, 1951), 316.
2. A BITTER FARCE
Morton Seif, "Fallen David and Goliath America: The Battle Report of Delmore Schwartz," *Jewish Social Studies* XIII (October, 1951), 320.
3. IN DREAMS BEGIN RESPONSIBILITIES
Irving Howe, "Tone in the Short Story," *Sewanee Review* LVII (Winter, 1949), 147-148.
4. THE WORLD IS A WEDDING
Isa Kapp, "Familial Relations," *Kenyon Review* XI (Winter, 1949), 163.
Heinz Politzer, "The Two Worlds of Delmore Schwartz," *Commentary* X (December, 1950), 564-565.

SCOTT, EVELYN

1. TURNSTILE
Alfred Dashiell, *Editor's Choice,* 212-213.

SEEGER, ALAN

1. THE CONQUEROR
Mary Orvis, *The Art of Writing Fiction,* 78.

SHAW, IRWIN

1. THE EIGHTY-YARD RUN
Stegner, Scowcroft, and Ilyin, *The Writer's Art,* 197-200.
2. THE GIRLS IN THEIR SUMMER DRESSES
Mary Orvis, *The Art of Writing Fiction,* 70-73, 98.

SHAW, IRWIN, Continued

3. SAILOR OFF THE BREMEN
   R. B. Heilman, *Modern Short Stories*, 172-173.

SHUMWAY, NAOMI

1. IKE AND US MOONS
   Edward J. O'Brien, *The Short Story Case Book*, 477-505.

SOLDATI, MARIO

1. THE WINDOW
   Bernard Wall, "New Italian Writers," *The Twentieth Century* CXLIX (May, 1951), 414-415.

STAFFORD, JEAN

1. THE INTERIOR CASTLE
   Richard A. Condon, "Stafford's 'The Interior Castle,'" *Explicator* XV, No. 1 (October, 1956), item 6.
2. CHILDREN ARE BORED ON SUNDAY
   James B. Hall and Joseph Langland, *The Short Story*, 357-358.
3. A REUNION
   Royal A. Gettmann and Bruce Harkness, *Teacher's Manual for "A Book of Stories,"* 58-60.

STEGNER, WALLACE

1. THE BLUE-WINGED TEAL
   Charles E. Eisinger, "Twenty Years of Wallace Stegner," *College English* XX (December, 1958), 115-116.
2. THE CITY OF THE LIVING
   Chester E. Eisinger, "Twenty Years of Wallace Stegner," *College English* XX (December, 1958), 115.
3. TWO RIVERS
   Mary Orvis, *The Art of Writing Fiction*, 22-26.
4. A VIEW FROM THE BALCONY
   Royal A. Gettmann and Bruce Harkness, *Teacher's Manual for "A Book of Stories,"* 3-4.

STEGNER, WALLACE, Continued

5. THE WOMEN ON THE WALL
Chester E. Eisinger, "Twenty Years of Wallace Stegner," *College English* XX (December, 1958), 115.
Wallace Stegner, "A Problem in Fiction," *Pacific Spectator* III (Autumn, 1949), 369-375. — reprinted in Stegner, Scowcroft, and Ilyin, *The Writer's Art*, 317-324.

STEIN, GERTRUDE

1. THE GOOD ANNA
Donald Sutherland, *Gertrude Stein*, 29-40.
2. MELANCTHA
Haldeen Braddy, "The Primitivism in Gertrude Stein's 'Melanctha,'" *New Mexico Quarterly Review* XX (Autumn, 1950), 358-365.
Oscar Cargill, *Intellectual America: Ideas on the March*, 315-316.
Katherine Mansfield, *Novels and Novelists*, 274.
Rosalind S. Miller, *Gertrude Stein*, 30-34.
Francis Russell, *Three Studies in Twentieth Century Obscurity*, 73-75.
Donald Sutherland, *Gertrude Stein*, 44-52.
3. THINGS AS THEY ARE
B. L. Reid, *Art by Subtraction: A Dissenting Opinion of Gertrude Stein*, 72-74.
Elizabeth Sprigge, *Gertrude Stein*, 44-49.
Donald Sutherland, *Gertrude Stein*, 46-47.
Edmund Wilson, *Shores of Light*, 580-586.

STEINBECK, JOHN

1. BREAKFAST
Sale, Hall, and Steinmann, *Critical Discussions for Teachers Using "Short Stories: Tradition and Direction,"* 50-52.
2. CHRYSANTHEMUMS
Joseph Warren Beach, *American Fiction: 1920-1940*, 311-314. — reprinted in E. W. Tedlock, Jr., and C. V. Wicker, *Steinbeck and His Critics*, 81-83.
Kenneth Kempton, *Short Stories for Study*, 120-124.
R. B. West, Jr., *The Short Story in America: 1900-1950*, 48-50.

STEINBECK, JOHN, Continued

3. FLIGHT
Norman Friedman, "What Makes a Short Story Short?" *Modern Fiction Studies* IV (Summer, 1958), 113-114.
Walter Havighurst, *Masters of the Modern Short Story*, viii-ix.
Peter Lisca, *The Wide World of John Steinbeck*, 98-100.
4. JOHNNY BEAR
Peter Lisca, *The Wide World of John Steinbeck*, 96.
5. THE LEADER OF THE PEOPLE
Adrian H. Jaffe and Virgil Scott, "Analysis" in Jaffe and Scott, *Studies in the Short Story*, 172-181.
Peter Lisca, *The Wide World of John Steinbeck*, 104-107.
6. THE RED PONY
Walter Gierasch, "Steinbeck's The Red Pony, II, 'The Great Mountains,'" *Explicator* IV (March, 1946), item 39.
D. W. Heiney, *Recent American Literature*, 234-235.
Peter Lisca, *The Wide World of John Steinbeck*, 101-104.
7. THE SHORT REIGN OF PIPPIN IV
Peter Lisca, *The Wide World of John Steinbeck*, 285-288.
8. ST. KATY THE VIRGIN
Peter Lisca, *The Wide World of John Steinbeck*, 94.
9. VIGILANTE
Peter Lisca, *The Wide World of John Steinbeck*, 97-98.
10. THE WHITE QUAIL
Peter Lisca, *The Wide World of John Steinbeck*, 95.

STEVENSON, ROBERT LOUIS

1. THE BEACH OF FALESA
Sidney Colvin, *The Letters of Robert Louis Stevenson*, III, 242-243.
2. THE BOTTLE IMP
Joseph Warren Beach, "The Sources of Stevenson's 'The Bottle Imp,'" *Modern Language Notes* XXV (January, 1910), 12-18.
George S. Hellman, "'Cue' Stories of Stevenson," *Bookman* (American) LXII (October, 1925), 160-164. — reprinted in Hellman, *The True Stevenson*, 221-230.
Peter Penzoldt, *The Supernatural in Fiction*, 105-106.
3. DR. JEKYLL AND MR. HYDE
(see "The Strange Case of Dr. Jekyll and Mr. Hyde")
4. A LODGING FOR THE NIGHT
William T. Going, "Stevenson's 'A Lodging for the Night,'" *Explicator* VIII (March, 1950), item 41.

STEVENSON, ROBERT LOUIS, Continued

5. MARKHEIM
Kenneth Kempton, *The Short Story*, 180-185.
Peter Penzoldt, *The Supernatural in Fiction*, 107-108.
Alfred C. Ward, *Aspects of the Modern Short Story*, 111-113.

6. THE MERRY MEN
Sidney Colvin, *The Letters of Robert Louis Stevenson*, II, 48-49, 50-51.
John Robert Moore, "Stevenson's Source for 'The Merry Men,'" *Philological Quarterly* XXIII (April, 1944), 135-140.

7. OLALLA
Sidney Colvin, *The Letters of Robert Louis Stevenson*, II, 359-360.

8. SIRE DE MALÉTROIT'S DOOR
Séan O'Faoláin, *The Short Story*, 193-197.

9. THE STRANGE CASE OF DR. JEKYLL AND MR. HYDE
George S. Hellman, "R. L. S. and the Streetwalker," *American Mercury* XXXVIII (July, 1936), 344.
Henry James, *Partial Portraits*, 169-171. — reprinted in Janet Adam Smith, *Henry James and Robert Louis Stevenson*, 155-157. — reprinted in James, *The House of Fiction* (Rupert Hart-Davis, 1957), 135-136.
G. B. Stern, *Robert Louis Stevenson*, 19.

10. THRAWN JANET
Coleman O. Parsons, "Stevenson's Use of Witchcraft in 'Thrawn Janet,'" *Studies in Philology* XLIII (July, 1946), 551-571.

11. THE WAIF WOMAN
George S. Hellman, " 'Cue' Stories of Stevenson," *Bookman* (American) LXII (October, 1925), 159-160. — reprinted in Hellman, *The True Stevenson*, 217-220.

12. WILL O' THE MILL
Henry James, *Partial Portraits*, 160-161. — reprinted in Janet Adam Smith, *Henry James and Robert Louis Stevenson*, 146-147. — reprinted in James, *The House of Fiction* (Rupert Hart-Davis, 1957), 129-130.
Alfred C. Ward, *Aspects of the Modern Short Story*, 108-111.

STUART, JESSE

1. ANOTHER APRIL
Jesse Stuart, Comment in Whit Burnett, *This Is My Best*, 407-408.

SUCKOW, RUTH

1. FOUR GENERATIONS
   Gorham Munson, "The Recapture of the Storyable," *University Review* X (Autumn, 1943) , 38-42.
2. GOLDEN WEDDING
   Douglas Bement, *Weaving the Short Story*, 221-251.
3. A START IN LIFE
   Royal A. Gettmann and Bruce Harkness, *Teacher's Manual for "A Book of Stories,"* 28-30.

TAYLOR, PETER

1. ALLEGIANCE
   Kenneth C. Cathey, "Peter Taylor: An Evaluation," *Western Review* XVIII (Autumn, 1953) , 13-14.
2. BAD DREAMS
   Kenneth C. Cathey, "Peter Taylor: An Evaluation," *Western Review* XVIII (Autumn, 1953) , 17-18.
3. A LONG FOURTH
   Kenneth C. Cathey, "Peter Taylor: An Evaluation," *Western Review* XVIII (Autumn, 1953) , 11-13.
4. TWO LADIES IN RETIREMENT
   Kenneth C. Cathey, "Peter Taylor: An Evaluation," *Western Review* XVIII (Autumn, 1953) , 17-18.
5. A WOMAN OF MEANS
   Kenneth C. Cathey, "Peter Taylor: An Evaluation," *Western Review* XVIII (Autumn, 1953) , 16-17.
   Roger Shattuck, "Six First Assignments of Guilt," *Western Review* XVI (Autumn, 1951) , 87-88.
   James Stern, "The Power of Charm," *New Republic* CXXII (June 26, 1950) , 20.
   R. P. Warren, "Father and Son," *New York Times Book Review* (June 11, 1950) , 8.
   Thomas Wilcox, "A Novelist of Means," *Sewanee Review* LIX (Winter, 1951) , 151-154,

THOMAS, DYLAN

1. ADVENTURES IN THE SKIN TRADE
   Derek Stanford, *Dylan Thomas*, 162-165.

Richard J. Stonesifer, "Thomas' 'Adventures in the Skin Trade,' "
Explicator XVII, No. 2 (November, 1958), item 10.

2. THE BURNING BABY
Jacob Korg, "The Short Stories of Dylan Thomas," *Perspective* I
(Spring, 1948), 188-189.
Derek Stanford, *Dylan Thomas,* 161-162.

3. THE DRESS
Jacob Korg, "The Short Stories of Dylan Thomas," *Perspective*
I (Spring, 1948), 185.

4. THE ENEMIES
Derek Stanford, *Dylan Thomas,* 158.

5. FOLLOWERS
Burton S. Glick, "A Brief Analysis of a Short Story by Dylan
Thomas," *American Imago* XIV (1957), 149-154.
Robert Phelps, "In Country Dylan," *Sewanee Review* LXIII
(Autumn, 1955), 683-684.

6. THE MAP OF LOVE
Frederick J. Hoffman, *Freudianism and the Literary Mind* (Second
Edition, 1957), 288-289.
Jacob Korg, "The Short Stories of Dylan Thomas," *Perspective*
I (Spring, 1948), 190.

7. THE MOUSE AND THE WOMAN
Frederick J. Hoffman, *Freudianism and the Literary Mind* (Second
Edition, 1957), 289-290.
Jacob Korg, "The Short Stories of Dylan Thomas," *Persepective*
I (Spring, 1948), 185-187.

8. ONE WARM SATURDAY
Frederick J. Hoffman, *Freudianism and the Literary Mind* (Second
Edition, 1957), 287-288.

9. PATRICIA, EDITH, AND ARNOLD
Herbert Barrows, *Suggestions for Teaching "15 Stories,"* 9-10.

10. THE TREE
Derek Stanford, *Dylan Thomas,* 158-159.

THOMPSON, THOMAS

1. A SHORE FOR THE SINKING
Richard B. Hudson, "Thompson's 'A Shore for the Sinking,' "
Explicator IX (June, 1951), item 59.

THORPE, T. B.

1. THE BIG BEAR OF ARKANSAS
Walter Blair, "The Technique of 'The Big Bear of Arkansas,' "
Southwest Review XXVIII (Summer, 1943), 426-435.
Carvel Collins, "Faulkner and Certain Earlier Southern Fiction,"
College English XVI (November, 1954), 96-97.

THURBER, JAMES

1. THE SECRET LIFE OF WALTER MITTY
Mary Orvis, *The Art of Writing Fiction*, 142-143.

TOLSTOY, LEO

1. ALBERT
Ernest J. Simmons, *Leo Tolstoy*, 156-157.
2. THE DEATH OF IVAN ILYICH
William Barrett, "Existentialism as a Symptom of Man's Contemporary Crisis," in Stanley R. Hopper, *Spiritual Problems in Contemporary Literature*, 143, 145.
E. M. Forster, *Two Cheers for Democracy*, 210-211.
Norman Friedman, "What Makes a Short Story Short?", *Modern Fiction Studies* IV (Summer, 1958), 115-116.
L. Hamalian and E. L. Volpe, *Ten Modern Short Novels*, 59-60.
Charles Neider, *Short Novels of the Masters*, 22-27.
Renato Poggioli, "The Art of Ivan Bunin," *Harvard Slavic Studies* I (1953), 257-258. — reprinted in Poggioli, *The Phoenix and the Spider*, 138-139.
Philip Rahv, "The Death of Ivan Ilyich and Joseph K.," *Southern Review* V (Summer, 1939), 174-185. — reprinted in Rahv, *Image and Idea*, 111-127.
Marc Slonim, *The Epic of Russian Literature*, 335.
3. THE DEVIL
Mark Van Doren, *Private Reader*, 148-150.
4. DOMESTIC HAPPINESS
(see "Family Happiness")
5. FAMILY HAPPINESS
Philip Rahv, *Image and Idea*, 81-82. — reprinted in William Phillips and Philip Rahv, *The New Partisan Reader, 1945-1953*, 217-218.

TOLSTOY, LEO, Continued

6. HOW MUCH LAND DOES A MAN NEED?
Royal A. Gettmann and Bruce Harkness, *Teacher's Manual for "A Book of Stories,"* 51-53.
West and Stallman, *The Art of Modern Fiction,* 131-133.

7. THE KREUTZER SONATA
Janko Lavrin, *Tolstoy: An Approach,* 126-127, 128-130.
Aylmer Maude, *Tolstoy on Art,* 12-16.
Tikhon Polner, *Tolstoy and His Wife,* 164-167.
Ernest J. Simmons, *Leo Tolstoy,* 437-446.
Marc Slonim, *The Epic of Russian Literature,* 338-341.

8. LUCERNE
V. V. Zenkovskii, *Russian Thinkers and Europe,* 120-121.

9. SEVASTOPOL IN DECEMBER, 1854
Avrahm Yarmolinsky, *A Treasury of Great Russian Short Stories,* xiii.

10. THREE ARSHINS OF LAND
(see "How Much Land Does a Man Need?")

11. THREE DEATHS
Beardsley, Daniel, and Leggett, *Aids to Study for "Theme and Form: An Introduction to Literature,"* 86.
Janko Lavrin, *Tolstoy: An Approach,* 84-85.
George Rapall Noyes, *Tolstoy,* 66-67.

12. THE THREE HERMITS
E. M. Forster, *Two Cheers for Democracy,* 211.

13. THE TWO HUSSARS
Waclaw Lednicki, *Russia, Poland and the West,* 211-213.
Renato Poggioli, *The Phoenix and the Spider,* 59-60.

14. WHERE LOVE IS, THERE IS GOD ALSO
Anon., "A Tolstoian Dispute," *Living Age* CCCXXXVI (March, 1929), 40.

TRILLING, LIONEL

1. OF THIS TIME, OF THAT PLACE
Felheim, Newman, Steinhoff, *Study Aids for Teachers for "Modern Short Stories,"* 19-21.

2. THE OTHER MARGARET
James T. Farrell, "Literature and Morality," *New International* XII (May, 1946), 143-145. — reprinted in James T. Farrell, *Literature and Morality,* 10-14.
Tom McAfee, "A Note on 'The Other Margaret,'" *Western Review* XIV (Winter, 1950), 143-144.

TURGENEV, IVAN

1. **BIRYUK**
[Mildred A. Martin, "The Last Shall Be First: A Study of Three Russian Short Stories," *Bucknell Review* VI (March, 1956), 13-23.]
2. **BYEZHIN MEADOW**
Frank O'Connor, "Turgenev and the Cult of the Will," in O'Connor, *The Mirror in the Roadway*, 130-131.
3. **A CORRESPONDENCE**
Henry James, *French Poets and Novelists*, 245-246.
4. **THE DIARY OF A SUPERFLUOUS MAN**
Waclaw Lednicki, *Russia, Poland, and the West*, 182-187.
5. **FIRST LOVE**
Ralph E. Matlaw, "Turgenev's Novels," *Harvard Slavic Studies*, IV (1957), 261-262.
Charles Morgan, "Turgenev's Treatment of a Love-Story," in Royal Society of Literature of the United Kingdom, *Essays by Divers Hands* XXV, n.s. (1950), 102-119.
6. **THE HISTORY OF LIEUTENANT ERGUNOV**
Edmund Wilson, "Turgenev and the Life-Giving Drop," *New Yorker* XXXIII (October 19, 1957), 202-203. — reprinted in Turgenev, *Literary Reminiscences,* (Farrar, 1958), 50-52.
7. **THE SINGERS**
Ashley Brown, "Turgenev," *Shenandoah* VI (Winter, 1954), 20-21.
8. **A TOUR OF THE FOREST**
Edmund Wilson, "Turgenev and the Life-Giving Drop," *New Yorker* XXXIII (October 19, 1957), 204-206. — reprinted in Turgenev, *Literary Reminiscences* (Farrar, 1958), 53-55.

TWAIN, MARK

1. **CAPTAIN STORMFIELD'S VISIT TO HEAVEN**
(see "Extract from Captain Stormfield's Visit to Heaven")
2. **THE CELEBRATED JUMPING FROG OF CALAVERAS COUNTY**
(see "The Notorious Jumping Frog of Calaveras County")
3. **THE DANDY FRIGHTENING THE SQUATTER**
Edgar M. Branch, *The Literary Apprenticeship of Mark Twain,* 7-10.
Fred W. Lorch, "A Source for Mark Twain's 'The Dandy Frightening the Squatter,'" *American Literature* III (November, 1931), 309.

4. A DOUBLE-BARRELLED DETECTIVE STORY
Lane Cooper, "Mark Twain's Lilacs and Laburnums," *Modern Language Notes* XLVII (February, 1932), 85-87.
Nathaniel S. Olds, "A Mark Twain Retort," *Saturday Review of Literature* VIII (May 7, 1932), 722.
Albert Bigelow Paine, *Mark Twain: A Biography* (Centenary Edition, 1935), II, 1136-1138.

5. EXTRACT FROM CAPTAIN STORMFIELD'S VISIT TO HEAVEN
Henry S. Canby, *Turn West, Turn East*, 243-244.
Albert Bigelow Paine, *Mark Twain's Notebook*, 130.
Isaac Rosenfeld, "A Boy's Heaven," *New Republic* CXXVII (December 1, 1952), 18-19.
Dixon Wecter, "Introduction," in Twain, *Report from Paradise* (Harper, 1952), ix-xxv.

6. GRANDFATHER'S RAM STORY
(see "The Story of the Old Ram")

7. THE MAN THAT CORRUPTED HADLEYBURG
Gladys C. Bellamy, *Mark Twain As a Literary Artist*, 308-309.
Everett Carter, *Howells and the Age of Realism*, 227-229.

8. THE MYSTERIOUS STRANGER
Gladys C. Bellamy, *Mark Twain As a Literary Artist*, 352-366, 372-376.
Henry S. Canby, *Turn West, Turn East*, 245-247.
Alexander Cowie, *The Rise of the American Novel*, 637-640.
Sherwood Cummings, "Mark Twain's Social Darwinism," *Huntington Library Quarterly* XX (February, 1957), 163-175, passim.
Bernard DeVoto, *Mark Twain at Work*, 127-130.
Theodore Dreiser, "Mark the Double Twain," *English Journal* XXIV (October, 1935), 615-627, passim.
E. B. Foote, "The Mysterious Paragraph," *Saturday Review of Literature* XII (October 26, 1935), 9.
E. S. Fussell, "The Structural Problem of 'The Mysterious Stranger,'" *Studies in Philology* XLIX (January, 1952), 95-104.
Carroll D. Laverty, "The Genesis of 'The Mysterious Stranger,'" *Mark Twain Quarterly* VII (Spring-Summer, 1947), 15-19.
R. M. Ludwig and M. B. Perry, *Nine Short Novels*, xlvii-li.
Edgar Lee Masters, *Mark Twain: A Portrait*, 221-234.
Albert Bigelow Paine, *Mark Twain's Notebook*, 337, 369.
Edward Wagenknecht, *Cavalcade of the American Novel*, 124-125.
Dixon Wecter, "Mark Twain," in Spiller, *Literary History of the United States*, II, 938-939.

TWAIN, MARK, Continued

Homer E. Woodbridge, "Mark Twain and the 'Gesta Romanorum,' " *Nation* CVIII (March 22, 1919) , 424-425.
9. THE NOTORIOUS JUMPING FROG OF CALAVERAS COUNTY
Gladys C. Bellamy, *Mark Twain As a Literary Artist,* 147-148.
Walter Blair, *Native American Humor (1800-1900),* (American Book, 1937) , 56-58.
Edgar M. Branch, *The Literary Apprenticeship of Mark Twain,* 120-129.
Roger Penn Cuff, "Mark Twain's Use of California Folklore in His Jumping Frog Story," *Journal of American Folklore* LXV (April-June, 1952) , 155-158.
Bernard DeVoto, *Mark Twain's America,* 172-178.
Albert Bigelow Paine, *Mark Twain: A Biography,* (Centenary Edition, 1935) I, 278-280.
10. THE STORY OF THE OLD RAM
J. W. Hollenbach, "Mark Twain, Story-Teller, at Work," *College English* VII (March, 1946) , 303-312.

UNAMUNO, MIGUEL DE

1. ABEL SÁNCHEZ
Arturo Barea, *Unamuno,* 43-46.
L. Hamalian and E. L. Volpe, *Ten Modern Short Novels,* 371-372.
2. AUNT TULA
Arturo Barea, *Unamuno,* 49-50.
3. LOVE AND PEDAGOGY
Arturo Barea, *Unamuno,* 38.
4. THE MARQUIS OF LUMBRIA
Angel Del Rio, "Introduction," in Unamuno, *Three Exemplary Novels* (Grove Press, 1956) , 24-33.
5. NOTHING LESS THAN A MAN
Arturo Barea, *Unamuno,* 46-49.
Angel Del Rio, "Introduction," in Unamuno, *Three Exemplary Novels* (Grove Press, 1956) , 24-33.
6. SAINT MANUEL BUENO, MARTYR
Arturo Barea, *Unamuno,* 50-55.
7. TWO MOTHERS
Angel Del Rio, "Introduction," in Unamuno, *Three Exemplary Novels* (Grove Press, 1956) , 24-33.

UNAMUNO, MIGUEL DE, Continued

8. LA VENDA
   Eleanor K. Paucker, "Unamuno's 'La Venda': Short Story and Drama," *Hispania* XXXIX (September, 1956), 309-312.

UPWARD, EDWARD

1. SUNDAY
   Stephen Spender, *The Destructive Element*, 237-243.

VAN DUYN, MONA

1. THE BELL
   Mary Orvis, *The Art of Writing Fiction*, 30-32.

WARREN, ROBERT PENN

1. BLACKBERRY WINTER
   Beardsley, Daniel, and Leggett, *Theme and Form: An Introduction to Literature*, 691-695, passim.
   John M. Bradbury, *The Fugitives: A Critical Account*, 199-200.
   Royal A. Gettmann and Bruce Harkness, *Teacher's Manual for "A Book of Stories,"* 56-58.
   Ray B. West, Jr., *The Short Story in America: 1900-1950*, 77-80.
2. THE CIRCUS IN THE ATTIC
   John M. Bradbury, *The Fugitives: A Critical Account*, 200-202.
   Robert Daniel, "No Place to Go," *Sewanee Review* LVI (Summer, 1948), 525.
   Anne Freemantle, Review of *The Circus in the Attic, Commonweal* XLVII (March 12, 1948), 547.
   Margaret Marshall, "Notes by the Way," *Nation* CLXVI (February 21, 1948), 216.
3. THE PATENTED GATE AND THE MEAN HAMBURGER
   Sale, Hall, and Steinmann, *Critical Discussions for Teachers Using "Short Stories: Tradition and Direction,"* 48-50.
4. PRIME LEAF
   John M. Bradbury, *The Fugitives: A Critical Account*, 196-197.

1. THE COUNTRY OF THE BLIND
Patrick Braybrooke, *Some Aspects of H. G. Wells,* 18-20.
Alfred C. Ward, *Aspects of the Modern Short Story,* 141-144.
2. THE DOOR IN THE WALL
Alfred C. Ward, *Aspects of the Modern Short Story,* 139-142.
3. THE TIME MACHINE
Patrick Braybrooke, *Some Aspects of H. G. Wells,* 13-18.

WELTY, EUDORA

1. ASPHODEL
Audrey Hodgins, "The Narrator as Ironic Device in a Short Story of Eudora Welty," *Twentieth Century Literature* I (January, 1956), 215-219.
2. AT THE LANDING
R. P. Warren, "The Love and the Separateness in Miss Welty," *Kenyon Review* VI (Spring, 1944), 255-256. — reprinted in Warren, *Selected Essays,* 165-166.
3. THE BRIDE OF THE INNISFALLEN
William Peden, "The Incomparable Welty," *Saturday Review* XXXVIII (April 9, 1955), 18.
Louis D. Rubin, Jr., "Two Ladies of the South," *Sewanee Review* XLIII (Autumn, 1955), 676-677.
4. THE BURNING
Thomas H. Carter, "Rhetoric and Southern Landscapes," *Accent* XV (Autumn, 1955), 294-295.
Robert G. Davis, *Instructor's Manual for "Ten Modern Masters,"* 53-54.
William H. McBurney, "Welty's 'The Burning,'" *Explicator* XVI, No. 2 (November, 1957), item 9.
5. CLYTIE
Granville Hicks, "Eurora Welty," *College English* XIV (October, 1952), 70-71. — reprinted in *English Journal* XLI (November, 1952), 462-463.
6. DEATH OF A TRAVELING SALESMAN
Eleanor Clark, "Old Glamour, New Gloom," *Partisan Review* XVI (June, 1949), 634-635.
Mark Schorer, *The Story,* 354-357.
7. FIRST LOVE
Winifred Lynskey, *Reading Modern Fiction,* (Second Edition, 1957), 483-485.

197

8. THE HITCH-HIKERS
   Granville Hicks, "Eudora Welty," *College English* XIV (November, 1952) , 70-71.
9. JUNE RECITAL
   Robert Daniel, "The World of Eudora Welty," in Rubin and Jacobs, *The Southern Renascence,* 312-313.
   H. C. Morris, "Zeus and the Golden Apples: Eudora Welty," *Perspective* V (Autumn, 1952) , 193-194.
10. KIN
    Louis D. Rubin, Jr., "Two Ladies of the South," *Sewanee Review* LXIII (Autumn, 1955) , 671-675.
11. LIVVIE
    Mary Orvis, *The Art of Writing Fiction,* 121-123.
    R. P. Warren, "The Love and the Separateness in Miss Welty," *Kenyon Review* VI (Spring, 1944) , 254-255. — reprinted in Warren, *Selected Essays,* 165-166.
12. A MEMORY
    Katherine Anne Porter, "Introduction" to Welty, *A Curtain of Green,* xxii. — reprinted in Porter, *The Days Before,* 108.
    R. P. Warren, "The Love and the Separateness in Miss Welty," *Kenyon Review* VI (Spring, 1944) , 252-253. — reprinted in Warren, *Selected Essays,* 162-163.
13. MUSIC FROM SPAIN
    Robert Daniel, "The World of Eudora Welty," in Rubin and Jacobs, *Southern Renascence,* 310.
    H. C. Morris, "Zeus and the Golden Apples: Eudora Welty," *Perspective* V (Autumn, 1952) , 196-197.
14. NO PLACE FOR YOU, MY LOVE
    Thomas H. Carter, "Rhetoric and Southern Landscapes," *Accent* XV (Autumn, 1955) , 293-294.
15. OLD MR. MARBLEHALL
    Brooks and Warren, *Understanding Fiction,* 470-480.
16. PETRIFIED MAN
    Robert G. Davis, *Instructor's Manual for "Ten Modern Masters,"* 52-53.
    William M. Jones, "Welty's 'The Petrified Man,'" *Explicator* XV, No. 4 (January, 1957) , item 21.
    Katherine Anne Porter, "Introduction" to Welty, *Curtain of Green,* xx-xxi. — reprinted in Porter, *The Days Before,* 107.
    Jarvis Thurston, *Reading Modern Short Stories,* 7, 13-14, 26.
17. A PIECE OF NEWS
    Brooks and Warren, *Understanding Fiction,* 143-145.

18. THE PONDER HEART
    Robert Martin Adams, "Formulas and Fictions," *Hudson Review* VII (Spring, 1954), 145.
    Robert Y. Drake, Jr., "The Reasons of the Heart," *Georgia Review* XI (Winter, 1957), 420-426.
    Warren French, "A Note on Eudora Welty's 'The Ponder Heart,' " *College English* XV (May, 1954), 474.
    Edwin Kennebeck, "People of Clay," *Commonweal* LIX (January 22, 1954), 410-411.
    William Peden, "A Trial With No Verdict," *Saturday Review* XXXVII (January 16, 1954), 14.
    V. S. Pritchett, "Bossy Edna Earle Had a Word for Everything," *New York Times Book Review* (January 10, 1954), 5.

19. POWERHOUSE
    Sale, Hall, and Steinmann, *Critical Discussions for Teachers Using "Short Stories: Tradition and Direction,"* 52-55.
    Ray B. West, Jr., "Three Methods of Modern Fiction," *College English* XII (January, 1951), 198-202. — reprinted in West and Stallman, *Art of Modern Fiction,* 403-408.

20. THE ROBBER BRIDEGROOM
    John Peale Bishop, "Violent Country," *New Republic* CVII (November 16, 1942), 646-647. — reprinted in Bishop, *Collected Essays,* 257-259.
    Eunice Glenn, "Fantasy in the Fiction of Eudora Welty," in Allen Tate, *A Southern Vanguard,* 85-88. — reprinted in John W. Aldridge, *Critiques and Essays on Modern Fiction,* 512-515.
    Marianne Hauser, "Miss Welty's Fairy Tale," *New York Times Book Review* (November 1, 1942), 6-7.
    Alfred Kazin, "An Enchanted World in America," *New York Herald Tribune Book Review* (October 25, 1942), 19.
    N. L. Rothman, "The Lost Realm," *Saturday Review of Literature* XXV (November 14, 1942), 16.
    Charles Shattuck, Review, *Accent* III (Winter, 1943), 124.
    Lionel Trilling, "American Fairy Tale," *Nation* CLV (December 12, 1942), 686-687.

21. SHOWER OF GOLD
    Felheim, Newman, and Steinhoff, *Study Aids for Teachers for "Modern Short Stories,"* 53-55.
    James B. Hall and Joseph Langland, *The Short Story,* 329-330.
    H. C. Morris, "Zeus and the Golden Apples: Eudora Welty," *Perspective* V (Autumn, 1953), 190-192.

WELTY, EUDORA, Continued

22. A STILL MOMENT

Royal A. Gettmann and Bruce Harkness, *Teacher's Manual for "A Book of Stories,"* 23-25.

Eunice Glenn, "Fantasy in the Fiction of Eudora Welty," in Allen Tate, *A Southern Vanguard*, 83-84. — reprinted in John W. Aldridge, *Critiques and Essays on Modern Fiction*, 510-512.

Isaac Rosenfeld, "Consolations of Poetry," *New Republic* CIX (October 18, 1943), 525-526.

Stallman and Watters, *Creative Reader*, 334.

R. P. Warren, "The Love and the Separateness in Miss Welty," *Kenyon Review* VI (Spring, 1944), 250-252. — reprinted in Warren, *Selected Essays*, 161-162.

23. A VISIT OF CHARITY

Lodwick Hartley, "Proserpina and the Old Ladies," *Modern Fiction Studies* III (Winter, 1957-1958), 350-354.

24. THE WIDE NET

R. P. Warren, "The Love and the Separateness in Miss Welty," *Kenyon Review* VI (Spring, 1944), 253-254. — reprinted in Warren, *Selected Essays*, 164-165.

25. A WORN PATH

Herbert Barrows, *Suggestions for Teaching "15 Stories,"* 31-32.

Robert G. Davis, *Instructor's Manual for "Ten Modern Masters,"* 51-52.

William M. Jones, "Welty's 'A Worn Path,'" *Explicator* XV, No. 9 (June, 1957), item 57.

WESCOTT, GLENWAY

1. THE PILGRIM HAWK

F. W. Dupee, "Return of Glenway Wescott," *New Republic* CIII (December 9, 1940), 807-808.

William Phillips, *Great American Short Novels*, xiii-xiv.

C. E. Schorer, "The Maturing of Glenway Wescott," *College English* XVIII (March, 1957), 323-324.

Katherine Woods, "A Strange Tale by Glenway Wescott," *New York Times Book Review* (December 1, 1940), 7.

M. D. Zabel, "The Whisper of the Devil," *Nation* CLI (December 21, 1940), 636-637.

WEST, JESSAMYN

1. HORACE CHOONEY, M.D.
   Jessamyn West, "The Story of a Story," *Pacific Spectator* III (Summer, 1949), 264-273. — reprinted in Stegner, Scowcroft, and Ilyin, *The Writer's Art*, 334-343.
2. LOVE, DEATH, AND THE LADIES' DRILL TEAM
   Kenneth Kempton, *Short Stories for Study*, 35-40.
3. SHIVAREE BEFORE BREAKFAST
   Robert B. Heilman, *Modern Short Stories*, 107-108.

WEST, NATHANAEL

1. A COOL MILLION
   Arthur Cohen, "Nathanael West's Holy Fool," *Commonweal* LXIV (June, 1956), 276-278.
   C. Carroll Hollis, "Nathanael West and the 'Lonely Crowd,'" *Thought* XXXIII (Autumn, 1958), 402-406.
   Alan Ross, "Novelist-Philosophers: XIV—The Dead Centre: an Introduction to Nathanael West," *Horizon* XVIII (October, 1948), 292-294. — reprinted in *Complete Works of Nathanael West* (Farrar, Straus, Cudahy, 1957), xvii-xix.
   Cyril M. Schneider, "The Individuality of Nathanael West,'" *Western Review* XX (Autumn, 1955), 16-20.*
2. THE DREAM LIFE OF BALSO SNELL
   Arthur Cohen, "Nathanael West's Holy Fool," *Commonweal* LXIV (June, 1956), 276-278.
   C. Carroll Hollis, "Nathanael West and the 'Lonely Crowd,'" *Thought* XXXIII (Autumn, 1958), 398-400.
   James Light, "Nathanael West, 'Balso Snell,' and the Mundane Millstone," *Modern Fiction Studies* IV (Winter, 1958-1959), 319-328.
   Alan Ross, "Novelist-Philosophers: XIV—The Dead Centre: an Introduction to Nathanael West," *Horizon* XVIII (October, 1948), 287-289. — reprinted in *Complete Works of Nathanael West* (Farrar, Straus, Cudahy, 1957), xi-xiii.
   Cyril M. Schneider, "The Individuality of Nathanael West," *Western Review* XX (Autumn, 1955), 8-10.*
   Edward G. Schwartz, "The Novels of Nathanael West," *Accent* XVII (Autumn, 1957), 251-256.
3. MISS LONELYHEARTS
   Robert M. Coates, "Introduction," in West, *Miss Lonelyhearts* (New Directions, 1933), xii-xiii.

Arthur Cohen, "Nathanael West's Holy Fool," *Commonweal* LXIV (June, 1956), 276-278.

James F. Light, *"Miss Lonelyhearts:* The Imagery of Nightmare," *American Quarterly* VIII (Winter, 1956), 316-327.

V. S. Pritchett, "Miss Lonelyhearts," *New Statesman and Nation* LIV (December, 1957), 791.

Alan Ross, "Novelist-Philosophers: XIV—The Dead Centre: an Introduction to Nathanael West," *Horizon* XVIII (October, 1948), 289-291. — reprinted in *Complete Works of Nathanael West* (Farrar, Straus, Cudahy, 1957), xiii-xvii.

Cyril M. Schneider, "The Individuality of Nathanael West," *Western Review* XX (Autumn, 1955), 10-16.*

Edward G. Schwartz, "The Novels of Nathanael West," *Accent* XVII (Autumn, 1957), 256-257.

WHARTON, EDITH

1. **AFTER HOLBEIN**
Anne Freemantle, "Edith Wharton: Values and Vulgarity," in Harold C. Gardiner, *Fifty Years of the American Novel*, 31-32.

William T. Going, "Wharton's 'After Holbein,'" *Explicator* X (November, 1951), item 8.

Blake Nevius, *Edith Wharton,* 193-194.

2. **AUTRES TEMPS**
Blake Nevius, *Edith Wharton,* 175-177.

3. **BUNNER SISTERS**
Blake Nevius, *Edith Wharton,* 124-126.

4. **ETHAN FROME**
Anne Freemantle, "Edith Wharton: Values and Vulgarity," in Harold C. Gardiner, *Fifty Years of the American Novel*, 24.

Alfred Kazin, *On Native Grounds,* 81.

Blake Nevius, "'Ethan Frome' and the Themes of Edith Wharton's Fiction," *New England Quarterly* XXIV (June, 1951), 204-207. — reprinted, with additional material, in Blake Nevius, *Edith Wharton,* 117-124, 127-130.

John Crowe Ransom, "Characters and Character: A Note on Fiction," *American Review* VI (January, 1936), 271-275.

----

* Readers of this article should consult *Western Review* (Spring, 1956), 254-256.

J. D. Thomas, "Marginalia on 'Ethan Frome,' " *American Literature* XXVII (November, 1955) , 405-409.
Lionel Trilling, "The Morality of Inertia," in R. M. MacIver, *Great Moral Dilemmas in Literature, Past and Present*, 37-46.
Edith Wharton, *A Backward Glance*, 209, 293, 295-296.
Edith Wharton, "Introduction," in Wharton, *Ethan Frome* (Modern Student's Library, Scribner's, 1922) , v-x.
Edith Wharton, "The Writing of 'Ethan Frome,' " *Colophon* III, Part 11 (1932) , 1-4. — reprinted in E. Adler and Others, *Breaking into Print* (Simon and Schuster, 1937) , 187-191. — reprinted in William Targ, *Reader for Writers* (Hermitage, 1951) , 145-147.

5. THE EYES
   Blake Nevius, *Edith Wharton*, 94-98.
6. THE FULLNESS OF LIFE
   Anne Freemantle, "Edith Wharton: Values and Vulgarity," in Harold C. Gardiner, *Fifty Years of the American Novel*, 21-22.
7. THE MISSION OF JANE
   Sale, Hall, and Steinmann, *Critical Discussions for Teachers Using "Short Stories: Tradition and Direction,"* 8-11.
8. THE PRETEXT
   Millicent Bell, "A James 'Gift' to Edith Wharton," *Modern Language Notes* LXXII (March, 1957) , 182-185.
9. ROMAN FEVER
   Royal A. Gettmann and Bruce Harkness, *Teacher's Manual for "A Book of Stories,"* 26-28.
10. SUMMER
    Blake Nevius, *Edith Wharton*, 168-173.
    Edith Wharton, *A Backward Glance*, 294.

WILLIAMS, TENNESSEE

1. ONE ARM
   Robert Roth, "Tennessee Williams in Search of a Form," *Chicago Review* IX (Summer, 1955) , 88-90.
2. DESIRE AND THE BLACK MASSEUR
   Robert Roth, "Tennessee Williams in Search of a Form," *Chicago Review* IX (Summer, 1955) , 91-92.

WILLIAMS, WILLIAM CARLOS

1. **THE BURDEN OF LOVELINESS**
Mona Van Duyn, "To 'Make Light of It' as Fictional Technique,"
Perspective VI (Autumn-Winter, 1953), 233-235.
2. **THE COLD WORLD**
Sale, Hall, and Steinmann, *Critical Discussions for Teachers Using
"Short Stories: Tradition and Direction,"* 47-48.
3. **THE DAWN OF ANOTHER DAY**
Vivienne Koch, *William Carlos Williams*, 223-225.
4. **THE DESCENDANT OF KINGS**
Vivienne Koch, *William Carlos Williams*, 211-212.
5. **A FACE OF STONE**
Vivienne Koch, *William Carlos Williams*, 218-220.
6. **THE GREAT AMERICAN NOVEL**
Hugh Kenner, "A Note on 'The Great American Novel,'"
Perspective VI (Autumn-Winter, 1953), 177-182.
7. **JEAN BEICKE**
Mona Van Duyn, "To 'Make Light of It' As Fictional Technique,"
Perspective VI (Autumn-Winter, 1953), 235-238.
8. **MIND AND BODY**
Vivienne Koch, *William Carlos Williams*, 213-214.
9. **OLD DOC RIVERS**
Vivienne Koch, *William Carlos Williams*, 215-217.
10. **THE USE OF FORCE**
Brooks, Purser, and Warren, *An Approach to Literature*, 33-34.
Royal A. Gettmann and Bruce Harkness, *Teacher's Manual for
"A Book of Stories,"* 61-62.
R. B. Heilman, *Modern Short Stories*, 373-374.
11. **THE VENUS**
Philip Rahv, *Image and Idea*, 153.

WILSON, ANGUS

1. **ET DONA FERENTES**
James B. Hall and Joseph Langland, *The Short Story*, 314-315.

WILSON, EDMUND

1. **ELLEN TERHUNE**
Alfred Kazin, "Le Misanthrope," *Partisan Review* XIII (Summer,
1946), 378-379.

WILSON, EDMUND, Continued

2. MR. AND MRS. BLACKBURN AT HOME
Alfred Kazin, "Le Misanthrope," *Partisan Review* XIII (Summer, 1946) , 379
3. THE PRINCESS WITH THE GOLDEN HAIR
Alfred Kazin, "Le Misanthrope," *Partisan Review* XIII (Summer, 1946) , 377-378.

WILSON, SLOAN

1. A LETTER OF ADMONITION
Kenneth Kempton, *Short Stories for Study,* 85-91.

WOLFE, THOMAS

1. BOOM TOWN
Floyd C. Watkins, *Thomas Wolfe's Characters,* 127-128.
2. CHICKAMAUGA
Edward C. Aswell, "A Note on Thomas Wolfe," in Thomas Wolfe, *The Hills Beyond* (First Edition, 1941) , 379.
Floyd C. Watkins, *Thomas Wolfe's Characters,* 142-146.
3. CHILD BY TIGER
Floyd C. Watkins, *Thomas Wolfe's Characters,* 102-109.
4. CIRCUS AT DAWN
Floyd C. Watkins, *Thomas Wolfe's Characters,* 68-69.
5. GOD'S LONELY MAN
Edward C. Aswell, "A Note on Thomas Wolfe," in Thomas Wolfe, *The Hills Beyond* (First Edition, 1941) , 380-383.
6. THE LION AT MORNING
Edward C. Aswell, "A Note on Thomas Wolfe," in Thomas Wolfe, *The Hills Beyond* (First Edition, 1941) , 380.
7. THE LOST BOY
Edward C. Aswell, "A Note on Thomas Wolfe," in Thomas Wolfe, *The Hills Beyond* (First Edition, 1941) , 377.
Herbert J. Muller, *Thomas Wolfe,* 159.
Louis D. Rubin, *Thomas Wolfe, the Weather of His Youth,* 46-51.
Stegner, Scowcroft, and Ilyin, *The Writer's Art,* 178-183.
Floyd C. Watkins, *Thomas Wolfe's Characters,* 138-141.
8. NO CURE FOR IT
Edward C. Aswell, "A Note on Thomas Wolfe," in Thomas Wolfe, *The Hills Beyond* (First Edition, 1941) , 377-378.

Aileen Pippett, *The Moth and the Star: A Biography of Virginia Woolf*, 103-105.

William Y. Tindall, *Forces in Modern British Literature, 1885-1946*, 302.

William Troy, "Virginia Woolf: The Poetic Method," *Symposium* III (January, 1932), 56.

5. MOMENTS OF BEING
Frank Baldanza, "Virginia Woolf's 'Moments of Being,'" *Modern Fiction Studies* II (February, 1956), 78.

Sylvia Berkman, *Katherine Mansfield*, 175-176.

James Hafley, "On One of Virginia Woolf's Short Stories," *Modern Fiction Studies* II (February, 1956), 13-16.

6. MONDAY OR TUESDAY
Bernard Blackstone, *Virginia Woolf*, 48.

David Daiches, *Virginia Woolf*, 47-48.

Dorothy Hoare, *Some Studies in the Modern Novel*, 47-49.

J. K. Johnstone, *The Bloomsbury Group*, 138, 328.

7. THE NEW DRESS
Robert B. Heilman, *Modern Short Stories*, 346-347.

8. A SOCIETY
David Daiches, *Virginia Woolf*, 45-47.

9. SOLID OBJECTS
Bernard Blackstone, *Virginia Woolf*, 152-154.

Marjorie Brace, "Worshipping Solid Objects: The Pagan World of Virginia Woolf," *Accent* IV (Summer, 1944), 249. — reprinted in Quinn and Shattuck, *Accent Anthology*, 493-494.

J. K. Johnstone, *The Bloomsbury Group*, 136-137.

10. THE STRING QUARTET
Bernard Blackstone, *Virginia Woolf*, 49-50.

David Daiches, *Virginia Woolf*, 48-50.

11. AN UNWRITTEN NOVEL
Marjorie Brace, "Worshipping Solid Objects: The Pagan World of Virginia Woolf," *Accent* IV (Summer, 1944), 248. — reprinted in Quinn and Shattuck, *Accent Anthology*, 491-492.

David Daiches, *Virginia Woolf*, 48.

James Hafley, *The Glass Roof: Virginia Woolf as Novelist*, 45.

Henry Lowenfeld, "Psychic Trauma and Productive Experience," in William Phillips, *Art and Psychoanalysis*, 303-304.

WRIGHT, RICHARD

1. BRIGHT AND MORNING STAR
   Edwin Berry Burgum, "The Art of Richard Wright's Short Stories," *Quarterly Review of Literature* I (Spring, 1944) , 209-210.
2. LONG BLACK SONG
   Edwin Berry Burgum, "The Art of Richard Wright's Short Stories," *Quarterly Review of Literature* I (Spring, 1944) , 206-209.

ZWEIG, STEFAN

1. FOUR-AND-TWENTY HOURS IN A WOMAN'S LIFE
   Sigmund Freud, "Dostoevsky and Parricide" in Freud, *Collected Papers,* Vol V, 239-241. — reprinted in William Phillips, *Art and Psychoanalysis,* 16-18.

PERIODICALS

Accent, I (1940) — XVIII, No. 4 (Autumn, 1958).

Alabama Review, I (1948) — XI, No. 3 (October, 1958).

American-German Review, I (1934) — XXV, No. 1 (October-November, 1958).

American Imago, I (1939) — X, No. 4 (Winter, 1953).

American Journal of Philology, XLVI (1925) — LXXIX, No. 4 (October, 1958).

American Literature, I (1929) — XXX, No. 3 (November, 1958).

American Prefaces, I, No. 1 (October, 1935) — VIII, No. 4 (Summer, 1943).

American Quarterly, I (1949) — X, No. 3 (Fall, 1958).

American Review, I (1933) — IX (October, 1937).

American-Scandinavian Review, XIII (1925) — XLVI, No. 2 (Summer, 1958).

American Scholar, I (1932) — XXVII, No. 3, (Summer, 1958).

American Slavic and East European Review, IV (1945) — XVII, No. 3 (October, 1958).

American Speech, I (1925) — XXXIII, No. 3 (October, 1958).

Analyst (Department of English, Northwestern University), No. I (March, 1953) —No. XV (March, 1958).

Antioch Review, I (1941) — XVIII, No. 3 (Autumn, 1958).

Arizona Quarterly, I (1945) — XIV, No. 3 (Autumn, 1958).

AUMLA (Journal of the Australian Universities Language and Literature Association), No. 1 (August, 1953) — No. 8 (May, 1958).

Bard Review, I (1945) — III, No. 3 (1950)

Books Abroad, I (1927) — XXXII (1958).

Boston Public Library Quarterly, I (1939) — X, No. 4 (October, 1958).

Boston University Studies in English, I (1955) — III, No. 4, (Winter, 1957).

Botteghe Oscure, I (1948) — XXII (Autumn, 1958).

Briarcliff Quarterly (formerly *Maryland Quarterly*), I, No. 1 (January, 1944) — III, No. 12, (January, 1947).

Bulletin of Hispanic Studies, I (1923) — XXXV (1958).

Bulletin of the New York Public Library, XXIX (1925) — LXII (1958).

California Quarterly, I (1951) — IV, No. 1 (1956).

Cambridge Journal, V (1951) — VII (1954).

Catholic World, CXLIV (1925) — CLXXXVII (September, 1958).

CEA Critic (previously the *News Letter* of the College English Association) , IX (1947) — XX (October, 1958) .

Character and Personality (see *Journal of Personality*) .

Chicago Review, I (1946) — XII, No. 3 (Autumn, 1958) .

Chimera, I (1942-1943) — V (1946-1947) .

College English, I (1939) — XX, No. 3 (December, 1958) .

Colorado Quarterly, I (1952) — IV (Spring, 1956) .

Commentary, I (1945) — XXVI, No. 5 (November, 1958) .

Commonweal, VI (1927) — LXVIII, No. 26 (September 26, 1958) .

Comparative Literature, I (1949) — X, No. 3 (Summer, 1958) .

Confluence, I (1952) — VII, No. 2 (Summer, 1958) .

Cornell Studies in English, IX (1925) — XLI (1958) .

Criterion, I, No. 1 (October, 1922) — XVIII, No. 71 (January, 1939) .

Critique: Studies in Modern Fiction, I, No. 1 (Winter, 1956) — II, No. 2 (Fall, 1958) .

Cross Currents, I (1950) — VIII, No. 4 (Fall, 1958) .

Dial, LXVIII (January, 1920) — LXXXVI (July, 1929) .

Discovery (Pocket Books, Inc.) , No. 1 (1952) — No. 6 (1955) .

Dublin Magazine, XXIII (1948) — XXXII (1957) .

Dublin Review, CLXXVI (1925) — CCXXXII (Summer, 1958) .

E. L. H.: A Journal of English Literary History, I (1934) — XXV, No. 3 (September, 1958) .

Encounter, I (1953) — XI, No. 6 (December, 1958) .

English (London) , I (1936) — XII, No. 69 (Autumn, 1958) .

English Fiction in Transition (1880-1920), I, No. 1 (Fall-Winter, 1957) — No. 3 (Fall, 1958) .

English Institute Essays, (1939) — (1957) .

English Journal, XIV (1925) — XLVII, No. 9 (December, 1958) .

English Miscellany, I (1950) — VII (1957) .

English Studies, I (1919) — XXXIX, No. 5 (October, 1958) .

Epoch, I (Fall, 1947) — IX, No. 2 (Autumn, 1958) .

Essays and Studies (by Members of the English Association) XI (1925) — XI, n.s. (1958) .

Essays by Divers Hands (Being the Transactions of the Royal Society of Literature) , I, n.s. (1921) — XXIX (1958) .

Essays in Criticism, I (1951) — VII, No. 4 (October, 1957) .

Ethics, XLIII (1932) — LXIX, No. 1 (October, 1958) .

European, No. 1 (March, 1953) — No. 52 (June, 1957) .

Evergreen Review, I, No. 1 (1957) — II, No. 6 (1958) .

Explicator, I (1942) — XVII, No. 3 (December, 1958) .

Faulkner Studies, I, No. 1 (Spring, 1952) — III, No. 4 (Winter, 1954) .

French Review, I (1927) — XXXII, No. 1 (October, 1958) .

French Studies, I (1947) — XII, No. 4 (October, 1958) .

Frontier, XIII (1932) — XIX (1939) .

Furioso, I (Summer, 1939) — VIII, No. 1 (Spring, 1953).
Georgia Review, I (1947) — XII, No. 3 (Fall, 1958).
Germanic Review, I (1926) — XXXIII, No. 4 (December, 1958).
German Life and Letters, I, n.s. (1947) — XI, No. 4, n.s. (July, 1958).
German Quarterly, I (1928) — XXXI, No. 4 (November, 1958).
Hibbert Journal, XXIX (1930) — LVII, No. 224 (October, 1958).
Hispania, VIII (1925) — XLI, No. 4 (December, 1958).
Hispanic Review, I (1933) — XXVI, No. 4 (October, 1958).
Hopkins Review, I (1947) — VI, No. 3-4 (Spring-Summer, 1953).
Horizon, I (1940) — XX, Nos. 120-121 (December, 1949 - January, 1950).
Hound and Horn, I, No. 1 (September, 1927) — VII, No. 4 (July, 1934).
Hudson Review, I (1947) — XI, No. 3 (Autumn, 1958).
Humanist, I, n.s. I (1941) — XVIII, n.s., No. 1 (1958).
Illinois Studies in Language and Litetrature, VI (November, 1926) — XLV (1958).
Irish Writing, No. 1 (1946) — No. 36 (Autumn-Winter, 1956-1957).
Italian Quarterly, I (1957) — II, No. 2 (Summer, 1958).
Italica, I (1924) — XXXV, No. 3 (September, 1958).
James Joyce Review, I (1957) — II, Nos. 1-2 (Autumn, 1958).
Jewish Social Studies, I (1939) — XX, No. 3 (July, 1958).
Journal of English and Germanic Philology, XXV (1925) — LVII, No. 3 (July, 1958).
Journal of General Education, I (1946) — XI (1958).
Journal of the History of Ideas, I (1940) — XIX, No. 4 (October, 1958).
Journal of Personality (formerly *Character and Personality*), I (1932) — XXVI, No. 3 (September, 1958).
Kenyon Review, I (1939) — XX, No. 4 (Autumn, 1958).
Life and Letters (formerly *Life and Letters Today*), XXI (1939) — LXV, No. 154 (June, 1950).
Life and Letters Today (see *Life and Letters*).
Listener, X (July 5, 1933) — LVI (July-December, 1956).
Literary Review, I, No. 1 (Autumn, 1957) — II, No. 1 (Autumn, 1958).
Literature and Psychology, I (1951) — VIII, No. 3 (Summer, 1958).
London Magazine, I (1954) — V, No. 11 (November, 1958).
Mandrake, I, No. 5, (October, 1947) — II, No. 11 (Autumn-Winter, 1955-1956).
Mark Twain Journal (formerly *Mark Twain Quarterly*), I (1936) — X, No. 1 (Summer, 1955).
Mark Twain Quarterly (see *Mark Twain Journal*).
Maryland Quarterly (see *Briarcliff Quarterly*).
Masses and Mainstream, I (1948) — VIII (December, 1955).
Meanjin Papers, II, No. 2 (Winter, 1943) — XV, No. 4 (Summer, 1956).

Measure, I (1950) —II, No. 4 (Fall, 1951).
Mind, XXXIV (1925) — LXVII, n.s., No. 268 (October, 1958).
Modern Fiction Studies, I (1955) — IV, No. 3 (Autumn, 1958).
Modern Language Journal, X (1925) — XLII, No. 7 (November, 1958).
Modern Language Notes, XL (1925) — LXXIII, No. 7 (November, 1958).
Modern Language Quarterly, I (1940) — XIX, No. 3 (September, 1958).
Modern Language Review, XX (1925) — LIII, No. 4 (October, 1958).
Modern Philology, XXIII (1925) — LVI, No. 2 (November, 1958).
Modern Quarterly (London), I (1938) -- II, No. 3 (July, 1939); I, n.s. (1945) — VIII, n.s., No. 4 (Autumn, 1953).
Monatshefte für Deutschen Unterricht, Deutsche Sprache und Literatur, XXV (1932) — L, No. 6 (November, 1958).
Month, CXLV (1925) — CLXXIV (December, 1939).
Nation, CXXI (1925) —CLXXXVII (November 29, 1958).
New England Quarterly, I (1928) — XXXI, No. 3 (September, 1958).
New Mexico Quarterly Review, I (1931) — XXVIII, No. 1 (Spring 1958).
New Republic, XLII (1925) — CXXXIX (December 1, 1958).
New World Writing (New American Library), No. 1 (April, 1952) — No. 14 (December, 1958).
New Yorker, XX (February 19, 1944) — XXXIV (November 15, 1958).
Nine, I, No. 1 (Winter, 1948-1949) — IV, No. 1 (Winter, 1953-1954).
Nineteenth Century and After, XCVII (1925) — CXLVIII, No. 886 (December, 1950).
Nineteenth Century Fiction, I (1945) — XIII, No. 3 (December, 1958).
Northern Review, I (1942) — VII, No. 4 (Summer, 1956).
Notes and Queries, CXLVIII (1925) — CCIII (1958).
Pacific Spectator, I (1947) — X, No. 4 (Autumn, 1956).
Partisan Review, I (February-March, 1934) — XXV, No. 4 (Fall, 1958).
Personalist, VI (1925) — XXXIX, No. 4 (Autumn, 1958).
Perspective, I (1947) — X, No. 3 (Summer-Autumn, 1958).
Perspectives USA, No. 1 (Autumn, 1952) — No. 16 (Summer, 1956).
Philological Quarterly, I (1922) — XXXVII, No. 3 (July, 1958).
PMLA (Publications of the Modern Language Association of America), XL (1925) — LXXIII, No. 5 (December, 1958).
Prairie Schooner, XI (1937) — XXXII, No. 3 (Fall, 1958).
Quarterly Journal of Speech, XI (1925) — XLIV, No. 3 (October, 1958).
Quarterly Review, CCXLIV (1925) — CCXCVI (October, 1958).
Quarterly Review of Literature, I (1943) — IX, No. 4 (1958).
Queen's Quarterly, XXXII (1925) — LXV, No. 3 (Autumn, 1958).
Review of English Studies, I (1925) — IX, No. 34 (May, 1958).

Rice Institute Pamphlets, XII (1925) – XLV, No. 3 (October, 1958).
Rocky Mountain Review (see *Western Review*).
Romance Philology, I (1947) – XII, No. 2 (November, 1958).
Romanic Review, XXVI (1935) – XLIX, No. 4 (December, 1958).
Russian Review, I (1941) – XVII, No. 4 (October, 1958).
Saturday Review (formerly *Saturday Review of Literature*), I (August 2, 1924) – XLI (September 30, 1958).
Saturday Review of Literature (see *Saturday Review*).
Science and Society, I (1936) – XXII, No. 4 (Fall, 1958).
Scrutiny, I (1932) – XIX, No. 4 (October, 1953).
Sewanee Review, XXXIII (1925) – LXVI, No. 4 (Autumn, 1958).
Shenandoah, I (1949) – IX, No. 3 (Summer, 1958).
Slavonic and East European Review, I (1922) – XXII (December, 1944).
South Atlantic Quarterly, XXIX (1930) – LVII, No. 4 (Autumn, 1958).
Southern Review, I (1935) – VII, No. 4 (Spring, 1942).
Southwest Review, X (1924) – XLIII, No. 4 (Autumn, 1958).
Studies in Philology, XXII (1925) – LV, No. 4 (October, 1958).
Symposium, I (1946) – XI, No. 2 (Fall, 1957).
Symposium: A Critical Review, I (1930) – IV (October, 1933).
Talisman, No. 2 (Winter, 1952) – No. 12 (Winter, 1957-Spring, 1958).
Tennessee Studies in Literature, I (1956) – III (1958).
Texas Quarterly, I, No. 1 (February, 1958) – I, No. 4 (Winter, 1958).
Thought, I (1926) – XXXIII, No. 130 (Autumn, 1958).
Tiger's Eye, No. 1 (October, 1947) -- No. 9 (October, 1949).
Times Literary Supplement (London), (January 1, 1925) – (December 26, 1958).
Tulane Studies in English, I (1949) – VII (1957).
Twentieth Century (formerly *Nineteenth Century and After*), CLXIX (1951) – CLXIV (September, 1958).
Twentieth Century Literature, I (1955) – IV, No. 3 (October, 1958).
Twice A Year, No. 1 (1938) – Nos. 16-17 (1948).
University of California Publications in English, I (1929) – XX (1949).
University of California Publications in Modern Philology, XII (1925) – L (1958).
University of Kansas City Review (formerly *University Review*), I (1935) – XXV, No. 1 (Autumn, 1958).
University of Michigan Contributions in Modern Philology, No. 1 (1947) – No. 21 (1957).
University of New Mexico Publications in Language and Literature, No. 1 (1949) – No. 13 (1958).
University of North Carolina Studies in Comparative Literature, No. 2 (1950) – No. 20 (1957).

University of North Carolina Studies in the Germanic Languages and Literatures, No. 1 (1949) — No. 22 (1958).

University Review (see *University of Kansas City Review*).

University of Texas Studies in English, V (1925) — XXXVI (1957).

University of Toronto Quarterly, I (1931) — XXVIII, No. 1 (October, 1958).

University of Upsala. Essays and Studies on American Language and Literature, I (1945) — XI (1954).

University of Upsala. Essays and Studies on English Language and Literature, VII (1950) — XVII (1957).

Utah Humanities Review (see *Western Humanities Review*).

Victorian Newsletter, No. 1 (April, 1952) — No. 13 (Spring, 1958).

Victorian Studies, I (1957) — II, No. 2 (December, 1958).

Views, II, No. 2 (Spring, 1954) — IV, No. 3 (n.d.)

Virginia Quarterly Review, I (1925) — XXXIV, No. 4 (Autumn, 1958).

Western Humanities Review (formerly *Utah Humanities Review*), I (1947) — XII, No. 4 (Autumn, 1958).

Western Review (formerly *Rocky Mountain Review*), VI, Nos. 3-4 (Spring-Summer, 1942) — XXIII, No. 1 (Autumn, 1958).

William and Mary Quarterly, I (1944) — XIV (1957).

Wind and the Rain, III (1945) — VII, Nos. 2-3, (1951).

Writer, LIII (1940) — LXXI, No. 9 (September, 1958).

Yale French Studies, No. 1 (1948) — No. 21 (Spring-Summer, 1958).

Yale Review, XV (1925) — XLVIII, No. 1 (September, 1958).

Yale Studies in English, LXX (1925) — CXXXIX (1958).

Year's Work in English Studies, VI (1925) — XXXVII (1956).

Year's Work in Modern Language Studies, I (1930) — XIX (1957).

BOOKS

I. GENERAL

Aldridge, John W., *After the Lost Generation.* New York: McGraw-Hill, 1951.

――――――, ed., *Critiques and Essays on Modern Fiction: 1920-1951.* New York: Ronald Press, 1952.

――――――, *In Search of Heresy: American Literature in an Age of Conformity.* New York: McGraw-Hill, 1956.

American Thought—1947. New York: Gresham Press, 1947.

Anderson, Margaret C., ed., *The Little Review Anthology.* New York: Hermitage House, 1953.

Angoff, Allan, ed., *American Writing Today.* New York: New York University Press, 1957.

Auden, W. H., *The Enchaféd Flood, or The Romantic Iconography of the Sea.* New York: Random House, 1950.

Bacourt, Pierre de, and J. W. Cunliffe, *French Literature During the Last Half-Century.* New York: Macmillan, 1923.

Barrows, Herbert, *Suggestions for Teaching "Fifteen Stories."* Boston: D. C. Heath, 1950.

Basler, Roy P., *Sex, Symbolism, and Psychology in Literature.* New Brunswick: Rutgers University Press, 1948.

Bates, H. E., *The Modern Short Story: A Critical Survey.* London: Thomas Nelson, 1943.

Beach, Joseph Warren, *American Fiction: 1920-1940.* New York: Macmillan, 1941.

——————, *The Twentieth Century Novel.* New York: Appleton-Century, 1932.

Beach, Stewart, *Short-Story Technique.* Boston: Houghton-Mifflin, 1929.

Beardsley, Monroe, Robert Daniel, and Glenn Leggett, *Aids to Study for "Theme and Form: An Introduction to Literature."* Englewood Cliffs: Prentice-Hall, 1956.

——————, eds., *Theme and Form: An Introduction to Literature.* Englewood Cliffs: Prentice-Hall, 1956.

Bement, Douglas, and Ross M. Taylor, *The Fabric of Fiction.* New York: Harcourt, 1951.

Bement, Douglas, *Weaving the Short Story.* New York: Long and Smith, 1932.

Bentley, Eric Russell, ed., *The Importance of Scrutiny.* New York: George W. Stewart, 1948.

Bewley, Marius, *The Complex Fate.* London: Chatto and Windus, 1952.

Bishop, John Peale, *The Collected Essays of John Peale Bishop.* New York: Scribner's, 1948.

Blackmur, R. P., *Anni Mirabiles, 1921-1925.* Washington, D. C.: Library of Congress, 1956.

——————, *The Double Agent: Essays in Craft and Elucidation.* New York: Arrow Editions, 1935.

——————, *The Lion and the Honeycomb.* New York: Harcourt, 1955.

Bogan, Louise, *Selected Criticism.* New York: Noonday Press, 1955.

Bowen, Elizabeth, *Collected Impressions.* New York: Knopf, 1950.

Boynton, Percy, *America in Contemporary Fiction.* Chicago: University of Chicago Press, 1940.

Bradbury, John M., *The Fugitives: A Critical Account.* Chapel Hill: University of North Carolina Press, 1958.

Brée, Germaine, and Margaret Guiton, *An Age of Fiction: The French*

Novel from Gide to Camus. New Brunswick: Rutgers University Press, 1957.

Brewster, Dorothy, and Angus Burrell, *Dead Reckonings in Fiction.* London: Longmans, Green, 1924.

Brewster, Dorothy, *East-West Passage: A Study in Literary Relationships.* London: Allen and Unwin, 1954.

Brewster, Dorothy, and Angus Burrell, *Modern Fiction.* New York: Columbia University Press, 1934.

Bronfeld, Stewart, ed., *A Treasury of New Short Fiction.* New York: National Publishing, 1955.

Brooks, Cleanth, and Robert B. Heilman, eds.. *Understanding Drama.* New York: Holt, 1945.

Brooks, Cleanth, and Robert Penn Warren, eds., *An Anthology of Stories from the Southern Review.* Baton Rouge: Louisiana State University Press, 1953.

————————, *Understanding Fiction.* New York: Crofts, 1943.

Brooks, Cleanth, John T. Purser, and Robert Penn Warren, eds., *An Approach to Literature.* New York: Appleton-Century-Crofts, 1952.

Brooks, Van Wyck, *The Flowering of New England, 1815-1865.* New York: Modern Library, 1941.

————————, *New England: Indian Summer, 1865-1915.* New York: Dutton, 1940.

————————, *The Opinions of Oliver Allston.* New York: Dutton, 1941.

————————, *The World of Washington Irving.* Philadelphia: Blakiston, 1945.

————————, *The Writer in America.* New York: Dutton, 1953.

Brown, Calvin S., *Music and Literature.* Athens: University of Georgia Press, 1948.

Brown, E. K., *Rhythm in the Novel.* Toronto: University of Toronto Press, 1950.

Brown, Francis, ed., *Highlights of Modern Literature* (Mentor Books). New York: New American Library, 1954.

Brown, Leonard, ed., *Modern American and British Short Stories.* New York: Harcourt, 1929.

Brownell, W. C., *American Prose Masters.* New York: Scribner's, 1925.

Burgum, Edwin Berry, *The Novel and the World's Dilemma.* New York: Oxford University Press, 1947.

Burke, Kenneth, *Counter-Statement* (Second Edition). Los Altos, California: Hermes Publications, 1953.

————————, *A Grammar of Motives.* New York: Prentice-Hall, 1945.

————————, *The Philosophy of Literary Form.* Baton Rouge: Louisiana State University Press, 1941.

————————, *A Rhetoric of Motives*. New York: Prentice-Hall, 1950.

Burnett, Whit and Hallie, eds., *Story: The Fiction of the Forties*. New York: Dutton, 1949.

Burnett, Whit, ed., *This Is My Best*. New York: Dial Press, 1942.

Burnett, Whit and Hallie, eds., *The Tough Ones: A Collection of Realistic Stories*. New York: Popular Library Eagle Book, 1954.

Butler, John F., *Exercises in Literary Understanding*. Chicago: Scott-Foresman, 1956.

Canby, Henry Seidel, and Robeson Bailey, eds., *The Book of the Short Story*. New York: Appleton-Century-Crofts, 1948.

Capetanakis, Demetrios, *The Shores of Darkness: Poems and Essays*. New York: Devin-Adair, 1949.

Cargill, Oscar, *Intellectual America: Ideas on the March*. New York: Macmillan, 1941.

Carter, Everett, *Howells and the Age of Realism*. Philadelphia: Lippincott, 1954.

Cecil, David, *Poets and Story-Tellers*. New York: Macmillan, 1949.

Cerf, Bennett A., ed., *Modern American Short Stories*. New York: World Publishing, 1945.

Chase, Richard, *The American Novel and Its Tradition*. Garden City: Doubleday, 1957.

Chesterton, G. K., *The Common Man*. New York: Sheed and Ward, 1950.

Connolly, Cyril, *The Condemned Playground, Essays: 1927-1944*. New York: Macmillan, 1946.

————————, *Enemies of Promise*. London: Routledge, 1938.

————————, ed., *The Golden Horizon*. New York: University Books, 1955.

Connolly, Francis *The Types of Literature*. New York: Harcourt, 1955.

Coveney, Peter, *Poor Monkey: The Child in Literature*. London: Rockliff, 1957.

Cowie, Alexander, *The Rise of the American Novel*. New York: American Book, 1951.

Cowley, Malcolm, ed., *Writers at Work: The "Paris Review" Interviews*. New York: Viking, 1958.

Cross, Ethan Allen, ed., *A Book of the Short Story*. New York: American Book, 1934.

Cross, Wilbur L., *Four Contemporary Novelists*. New York: Macmillan, 1930.

Current-Garcia, Eugene, and Walton R. Patrick, eds., *American Short Stories: 1820 to the Present*. Chicago: Scott, Foresman, 1952.

Daiches, David, *The Novel and the Modern World*. Chicago: University of Chicago Press, 1939.

Dashiell, Alfred, *Editor's Choice*. New York: Putnam's, 1934.

Davis, Robert G., *Instructor's Manual for "Ten Modern Masters,"* New York: Harcourt, 1953.

—————————, ed., *Ten Modern Masters*. New York: Harcourt, 1953.

Day, A. Grove, and Willian F. Bauer, eds., *The Greatest American Short Stories*. New York: McGraw-Hill, 1953.

Douglas, Wallace, et al., eds., *The Critical Reader: Poems, Studies, and Essays*. New York: W. W. Norton, 1949.

Duffey, Bernard, *The Chicago Renaissance in American Letters: A Critical History*. East Lansing: Michigan State College Press, 1954.

Dupuy, Ernest, *The Great Masters of Russian Literature*. New York: T. Y. Crowell, 1886.

Edel, Leon, *The Psychological Novel, 1900-1950*. Philadelphia: Lippincott, 1955.

Edgar, Pelham, *The Art of the Novel*. New York: Macmillan, 1933.

Eliot, T. S., *After Strange Gods*. London: Faber, 1934.

Eloesser, Arthur, *Modern German Literature*. New York: Knopf, 1933.

Fadiman, Clifton, ed., *Reading I've Liked*. New York: Simon and Schuster, 1941.

Farrell, James T., *The League of Frightened Philistines*. New York: Vanguard, 1945.

—————————, *Literature and Morality*. New York: Vanguard, 1947.

Feibleman, James K., *Aesthetics: A Study of the Fine Arts in Theory and Practice*. New York: Duell, Sloan and Pearce, 1949.

Feidelson, Charles, Jr., *Symbolism and American Literature*. Chicago: University of Chicago Press, 1953.

Felheim, Marvin, Franklin Newman, and William Steinhoff, *Study Aids for Teachers for "Modern Short Stories."* New York: Oxford University Press, 1951.

Fiedler, Leslie, *An End to Innocence*. Boston: Beacon Press, 1955.

Ford, Ford Madox, *Portraits from Life* (English edition titled *Mightier Than the Sword*). Boston: Houghton Mifflin, 1937.

Forster, E. M., *Two Cheers for Democracy*. New York: Harcourt, 1951.

Fowlie, Wallace, *Clowns and Angels: Studies in Modern French Literature*. New York: Sheed and Ward, 1943.

Fraser, G. S., *The Modern Writer and His World*. London: Andre Deutsch, 1955.

Freud, Sigmund, *Collected Papers*, Vol. V. London: Hogarth, 1950.

Friederich, Werner P., *An Outline-History of German Literature*. New York: Barnes and Noble, 1948.

Friedman, Melvin J., *Stream of Consciousness: A Study in Literary Method*. New Haven: Yale University Press, 1955.

Frohock, W. M., *The Novel of Violence in America, 1920-1950*. Dallas: Southern Methodist University Press, 1950.

Fromm, Erich, *The Forgotten Language.* New York: Rinehart, 1951.

Gardiner, Harold C., S. J., ed., *American Classics Reconsidered: A Christian Appraisal.* New York: Scribner's, 1958.

――――――, *Fifty Years of the American Novel.* New York: Scribner's, 1951.

Geismar, Maxwell, *The Last of the Provincials.* London: Secker & Warburg, 1947.

――――――, *Writers in Crisis: 1925-1940.* Boston: Houghton Mifflin, 1942.

Gettmann, Royal A., and Bruce Harkness, *Teacher's Manual for "A Book of Stories."* New York: Rinehart, 1955.

Gilkes, Lillian, and Warren Bower, *Short Story Craft: An Introduction to Short Story Writing.* New York: Macmillan, 1949.

Goodman, Paul, *The Structure of Literature.* Chicago: University of Chicago Press, 1954.

Gordon, Caroline, and Allen Tate, eds., *The House of Fiction.* New York: Scribner's, 1950.

Gordon, Caroline, *How to Read a Novel.* New York: Viking ,1957.

Grabo, Carl H., *The Technique of the Novel.* New York: Schribner's, 1928.

Gray, James, *On Second Thought.* Minneapolis: University of Minnesota Press, 1946.

Greene, Graham, *The Lost Childhood and Other Essays.* New York: Viking, 1952.

Hall, James B., and Joseph Langland, eds., *The Short Story.* New York: Macmillan, 1956.

Halle, Morris, ed., *For Roman Jakobson.* The Hague: Mouton, 1956.

Hamalian, Leo, and Edmond L. Volpe, eds., *Ten Modern Short Novels.* New York: Putnam's, 1958.

Hamilton, Clayton, *A Manual of the Art of Fiction.* Garden City: Doubleday, Page, 1922.

Hartwick, Harry, *Foreground of American Fiction.*_ New York: American Book, 1934.

Harvard Slavic Studies, I. Cambridge: Harvard University Press, 1953.

――――――, IV. Cambridge: Harvard University Press, 1957.

Hastings, Harry W., ed., *The College Short Story Reader.* New York: Odyssey, 1948.

Hatcher, Harlan H., *Creating the Modern American Novel.* New York: Farrar and Rinehart, 1935.

Havighurst, Walter, *Instructor's Manual: "Masters of the Modern Short Story."* New York: Harcourt, 1955.

――――――, ed., *Masters of the Modern Short Story.* New York: Harcourt, 1945.

Haydn, Hiram, and John Cournos, eds., *A World of Great Stories*. New York: Crown, 1947.

Heilman, R. B., ed., *Modern Short Stories*. New York: Harcourt, 1950.

Heiney, Donald, *Recent American Literature*. Great Neck, N. Y.: Barron's Educational Series, 1958.

Heller, Erich, *The Disinherited Mind*. New York: Farrar, Straus and Cudahy, 1957.

Henderson, Philip, *The Novel Today*. London: Bodley Head, 1936.

Hicks, Granville, *The Great Tradition: An Interpretation of American Literature since the Civil War* (Revised Edition). New York: Macmillan, 1935.

Highet, Gilbert, *People, Places, and Books*. New York: Oxford University Press, 1953.

Hoare, Dorothy M., *Some Studies in the Modern Novel*. London: Chatto & Windus, 1938.

Hodin, J. P., *The Dilemma of Being Modern*. London: Routledge, 1956.

Hoffman, Frederick J., *Freudianism and the Literary Mind* (Second Edition). Baton Rouge: Louisiana State University Press, 1957.

——————, *The Modern Novel in America, 1900-1950*. Chicago: Regnery, 1951.

Holroyd, Stuart, *Emergence from Chaos*. Boston: Houghton Mifflin, 1957.

Hopper, Stanley R., ed., *Spiritual Problems in Contemporary Literature*. New York: Harper, 1952.

Horn, Francis H., ed., *Literary Masterpieces of the Western World*. Baltimore: Johns Hopkins Press, 1953.

Howe, Irving, *Politics and the Novel* (Meridian Books). New York: Horizon Press, 1957.

Index to Little Magazines 1948 (Compiled by Smith, Colegrove, Swallow). Denver: Swallow, 1949.

Index to Little Magazines 1949 (Compiled by Smith, Colegrove, Stephens, Swallow). Denver: Swallow, 1950.

Index to Little Magazines 1950 (Compiled by Colegrove, Smith, Culliton, Swallow). Denver: Swallow, 1951.

Index to Little Magazines 1951 (Compiled by Colegrove, Swallow, Woodford). Denver: Swallow, 1953.

Index to Little Magazines 1952 (Compiled by Colegrove, Felton, Swallow). Denver: Swallow, n.d.

Index to Little Magazines 1953-1954-1955 (Compiled by Sheehy, Lohf). Denver: Swallow, n.d.

Index to Little Magazines 1956-1957 (Compiled by Sheehy, Lohf). Denver: Swallow, n.d.

Jaffe, Adrian H., and Virgil Scott, eds., *Studies in the Short Story*. New York: Dryden, 1949.

James, Henry, *French Poets and Novelists*. London: Macmillan, 1908.

—————— ——————, *The House of Fiction: Essays on the Novel* (ed., Leon Edel). London: Rupert Hart-Davis, 1957.

——————————, *Notes on Novelists*. New York: Scribner's, 1914.

——————————, *Partial Portraits*. London: Macmillan, 1905.

——————————, *The Question of Our Speech*. Boston: Houghton Mifflin, 1905.

Jameson, Storm, *The Writer's Situation*. London: Macmillan, 1950.

Jessup, Alexander, and Henry Seidel Canby, eds., *The Book of the Short Story*. New York: Appleton, 1929.

Jessup, Josephine Lurie, *The Faith of Our Feminists: A Study in the Novels of Edith Wharton, Ellen Glassgow, Willa Cather*. New York: Richard R. Smith, 1950.

Jones, Howard Mumford, *The Bright Medusa*. Urbana: University of Illinois Press, 1952.

Josephson, Matthew, *Portrait of the Artist As American*. New York: Harcourt, 1930.

Kaufmann, Walter, ed., *Existentialism from Dostoevsky to Sartre*. New York: Meridian Books, 1957.

Kazin, Alfred, *The Inmost Leaf: A Selection of Essays*. New York: Harcourt, 1955.

——————————, *On Native Grounds*. New York: Reynal and Hitchcock, 1942.

Kempton, Kenneth Payson, *Short Stories for Study*. Cambridge: Harvard University Press, 1953.

——————————, *The Short Story*. Cambridge: Harvard University Press, 1947.

Kettle, Arnold, *An Introduction to the English Novel*. London: Hutchinson University Library, 1957.

Knickerbocker, Edwin Van B., ed., *Notable Short Stories of Today*. New York: Harper, 1929.

Knight, Grant C., *The Critical Period in American Literature*. Chapel Hill: The University of North Carolina Press, 1951.

Knights, L. C., *Explorations: Essays in Criticism*. New York: George W. Stewart, 1947.

Kunitz, Joshua, ed., *Azure Cities: Stories of New Russia*. New York: International, 1929.

Larsen, Thorleif, and W. L. MacDonald, eds., *A Century of Short Stories (1824-1927)*. Toronto: Macmillan, 1935.

Lavrin, Janko, *An Introduction to the Russian Novel*. London: Methuen, 1942.

——————, *Russion Writers: Their Lives and Literature.* New York: Van Nostrand, 1954.

Lawrence, D. H., *Studies in Classic American Literature.* New York: Thomas Seltzer, 1923.

Leary, Lewis, ed., *Articles on American Literature, 1900-1950.* Durham: Duke University Press, 1954.

Leavis, F. R., *The Common Pursuit.* New York: George W. Stewart, 1952.

——————, *The Great Tradition.* London: Chatto and Windus, 1948.

Lednicki, Waclaw, *Bits of Table Talk on Pushkin, Mickiewicz, Goethe, Turgenev, and Sienkiewicz.* The Hague: Martinus Nijhoff, 1956.

——————, *Russia, Poland, and the West: Essays in Literary and Cultural History.* New York: Roy, 1954.

Lehmann, John, *The Open Night.* London: Longmans, Green, 1952.

Lerner, Max, *Actions and Passions.* New York: Simon and Schuster, 1949.

Lesser, Simon O., *Fiction and the Unconscious.* Boston: Beacon Press, 1957.

Levin, Harry, *Contexts of Criticism.* Cambridge: Harvard University Press, 1957.

Lewis, R. W. B., *The American Adam: Innocence Tragedy and Tradition in the Nineteenth Century.* Chicago: University of Chicago Press, 1955.

Lewis, Wyndham, *Men Without Art.* London: Cassell, 1934.

Leyburn, Ellen Douglass, *Satiric Allegory: Mirror of Man.* New Haven: Yale University Press, 1956.

Liddell, Robert, *A Treatise on the Novel.* London: Cape, 1947.

Locke, Louis G., William Gibson, and George Arms, eds., *Introduction to Literature* (Vol II, *Readings for Liberal Education*). New York: Rinehart, 1948, 1952, 1957.

Loggins, Vernon, *I Hear America: Literature in the United States Since 1900.* New York: Crowell, 1937.

Lubbock, Percy, *The Craft of Fiction.* New York: Peter Smith, 1945.

Luccock, Halford E., *American Mirror: Social, Ethical and Religious Aspects of American Literature 1930-1940.* New York: Macmillan, 1940.

Ludwig, Jack Barry, and W. Richard Poirer, *Instructor's Manual to Accompany "Stories: British and American."* Cambridge: Houghton Mifflin, 1953.

——————, eds., *Stories: British and American.* Boston: Houghton Mifflin, 1953.

Ludwig, Richard M., and Marvin B. Perry, eds., *Nine Short Novels.* Boston: D. C. Heath, 1952.

Lynd, Robert, *Books and Writers*. London: Dent, 1952.

Lynskey, Winifred C., ed., *Reading Modern Fiction* (Second Edition). New York: Scribner's, 1957.

MacCarthy, Desmond, *Memories*. London: MacGibbon and Kee, 1953.

MacIver, R. M., ed., *Great Moral Dilemmas in Literature, Past and Present*. New York: Harper, 1956.

Mann, Klaus, and Hermann Kesten, eds., *Heart of Europe: An Anthology of Creative Writing in Europe, 1920-1940*. New York: Fischer, 1943.

Mann, Thomas, *Essays of Three Decades*. New York: Knopf, 1947.

——————————, *Three Essays*. New York: Knopf, 1929.

Mansfield, Katherine, *Novels and Novelists*. London: Constable, 1930.

Marcel, Gabriel, *Homo Viator*. Chicago: Regnery, 1951.

Martin, E. W. L., *The New Spirit*. London: Dennis Dobson, 1946.

Matthiessen, F. O., *The American Renaissance*. New York: Oxford University Press, 1941.

——————————, *The Responsibilities of the Critic*. New York: Oxford University Press, 1952.

Maurois, Andre, *Prophets and Poets*. New York: Harper, 1935.

McIlwaine, Shields, *The Southern Poor-White from Lubberland to Tobacco Road*. Norman: University of Oklahoma Press, 1939.

McKeon, Richard, *Thought, Action, and Passion*. Chicago: University of Chicago Press, 1954.

McNamee, Maurice B., S.J., ed., *Reading for Understanding*. New York: Rinehart, 1952.

Melchiori, Giorgio, *The Tightrope Walkers: Studies of Mannerism in Modern English Literature*. New York: Macmillan, 1956.

Mencken, H. L., *A Mencken Chrestomathy*. New York: Knopf, 1949.

Millett, Fred B., *Contemporary American Authors*. New York: Harcourt, 1944.

——————————, ed., *Reading Fiction*. New York: Harper, 1950.

Mirsky, D. S., *Contemporary Russian Literature, 1881-1925*. London: Routledge, 1926.

——————————, *A History of Russian Literature* (Comprising *A History of Russian Literature* and *Contemporary Russian Literature*, edited and abridged by Francis J. Whitfield). New York: Knopf, 1949.

Monroe, N. Elizabeth, *The Novel and Society: A Critical Study of the Modern Novel*. Chapel Hill: University of North Carolina Press, 1941.

Mueller, Gustav E., *Philosophy of Literature*. New York: Philosophical Library, 1948.

Muir, Edwin, *Essays on Literature and Society*. London: Hogarth, 1949.

Muller, Herbert J., *Modern Fiction: A Study of Values*. New York: Funk & Wagnalls, 1937.

Murry, John M., *Between Two Worlds: The Autobiography of John Middleton Murry*. New York: Messner, 1936.

——————, *Countries of the Mind* (First and Second Series). Oxford University Press, 1937.

——————, *John Clare and Other Studies*. London: Peter Nevill, 1950.

——————, *Love, Freedom and Society*. London: J. Cape, 1957.

Neider, Charles, ed., *Short Novels of the Masters*. New York: Rinehart, 1948.

New Directions in Prose and Poetry No. 14. New York: New Directions, 1953.

Nuhn, Ferner, *The Wind Blew from the East*. New York: Harper, 1942.

O'Brien, Edward J., *The Short Story Case Book*. New York: Farrar and Rinehart, 1935.

O'Brien, Justin, ed., *From the N.R.F.* New York: Farrar, Straus, Cudahy, 1958.

O'Connor, Frank, *The Mirror in the Roadway: A Study of the Modern Novel*. New York: Knopf, 1956.

O'Connor, William Van, ed., *Forms of Modern Fiction*. Minneapolis: University of Minnesota Press, 1948.

——————, *Modern Prose: Form and Style*. New York: Crowell, 1959.

O'Faoláin, Séan, *The Short Story*. New York: Devin-Adair, 1951.

Orvis, Mary, *The Art of Writing Fiction*. New York: Prentice-Hall, 1948.

Penzoldt, Peter, *The Supernatural in Fiction*. London: Peter Nevill, 1952.

Peyre, Henri, *The Contemporary French Novel*. New York: Oxford University Press, 1955.

Pfleger, Karl, *Wrestlers with Christ*. New York: Sheed and Ward, 1936.

Phillips, William, ed., *Art and Psychoanalysis*. New York: Criterion Books, 1957.

——————, ed., *Great American Short Novels*. New York: Dial, 1950.

——————, and Philip Rahv, eds., *The New Partisan Reader, 1945-1953*. New York: Harcourt, 1952.

Pick, Robert, ed., *German Stories and Tales*. New York: Knopf, 1954.

Poggioli, Renato, *The Phoenix and the Spider: A Book of Essays about Some Russian Writers and Their Views of the Self*. Cambridge: Harvard University Press, 1957.

Porter, Katherine Anne, *The Days Before*. New York: Harcourt, 1952.

Pound, Ezra, *Literary Essays of Ezra Pound*. London: Faber, 1954.

Prescott, Orville, *In My Opinion*. Indianapolis: Bobbs-Merrill, 1952.

Pritchett, V. S., *Books in General*. New York: Harcourt, 1953.

——————, *The Living Novel*. New York: Reynal and Hitchcock, 1947.

Quinn, Arthur Hobson, *American Fiction: An Historical and Critical Survey*. New York: Appleton-Century-Crofts, 1936.

——————, ed., *The Literature of The American People: An Historical and Critical Survey*. New York: Appleton-Century-Crofts, 1951.

Quinn, Kerker, and Charles Shattuck, eds., *Accent Anthology*. New York: Harcourt, 1946.

Rahv, Philip, ed., *Great Russian Short Novels*. New York: Dial, 1951.

——————, *Image and Idea*. Norfolk: New Directions, 1949.

Rajan, B., ed., *The Novelist As Thinker*. London: Dennis Dobson, 1947.

Ransom, John Crowe, ed., *The Kenyon Critics*. Cleveland: World Publishing, 1951.

Rideout, Walter B., *The Radical Novel in the United States, 1900-1954*. Cambridge: Harvard University Press, 1956.

Roditi, Edouard, *Oscar Wilde*. Norfolk: New Directions, 1947.

Rosenfeld, Paul, *Port of New York: Essays on Fourteen American Moderns*. New York: Harcourt, 1924.

Rosenthal, M. L., and A. J. M. Smith, eds., *Exploring Poetry*. New York: Macmillan, 1955.

Ross, Woodburn O., and A. Doyle Wallace, eds., *Short Stories in Context*. New York: American Book, 1953.

Rowse, A. L., *The English Past: Evocations of Persons and Places*. New York: Macmillan, 1952.

Rubin, Louis D., and Robert D. Jacobs, eds., *Southern Renascence: The Literature of the Modern South*. Baltimore: Johns Hopkins Press, 1953.

Russell, Francis, *Three Studies in Twentieth Century Obscurity*. Aldington, Ashford, Kent: The Hand and Flower Press, 1954.

Sale, William M., Jr., James Hall, and Martin J. Steinmann, Jr., *Critical Discussions for Teachers Using "Short Stories: Tradition and Direction."* Norfolk: New Directions, 1949.

Sale, William M., Jr., James Hall, and Martin Steinmann, Jr., eds., *Short Stories: Tradition and Direction*. Norfolk: New Directions, 1949.

Sartre, Jean-Paul, *Literary and Philosophical Essays*. London: Rider, 1955.

——————, *Literary Essays*. New York: Wisdom Library, 1957.

Savage, D. S., *The Withered Branch*. New York: Pellegrini and Cudahy, 1952.

Schoolfield, George C., *The Figure of the Musician in German Literature*. Chapel Hill: University of North Carolina Press, 1956.

Schorer, Mark, Josephine Miles, and Gordon McKenzie, eds., *Criticism: The Foundations of Modern Literary Judgment*. New York: Harcourt, 1948.

——————, ed., *The Story*. New York: Prentice-Hall, 1950.

Schweikert, Harry C., ed., *Russian Short Stories*. Chicago: Scott, Foresman, 1919.

Scott, Nathan A., Jr., *Rehearsals of Discomposure*. New York: King's Crown, 1952.

——————, ed., *The Tragic Vision and the Christian Faith*. New York: Association Press, 1957.

Scott-James, R. A., *Fifty Years of English Literature*. London: Longmans, Green, 1957.

Shaw, Harry, and Douglas Bement, *Reading the Short Story*. New York: Harper, 1954.

Short, Raymond W., and Richard B. Sewall, *A Manual of Suggestions for Teachers Using "Short Stories for Study."* (Third Edition). New York: Holt, 1956.

——————, eds., *Short Stories for Study: An Anthology* (Third Edition). New York: Holt, 1956.

Silz, Walter, *Realism and Reality: Studies in the German Novelle of Poetic Realism*. Chapel Hill: University of North Carolina Press, 1954.

Slochower, Harry, *No Voice is Wholly Lost*. New York: Creative Age Press, 1945.

——————, *Three Ways of Modern Man*. New York: International Publishers, 1937.

Slonim, Marc, *The Epic of Russian Literature*. New York: Oxford University Press, 1950.

——————, *Modern Russian Literature*. New York: Oxford University Press, 1953.

——————, *An Outline of Russian Literature*. New York: Oxford University Press, 1958.

Smith, Horatio, ed., *Columbia Dictionary of Modern European Literature*. New York: Columbia University Press, 1947.

Snell, George, *The Shapers of American Fiction*. New York: Dutton, 1947.

Spender, Stephen, *The Creative Element: A Study of Vision, Despair and Orthodoxy among some Modern Writers*. London: Hamish Hamilton, 1953.

226

——————, *The Destructive Element: A Study of Modern Writers and Beliefs.* Boston: Houghton Mifflin, 1936.

Spiller, Robert, Willard Thorp, Thomas H. Johnson, and Henry Seidel Canby, eds., *Literary History of the United States* (Vols. I, II, III). New York: Macmillan, 1948.

Stallman, R. W., and R. E. Watters, eds., *The Creative Reader.* New York: Ronald Press, 1954.

——————, *The Critic's Notebook.* Minneapolis: The University of Minnesota Press, 1950.

——————, ed., *Critiques and Essays in Criticism, 1920-1948.* New York: Ronald Press, 1949.

Stegner, Wallace, Richard Scowcroft, and Boris Ilyin, eds., *The Writer's Art.* Boston: D. C. Heath, 1950.

Stewart, Randall, *American Literature and Christian Doctrine.* Baton Rouge: Louisiana State University Press, 1958.

——————, and Dorothy Bethurum, eds., *Classic American Fiction* (*Living Masterpieces of American Literature,* Vol. 2). Chicago: Scott-Foresman, 1954.

——————, *Modern American Narration* (*Living Masterpieces of American Literature,* Vol 3). Chicago: Scott-Foresman, 1954.

Stovall, Floyd, ed., *Eight American Authors: A Review of Research and Criticism.* New York: Modern Language Association of America, 1956.

Strachey, Lytton, *Literary Essays.* New York: Harcourt, 1949.

Studies in Memory of John Jay Parry (English Department of the University of Illinois). Urbana: University of Illinois Press, 1955.

Summers, Richard, ed., *Craft of the Short Story.* New York: Rinehart, 1948.

Swinnerton, Frank, *The Georgian Scene.* New York: Farrar and Rinehart, 1934.

Tate, Allen, *The Forlorn Demon.* Chicago: Regnery, 1953.

——————, *The Hovering Fly and Other Essays.* Cummington, Mass.: Cummington Press, 1949.

——————, *The Man of Letters in the Modern World, Selected Essays: 1928-1955.* New York: Meridian Books, 1955.

——————, *Reason in Madness: Critical Essays.* New York: Putnam's, 1941.

——————, ed., *A Southern Vanguard, The John Peale Bishop Memorial Volume.* New York: Prentice-Hall, 1947.

Thomas, Wright, and Stuart Gerry Brown, eds., *Reading Prose: An Introduction to Critical Study.* New York: Oxford University Press, 1952.

Thurston, Jarvis, ed., *Reading Modern Short Stories*. Chicago: Scott-Foresman, 1955.

Tindall, William York, *Forces in Modern British Literature, 1885-1946*. New York: Knopf, 1947.

————————, *The Literary Symbol*. Bloomington: Indiana University, 1955.

Trilling, Lionel, *The Liberal Imagination*. New York: Viking, 1950.

————————, *The Opposing Self*. London: Secker and Warburg, 1955.

Turnell, Martin, *The Novel in France*. New York: Vintage Books, 1958.

Tymms, Ralph, *Doubles in Literary Psychology*. Cambridge: Bowes and Bowes, 1949.

Ullmann, Stephen, *Style in the French Novel*. Cambridge: Cambridge University Press, 1957.

Undset, Sigrid, *Men, Women, and Places*. New York: Knopf, 1939.

Unger, Leonard, *The Man in the Name*. Minneapolis: University of Minnesota Press, 1956.

University of Virginia, *English Studies in Honor of James Southall Wilson*. Charlottesville: University of Virginia, 1951.

Van Doren, Mark, ed., *The New Invitation to Learning*. New York: New Home Library, 1942.

————————, *Private Reader*. New York: Holt, 1942.

Verschoyle, Derek, ed., *The English Novelists: A Survey of the Novel by Twenty Contemporary Novelists*. London: Chatto and Windus, 1936.

Vivas, Elisio, *Creation and Discovery*. New York: Noonday, 1955.

Wagenknecht, Edward, *Cavalcade of the American Novel*. New York: Holt, 1952.

————————, *Cavalcade of the English Novel* (1954 Edition). New York: Holt, 1954.

————————, ed., *A Preface to Literature*. New York: Holt, 1954.

Wain, John, *Preliminary Essays*. London: Macmillan, 1957.

Walcutt, Charles Child, *American Literary Naturalism, A Divided Stream*. Minneapolis: University of Minnesota Press, 1956.

Wallace, Irving, *The Fabulous Originals*. New York: Knopf, 1955.

Ward, Alfred C., *Aspects of the Modern Short Story: English and American*. New York: Lincoln MacVeagh, Dial Press, 1925.

Warner, Rex, *The Cult of Power*. London: John Lane, 1946.

Warren, Austin, *Rage for Order*. Chicago: University of Chicago Press, 1948.

Warren, Robert Penn, *Selected Essays*. New York: Random House, 1958.

Watts, Harold H., *Hound and Quarry*. London: Routledge and Kegan Paul, 1953.

Wellek, René, and Austin Warren, *Theory of Literature*. New York: Harcourt, 1949.

West, Ray B., Jr., ed., *Essays in Modern Literary Criticism*. New York: Rinehart, 1952.

West, Ray B., Jr., *The Short Story in America: 1900-1950*. Chicago: Regnery, 1952.

——————, and Robert Wooster Stallman, eds., *The Art of Modern Fiction*. New York: Rinehart, 1949.

West, Rebecca, *The Court and the Castle*. New Haven: Yale University Press, 1957.

——————, *The Strange Necessity*. London: J. Cape, 1928.

Whipple, T. K., *Study Out the Land*. Berkeley: University of California Press, 1943.

Wilson, Edmund, *The American Earthquake: A Documentary of the Twenties and Thirties*. Garden City: Doubleday, 1958.

——————, *The Boys in the Back Room*. San Francisco: Colt Press, 1941.

——————, *Classics and Commercials*. New York: Farrar, Straus, 1950.

——————, *Eight Essays* (Anchor Books). New York: Doubleday, 1954.

——————, *A Piece of My Mind: Reflections at Sixty*. New York: Farrar, Straus, and Cudahy, 1956.

——————, ed., *The Shock of Recognition*. Garden City: Doubleday, Doran, 1943.

——————, *Shores of Light: A Literary Chronicle of the Twenties and Thirties*. New York: Farrar, Straus, and Young, 1952.

——————, *The Triple Thinkers*. New York: Harcourt, 1938.

——————, *The Wound and the Bow*. Boston: Houghton Mifflin, 1941.

Winters, Yvor, *In Defense of Reason*. New York: Swallow Press and William Morrow, 1947.

——————, *Maule's Curse: Seven Studies in the History of American Obscurantism*. Norfolk: New Directions, 1938.

Wood, William Ransom, ed., *Short Short Stories*. New York: Harcourt, 1951.

Woolf, Virginia, *The Moment and Other Essays*. New York: Harcourt, 1948.

Yarmolinsky, Avrahm, ed., *A Treasury of Great Russian Short Stories*. New York: Macmillan, 1946.

Zabel, Morton D., *Craft and Character in Modern Fiction*. New York: Viking, 1957.

----------------, ed., *Literary Opinion in America* (Revised Edition). New York: Harper, 1951.

Zenkovskii, V. V., *Russian Thinkers and Europe*. Ann Arbor: J. W. Edwards (for The American Council of Learned Societies), 1953.

Zweig, Stefan, *Master Builders: A Typology of the Spirit*. New York: Viking, 1939.

II. AUTHOR CHECKLISTS

ANDERSON, SHERWOOD:

    Anderson, Sherwood, *Sherwood Anderson's Memoirs*. New York: Harcourt, 1942.

    Chase, Cleveland B., *Sherwood Anderson*. New York: McBride, 1927.

    Howe, Irving, *Sherwood Anderson*. New York: William Sloane Associates, 1951.

    Rosenfeld, Paul, ed., *The Sherwood Anderson Reader*. Boston: Houghton Mifflin, 1947.

    Schevill, James, *Sherwood Anderson: His Life and Work*. Denver: University of Denver Press, 1951.

BALZAC, HONORÉ DE:

    Burton, J. M., *Honoré de Balzac and His Figures of Speech*. Princeton: Princeton University Press, 1921.

    Dargan, E. Preston, and Bernard Weinberg, eds., *The Evolution of Balzac's "Comédie humaine."* Chicago: University of Chicago Press, 1942.

    Dargan, E. Preston, *Honoré de Balzac: A Force of Nature*. Chicago: University of Chicago Press, 1932.

    Dargan, E. Preston, W. L. Crain, and Others, *Studies in Balzac's Realism*. Chicago: University of Chicago Press, 1932.

    Dedinsky, Brucia, *Development of the Scheme of the "Comédie humaine": Distribution of the Stories*. Chicago: University of Chicago Libraries, 1943.

    Floyd, Juanita Helm, *Women in the Life of Honoré de Balzac*. New York: Holt, 1921.

    Garnand, H. J., *The Influence of Walter Scott on the Works of Balzac*. New York: Columbia University, 1926.

    Garrett, Helen T., *Clothes and Character: The Function of Dress in Balzac*. Philadelphia: University of Pennsylvania (Ph. D. Dissertation), 1941.

    Giraud, Raymond, *The Unheroic Hero in the Novels of Stendhal, Balzac, and Flaubert*. New Brunswick: Rutgers University Press, 1957.

Hastings, Walter Scott, ed., *Balzac and Souverain: An Unpublished Correspondence*. Garden City: Doubleday, Page, 1927.

Hunt, Herbert J., *Honoré de Balzac: A Biography*. London: University of London, Athlone Press, 1957.

Lawton, Frederick, *Balzac*. London: Richards, 1910.

Levin, Harry, *Toward Balzac*. Norfolk: New Directions, 1947.

Pfeiffer, Charles Leonard, *Taste and Smell in Balzac's Novels*. Tucson: University of Arizona Press, 1949.

Rogers, Samuel, *Balzac and the Novel*. Madison: University of Wisconsin Press, 1953.

Romains, Jules, ed., *The Short Novels of Balzac*. New York: Dial, 1948.

Royce, William Hobart, *Balzac As He Should Be Read*. New York: Auguste Giraldi, 1946.

——————, *A Balzac Bibliography*. Chicago: University of Chicago Press, 1929.

——————, *Indexes to A Balzac Bibliography*. Chicago: University of Chicago Press, 1930.

Scott, Mary Wingfield, *Art and Artists in Balzac's "Comédie humaine."* Chicago: University of Chicago Libraries, 1937.

Zweig, Stefan, *Balzac*. New York: Viking, 1946.

BENÉT, STEPHEN VINCENT:

Fenton, Charles A., *Stephen Vincent Benét: The Life and Times of an American Man of Letters, 1898-1943*. New Haven: Yale University Press, 1958.

BIERCE, AMBROSE:

De Castro, Adolphe D., *Portrait of Ambrose Bierce*. New York: Century, 1929.

Fadiman, Clifton, ed., *The Collected Writings of Ambrose Bierce*. New York: Citadel, 1946.

Fatout, Paul, *Ambrose Bierce and the Black Hills*. Norman: University of Oklahoma Press, 1956.

——————, *Ambrose Bierce: The Devil's Lexicographer*. Norman: University of Oklahoma Press, 1951.

Grattan, C. Hartley, *Bitter Bierce: A Mystery of American Letters*. Garden City: Doubleday, Doran, 1929.

McWilliams, Carey, *Ambrose Bierce: A Biography*. New York: Boni, 1929.

Neale, Walter, *Life of Ambrose Bierce*. New York: Walter Neale, 1929.

Noel, Joseph, *Footloose in Arcadia: A Personal Record of Jack London, George Sterling, Ambrose Bierce*. New York: Carrick and Evans, 1940.

Walker, Franklin, *Ambrose Bierce: The Wickedest Man in San Francisco*. San Francisco: Colt Press, 1941.

BOWEN, ELIZABETH:

Brooke, Jocelyn, *Elizabeth Bowen* (Supplement to *British Book News*). London: Longmans, Green, 1952.

BROWN, CHARLES BROCKDEN:

Clark, David Lee, *Charles Brockden Brown: Pioneer Voice of America*. Durham: Duke University Press, 1952.

Warfel, Harry R., *Charles Brockden Brown: American Gothic Novelist*. Gainesville: University of Florida Press, 1949.

Warfel, Harry R., ed., *The Rhapsodist and Other Uncollected Writings by Charles Brockden Brown*. New York: Scholars' Facsimiles and Reprints, 1943.

CABLE, GEORGE W.:

Biklé, Lucy Leffingwell Cable, *George W. Cable: His Life and Letters*. New York: Scribner's, 1928.

Cardwell, Guy A., *Twins of Genius*. East Lansing: Michigan State College Press, 1953.

Ekström, Kjell, *George Washington Cable: A Study of His Early Life and Work*. Upsala: A.-B. Lundequistska Bokhandeln, 1950.

Turner, Arlin, *George W. Cable: A Biography*. Durham: Duke University Press, 1956.

CAMUS, ALBERT:

Brée, Germaine, *Camus*. New Brunswick: Rutgers University Press, 1959.

Hanna, Thomas, *The Thought and Art of Albert Camus*. Chicago: Regnery, 1958.

Maquet, Albert, *Albert Camus: The Invincible Summer*. New York: George Braziller, 1958.

Thody, Philip, *Albert Camus: A Study of His Work*. London: Hamish Hamilton, 1957.

CATHER, WILLA:

Bennett, Mildred R., ed., *Early Stories of Willa Cather*. New Yord: Dodd, Mead, 1957.

Daiches, David, *Willa Cather: A Critical Introduction*. Ithaca: Cornell University Press, 1951.

Kates, George N., *Willa Cather in Europe: Her Own Story of the First Journey*. New York: Knopf, 1956.

Lewis, Edith, *Willa Cather Living*. New York: Knopf, 1953.

Rapin, René, *Willa Cather*. New York: McBride, 1930.

Sergeant, Elizabeth Shepley, *Willa Cather: A Memoir*. Philadelphia: Lippincott, 1953.

Shively, James R., ed., *Writings from Willa Cather's Campus Years*. Lincoln: University of Nebraska Press, 1950.

CHEKHOV, ANTON:

Avilov, Lydia, *Chekhov in My Life*. New York: Harcourt, 1950.

Bruford, W. H., *Anton Chekhov*. New Haven: Yale University Press, 1957.

————, *Chekhov and His Russia*. London: Paul, Trench, Trubner, 1948.

Chekhov, Anton, *Letters of Anton Chekhov to His Family and Friends*. New York: Macmillan, 1920.

————, *The Personal Papers of Anton Chekhov*. New York: Lear, 1948.

Gerhardi, William, *Anton Chekhov: A Critical Study*. New York: Duffield, 1923.

Hingley, Ronald, *Chekhov: A Biographical and Critical Study*. London: Allen and Unwin, 1950.

Koteliansky, S. S., and Philip Tomlinson, eds., *The Life and Letters of Anton Tchekhov*. London: Cassell, 1925.

Magarshack, David, *Chekhov the Dramatist*. London: Lehmann, 1952.

————, *Chekhov: A Life*. New York: Grove, 1953.

Toumanova, Princess Nina Andronikova, *Anton Chekhov: The Voice of Twilight Russia*. New York: Columbia University Press, 1937.

Wilson, Edmund, ed., *Peasants and Other Stories* (Anchor Books). Garden City: Doubleday, 1956.

Yarmolinsky, Avrahm, ed., *The Portable Chekhov*. New York: Viking, 1947.

————, *The Unknown Chekhov: Stories and Other Writings Hitherto Untranslated*. New York: Noonday, 1954.

CONRAD, JOSEPH:

Allen, Jerry, *The Thunder and the Sunshine: A Biography of Joseph Conrad*. New York: Putnam's, 1958.

Bancroft, William Wallace, *Joseph Conrad: His Philosophy of Life*. Boston: Stratford, 1933.

Bradbrook, M. C., *Joseph Conrad: Poland's English Genius*. Cambridge: Cambridge University Press, 1941.

Conrad, Joseph, *Conrad's Prefaces to His Works*. London: Dent, 1937.

————, *Notes on Life and Letters*. London: Dent, 1921.

Crankshaw, Edward, *Joseph Conrad: Some Aspects of the Art of the Novel*. London: John Lane, 1936.

Curle, Richard, *Joseph Conrad and His Characters: A Study of Six Novels*. London: Heinemann, 1957.

233

——————————, *Joseph Conrad: A Study*. London: Kegan Paul, Trench, Trübner, 1914.

Cushwa, Frank W., *An Introduction to Conrad*. Garden City: Doubleday, Doran, 1933.

Gordan, John Dozier, *Joseph Conrad: The Making of a Novelist*. Cambridge: Harvard University Press, 1941.

Guerard, Albert J., *Conrad: The Novelist*. Cambridge: Harvard University Press, 1958.

——————————, *Joseph Conrad*. New York: New Directions, 1947.

Haugh, Robert F., *Joseph Conrad: Discovery in Design*. Norman: University of Oklahoma Press, 1957.

Hewitt, Douglas, *Conrad: A Reassessment*. Philadelphia: Dufour and Saifer, 1952.

Jean-Aubry, Gérard, *The Sea Dreamer: A Definitive Biography of Joseph Conrad*. New York: Doubleday, 1957.

Lohf, Kenneth A., and Eugene P. Sheehy, *Joseph Conrad at Mid-Century: Editions and Studies, 1895-1955*. Minneapolis: University of Minnesota Press, 1957.

Mégroz, R. L., *Joseph Conrad's Mind and Method*. London: Faber, 1931.

Morf, Gustav, *The Polish Heritage of Joseph Conrad*. London: Sampson Low, Marston, 1930.

Moser, Thomas, *Joseph Conrad: Achievement and Decline*. Cambridge: Harvard University Press, 1957.

Visiak, E. H., *The Mirror of Conrad*. New York: Philosophical Library, 1956.

Warner, Oliver, *Joseph Conrad* (Supplement to *British Book News*.) London: Longmans, Green, 1950.

——————————, *Joseph Conrad*. London: Longmans, Green, 1951.

Wiley, Paul L., *Conrad's Measure of Man*. Madison: University of Wisconsin Press, 1954.

Wright, Walter E., *Romance and Tragedy in Joseeph Conrad*. Lincoln: University of Nebraska Press, 1949.

Zabel, M. D., ed., *The Portable Conrad*. New York: Viking, 1954.

COPPARD, A. E.:

Jehin, A., *Remarks on the Style of A. E. Coppard*. Buenos Aires: English Pamphlet Series No. 8, 1944.

Schwartz, Jacob, *The Writings of Alfred Edgar Coppard*. London: Ulysses Bookshop, 1931.

CRANE, STEPHEN:

Beer, Thomas, *Stephen Crane: A Study in American Letters*. Garden City: Garden City Publishing, 1927.

Berryman, John, *Stephen Crane*. New York: William Sloane Assiates, 1950.

234

Follett, Wilson, ed., *The Works of Stephen Crane*, 12 Vols. New York: Knopf, 1925-1926.

Hoffman, Daniel G., *The Poetry of Stephen Crane*. New York: Columbia University Press, 1957.

Linson, Corwin K., *My Stephen Crane*. Syracuse: Syracuse University Press, 1958.

Schoberlin, Melvin, ed., *The Sullivan County Sketches of Stephen Crane*. Syracuse: Syracuse University Press, 1949.

Stallman, Robert Wooster, ed., *Stephen Crane: An Omnibus*. New York: Knopf, 1952.

Van Doren, Carl, ed., *Twenty Stories by Stephen Crane*. New York: World Publishing, 1945.

Williams, Ames W., and Vincent Starrett, *Stephen Crane: A Bibliography*. Glendale: Valentine, 1948.

DOSTOEVSKY, FYODOR:

Berdyaev, Nicholas, *Dostoievsky: An Interpretation*. London: Sheed and Ward, 1934.

Carr, Edward Hallett, *Dostoevsky, 1821-1881: A New Biography*. Boston: Houghton Mifflin, 1931.

Dostoevsky, Anna G., *Dostoevsky Portrayed By His Wife*. London: Routledge, 1926.

Dostoievsky, F. M., *The Diary of a Writer*. New York: Braziller, 1954.

Fayer, Mischa H., *Gide, Freedom and Dostoevsky*. Burlington, Vermont: Lane Press, 1946.

Fueloep-Miller, Rene, *Fyodor Dostoevsky: Insight, Faith, and Prophecy*. New York: Scribner's, 1950.

Gide, André, *Dostoevsky*. Norfolk: New Directions, 1949.

Hubben, William, *Four Prophets of Our Destiny: Kierkegaard, Dostoevsky, Nietzsche, Kafka*. New York: Macmillian, 1952.

Ivanov, Vyacheslav, *Freedom and the Tragic Life: A Study in Dostoevsky*. New York: Noonday, 1952.

Lavrin, Janko, *Dostoevsky and His Creation: A Psycho-Critical Study*. London: Collins, 1920.

————————, *Dostoevsky: A Study*. New York: Macmillan, 1947.

Lloyd, J. A. T., *Fyodor Dostoevsky*. New York: Scribner's, 1947.

Mackiewicz, Stanislaw, *Dostoevsky*. London: Orbis, 1948.

Magarshack, David, ed., *The Best Short Stories of Dostoevsky*. New York: Modern Library, 1955.

Meier-Graefe, Julius, *Dostoevsky: The Man and His Work*. New York: Harcourt, 1928.

Muchnic, Helen, *Dostoevsky's English Reputation (1881-1936)*. *Smith College Studies in Modern Languages*, XX, Nos. 3-4 (Northampton, 1939).

235

Murry, J. Middleton, *Fyodor Dostoevsky: A Critical Study.* London: Secker, 1916.

Passage, Charles E., *Dostoevski the Adapter: A Study in Dostoevski's Use of the Tales of Hoffmann.* Chapel Hill: University of North Carolina Press, 1954.

Phillips, William, ed., *The Short Stories of Dostoevsky.* New York: Dial, 1946.

Powys, John Cowper, *Dostoievsky: A Study.* London: Lane, 1946.

Seduro, Vladimir, *Dostoyevski in Russian Literary Criticism, 1846-1956.* New York: Columbia University Press, 1957.

Simmons, Ernest J., *Dostoevski: The Making of a Novelist.* New York: Oxford University Press, 1940; London: John Lehmann, 1950.

Slonim, Marc, *Three Loves of Dostoevsky.* New York: Rinehart, 1955.

Smith, S. Stephenson, and Andrei Isotoff, *The Abnormal from Within: Dostoevsky.* Eugene: University of Oregon, 1935.

Soloviev, Evgenii, *Dostoievsky: His Life and Literary Activity.* London: Allen and Unwin, 1916.

Steiner, George, *Tolstoy or Dostoevsky: An Essay in the Old Criticism.* New York: Knopf, 1959.

Troyat, Henry, *Firebrand: The Life of Dostoevsky.* New York: Roy, 1946.

Woodhouse, C. M., *Dostoievsky.* New York: Roy, 1951.

Yarmolinsky, Avrahm, *Dostoevsky: His Life and Art.* New York: Criterion Books, 1957.

———————, *Dostoievsky: A Study in His Ideology.* New York: Columbia University, 1921.

Zander, L. A., *Dostoevsky.* London: SCM Press, 1948.

DREISER, THEODORE:

Dreiser, Helen, *My Life with Dreiser.* New York: World Publishing, 1951.

Dreiser, Theodore, *The Best Short Stories of Theodore Dreiser* (with an Introduction by James T. Farrell) . Cleveland: World Publishing, 1956.

Dudley, Dorothy, *Forgotten Frontiers: Dreiser and the Land of the Free.* New York: Smith and Haas, 1932.

Elias, Robert H., *Theodore Dreiser: Apostle of Nature.* New York: Knopf, 1949.

Kazin, Alfred, and Charles Shapiro, eds., *The Stature of Theodore Dreiser.* Bloomington: Indiana University Press, 1955.

Matthiessen, F. O., *Theodore Dreiser.* New York: William Sloane Associates, 1951.

McDonald, Edward D., *A Bibliography of the Writings of Theodore Dreiser*. Philadelphia: Centaur Book Shop, 1928.

Rascoe, Burton, *Theodore Dreiser*. New York: McBride, 1925.

FAULKNER, WILLIAM:

Campbell, Harry M., and Ruel E. Foster, *William Faulkner: A Critical Appraisal*. Norman: University of Oklahoma Press, 1951.

Coughlan, Robert, *The Private World of William Faulkner*. New York: Harper, 1954.

Daniel, Robert W., *A Catalogue of the Writings of William Faulkner*. New Haven: Yale University, 1942.

Hoffman, Frederick J., and Olga W. Vickery, eds., *William Faulkner: Two Decades of Criticism*. East Lansing: Michigan State College Press, 1951.

Howe, Irving, *William Faulkner: A Critical Study*. New York: Random House, 1952.

Jelliffe, Robert A., ed., *Faulkner at Nagano*. Tokyo: Kenkyusha, 1956.

Malin, Irving, *William Faulkner: An Interpretation*. Stanford: Stanford University Press, 1957.

Miner, Ward L., *The World of William Faulkner*. Durham: Duke University Press, 1952.

O'Connor, William Van, *The Tangled Fire of William Faulkner*. Minneapolis: University of Minnesota Press, 1954.

Robb, Mary Cooper, *William Faulkner, An Estimate of His Contribution to the American Novel*. Pittsburgh: University of Pittsburgh Press, 1957.

FITZGERALD, F. SCOTT:

Kazin, Alfred, ed., *F. Scott Fitzgerald: The Man and His Work*. Cleveland: World Publishing, 1951.

Miller, James E., Jr., *The Fictional Technique of Scott Fitzgerald*. The Hague: Martinus Nijhoff, 1957.

Mizener, Arthur, ed., *Afternoon of an Author: A Selection of Uncollected Stories and Essays by F. Scott Fitzgerald*. Princeton: Princeton University Library, 1957.

----------------------, *The Far Side of Paradise: A Biography of F. Scott Fitzgerald*. Boston: Houghton Mifflin, 1951; New York: Vintage Books, 1959.

Parker, Dorothy, ed., *The Portable F. Scott Fitzgerald*. New York: Viking, 1945.

FLAUBERT, GUSTAVE:

Bart, Benjamin F., *Flaubert's Landscape Descriptions*. Ann Arbor: University of Michigan Press, 1957.

Flaubert, Gustave, *Bouvard and Pécuchet* (Translated by T. W.

Earp and G. W. Stonier, with an Introduction by Lionel Trilling) . Norfolk: New Directions, 1954.

Giraud, Raymond, *The Unheroic Hero in the Novels of Stendhal, Balzac and Flaubert.* New Brunswick: Rutgers University Press, 1957.

Riddell, Agnes Rutherford, *Flaubert and Maupassant: A Literary Relationship.* Chicago: University of Chicago Press, 1920.

Spencer, Philip, *Flaubert: A Biography.* London: Faber, 1952.

Steegmuller, Francis, *Flaubert and Madame Bovary* (Second Edition) . New York: Farrar, Straus, and Cudahy, 1950; New York: Vintage Books, 1957.

————————, ed., *Selected Letters of Gustave Flaubert.* New York: Farrar, Straus, and Cudahy, 1953; New York: Vintage Books, 1957.

Tarver, John Charles, *Gustave Flaubert: As Seen in His Works and Correspondence.* Edinburgh: Constable, 1895.

Thorlby, Anthony, *Gustave Flaubert and the Art of Realism.* New Haven: Yale University Press, 1957.

Whyte, Frederic, ed., *Stories by Gustave Flaubert.* New York: Dutton, 1910.

FORSTER, E. M.:

Johnstone, J. K., *The Bloomsbury Group: A Study of E. M. Forster, Lytton Strachey, Virginia Woolf, and their Circle.* New York: Noonday, 1954.

Macaulay, Rose, *The Writings of E. M. Forster.* London: Hogarth, 1938.

McConkey, James, *The Novels of E. M. Forster.* Ithaca: Cornell University Press, 1957.

Trilling, Lionel, *E. M. Forster.* Norfolk: New Directions, 1943.

Warner, Rex, *E. M. Forster* (Supplement to *British Book News*) . London: Longmans, Green, 1950.

FREEMAN, MARY E. WILKINS:

Forster, Edward, *Mary E. Wilkins Freeman.* New York: Hendricks House, 1956.

GALSWORTHY, JOHN:

Chevrillon, André, *Three Studies in English Literature: Kipling, Galsworthy, Shakespeare.* London: Heinemann, 1923.

Croman, N., *John Galsworthy.* London: Oxford University Press, 1933.

Cross, Wilbur L., *Four Contemporary Novelists.* New York: Macmillan, 1930.

Galsworthy, Ada, *Over the Hills and Far Away.* London: Hale, 1937.

Garnett, Edward, ed., *Letters from John Galsworthy, 1900-1932.*
London: J. Cape, 1934.

Marrot, H. V., *A Bibliography of the Works of John Galsworthy.*
London: Elkin Mathews and Marrot, 1928.

————————, *The Life and Letters of John Galsworthy.* New
York: Scribner's, 1936.

Mottram, R. H., *For Some We Loved: An Intimate Portrait of
Ada and John Galsworthy.* London: Hutchinson, 1956.

————————, *John Galsworthy* (Supplement to *British Book
News*). London: Longmans, Green, 1956.

Reynolds, M. E., *Memories of John Galsworthy* (by His Sister).
London: Hale, 1936.

Schalit, Leon, *John Galsworthy: A Survey.* London: Heinemann,
1929.

GIDE, ANDRÉ:

Ames, Van Meter, *André Gide.* Norfolk: New Directions, 1947.

Fayer, Mischa H., *Gide, Freedom and Dostoevsky.* Burlington,
Vermont: Lane Press, 1946.

Guerard, Albert J., *André Gide.* Cambridge: Harvard University
Press, 1951.

Mann, Klaus, *André Gide and the Crisis of Modern Thought.*
New York: Creative Age, 1943.

March, Harold, *Gide and the Hound of Heaven.* Philadelphia:
University of Pennsylvania Press, 1952.

O'Brien, Justin, *Portrait of André Gide: A Critical Biography.*
New York: Knopf, 1953.

Painter, George D., *André Gide: A Critical and Biographical
Study.* New York: Roy Publishers, 1951.

Pierre-Quint, Léon, *André Gide: His Life and His Work.* New
York: Knopf, 1934.

Starkie, Enid, *André Gide.* New Haven: Yale University Press,
1954.

Thomas, Lawrence, *André Gide: The Ethic of the Artist.* London:
Secker and Warburg, 1950.

GOGOL, NIKOLAI:

Lavrin, Janko, *Gogol.* London: Routledge, 1926.

————————, *Nikolai Gogol (1809-1852): A Centenary Survey.*
London: Sylvan Press, 1951.

Magarshack, David, *Gogol: A Life.* New York: Grove, 1957.

Nabokov, Vladimir, *Nikolai Gogol.* Norfolk: New Directions,
1944.

HARDY, THOMAS:

Abercrombie, Lascelles, *Thomas Hardy: A Critical Study.* London:
Secker, 1924.

Bailey, J. O., *Thomas Hardy and the Cosmic Mind: A New Reading of 'The Dynasts.'* Chapel Hill: University of North Carolina Press, 1956.

Beach, Joseph Warren, *The Technique of Thomas Hardy.* Chicago: University of Chicago Press, 1922.

Blunden, Edmund, *Thomas Hardy.* London: Macmillan, 1951.

Braybrooke, Patrick, *Thomas Hardy and His Philosophy.* London: Daniel, 1928.

Brennecke, Ernest, Jr., *The Life of Thomas Hardy.* New York: Greenberg, 1925.

Cecil, David, *Hardy the Novelist: An Essay in Criticism.* Indianapolis: Bobbs-Merrill, 1946.

Chase, Mary Ellen, *Thomas Hardy from Serial to Novel.* Minneapolis: University of Minnesota Press, 1927.

Chew, Samuel C., *Thomas Hardy: Poet and Novelist.* New York: Knopf, 1929.

Child, Harold, *Thomas Hardy.* London: Nisbet, 1925.

Duffin, H. C., *Thomas Hardy: A Study of the Wessex Novels.* Manchester: University Press, 1921.

Fowler, J. H., *The Novels of Thomas Hardy* (Pamphlet) . Oxford: English Association, 1928.

Grimsditch, Herbert B., *Character and Environment in the Novels of Thomas Hardy.* London: Witherby, 1925.

Guerard, Albert J., *Thomas Hardy: The Novels and Stories.* Cambridge: Harvard University Press, 1949.

Hardy, Evelyn, *Thomas Hardy: A Critical Biography.* London: Hogarth, 1954.

Hardy, Evelyn, ed., *Thomas Hardy's Notebooks: And Some Letters from Julia Augusta Martin.* London: Hogarth, 1955.

Hardy, Florence, *Early Life of Thomas Hardy, 1840-1891.* New York: Macmillan, 1928.

——————, *Later Years of Thomas Hardy, 1892-1928.* London: Macmillan, 1930.

Hardy, Thomas, *Life and Art: Essays, Notes, and Letters Collected for the First Time* (with Introduction by Ernest Brennecke, Jr.) . New York: Greenberg, 1925.

Hawkins, Desmond, *Thomas Hardy.* London: A. Barker, 1951.

Johnson, Lionel, *The Art of Thomas Hardy* (Revised Edition) . London: John Lane, 1928.

Macdonell, Annie, *Thomas Hardy.* London: Hodder and Stoughton, 1894.

McDowall, Arthur, *Thomas Hardy: A Critical Study.* London: Faber, 1931.

Purdy, Richard Little, *Thomas Hardy: A Bibliographical Study.* London: Oxford University Press, 1954.

Scott-James, Rolfe A., *Thomas Hardy, 1840-1928* (Supplement to *British Book News*). London: Longmans, Green, 1951.

Southern Review (Thomas Hardy Centennial Issue). Summer, 1940.

Tomlinson, H. M., *Thomas Hardy.* New York: Crosby Gaige, 1929.

Weber, Carl J., *Hardy and the Lady From Madison Square.* Waterville, Maine: Colby College Press, 1952.

——————, *Hardy at Colby: A Check-List of the Writings By and About Thomas Hardy Now in the Library of Colby College.* Waterville, Maine: Colby College Library, 1936.

——————, *Hardy in America: A Study of Thomas Hardy and His American Readers.* Waterville, Maine: Colby College Library, 1946.

——————, *Hardy of Wessex.* New York: Columbia University Press, 1940.

Weber, Carl J., ed., *The Letters of Thomas Hardy.* Waterville, Maine: Colby College Press, 1954.

Weber, Carl J., *Rebekah Owen and Thomas Hardy.* Waterville, Maine: Colby College Library, 1939.

Webster, H. C., *On a Darkling Plain.* Chicago: University of Chicago Press, 1947.

HARTE, BRET:

Harrison, Joseph B., ed. *Bret Harte: Representative Selections.* New York: American Book, 1941.

Harte, Geoffrey Bret, ed., *The Letters of Bret Harte.* Boston: Houghton Mifflin, 1926.

Stewart, George R., Jr., *A Bibliography of the Writings of Bret Harte in the Magazines and Newspapers of California, 1857-1871.* Berkeley: University of California Press, 1933.

——————, *Bret Harte: Argonaut and Exile.* Boston: Houghton Mifflin, 1931.

HAWTHORNE, NATHANIEL:

Arvin, Newton, *Hawthorne.* London: Noel Douglas, 1930.

Arvin, Newton, ed., *Hawthorne's Short Stories* (Vintage Books). New York: Knopf, 1955.

Cantwell, Robert, *Nathaniel Hawthorne: The American Years.* New York: Rinehart, 1948.

Davidson, Edward H., ed., *Hawthorne's "Doctor's Grimshaws's Secret."* Cambridge: Harvard University Press, 1954.

Davidson, Edward H., *Hawthorne's Last Phase.* New Haven: Yale University Press, 1949.

Fogle, Richard H., *Hawthorne's Fiction: The Light and the Dark*. Norman: University of Oklahoma Press, 1952.

Gorman, Herbert, *Nathaniel Hawthorne: A Study in Solitude*. New York: Doran, 1927.

Hall, Lawrence Sargent, *Hawthorne: Critic of Society*. New Haven: Yale University Press, 1944.

Hawthorne, Nathaniel, *Passages from the American Note-Books*. Boston: Houghton, Mifflin, 1896.

James, Henry, *Hawthorne*. New York: Harper, 1879.

Lundblad, Jane, *Nathaniel Hawthorne and European Literary Tradition*. Upsala: A.-B. Lundequistska Bokhandlen, 1947.

——————————, *Nathaniel Hawthorne and the Tradition of Gothic Romance*. Upsala: A.-B. Lundequistska Bokhandlen, 1946.

Male, Roy R., *Hawthorne's Tragic Vision*. Austin: University of Texas Press, 1957.

Mather, Edward, *Nathaniel Hawthorne: A Modest Man*. New York: Crowell, 1940.

Schubert, Leland, *Hawthorne, the Artist: Fine-Art Devices in Fiction*. Chapel Hill: University of North Carolina Press, 1944.

Stein, William Bysshe, *Hawthorne's Faust: A Study of the Devil Archetype*. Gainesville: University of Florida Press, 1953.

Stewart, Randall, ed., *The American Notebooks by Nathaniel Hawthorne*. New Haven: Yale University Press, 1932.

Stewart, Randall, *Nathaniel Hawthorne: A Biography*. New Haven: Yale University Press, 1948.

Turner, Arlin, ed., *Hawthorne As Editor: Selections from His Writings in "The American Magazine of Useful and Entertaining Knowledge."* University, Louisiana: Louisiana State University Press, 1941.

Van Doren, Mark, ed., *The Best of Hawthorne*. New York: Ronald, 1951.

Van Doren, Mark, *Nathaniel Hawthorne*. New York: William Sloane, 1949.

Von Abele, Rudolph, *The Death of the Artist: A Study of Hawthorne's Disintegration*. The Hague: Martinus Nijhoff, 1955.

Waggoner, Hyatt H., *Hawthorne: A Critical Study*. Cambridge: Harvard University Press, 1955.

Waggoner, Hyatt H., ed., *Nathaniel Hawthorne: Selected Tales and Sketches* (Rinehart Editions). New York: Rinehart, 1950.

Warren, Austin, ed., *Nathaniel Hawthorne: Representative Selections*. Cincinnati: American Book, 1934.

Woodberry, George E., *Nathaniel Hawthorne*. Boston: Houghton Mifflin, 1902.

HEMINGWAY, ERNEST:
Atkins, John, *The Art of Ernest Hemingway: His Work and Personality*. London: Peter Nevill, 1952.
Baker, Carlos, *Hemingway: The Writer As Artist*. Princeton: Princeton University Press, 1952; Second Edition, 1956.
McCaffery, John K. M., ed., *Ernest Hemingway: The Man and His Work*. Cleveland: World Publishing, 1950.
Young, Philip, *Ernest Hemingway*. New York: Rinehart, 1952.
HESSE, HERMANN:
Mileck, Joseph, *Hermann Hesse and His Critics: The Criticism and Bibliography of Half a Century*. Chapel Hill: University of North Carolina Press, 1957.
——————————, *Hermann Hesse's "Glasperlenspiel."* Berkeley: University of California Press, 1952.
HUXLEY, ALDOUS:
Atkins, John, *Aldous Huxley: A Literary Study*. London: John Calder, 1956.
Brooke, Jocelyn, *Aldous Huxley* (Supplement to *British Book News*). London: Longmans, Green, 1954.
Joad, C. E. M., *Return to Philosophy*. London: Faber, 1935.
Rolo, Charles J., ed., *The World of Aldous Huxley: An Omnibus of His Fiction and Non-Fiction Over Three Decades*. New York: Harper, 1947.
Savage, D. S., *Mysticism and Aldous Huxley: An Examination of Gerald Heard-Aldous Huxley Theories* (Pamphlet). Yonkers, New York: Alicat Bookshop Press, 1947.
Weaver, Raymond, and Others. *Aldous Huxley: Satirist and Humanist*. Garden City: Doubleday, Doran, n.d.
IRVING, WASHINGTON:
Langfeld, William R., and Philip C. Blackburn. *Washington Irving: A Bibliography*. New York: New York Public Library 1933.
McDermott, John F., ed., *The Western Journals of Washington Irving*. Norman: University of Oklahoma Press, 1944.
Penny, Clara Louisa, ed., *Washington Irving Diary: Spain, 1828-1829*. New York: Hispanic Society of America, 1926.
Pochmann, Henry A., ed., *Washington Irving: Representative Selections*. New York: American Book, 1934.
Reichart, Walter A., *Washington Irving and Germany*. Ann Arbor: University of Michigan Press, 1957.
Trent, William P., and George S. Hellman, *The Journals of Washington Irving*. Boston: Bibliophile Society, 1919.
Williams, Stanley T., and Mary Allen Edge, *A Bibliography of the*

Writings of Washington Irving: A Checklist. New York: Oxford University Press, 1936.

Williams, Stanley T., ed., *Journal of Washington Irving (1823-1824).* Cambridge: Harvard University Press, 1931.

——————, *Journal of Washington Irving, 1828.* New York: American Book, 1937.

Williams, Stanley T., *The Life of Washington Irving.* New York: Oxford University Press, 1935.

JAMES, HENRY:

Anderson, Quentin, *The American Henry James.* New Brunswick: Rutgers University Press, 1957.

Andreas, Osborne, *Henry James and the Expanding Horizon: A Study of the Meaning and Basic Themes of James's Fiction.* Seattle: University of Washington Press, 1948.

Beach, Joseph Warren, *The Method of Henry James.* New Haven: Yale University Press, 1918.

Bosanquet, Theodora, *Henry James at Work* (Hogarth Essays). London: Hogarth Press, 1924.

Bowden, Edwin T., *The Themes of Henry James.* New Haven: Yale University Press, 1956.

Brooks, Van Wyck, *The Pilgrimage of Henry James.* New York: Dutton, 1925.

Canby, Henry Seidel, *Turn West, Turn East: Mark Twain and Henry James.* Boston: Houghton Mifflin, 1951.

Crews, Frederick C., *The Tragedy of Manners: Moral Drama in the Later Novels of Henry James.* New Haven: Yale University Press, 1957.

Dupee, F. W., *Henry James.* New York: William Sloane Associates, 1951; Revised Edition (Anchor Books), Garden City: Doubleday, 1956.

Dupee, F. W., ed., *The Question of Henry James.* New York: Holt, 1945.

Edel, Leon, ed., *The Ghostly Tales of Henry James.* New Brunswick: Rutgers University Press, 1949.

——————, *Henry James: Selected Fiction* (Everyman's Library). New York: Dutton, 1953.

Edel, Leon, *Henry James: The Untried Years, 1843-1870.* Philadelphia: Lippincott, 1953.

Edel, Leon, ed., *The Selected Letters of Henry James.* New York: Farrar, Straus and Cudahy, 1955.

Edel, Leon, and Dan H. Laurence, *A Bibliography of Henry James.* London: Rupert Hart-Davis, 1957.

Edel, Leon, and Gordon N. Ray, eds., *Henry James and H. G. Wells.* Urbana: University of Illinois Press, 1958.

Edgar, Pelham, *Henry James: Man and Author*. Boston: Houghton Mifflin, 1927.

Fadiman, Clifton, ed., *The Short Stories of Henry James*. New York: Modern Library, 1945.

Grattan, C. Hartley, *The Three Jameses*. London: Longmans, Green, 1932.

Hoffmann, Charles G., *The Short Novels of Henry James*. New York: Bookman Associates, 1957.

James, Henry, *The Art of the Novel: Critical Prefaces*. New York: Scribner's, 1946.

Kelley, Cornelia P., *The Early Development of Henry James* (University of Illinois Studies in Language and Literature, XV). Urbana: University of Illinois Press, 1930.

Kenton, Edna, ed., *Eight Uncollected Tales of Henry James*. New Brunswick: Rutgers University Press, 1950.

LeClair, Robert C., *Young Henry James: 1843-1870*. New York: Bookman Associates, 1955.

Levy, Leo B., *Versions of Melodrama: A Study of the Fiction and Drama of Henry James, 1865-1897* (University of California Publications, English Studies, Vol. 16). Berkeley: University of California Press, 1957.

Lubbock, Percy, ed., *The Letters of Henry James*. Vols. I, II. New York: Scribner's, 1920.

Matthiessen, F. O., ed., *The American Novels and Stories of Henry James*. New York: Knopf, 1947.

Matthiessen, F. O., *Henry James: The Major Phase*. New York: Oxford University Press, 1944.

Matthiessen, F. O., ed., *Henry James' Stories of Writers and Artists*. Norfolk: New Directions, 1944.

Matthiessen, F. O., *The James Family*. New York: Knopf, 1947.

Matthiessen, F. O., and Kennth B. Murdoch, eds., *The Notebooks of Henry James*. New York: Oxford University Press, 1947.

McCarthy, Harold T., *Henry James: The Creative Process*. New York: Thomas Yoseloff, 1958.

Nowell-Smith, Simon, ed., *The Legend of the Master*. New York: Scribner's, 1948.

Phillips, LeRoy, *A Bibliography of the Writings of Henry James* (Revised Edition). New York: Coward-McCann, 1930.

Rahv, Philip, ed., *The Great Short Novels of Henry James*. New York: Dial Press, 1944.

Richardson, Lyon P., ed., *Henry James: Representative Selections*. Cincinnati: American Book, 1941.

Roberts, Morris, *Henry James's Criticism*. Cambridge: Harvard University Press, 1929.

Smith, Janet Adam, *Henry James and Robert Louis Stevenson: A Record of Friendship and Criticism*. London: Rupert Hart-Davis, 1948.

Stevenson, Elizabeth, *The Crooked Corridor: A Study of Henry James*. New York: Macmillan, 1949.

Swan, Michael, *Henry James*. New York: Roy Publishers, 1952.

Wegelin, Christof, *The Image of Europe in Henry James*. Dallas: Southern Methodist University Press, 1958.

West, Rebecca, *Henry James*. London: Nisbet, 1916.

Zabel, Morton D., ed., *The Portable Henry James*. New York: Viking, 1951.

JEWETT, SARAH ORNE:

Cary, Richard, ed., *Sarah Orne Jewett Letters*. Waterville, Maine: Colby College Press, 1956.

Cather, Willa, ed., *The Best Stories of Sarah Orne Jewett*. Boston: Houghton Mifflin, 1927.

Fields, Annie, ed., *Letters of Sarah Orne Jewett*. Boston: Houghton Mifflin, 1911.

Matthiessen, F. O., *Sarah Orne Jewett*. Boston: Houghton Mifflin, 1929.

Weber, Clara W., and Carl J. Weber, *A Bibliography of the Published Writings of Sarah Orne Jewett*. Waterville, Maine: Colby College Press, 1949.

Weber, Carl J., ed., *Letters of Sarah Orne Jewett*. Waterville, Maine: Colby College Press, 1947.

JOYCE, JAMES:

Beckett, Samuel, and Others, *An Exagmination of James Joyce*. Norfolk: New Directions, 1939.

Budgen, Frank, *James Joyce and the Making of Ulysses*. New York: Smith and Haas, 1934.

Campbell, Joseph, and Henry Morton Robinson, *A Skeleton Key to Finnegans Wake*. New York: Harcourt, 1947.

Colum, Mary and Padraic, *Our Friend James Joyce*. Garden City: Doubleday, 1958.

Edel, Leon, *James Joyce: The Last Journey*. New York: Gotham Book Mart, 1947.

Gilbert, Stuart, *James Joyce's Ulysses, A Study*. New York: Knopf, 1938.

Gilbert, Stuart, ed., *Letters of James Joyce*. New York: Viking, 1957.

Gillet, Louis, *Claybook for James Joyce*. London: Abelard-Schuman, 1958.

Givens, Seon, ed., *James Joyce: Two Decades of Criticism*. New York: Vanguard, 1948.

Glasheen, Adaline, *A Census of Finnegans Wake.* Evanston: Northwestern University Press, 1956.

Golding, Louis, *James Joyce.* London: Butterworth, 1933.

Gorman, Herbert, *James Joyce.* New York: Rinehart, 1948.

——————, *James Joyce: His First Forty Years.* New York: Huebsch, 1924.

Hutchins, Patricia, *James Joyce's Dublin.* London: Grey Walls Press, 1950.

——————, *James Joyce's World.* London: Methuen, 1957.

Jones, William Powell, *James Joyce and the Common Reader.* Norman: University of Oklahoma Press, 1955.

Joyce, Stanislaus, *My Brother's Keeper: James Joyce's Early Years.* New York: Viking, 1958.

Kain, Richard M., *Fabulous Voyager: James Joyce's "Ulysses."* Chicago: University of Chicago Press, 1947.

Kenner, Hugh, *Dublin's Joyce.* Bloomington: Indiana University Press, 1956.

Levin, Harry, *James Joyce: A Critical Introduction.* Norfolk: New Directions, 1941.

Loehrich, Rolf R., *The Secret of Ulysses: An Analysis of James Joyce's "Ulysses."* McHenry, Illinois: Compass Press, 1953.

Magalaner, Marvin and Richard M. Kain, *Joyce: The Man, the Work, the Reputation.* New York: New York University Press, 1956.

Magalaner, Marvin, ed., *A James Joyce Miscellany.* New York: James Joyce Society, 1957.

Noel, Lucie, *James Joyce and Paul L. Leon: The Story of a Friendship.* New York: Gotham Book Mart, 1950.

Noon, William T., S.J., *Joyce and Aquinas.* New Haven: Yale University Press, 1957.

Parker, Alan, *James Joyce: A Bibliography of His Writings, Critical Material and Miscellanea.* Boston: F. W. Faxon, 1948.

Schutte, William, *Joyce and Shakespeare: A Study in the Meaning of Ulysses.* New Haven: Yale University Press, 1957.

Slocum, John J., and Herbert Cahoon, *A Bibliography of James Joyce, 1882-1941.* New Haven: Yale University Press, 1953.

Smidt, Kristian, *James Joyce and the Cultic Use of Fiction.* Oslo: Akademisk Forlag, 1955.

Smith, Paul Jordan, *A Key to the "Ulysses" of James Joyce.* New York: Covici, Friede, 1934.

Stewart, J. I. M., *James Joyce* (Supplement to *British Book News*). London: Longmans, Green, 1957.

Strong, L. A. G., *The Sacred River: An Approach to James Joyce.* New York: Pellegrini and Cudahy, 1951.

Sullivan, Kevin, *Joyce Among the Jesuits.* New York: Columbia University Press, 1958.

Tindall, William York, *James Joyce: His Way of Interpreting the Modern World.* New York: Scribner's, 1950.

Ussher, Arland, *Three Great Irishmen: Shaw, Yeats, Joyce* (Mentor Books). New York: New American Library, 1957.

KAFKA, FRANZ:

Flores, Angel, and Homer Swander, eds., *Franz Kafka Today.* Madison: University of Wisconsin Press, 1958.

Flores, Angel, ed., *The Kafka Problem.* New York: New Directions, 1946.

A Franz Kafka Miscellany (Second Edition). New York: Twice A Year Press, 1946.

Goodman, Paul, *Kafka's Prayer.* New York: Vanguard, 1947.

Gray, Ronald, *Kafka's Castle.* Cambridge: Cambridge University Press, 1956.

Hubben, William, *Four Prophets of Our Destiny: Kierkegaard, Dostoevsky, Nietzsche, Kafka.* New York: Macmillan, 1952.

Kafka, Franz, *The Great Wall of China* (Translated by Willa and Edwin Muir). New York: Schocken Books, 1946.

——————, *Metamorphosis* (Translated by A. L. Lloyd). New York: Vanguard, 1946.

Neider, Charles, *The Frozen Sea: A Study of Franz Kafka.* New York: Oxford University Press, 1948.

Tauber, Herbert, *Franz Kafka: An Interpretation of His Works* (translated by G. Humphreys Roberts and Roger Senhouse.) New Haven: Yale University Press, 1948.

KIPLING, RUDYARD:

Beresford, G. C., *Schooldays With Kipling.* New York: Putnam's 1936.

Brown, Hilton, *Rudyard Kipling.* New York: Harper, 1945.

Carpenter, Lucile Russell, *Rudyard Kipling: A Friendly Profile.* Chicago: Argus Books, 1942.

Carrington, C. E., *The Life of Rudyard Kipling.* Garden City: Doubleday, 1955.

Chevrillon, André, *Three Studies in English Literature: Kipling, Galsworthy, Shakespeare.* London: Heinemann, 1923.

Cobb, Irvin S., Anice P. Page, and Others. *Around the World with Kipling.* Garden City: Doubleday, Page, 1926.

Cooper, Anice Page, *Rudyard Kipling.* Garden City: Doubleday, Doran, 1928.

Croft-Cooke, Rupert, *Rudyard Kipling.* Denver: Alan Swallow, 1948.

Dobrée, Bonamy, *Rudyard Kipling* (Supplement to *British Book News*). London: Longmans, Green, 1951.

Eliot, T. S., ed., *A Choice of Kipling's Verse*. New York: Scribner's, 1943.

Hart, Walter Morris, *Kipling: The Story Writer*. Berkeley: University of California Press, 1918.

Hopkins, R. Thurston, *Rudyard Kipling: A Literary Appreciation*. London: Simpkin, Marshall, Hamilton, Kent, 1915.

Kipling, Rudyard, *Something of Myself for My Friends Known and Unknown*. Garden City: Doubleday, Doran, 1937.

Livingston, Flora V., *Bibliography of the Works of Rudyard Kipling*. New York: Edgar H. Wells, 1927.

———————, *Suplement to Bibliography of the Works of Rudyard Kipling*. Cambridge: Harvard University Press, 1938.

Monkshood, G. F., [William James Clark], *The Less Familiar Kipling, and Kiplingana*. London: Jarrold, 1917.

Palmer, John, *Rudyard Kipling* (Third Edition). London: Nisbet, 1928.

Rice, Howard C., *Rudyard Kipling in New England*. Brattleboro, Vermont: Stephen Daye Press, 1936.

Shanks, Edward, *Rudyard Kipling: A Study in Literature and Political Ideas*. London: Macmillan, 1940.

Weygandt, Ann M., *Kipling's Reading and Its Influence on His Poetry*. Philadelphia: University of Pennsylvania Press, 1939.

LARDNER, RING:

Elder, Donald, *Ring Lardner: A Biography*. Garden City: Doubleday, 1956.

Seldes, Gilbert, ed., *The Portable Ring Lardner*. New York: Viking, 1946.

LAWRENCE, D. H.:

Aldington, Richard, *D. H. Lawrence*. London: Chatto and Windus, 1930.

———————, *D. H. Lawrence: An Indiscretion*. Seattle: University of Washington Book Store, 1927.

———————, *D. H. Lawrence: Portrait of a Genius, But . . . .* New York: Duell, Sloan, Pearce, 1950.

Brett, Dorothy, *Lawrence and Brett: A Friendship*. Philadelphia: Lippincott, 1933.

Bynner, Witter, *Journey with Genius*. New York: John Day, 1951.

Carswell, Catherine, *The Savage Pilgrimage: A Narrative of D. H. Lawrence*. New York: Harcourt, 1932.

Fay, Eliot, *Lorenzo in Search of the Sun*. New York: Bookman Associates, 1953.

249

Freeman, Mary, *D. H. Lawrence: A Basic Study of His Ideas.* Gainesville: University of Florida, 1955.

Gregory, Horace, *Pilgrim of the Apocalypse: A Critical Study of D. H. Lawrence.* New York: Viking, 1933.

Hoffman, Frederick J., and Harry T. Moore, eds., *The Achievement of D. H. Lawrence.* Norman: University of Oklahoma Press, 1953.

Hough, Graham, *The Dark Sun: A Study of D. H. Lawrence.* London: Duckworth, 1956.

Huxley, Aldous, ed., *The Letters of D. H. Lawrence.* New York: Viking, 1932.

Kenmare, D., *Firebird: A Study of D. H. Lawrence.* New York: Philosophical Library, 1952.

Kingsmill, Hugh, *The Life of D. H. Lawrence.* New York: Dodge, 1938.

Lawrence, Frieda, *Not I But the Wind.* New York: Viking, 1934.

Luhan, Mable Dodge, *Lorenzo in Taos.* New York: Knopf, 1932.

McDonald, Edward D., *A Bibliography of the Writings of D. H. Lawrence.* Philadelphia: Centaur Book Shop, 1925.

————————, *The Writings of D. H. Lawrence, 1925-1940: A Bibliographical Supplement.* Philadelphia: Centaur Book Shop, 1931.

Moore, Harry T., ed., *D. H. Lawrence's Letters to Bertrand Russell.* New York: Gotham Book Mart, 1948.

Moore, Harry T., *The Intelligent Heart: The Story of D. H. Lawrence.* New York: Farrar, Straus and Young, 1954.

————————, *The Life and Works of D. H. Lawrence.* New York: Twayne Publishers, 1951.

Murry, J. Middleton, *Son of Woman: The Story of D. H. Lawrence.* London: J. Cape, 1931.

Nehls, Edward, ed., *D. H. Lawrence: A Composite Biography* (Vols. I, II, III). Madison: University of Wisconsin Press, 1957-1959.

Nin, Anaïs, *D. H. Lawrence: An Unprofessional Study.* Paris: Edward W. Titus, 1932.

Potter, Stephen, *D. H. Lawrence, A First Study.* London: J. Cape, 1930.

Rees, Richard, *Brave Men: A Study of D. H. Lawrence and Simone Weil.* London: Gollancz, 1958.

Seligmann, Herbert J., *D. H. Lawrence: An American Interpretation.* New York: Thomas Seltzer, 1924.

Spilka, Mark, *The Love Ethic of D. H. Lawrence.* Bloomington: Indiana University Press, 1955.

T. E. [Jessie Chambers], *D. H. Lawrence: A Personal Record.* London: J. Cape, 1935.

Tedlock, E. W., Jr., *The Frieda Lawrence Collection of D. H. Lawrence Manuscripts: A Descriptive Bibliography.* Albuquerque: University of New Mexico Press, 1948.

Tindall, William York, *D. H. Lawrence and Susan His Cow.* New York: Columbia University Press, 1939.

Tindall, William York, ed., *The Later D. H. Lawrence.* New York: Knopf, 1952.

Tiverton, Father William, *D. H. Lawrence and Human Existence.* London: Rockcliff Press, 1951.

Trilling, Diana, ed., *The Portable D. H. Lawrence.* New York: Viking, 1950.

————, *The Selected Letters of D. H. Lawrence.* New York: Farrar, Straus, Cudahy, 1958.

White, William, *D. H. Lawrence: A Checklist, 1931-1950.* Detroit: Wayne University Press, 1950.

Young, Kenneth, *D. H. Lawrence* (Supplement to *British Book News*). London: Longmans, Green, 1952.

LONDON, JACK:

London, Charmian, *The Book of Jack London.* New York: Century, 1921.

London, Joan, *Jack London and His Times: An Unconventional Biography.* New York: Book League of America, 1939.

Stone, Irving, *Sailor on Horseback: The Biography of Jack London.* Boston: Houghton Mifflin, 1938.

MANN, THOMAS:

Baer, Lydia, *The Concept and the Function of Death in the Works of Thomas Mann* (Condensation of Ph.D. dissertation, University of Pennsylvania). Freiburg im Breisgau, Germany: Jos. Waibel'sche Buchdruckerie, 1932.

Brennan, Joseph Gerard, *Thomas Mann's World.* New York: Columbia University Press, 1942.

Hatfield, Henry, *Thomas Mann.* Norfolk: New Directions, 1951.

Heller, Erich, *The Ironic German: A Study of Thomas Mann.* Boston: Little, Brown, 1958.

Hirschbach, Frank Donald, *The Arrows and the Lyre: A Study of the Role of Love in the Works of Thomas Mann.* The Hague: Martinus Nijhoff, 1955.

Jonas, Klaus W., *Fifty Years of Thomas Mann Studies: A Bibliography of Criticism.* Minneapolis: University of Minnesota Press, 1955.

Kaufmann, Fritz, *Thomas Mann, The World as Will and Representation.* Boston: Beacon Press, 1957.

Letters, F. J. H., *An Introduction to Thomas Mann.* Armidale, N.S.W.: New England University College, n.d.

Lindsay, J. M., *Thomas Mann.* Oxford: Blackwell, 1954.

Mann, Erika, *The Last Year of Thomas Mann.* New York: Farrar, Straus and Cudahy, 1958.

Neider, Charles, ed., *The Stature of Thomas Mann.* Norfolk: New Directions, 1947.

Nicholls, R. A., *Nietzsche in the Early Work of Thomas Mann.* Berkeley: University of California Press, 1955.

Slochower, Harry, *Thomas Mann's Joseph Story: An Interpretation.* New York: Knopf, 1938.

Thomas, R. Hinton, *Thomas Mann, The Mediation of Art.* Oxford: Clarendon Press, 1956.

Weigand, Hermann J., *Thomas Mann's Novel, "Der Zauberberg."* New York: Appleton-Century, 1933.

MANSFIELD, KATHERINE:

Alpers, Antony, *Katherine Mansfield: A Biography.* New York: Knopf, 1953.

Berkman, Sylvia, *Katherine Mansfield: A Critical Study.* New Haven: Yale University Press, 1951.

Bowen, Elizabeth, ed., *Stories by Katherine Mansfield.* New York: Vintage Books, 1956.

Friis, Anne, *Katherine Mansfield: Life and Stories.* Copenhagen: Einar Munksgaard, 1946.

Lawlor, P. A., *The Loneliness of Katherine Mansfield.* Wellington, New Zealand: Beltane Book Bureau, 1950.

————————, *The Mystery of Maata, A Katherine Mansfield Novel.* Wellington, New Zealand: Beltane Book Bureau, 1946.

Mantz, Ruth Elvish, *The Critical Bibliography of Katherine Mansfield.* London: Constable, 1931.

Morris, G. N., *Mansfieldana: A Brief Katherine Mansfield Bibliography.* Wellington: Beltane Book Bureau, 1948.

Murry, John Middleton, ed., *Katherine Mansfield's Letters to John Middleton Murry, 1913-1922.* New York: Knopf, 1951.

————————, *The Scrapbook of Katherine Mansfield.* New York: Knopf, 1940.

MAUGHAM, W. SOMERSET:

Aldington, Richard, *W. Somerset Maugham: An Appreciation* (Pamphlet). New York: Doubleday, Doran, 1939.

Brophy, John, *Somerset Maugham* (Supplement to *British Book News*). London: Longmans, Green, 1952.

Cordell, Richard A., *W. Somerset Maugham.* Toronto: Nelson, 1937.

Jonas, Klaus W., *A Bibliography of the Writings of W. Somerset Maugham*. South Hadley, Massachusetts: n.p., 1950.

————————, *The Gentleman from Cap Ferrat*. New Haven: Center of Maugham Studies, 1956.

Jonas, Klaus W., ed., *The Maugham Enigma*. New York: Citadel, 1954.

Maugham, W. Somerset, *The Summing Up*. New York: Doubleday, Doran, 1938.

————————, *A Writer's Notebook*. Garden City: Doubleday, 1955.

McIver, Claude Searcy, *William Somerset Maugham: A Study of Technique and Literary Sources*. Philadelphia: University of Pennsylvania (Ph.D. Dissertation), 1936.

Stott, Raymond Toole, *The Writings of William Somerset Maugham: A Bibliography*. London: B. Rota, 1956.

Towne, Charles H., Carl Van Doren, Mark Van Doren, and Others, *W. Somerset Maugham: Novelist, Essayist, Dramatist* (Pamphlet). New York: Doran, 1925.

Ward, Richard H., *W. Somerset Maugham*. London: Geoffrey Bles, 1937.

MAUPASSANT, GUY DE:

Artinian, A., *Maupassant Criticism in France, 1880-1940*. New York: King's Crown Press, 1941.

Boyd, Ernest, *Guy de Maupassant: A Biographical Study*. Boston: Little, Brown, 1928.

Galantière, Lewis, ed., *The Portable Maupassant*. New York: Viking, 1947.

Jackson, Samuel, *Guy de Maupassant*. London: Duckworth, 1938.

Riddell, Agnes Rutherford, *Flaubert and Maupassant: A Literary Relationship*. Chicago: University of Chicago Press, 1920.

Sherard, Robert H., *The Life, Work and Evil Fate of Guy de Maupassant*. London: Laurie, 1926.

Steegmuller, Francis, *Maupassant: A Lion in the Path*. New York: Random House, 1949.

Sullivan, Edward D., *Maupassant the Novelist*. Princeton: Princeton University Press, 1954.

MELVILLE, HERMAN:

Anderson, Charles Roberts, *Melville in the South Seas*. New York: Columbia University Press, 1951.

Arvin, Newton, *Herman Melville*. New York: William Sloane Associates, 1950.

Baird, James, *Ishmael*. Baltimore: Johns Hopkins Press, 1956.

Braswell, William, *Melville's Religious Thought*. Durham: Duke University Press, 1943.

Chase, Richard, *Herman Melville: A Critical Study.* New York: Macmillan, 1949.

Davis, Merrell R., *Melville's Mardi: A Chartless Voyage.* New Haven: Yale University Press, 1952.

Freeman, F. Barron, ed., *Herman Melville's Billy Budd.* Cambridge: Harvard University Press, 1948.

Freeman, John, *Herman Melville.* New York: Macmillan, 1926.

Gilman, William H., *Melville's Early Life and "Redburn."* New York: New York University Press, 1951.

Hillway, Tyrus and Luther S. Mansfield, eds., *Moby-Dick Centennial Essays.* Dallas: Southern Methodist University Press, 1953.

Howard, Leon, *Herman Melville: A Biography.* Berkeley: University of California Press, 1951.

Leyda, Jay, ed., *The Complete Stories of Herman Melville.* New York: Random House, 1949.

Leyda, Jay, *The Melville Log: A Documentary Life of Herman Melville, 1819-1891.* Two Volumes. New York: Harcourt, 1951.

Mason, Ronald, *The Spirit Above the Dust: A Study of Herman Melville.* London: John Lehmann, 1951.

Metcalf, Eleanor Melville, *Herman Melville: Cycle and Epicycle.* Cambridge: Harvard University Press, 1953.

Mumford, Lewis, *Herman Melville.* New York: Harcourt, 1929.

Oliver, Egbert S., ed., *Piazza Tales by Herman Melville.* New York: Hendricks House, Farrar Straus, 1948.

Olson, Charles, *Call Me Ishmael.* New York: Reynal and Hitchcock, 1947.

Percival, M. O., *A Reading of Moby Dick.* Chicago: University of Chicago Press, 1950.

Pommer, Henry F., *Milton and Melville.* Pittsburgh: University of Pittsburgh Press, 1950.

Rosenberry, Edward H., *Melville and the Comic Spirit.* Cambridge: Harvard University Press, 1955.

Sedgwick, William Ellery, *Herman Melville: The Tragedy of Mind.* Cambridge: Harvard University Press, 1944.

Stern, Milton R., *The Fine Hammered Steel of Herman Melville.* Urbana: University of Illinois Press, 1957.

Stern, Milton R., ed., *Typee and Billy Budd* (Dutton Paperbacks). New York: Dutton, 1958.

Stone, Geoffrey, *Melville.* New York: Sheed and Ward, 1949.

Thompson, Lawrence, *Melville's Quarrel With God.* Princeton: Princeton University Press, 1952.

Thorp, Willard, ed., *Herman Melville: Representative Selections.* New York: American Book, 1938.

Weaver, Raymond M., *Herman Melville: Mariner and Mystic.* New York: Doran, 1921.

Weaver, Raymond, ed., *Shorter Novels of Herman Melville.* New York: Liveright, 1928.

Wright, Nathalia, *Melville's Use of the Bible.* Durham: Duke University Press, 1949.

MEREDITH, GEORGE:

Beach, Joseph Warren, *The Comic Spirit in George Meredith.* London: Longmans, Green, 1911.

Coolidge, Bertha, *A Catalogue of the Altschul Collection of George Meredith in the Yale University Library.* New Haven: Privately Printed, 1931.

Forman, M. Buxton, *A Bibliography of the Writings in Prose and Verse of George Meredith.* Edinburgh: Bibliographical Society, 1922.

————————, *Meredithiana, Being a Supplement to the Bibliography of Meredith.* Edinburgh: Bibliographical Society, 1924.

Gretton, Mary Sturge, *The Writings and Life of George Meredith: A Centenary Study.* Cambridge: Harvard University Press, 1926.

Lindsay, Jack, *George Meredith: His Life and Work.* London: Bodley Head, 1956.

Meredith, W. M., ed., *Letters of George Meredith* (Two Volumes). New York: Scribner's, 1912.

Priestley, J. B., *George Meredith.* New York: Macmillan, 1926.

Sassoon, Siegfried, *Meredith.* New York: Viking, 1948.

Sencourt, Robert E. [Robert E. G. George], *The Life of George Meredith.* New York: Scribner's, 1929.

Sitwell, Osbert, *The Novels of George Meredith and Some Notes on the English Novel* (Pamphlet). London: The English Associate, November, 1947.

Stevenson, Lionel, *The Ordeal of George Meredith.* New York: Scribner's, 1953.

Wright, Walter F., *Art and Substance in George Meredith.* Lincoln: University of Nebraska Press, 1953.

MÉRIMÉE, PROSPER:

Johnstone, G. H., *Prosper Mérimée: A Mask and a Face.* New York: Dutton, 1927.

Lyon, Sylvia, *The Life and Times of Prosper Mérimée.* New York: Dial, 1948.

O. HENRY:

Clarkson, Paul S., *A Bibliography of William Sydney Porter* (O. Henry). Caldwell, Idaho: Caxton, 1938.

Davis, Robert H., and A. B. Maurice, *The Caliph of Bagdad.* New York: Appleton, 1931.

Kramer, Dale, *The Heart of O. Henry.* New York: Rinehart, 1954.

Langford, Gerald, *Alias O. Henry: A Biography of William Sydney Porter.* New York: Macmillan, 1957.

Long, E. Hudson, *O. Henry: The Man and His Work.* Philadelphia: University of Pennsylvania Press, 1949.

Nolan, Jeannette, *O. Henry: The Story of William Sydney Porter.* New York: Messner, 1943.

O. Henry Papers (Containing Some Sketches of His Life Together with an Alphabetical Index to His Complete Works) . Garden City: Doubleday, Page, n.d.

Smith, Charles A., *O. Henry Biography.* Garden City: Doubleday, Page, 1916.

Williams, William Wash, *The Quiet Lodger of Irving Place.* New York: Dutton, 1936.

Wilson, Lollie C., *Hard to Forget: The Young O. Henry.* Los Angeles: Lymanhouse, 1939.

ORWELL, GEORGE:

Atkins, John, *George Orwell: A Literary Study.* London: John Calder, 1954.

Brander, Laurence, *George Orwell.* London: Longmans, Green, 1954.

Hollis, Christopher, *A Study of George Orwell: The Man and His Works.* London: Hollis and Carter, 1956.

Hopkinson, Tom, *George Orwell* (Supplement to *British Book News*) . London: Longmans, Green, 1953.

Rovere, Richard H., ed., *The Orwell Reader: Fiction, Essays, and Reportage.* New York: Harcourt, 1956.

POE, EDGAR ALLAN:

Allen, Hervey, *Israfel: The Life and Times of Edgar Allan Poe.* New York: Doran, 1927.

Bonaparte, Marie, *The Life and Works of Edgar Allan Poe: A Psycho-Analytic Interpretation.* London: Imago Publishing, 1949.

Braddy, Haldeen, *Glorious Incense: The Fulfillment of Edgar Allan Poe.* Washington, D. C.: Scarecrow Press, 1953.

Campbell, Killis, *The Mind of Poe and Other Studies.* Cambridge: Harvard University Press, 1933.

Davidson, Edward H., *Poe: A Critical Study.* Cambridge: Harvard University Press, 1957.

Fagin, N. Bryllion, *The Histrionic Mr. Poe.* Baltimore: John Hopkins Press, 1949.

Harrison, James A., ed., *The Complete Works of Edgar Allan Poe.* New York: Crowell, 1902.

Heartman, Charles F., and James R. Canny, *A Bibliography of First Printings of the Writings of Edgar Allan Poe.* Hattiesburg, Mississippi: The Book Farm, 1940.

Hyslop, Lois and Francis E., Jr., ed., *Baudelaire on Poe.* State College, Pennsylvania: Bald Eagle Press, 1952.

Krutch, Joseph Wood, *Edgar Allan Poe: A Study in Genius.* New York: Knopf, 1926.

Lauvrière, Emile, *The Strange Life and Strange Loves of Edgar Allan Poe.* (Translated by Edwin Gile Rich). Philadelphia: Lippincott, 1935.

Lindsay, Philip, *The Haunted Man: A Portrait of Edgar Allan Poe.* New York: Philosophical Library, 1954.

Phillips, Mary E., *Edgar Allan Poe: The Man.* Philadelphia: Winston, 1926.

Pope-Hennessy, Una, *Edgar Allan Poe, 1809-1849: A Critical Biography.* London: Macmillan, 1934.

Quinn, Arthur Hobson, *Edgar Allan Poe: A Critical Biography.* New York: Appleton-Century, 1941.

Quinn, Patrick F., *The French Face of Edgar Poe.* Carbondale: Southern Illinois University Press, 1957.

Shanks, Edward, *Edgar Allan Poe.* New York: Macmillan, 1937.

Stern, Philip Van Doren, ed., *The Portable Edgar Allan Poe.* New York: Viking, 1945.

Whitman, Sarah Helen, *Edgar Poe and His Critics.* New Brunswick: Rutgers University Press, 1949.

Woodberry, G. E., *The Life of Edgar Allan Poe, Personal and Literary, with his Chief Correspondence with Men of Letters.* Boston: Houghton Mifflin, 1909.

PORTER, KATHERINE ANNE:

Mooney, Harry John, Jr., *The Fiction and Criticism of Katherine Anne Porter.* Pittsburgh: University of Pittsburgh Press, 1957.

Schwartz, Edward, *Katherine Anne Porter: A Critical Bibliography.* New York: New York Public Library, 1953.

PUSHKIN, ALEXANDER:

Beckwith, Martha Warren, and Others, *Pushkin: The Man and the Artist.* New York: Paisley Press, 1937.

Cross, Samuel H., and Ernest J. Simmons, *Alexander Pushkin, 1799-1837: His Life and Literary Heritage.* New York: American Russian Institute for Cultural Relations with the Soviet Union, 1937.

Herford, C. H., *The Post-War Mind of Germany and Other European Studies.* Oxford: Clarendon Press, 1927.

Lambert, Lydia, *Pushkin: Poet and Lover*. Garden City, Doubleday, 1946.

Lavrin, Janko, *Pushkin and Russian Literature*. New York: Macmillan, 1948.

Mirsky, D. S., *Pushkin*. London: Routledge, 1926.

Pushkin: A Collection of Articles and Essays on the Great Russian Poet, A. S. Pushkin. Moscow: The U.S.S.R. Society for Cultural Relations with Foreign Countries, 1939.

Simmons, Ernest J., *Pushkin*. Cambridge: Harvard University Press, 1937.

Troyat, Henri, *Pushkin: A Biography*. New York: Pantheon, 1950.

Weidle, Wladimir, *Pushkin, 1799-1837*. Paris: Unesco, 1949.

STEIN, GERTRUDE:

Gallup, Donald, ed., *The Flowers of Friendship: Letters Written to Gertrude Stein*. New York: Knopf, 1953.

Haas, Robert B., and Donald C. Gallup, *A Catalogue of the Published and Unpublished Writings of Gertrude Stein*. New Haven: Yale University Press, 1941.

Miller, Rosalind S., *Gertrude Stein: Form and Intelligibility*. New York: Exposition, 1949.

Reid, B. L., *Art by Subtraction: A Dissenting Opinion of Gertrude Stein*. Norman: University of Oklahoma Press, 1958.

Sawyer, Julian, *Gertrude Stein: A Bibliography*. New York: Arrow Editions, 1940.

Sprigge, Elizabeth, *Gertrude Stein: Her Life and Work*. New York: Harper, 1957.

Stein, Gertrude, *Alphabets and Birthdays* (Introduction by Donald Gallup). New Haven: Yale University Press, 1957.

——————, *As Fine as Melanctha* (Foreword by Natalie Clifford Barney). New Haven: Yale University Press, 1954.

——————, *The Autobiography of Alice B. Toklas*. New York: Literary Guild, 1933.

——————, *Bee Time Vine and Other Pieces* (Preface and Notes by Virgil Thomson). New Haven: Yale University Press, 1953.

——————, *Everybody's Autobiography*. New York: Random House, 1937.

——————, *Mrs. Reynolds, and Five Earlier Novelettes* (Introduction by Lloyd Frankenberg). New Haven: Yale University Press, 1952.

——————, *A Novel of Thank You* (Introduction by Carl Van Vechten). New Haven: Yale University Press, 1958.

——————, *Painted Lace and Other Pieces* (Introduction by

Daniel-Henry Kahnweiler). New Haven: Yale University Press, 1955.

————————, *Stanzas in Meditation and Other Poems* (Preface by Donald Sutherland). New Haven: Yale University Press, 1955.

————————, *Two: Gertrude Stein and Her Brother and Other Early Portraits* (Foreword by Janet Flanner). New Haven: Yale University Press, 1951.

Sutherland, Donald, *Gertrude Stein: A Biography of Her Work.* New Haven: Yale University Press, 1951.

Van Vechten, Carl, ed., *Selected Writings of Gertrude Stein.* New York: Random House, 1946.

STEINBECK, JOHN:

Lisca, Peter, *The Wide World of John Steinbeck.* New Brunswick: Rutgers University Press, 1958.

Tedlock, E. W., Jr., and C. V. Wicker, eds., *Steinbeck and His Critics: A Record of Twenty-Five Years.* Albuquerque: University of New Mexico Press, 1957.

STEVENSON. ROBERT LOUIS:

Balfour, Graham, *The Life of Robert Louis Stevenson.* London: Methuen, 1908.

Bermann, Richard A., *Home from the Sea: Robert Louis Stevenson in Samoa.* Indianapolis: Bobbs-Merrill, 1939.

Carré, Jean Marie, *The Frail Warrior.* New York: Coward-McCann, 1930.

Chesterton, G. K., *Robert Louis Stevenson.* New York: Dodd, Mead, 1928.

Colvin, Sidney, ed., *The Letters of Robert Louis Stevenson* (Four Volumes). New York: Scribner's, 1911.

Commins, Saxe, ed., *Selected Writings of Robert Louis Stevenson.* New York: Random House, 1947.

Cooper, Lettice, *Robert Louis Stevenson.* Denver: Alan Swallow, 1948.

Dalglish, Doris N., *Presbyterian Pirate: A Portrait of Stevenson.* London: Oxford University Press, 1937.

Dark, Sidney, *Robert Louis Stevenson.* London: Hodder and Stoughton, 1931.

Ferguson, DeLancey, and Marshall Waingrow, eds., *RLS: Stevenson's Letters to Charles Baxter.* New Haven: Yale University Press, 1956.

Fisher, Anne B., *No More a Stranger.* Stanford: Stanford University Press, 1946.

Furnas, J. C., *Voyage to Windward: The Life of Robert Louis Stevenson.* New York: William Sloane Associates, 1951.

Hellman, George S., *The True Stevenson: A Study in Clarification.* Boston: Little, Brown, 1925.

Hinkley, Laura L., *The Stevensons: Louis and Fanny.* New York: Hastings House, 1950.

Issler, Anne R., *Happier for His Presence: San Francisco and Robert Louis Stevenson.* Stanford: Stanford University Press, 1949.

——————, *Our Mountain Hermitage: Silverado and Robert Louis Stevenson.* Stanford: Stanford University Press, 1950.

——————, *Stevenson at Silverado.* Caldwell, Idaho: Caxton, 1939.

Lockett, W. G., *Robert Louis Stevenson at Davos.* London: Hurst and Blackett, 1934.

Masson, Rosaline O., ed., *I Can Remember Robert Louis Stevenson.* New York: Stokes, 1923.

McGaw, Sister Martha Mary, *Stevenson in Hawaii.* Honolulu: University of Hawaii Press, 1950.

McKay, George L., *A Stevenson Library: Catalogue of Writings By and About Robert Louis Stevenson Formed by Edwin J. Beinecke* (Four Volumes). New Haven: Yale University Library, 1951-1958.

Prideaux, W. F., *A Bibliography of the Works of Robert Louis Stevenson* (Revised Edition). London: Hollings, 1917.

Smith, Janet Adam, ed., *Henry James and Robert Louis Stevenson: A Record of Friendship and Criticism.* London: Rupert Hart-Davis, 1948.

Smith, Janet Adam, *R. L. Stevenson.* London: Duckworth, 1937.

Stern, G. B., *Robert Louis Stevenson* (Supplement to *British Book News*). London: Longmans, Green, 1952.

Steuart, J. A., *Robert Louis Stevenson: Man and Writer.* London: Low, Marston, 1924.

Stevenson, Fanny and Robert Louis, *Our Samoan Adventure* (Edited by Charles Neider, with an Introduction and Notes). New York: Harper, 1955.

SUCKOW, RUTH:

Suckow, Ruth, *A Memoir.* New York: Rinehart, 1952.

THOMAS, DYLAN:

Fraser, G. S., *Dylan Thomas* (Supplement to *British Book News*). London: Longmans, Green, 1957.

Huff, William H., "Bibliography," in Elder Olson, *The Poetry of Dylan Thomas.* Chicago: University of Chicago Press, 1954.

——————, *Dylan Thomas, A Bibliography.* Evanston: Northwestern University Library, 1953.

260

Olson, Elder, *The Poetry of Dylan Thomas.* Chicago: University of Chicago Press, 1954.

Rolph, J. Alexander, *Dylan Thomas: A Bibliography.* London: J. M. Dent, 1956.

Stanford, Derek, *Dylan Thomas.* New York: Citadel Press, 1954.

Treece, Henry, *Dylan Thomas: 'Dog Among the Fairies.'* London: L. Drummond, 1949.

TOLSTOY, LEO:

Berlin, Isaiah, *The Hedgehog and the Fox: An Essay on Tolstoy's View of History.* New York: Simon and Schuster, 1953.

Birukoff, Paul, *The Life of Tolstoy.* London: Cassell, 1911.

Bodde, D., *Tolstoy and China.* Princeton: Princeton University Press, 1950.

Davis, Helen E., *Tolstoy and Nietzsche: A Problem in Biographical Ethics.* New York: New Republic, 1929.

Dole, Nathan Haskell, *The Life of Count Lyof N. Tolstoi.* New York: Crowell, 1911.

Fausset, Hugh I'Anson, *Tolstoy: The Inner Drama.* New York: Harcourt, 1928.

Hofmann, Modest, and André Pierre, *By Deeds of Truth: The Life of Leo Tolstoy.* New York: Orion Press, 1958.

Joy, Charles R., ed., *Lyof Tolstoy: An Anthology.* Boston: Beacon, 1958.

Kuzminskaya, Tatyana, *Tolstoy As I Knew Him: My Life at Home and at Yasnaya Polyana.* New York: Macmillan, 1948.

Kvitko, David, *A Philosophic Study of Tolstoy.* New York: Ph.D. Dissertation, Columbia University, 1927.

Lavrin, Janko, *Tolstoy: An Approach.* New York: Macmillan, 1946.

Maude, Aylmer, *Leo Tolstoy and His Works.* ·New York: Oxford University Press, 1931.

——————, *Tolstoy on Art.* Boston: Small, Maynard, 1924.

Nazaroff, Alexander I., *Tolstoy: The Inconstant Genius.* New York: Stokes, 1929.

Noyes, George Rapall, *Tolstoy.* New York: Duffield, 1918.

Polner, Tikhon, *Tolstoy and His Wife.* New York: Norton, 1945.

Simmons, Ernest J., *Leo Tolstoy.* Boston: Little, Brown, 1946.

Steiner, George, *Tolstoy or Dostoevsky: An Essay in the Old Criticism.* New York: Knopf, 1959.

Tolstaya, Sophie, *The Countess Tolstoy's Later Diary.* London: Gollancz, 1929.

——————, *The Diary of Tolstoy's Wife, 1860-1891.* London: Gollancz, 1928.

Tolstoy, Alexandra, *Tolstoy: A Life of My Father*. New York: Harper, 1953.

TURGENEV, IVAN:

Gettmann, Royal A., *Turgenev in England and America*. Urbana: University of Illinois Press, 1941.

Magarshack, David, *Turgenev: A Life*. New York: Grove, 1954.

Turgenev, Ivan, *Literary Reminiscences and Autobiographical Fragments*. New York: Farrar, Straus and Cudahy, 1958.

Yarmolinsky, Avrahm, ed., *The Borzoi Turgenev*. New York: Knopf, 1950.

Yarmolinsky, Avrahm, *Turgenev: The Man, His Art, and His Age*. London: Hodder and Stoughton, 1926.

Zhitova, Mme. V., *The Turgenev Family*. London: Harvill Press, 1947.

TWAIN, MARK:

Allen, Jerry, *The Adventures of Mark Twain*. Boston: Little, Brown, 1954.

Andrews, Kenneth R., *Nook Farm: Mark Twain's Hartford Circle*. Cambridge: Harvard University Press, 1950.

Asselineau, Roger, *The Literary Reputation of Mark Twain from 1910 to 1950: A Critical Essay and a Bibliography*. Paris: Didier, 1954.

Bellamy, Gladys C., *Mark Twain As a Literary Artist*. Norman: University of Oklahoma Press, 1950.

Benson, Ivan, *Mark Twain's Western Years*. Stanford: Stanford University Press, 1938.

Branch, Edgar M., *The Literary Apprenticeship of Mark Twain*. Urbana: University of Illinois Press, 1950.

Brashear, Minnie M., *Mark Twain: Son of Missouri*. Chapel Hill: University of North Carolina Press, 1934.

Brooks, Van Wyck, *The Ordeal of Mark Twain*. New York: Dutton, 1920.

Canby, Henry Seidel, *Turn West, Turn East: Mark Twain and Henry James*. Boston: Houghton Mifflin, 1951.

Cardwell, Guy A., *Twins of Genius*. East Lansing: Michigan State College Press, 1953.

Clemens, Clara, *My Father Mark Twain*. New York: Harper, 1931.

DeVoto, Bernard, *Mark Twain at Work*. Cambridge: Harvard University Press, 1942.

------------------------, *Mark Twain's America*. Boston: Houghton Mifflin, 1951.

DeVoto, Bernard, ed., *The Portable Mark Twain*. New York: Viking, 1946.

Ferguson, De Lancey, *Mark Twain: Man and Legend*. Indianapolis: Bobbs-Merrill, 1943.

Frear, Walter Francis, *Mark Twain and Hawaii*. Chicago: Lakeside Press, 1947.

Johnson, Merle, *A Bibliography of the Works of Mark Twain*. New York: Harper, 1935.

Hemminghaus, Edgar H., *Mark Twain in Germany*. New York: Columbia University Press, 1939.

Mack, Effie Mona, *Mark Twain in Nevada*. New York: Scribner's, 1947.

Masters, Edgar Lee, *Mark Twain: A Portrait*. New York: Scribner's, 1938.

Neider, Charles, ed., *The Complete Short Stories of Mark Twain*. Garden City: Hanover House, 1957; New York: Bantam Books, 1958.

Paine, Albert Bigelow, ed., *Mark Twain's Letters*. New York: Harper, 1917.

Paine, Albert Bigelow, *Mark Twain: A Biography* (Centenary Edition, Two Volumes). New York: Harper, 1935.

Paine, Albert Bigelow, ed., *Mark Twain's Notebook*. New York: Harper, 1935.

Pattee, Fred Lewis, ed., *Mark Twain: Representative Selections*. New York: American Book, 1935.

Pellowe, William C. S., *Mark Twain: Pilgrim from Hannibal*. New York: Hobson Book Press, 1945.

Scott, Arthur L., ed., *Mark Twain: Selected Criticism*. Dallas: Southern Methodist University Press, 1955.

Smith, Henry Nash, and Frederick Anderson, eds., *Mark Twain of the 'Enterprise': Newspaper Articles and Other Documents 1862-1864*. Berkeley: University of California Press, 1957.

Twain, Mark, *Mark Twain's Autobiography*. New York: Harper, 1924.

———————————, *Report from Paradise*. New York: Harper, 1952.

Wagenknecht, Edward, *Mark Twain: The Man and His Work*. New Haven: Yale University Press, 1935.

Webster, Samuel Charles, *Mark Twain, Business Man*. Boston: Little, Brown, 1946.

Wecter, Dixon, ed., *The Love Letters of Mark Twain*. New York: Harper, 1949.

Wecter, Dixon, *Sam Clemens of Hannibal*. Boston: Houghton Mifflin, 1952.

West, Victor Royce, *Folklore in the Works of Mark Twain*. Lincoln, Nebraska: University of Nebraska, 1930.

UNAMUNO, MIGUEL DE:
Barea, Arturo, *Unamuno*. New Haven: Yale University Press, 1952.
WELLS, H. G.:
Belgion, Montgomery, *H. G. Wells* (Supplement to *British Book News*). London: Longmans, Green, 1953.
Braybrooke, Patrick, *Some Aspects of H. G. Wells*. London: Daniel, 1928.
Brome, Vincent, *H. G. Wells: A Biography*. London: Longmans, Green, 1951.
Brown, Ivor J. C., *H. G. Wells*. London: Nisbet, 1923.
Cross, Wilbur L., *Four Contemporary Novelists*. New York: Macmillan, 1930.
Dark, Sidney, *An Outline of Wells: The Superman in the Street*. Putnam's, 1922.
Doughty, F. H., *H. G. Wells: Educationist*. New York: Doran, 1927.
Edel, Leon, and Gordon N. Ray, eds., *Henry James and H. G. Wells: A Record of Their Friendship, Their Debate on the Art of Fiction, and Their Quarrel*. Urbana: University of Illinois Press, 1958.
Nicholson, Norman C., *H. G. Wells*. Denver: Alan Swallow, 1950.
Wells, Geoffrey H. [Geoffrey West], *The Works of H. G. Wells, 1887-1925: A Bibliography*. London: Routledge, 1926.
WEST, NATHANAEL:
Ross, Alan, ed., *The Complete Works of Nathanael West*. New York: Farrar, Straus and Cudahy, 1957.
WHARTON, EDITH:
Cross, Wilbur L., *Edith Wharton* (Pamphlet). New York: Appleton, 1927.
Lubbock, Percy, *Portrait of Edith Wharton*. New York: Appleton-Century, 1947.
Nevius, Blake, *Edith Wharton: A Study of Her Fiction*. Berkeley: University of California Press, 1953.
Quinn, Arthur Hobson, ed., *An Edith Wharton Treasury*. New York: Appleton-Century-Crofts, 1950.
Wharton, Edith, *A Backward Glance*. New York: Appleton-Century, 1934.
WILLIAMS, WILLIAM CARLOS:
Koch, Vivienne, *William Carlos Williams*. Norfolk: New Directions, 1950.
Thirlwall, John C., ed., *The Selected Letters of William Carlos Williams*. New York: McDowell, Obolensky, 1957.

WOLFE, THOMAS:
   Geismar, Maxwell, ed., *The Portable Thomas Wolfe*. New York: Viking, 1946.
   Johnson, Pamela H., *Thomas Wolfe: A Critical Study*. London: Heinemann, 1947.
   Muller, Herbert J., *Thomas Wolfe*. Norfolk: New Directions, 1947.
   Pollock, Thomas Clark, and Oscar Cargill, *Thomas Wolfe at Washington Square*. New York: New York University Press, 1954.
   Preston, George R., Jr., *Thomas Wolfe: A Bibliography*. New York: Charles S. Boesen, 1943.
   Rubin, Louis D., Jr., *Thomas Wolfe, The Weather of His Youth*. Baton Rouge: Louisiana State University Press, 1955.
   Walser, Richard, ed., *The Enigma of Thomas Wolfe: Biographical and Critical Selections*. Cambridge: Harvard University Press, 1953.
   Watkins, Floyd C., *Thomas Wolfe's Characters: Portraits from Life*. Norman: University of Oklahoma Press, 1957.
   Wolfe, Thomas, *The Hills Beyond* (with notes by Edward C. Aswell). New York: Harper, 1941.
WOOLF, VIRGINIA:
   Blackstone, Bernard, *Virginia Woolf*. New York: Harcourt, 1949.
   Chambers, R. L., *The Novels of Virginia Woolf*. Edinburgh: Oliver and Boyd, 1955.
   Daiches, David, *Virginia Woolf*. Norfolk: New Directions, 1942.
   Forster, E. M., *Virginia Woolf*. New York: Harcourt, 1942.
   Hafley, James, *The Glass Roof: Virginia Woolf as Novelist*. Berkeley: University of California Press, 1954.
   Johnstone, J. K., *The Bloomsbury Group: A Study of E. M. Forster, Lytton Strachey, Virginia Woolf, and their Circle*. New York: Noonday, 1954.
   Kirkpatrick, B. J., *A Bibliography of Virginia Woolf*. London: Rupert Hart-Davis, 1957.
   Pippett, Aileen, *The Moth and the Star: A Biography of Virginia Woolf*. Boston: Little, Brown, 1955.